COUNTRY HOUSE TREASURES

ABOVE *Silver cup and cover
by Paul Taylor, 1746;
Anglesey Abbey.*
OVERLEAF *View into
the Drawing Room,
Sledmere House.*
ENDPAPERS *Detail of
wood-carving by
Grinling Gibbons at
Petworth House.*

COUNTRY HOUSE TREASURES

Arthur Foss

*with Scottish country house contributions
by Rosemary Joekes*

BOOK CLUB ASSOCIATES
London

To Clare, Alexander and Caroline

This edition published 1980 by Book Club
Associates by arrangement with Weidenfeld and
Nicolson and the National Trust

Designed by Tim Higgins

Printed in Great Britain by
Jarrold and Sons Ltd, Norwich

Contents

Picture Acknowledgments

The author and publishers would like to thank the following for permission to reproduce illustrations and for supplying photographs (numbers in italics refer to colour illustrations):

The National Trust: 1 (photo John Bethell), 17 (photo John Bethell), 22 (photo John Bethell), 26, 29 left and right (photos John Bethell), 30, 33 (photo John Bethell), 40 (photo Jonathan M. Gibson), 47 (photo J. Whitaker), 49 (photo Gordon Fraser Gallery Ltd), 52 (photo A. F. Kersting), 56, 77 (photo The Courtauld Institute of Art), 85 (photo Edwin Smith), 93 (photo Alan North), 96 left (photo J. Whitaker), 96 right, 97 (photo John Bethell), 105 (photo J. Whitaker), 107 left and right, 108, 115, 116 (photo The Courtauld Institute of Art), 118, 122, 131, *142* (photo J. Whitaker), 133, 136 above (photo John Bethell), 136 below, 148 (photo A. Hornak), *168* (photo Horst Kolo), 169 left and right, 171 (photo Jonathan M. Gibson), 172 (photo J. Whitaker), 173 (photo Edwin Smith), 188 (photo John Bethell), 189, 190 left and right, 203 (photo A. Hornak), 204 (photo John Bethell), 215 above and below (photos J. Whitaker), *242* (photo John Bethell), 234 (photo J. Whitaker), 237 (photo Royal Academy of Arts), 237, 247 (photo J. Whitaker), 252 left and right, 253 (photo J. Whitaker), 259 (photo J. Whitaker), 261, 263 (photo J. Whitaker), 265 left and right (photos J. Whitaker), 266 below, *268* below left (photo J. Whitaker), 284, 287, 288, 291 below, 297 (photo A. F. Kersting), 298 (photo A. F. Kersting), 301 (photo John Bethell), 302 (photo Peter Pritchard), 306, 310 (photo John Bethell), 321 (photo Country Life), 326, 333 left (photo John Bethell), 333 right (photo Blinkhorns), 335 above (photo C. D. Reddie), 335 below, 336 left and right (photos The Courtauld Institute of Art), 338 above (photo A. Hornak), 340, 341 (photo John Bethell), 342, 344, 346 (photo J. Whitaker).

John Bethell: 2, 25, 44, 50, 84 above and below, *91*, 106, 178, 194, 195, 222, 228, 266 above, 275, 279, 280 left, *293*, *294*, 300, 312, *319*.

Woodmansterne Ltd: 18 (photo Clive Friend), *141* (photo Nicholas Servian), 196 (photo Nicholas Servian), *241* above and below, 286 (photo Jeremy Marks).

The Duke of Northumberland: 20 above and below, 318 above and below (photos English Life Publications).

The Spencer Collection, Althorp: 21 left and right, 65.

Weidenfeld Archive: 23, 41 above (photo The Press Association), 110 (photo Edwin Smith), 111 (photo Edwin Smith), 121, 126, 146, *167* above, 180, 185 (photo Edwin Smith), 210 below, 217 (photo The Courtauld Institute of Art), 224 (photo Country Life), 227, 233, 258 below (photo Jonathan M. Gibson), 273, 303, 317, 327 left and right (photos Jarrold, Norwich), 328 (photo Country Life), endpapers.

The Count and Countess Blase de Pomeroy: 27 left.

Arundel Castle Trustees Ltd: 27 right, 28 (photo The Connoisseur).

The City of Birmingham Museums and Art Gallery: 31.

A. F. Kersting: 32, 55, 80, 82, 98, 174, 182 below, 205, 208, 229, 231, 243, 255, 262, *267*, 283.

The Department of the Environment, crown copyright: 34, 170, 197, 201.

Jeremy Whitaker: 36, *66*, 68, 144, 152, 165, 182 above, 232, 238.

Mr J. B. Hickson: 37.

The Lord Armstrong Collection, Bamburgh Castle: 38.

The Lord Montagu of Beaulieu: 41 below.

Leicestershire Museums: 42.

Mr E. S. Curwen: 43.

The Duke of Rutland: 46 (photo The Courtauld Institute of Art).

The Duke of Atholl Collection, Blair Castle: 53.

Bradford Art Galleries and Museums: 58.

The Duke of Buccleuch and Queensberry: 59, 61, 129.

Stockport Metropolitan Borough Council: 62.

Mr and Mrs George Lane Fox: 64 left and right.

Angelo Hornak: *66*.

Sir Westrow Hulse: 67.

The National Trust for Scotland: 69, 87, 120 (photo Woodmansterne Ltd), 124, 143, 163, 187.

The Lord Saye and Sele: 71.

Plymouth Corporation: 73.

The Marquess of Exeter: 74 left and right (photos The Courtauld Institute of Art).

Trustees of Burton Agnes Hall Preservation Trust Ltd: 75, 76 (photos Jarrold, Norwich).

Trustees of the Faringdon Collection, Buscot Park: 78.

Major A. S. C. Browne: 79.

The Marquess of Northampton: 83, 112.

Sir Alfred Munnings Art Museum: 86.

Mr George Howard: 89.

The Earl of Cawdor: 94 (photo British Tourist Association).

Trustees of the Chatsworth Settlement: 99 above, 99 below (photo A. Hornak).

David Lowsley-Williams: 100.

Cooper-Bridgeman Library: *92*, 114, 147, *167* below, 175, *268* above, *320*, *332*.

The Jane Austen Memorial Trust: 101 (photo J. Butler-Kearney).

Trustees of the Hon. Nicholas Beatty: 102.

Executors of the late Mr Denys E. Bower: 103 left and right.

Mr P. R. de L. Giffard: 104.

The American Museum in Britain: 109 left and right.

Mr and Mrs Bryce McCosh: 124.

Mr and Mrs A. G. Jarvis: 125.

The Countess of Sutherland: 130.

John Macleod of Macleod: 132.

The Hon. Mrs Hervey-Bathurst: 135.

The Duke of Grafton: 140 left and right (photos The Courtauld Institute of Art).

Antique Collector: 139 (photo John Bullough), 230.

The Viscount Gage: 149.

The Duke of Roxburghe: 151.

The Earl of Strathmore and Kinghorne: 155 above and below.

Viscount Hampden: 157.

Mr Alan Wyndham Green: 158.

The Goodwood Estate Co. Ltd: 160, 161 (photo J. Whitaker).

The Earl of Verulam: 162.

The Marquess of Salisbury: 177 (photo The Courtauld Institute of Art).

The Lord Astor of Hever: 179 above and below.

The Marquess of Linlithgow: 184 (photo English Life Publications).

Mr C. H. Robinson: 191.

The Pilgrim Press: 193.

The Greater London Council: 199, 200 above and below (Iveagh Bequest, Kenwood), 226, 280 right (Suffolk Collection, Ranger's House).

Mr G. R. Spencer: 207.

City of Edinburgh Council: 209.

Leeds Castle Trustees: 210 left and right (photos A. Hornak).

Mr O. R. Bagot: 212 (photo J. Whitaker).

Mr D. S. Wills: 213, 214.

The Marquess of Bath: 216 left and right.

Leeds Metropolitan District Council: 218, 322, 323 above.

The Wernher Family: 220 above left and right.

J. J. Eyston: 225.

Oulston Hall: 240 left (photo Country Life), 240 right (photo Paul Mellon Centre for Studies in British Art).

George Jeffreys: 244 (photo John Brealey).

Nottingham City Council: 245 left and right.

Scunthorpe Corporation: 246.

Mrs Bagchase: 248, 249 (photos R. Brightman).

Kirklees Metropolitan Council: 250.

Packwood House: 254.

John Makepeace Ltd: 256.

Mr Molesworth St-Aubyn: 258 above.

Viscount De L'Isle: 260 left and right.

Commander Michael Watson: *268* below right, 281 (photos English Life Publications).

The Earl of Devon: 271 (photo English Life Publications).

The Earl of Powis: 272.

David Beevers: 274.

Squire de Lisle: 276 (photo James Mortimer).

Lord Bernard: 278 (photo English Life Publications).

Welsh Folk Museum, St Fagan's: 285.

H.M. the Queen: 289.

The Earl of Mansfield: 291 above left and right (photo Scottish Field).

Mr and Mrs P. J. Radford: 292 above and below.

Simon Wingfield Digby: 296 (photo Percy Hennell).

Mr J. St A. Warde: 305 (photo Sydney W. Newbery).

Lord and Lady Braye: 307 (photo English Life Publications).

Lord Gretton: 308.

Stonor Enterprises: 309.

The Dent-Brocklehurst Family Trust: 314 above (photo Paul Mellon Centre for Studies in British Art), 314 below.

Sulgrave Manor Board: 315.

Mr and Mrs S. H. Crabtree: 323 below.

Towneley Hall Art Gallery and Museums, Burnley Borough Council: 325.

Newport Museum and Art Gallery: 325.

Warwick Castle Ltd: 338 below, 339 (photos John Wright).

The Earl of Bradford: 343.

Trustees of the Bedford Estate: 349.

Picture research by Julia Brown and Jane Beamish.

Introduction

Since the end of the Second World War and especially during the last decade, there has been an enormous increase in country house visiting. The enjoyment of such visits may lie simply in a day spent in the country or in the brief retreat from the humdrum surroundings in which most of us live. There is a strong element of curiosity about how others, particularly the famous, live or have lived, and the media have no doubt stimulated a wider awareness of the pleasure to be gained from seeing the homes of distinguished individuals or families and an increased appreciation of the past achievements of architects, artists and craftsmen.

Britain's country houses in all their variety and richness of contents form the most finely preserved architectural and cultural heritage in the world and offer perspectives of human history and artistic variety that no museum collection can provide. The growth in country house visiting has done a little to help owners protect their properties from decay through overtaxation. Private owners have formed the Historic Houses Association to win recognition from government of the value of the country house to the nation. In other circumstances, many properties with endowments to maintain them have come into the care of the National Trust and the National Trust for Scotland, both of them charities.

There is, however, nothing new in country house visiting. Celia Fiennes in her *Journeys* in the late-17th and early-18th centuries has much to record about individual properties. The 3rd Duke of Dorset, not in anyway to be confused with Max Beerbohm's character of that name in *Zuleika Dobson* but the master of fabulous Knole, gave instructions in about 1792 that all visitors should be asked to sign their names in a book. In *Pride and Prejudice*, published in 1813, Jane Austen's heroine, Elizabeth Bennett, goes as a sightseer to the large house in Derbyshire owned by her suitor, Mr Darcy.

In the past, owners were happy for strangers to be welcomed into their houses because such visits were an indication of the importance both of their properties and themselves. They did not charge admission fees but the visitor was expected to pay handsomely – in value very much more than is asked today – for the opportunity to the caretaker or servant who conducted him round the interior. Certainly far more than a tip was expected, especially if the tour of the house involved opening the window shutters in the state rooms and taking off and later putting back the protective coverings over the furniture and carpets if the rooms were not actually in use. Few families spent all their time in the country and the state rooms would be opened up only on important occasions. Today, country house enthusiasts can for a modest sum join the Historic Houses Association and one or other of the National Trusts and thus enjoy the privilege of seeing nearly all the important houses open to the public without further payment.

These islands have been fortunate in that our ancestors in the 16th, 17th and 18th centuries were able through their wealth, energy, good taste and shrewdness to acquire many fine paintings and much good furniture and porcelain for their country houses and because of a relatively stable society and the tradition of the country house as a permanent family home, these treasures have been remarkably well safeguarded. The private collections to be found at Alnwick Castle, Althorp, Bowhill and Drumlanrig Castle, at Burghley House, Castle Howard, Chatsworth, Corsham Court, Firle Place, Harewood House, Hopetoun House, Petworth House, Polesden Lacey, Upton House and Wilton House – to mention but a few – are surely unrivalled anywhere.

Moreover, these treasures throw a fascinating light on many aspects of our history. The allegorical group of Henry VIII and his family at Sudeley Castle and the two remarkable portraits of Queen Elizabeth I at Hatfield House, one by Hilliard and the other perhaps by Zuccaro pay tribute to the monarchy at the peak of its power. At Chiddingstone Castle, Coughton Court, Sizergh Castle, Stanford Hall, Stonor Park and at Falkland Palace and the House of Traquair are reminders of the Stuart tragedy. Portraits by Batoni to be found in many houses, including Newby Hall, Norton Conyers and Uppark, recall visits to Italy and the Grand Tour, which are likewise reflected by views of the Campagna in the Cabinet at Felbrigg and the caricature by Reynolds of English visitors in Rome, which hangs in the Billiards Room at Holker Hall.

From Blenheim Palace, Powis Castle and Shugborough come the echoes of battles in Europe and India, marking the ascendancy of the British Empire, while at Parham and Shugborough are reminders of distant exploration and high adventure in the Antipodes and the Pacific. At Anglesey Abbey and Hever Castle are two remarkable collections of paintings, furniture, armour, ivory and silver, eclectic selections of the finest quality which both intrigue and enchant; Scone Palace houses similar wide-ranging treasures. The French 18th century in its many aspects is nowhere to be seen to greater advantage than at Waddesdon Manor. The list could be extended for pages.

There are houses associated with the North American continent, such as Washington Old Hall and Sulgrave Manor which will always be connected with the forebears of George Washington, the first President of the United States. A much later President, General Eisenhower, is remembered at Culzean Castle, while Haddow House, Leith Hall, and Quebec House in Westerham, Kent, where General Wolfe was born, have strong links with Canada. There are also a very few houses for which it would be difficult to claim treasures but which nevertheless retain something of the personality of their erstwhile owners. Among them are Abbotsford House, the home of Sir Walter Scott, Lamb House, Rye, where Henry James spent most of his later years, and Cloud's Hill in Dorset, which was T.E. Lawrence's retreat.

A major interest in any visit to a country house is the interior and its contents. Either guidebooks or guides or both are available at most if not all of the properties open to the public but among the many books which have recently been written about them, there is no one volume in which there are details in some depth about the contents of houses in the possession of the National Trusts and in private ownership. This book attemps to fill this gap so that those interested in particular aspects of the arts can inform themselves where good examples are to be found. In addition there is, it is hoped, sufficient information about the history of the houses and their owners to give the reader a background to the treasures and show how they came to be there.

'Treasures' in the context of this book has been given a wide interpretation. The decorative as well as the fine arts have been included under this heading, together with outstanding examples of craftsmanship. To exclude such marvels as the plasterwork ceilings executed by, for example, the younger Joseph Rose, or the treads and balusters of the main staircase at Claydon House, the stone and marble inlaid floors at Dodington House near Chipping Sodbury, and at Newby Hall, or the outstanding joinery to be found at Castle Coole would surely be wrong in a book such as this.

The houses discussed in this volume are listed in the *Historic Houses, Castles and Gardens Annual* and are open to visitors on at least twenty advertised days in the year; information about the days and hours of opening and other relevant details will also be found in this publication. In addition to privately owned properties and those in the care of the two National Trusts, several museums which were once country houses have been included. Acquired in recent years by local authorities, they now contain paintings, furniture, porcelain and other treasures from houses in the country. Three excellent examples are Temple Newsam, Cannon Hall and Pollok House, administered respectively by the Leeds and Barnsley Metropolitan District Councils and by the City of Glasgow District Council. Tredegar House on the outskirts of Newport, Gwent, is being imaginatively restored by the Newport Borough Council to its former glory as the finest mansion of its period in Wales. Happily, private owners are also active in carefully restoring country houses, as can be seen, among others, at Bryn Bras Castle, Kentwell Hall, Penhow Castle and Sheffield Park.

It has not been possible to include every house open to the public on twenty advertised occasions each year. In some cases the interior may be devoid of interest, or it may be that the owner does not wish his property mentioned, or that a visit has proved impossible to plan in the time available. The exclusion of a particular property in no way implies criticism of the house, its content or its owner. It may also be that an important new house has been opened after this book went to press or that another house described here has subsequently been closed to the public.

Owners naturally reserve the right to re-arrange their belongings, to withdraw an item from a public to a private room, and indeed, to sell a painting or piece of furniture described in this book. The chance discovery of an old account book or the use of X-ray equipment to examine the canvas of a painting may occasionally reveal that the original attribution to a particular artist has been incorrect; this has happened to a number of 16th- and early-17th-century portraits and on occasion with artists of a much later date. For example, many paintings until recently confidently attributed to John Constable are now known to have been painted by his nephew. In order to reduce mistakes to a minimum each entry has been submitted to its owner, curator or to the relevant Historic Buildings Representative of the National Trust.

A word about attributions, especially with regard to paintings. If a particular painting is signed or known to be by a particular artist, the surname only will be given. Space does not permit describing, for example, Reynolds as Sir Joshua Reynolds PRA each time his name appears, but names in full will be found in the Index. If a painting is thought to be by a particular artist, then the fact that it is attributed will be stated.

A final element to be taken into account is why the particular paintings, pieces of furniture, porcelain and other objects of art have been selected for mention. Here the author is at his most vulnerable. It is merely a question of personal taste; it is highly unlikely that any other compiler of such a book would have chosen exactly the same items or described them in exactly the same way.

I owe an enormous debt to a great many people. I would first like warmly to thank Mr Edward Fawcett, Director of Public Relations of the National Trust, who originally invited me to contribute a book to the joint National Trust/Weidenfeld and Nicolson publishing venture. I am delighted that Rosemary Joekes, who co-edited with the late Robin Fedden *The National Trust Guide* and *Treasures of the National Trust*, has written the section of the book which deals with the country house treasures in her native Scotland. I am also grateful to Miss Ann Wilson for all her help as the publisher's editor during the two and a half years which it has taken to collect and present the material in this book.

I would like to record my gratitude to the owners and museum authorities who have so generously gone to much trouble, first to allow me to see or personally to conduct me through their houses at times not always convenient to themselves and later to check what I have written and on occasion provide extra valuable information. In the same way I would like to thank my colleagues in the National Trust and especially the Historic Buildings Representatives and Administrators who have done so much to save me from error, and I join with Rosemary Joekes in acknowledging the debt owed to the equally helpful staff of the National Trust for Scotland. In conclusion, I would like to thank Miss Bridget Bates for her patience and cheerfulness in typing this book and last but not least my wife for her help and encouragement in so many ways.

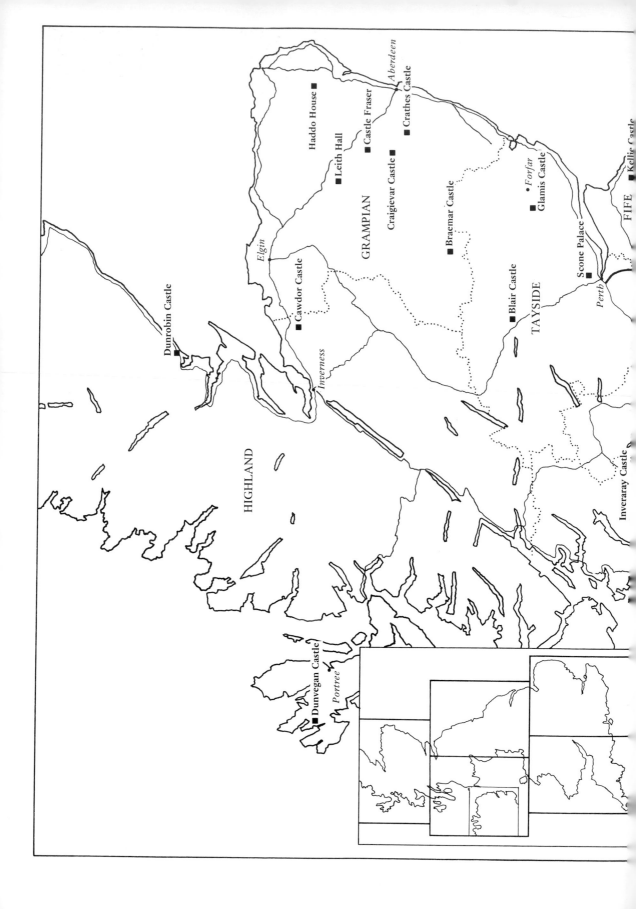

HIGHLAND

GRAMPIAN

TAYSIDE

FIFE

Dunrobin Castle

Dunvegan Castle

Portree

Cawdor Castle

Elgin

Inverness

Haddo House

Leith Hall

Castle Fraser

Craigievar Castle

Crathes Castle

Aberdeen

Braemar Castle

Blair Castle

Glamis Castle

Forfar

Scone Palace

Perth

Kellie Castle

Inveraray Castle

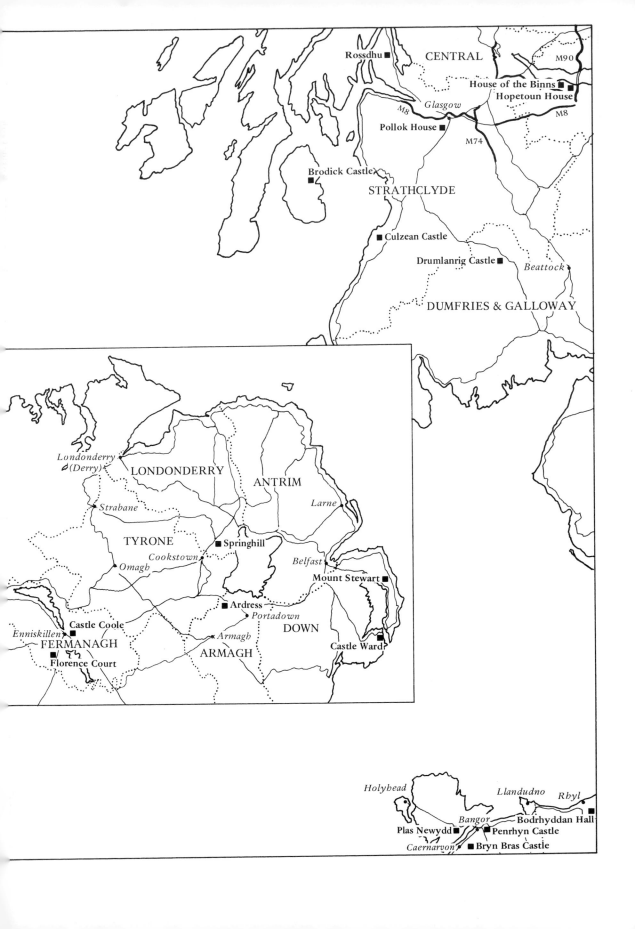

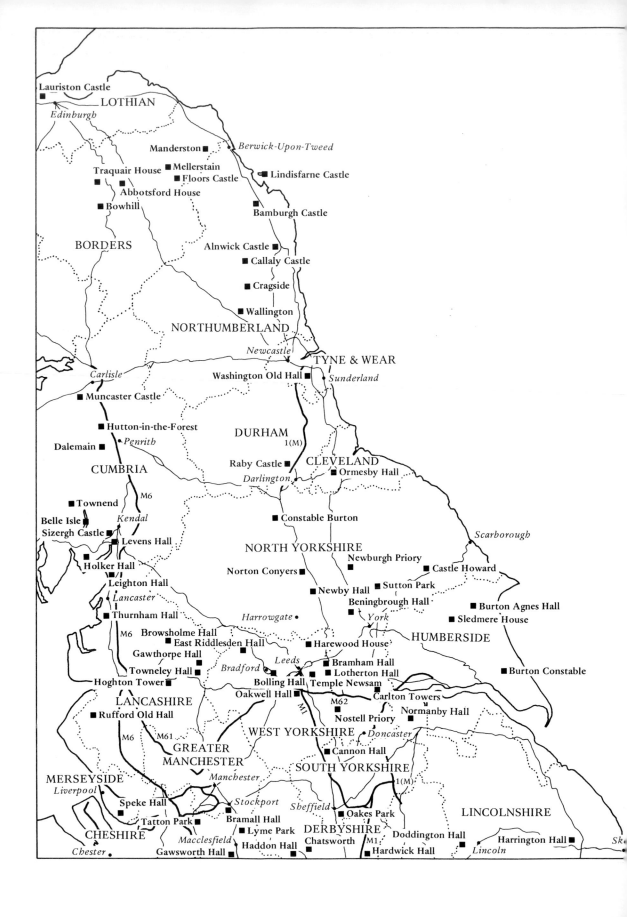

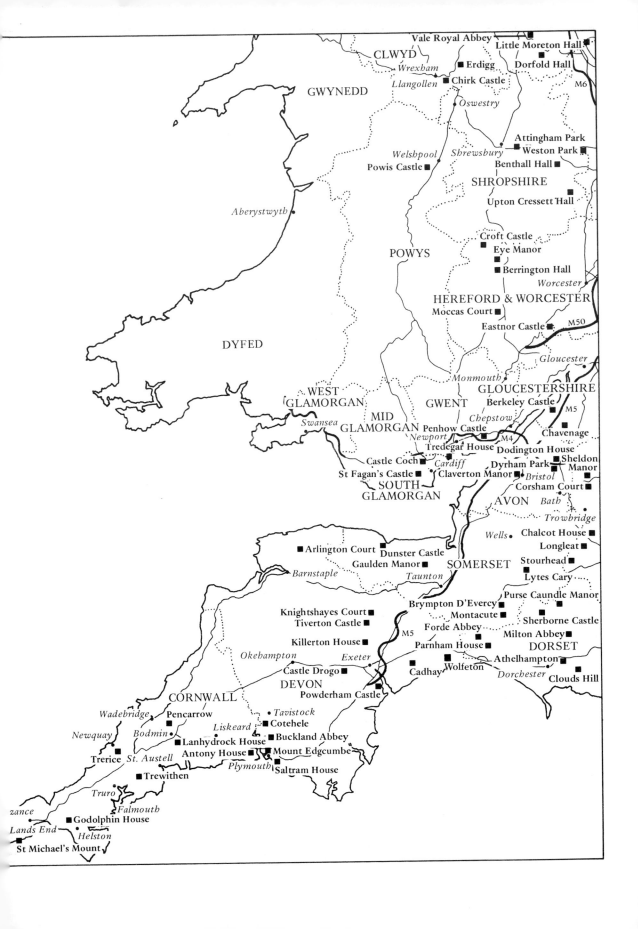

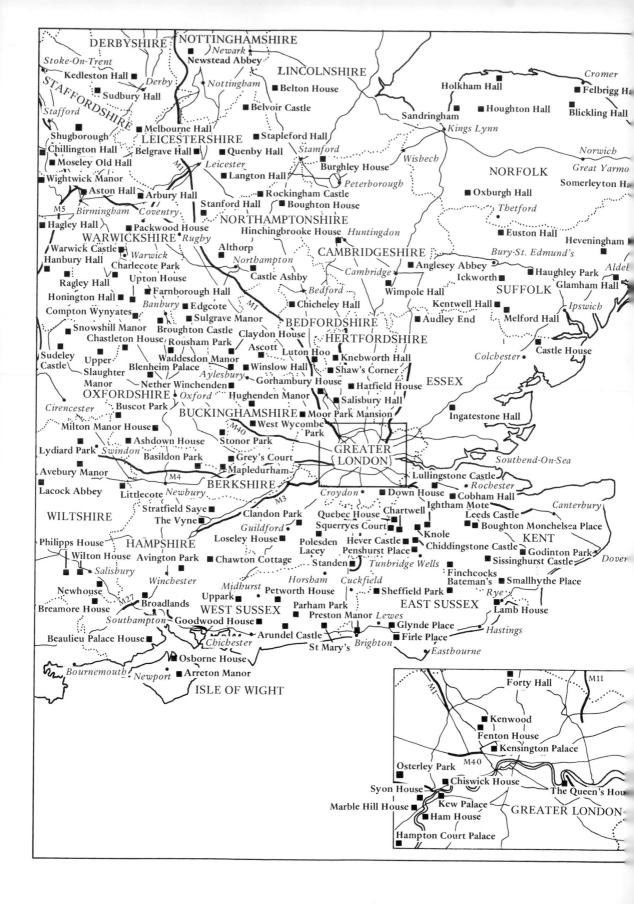

COUNTRY
HOUSE
TREASURES

*Chelsea-Derby biscuit porcelain group,
c. 1780; Upton House.*

*The Entrance Hall, Abbotsford House, the home of Sir Walter Scott
whose antiquarian interests are reflected throughout the house.*

Abbotsford House Borders

Mrs Patricia Maxwell-Scott OBE

3 miles NW of Melrose S of A72

In 1811 the sheriff-depute of Selkirk moved into a modest farmhouse on·the bank of the Tweed. By 1818 he was in a position to build a new house in its place, which he romantically christened Abbotsford. The owner of the grand new house was Sir Walter Scott, the building of Abbotsford the tangible evidence of the success of his poems and of the Waverley novels written there between 1812 and 1818. His wealth was, sadly, temporary, but his vast reputation has endured both at home and throughout Europe. Few men can have had so much influence on the literature, music and attitudes of their day. During his lifetime, the home Scott loved welcomed many distinguished visitors who responded to his warm personality, and even as early as 1833, the year after his death, Abbotsford had become, as it remains, a place of pilgrimage.

The house is not architecturally or decoratively distinguished – rather muddled and vaguely Gothic with predominantly English medieval features: battlements, turrets and machicolation – but inside, it reflects Scott's antiquarian enthusiasms no less than his personality as a man and writer. The Library and galleried Study contain over 9,000 volumes, his desk and the last suit of clothes he wore, with plaid trousers, kid gloves and walking stick. The Drawing Room, hung with somewhat garish Chinese wallpaper, contains a second desk – Portuguese and made of ebony – given with its matching set of chairs to Scott by George IV. Another gift, this time from his publishers, is a pair of large and ornate carved boxwood chairs, attributed to the Venetian carver Andrea Brustolon (1662–1732).

Sir Walter Scott's passion for the more romantic aspects of Scottish history led him to collect a varied and at times indiscriminate assortment of objects; they include a pocket-book embroidered by Flora Macdonald (presented to him by the heroine's niece), Rob Roy's battered leather purse, a lock of Prince Charles Edward's hair, his touchingly simple little wooden quaich with a glass bottom, and the prince's superb chased silver set of hunting knives of the Louis XIV period, together with Montrose's cabinet found on the battlefield of Philiphaugh and his sword, once belonging to James VI and I, given him by Charles I. There are also mementos of European history, among them the golden bee-clasp of Napoleon's cloak found in his carriage after Waterloo. Abbotsford contains an interesting collection of arms and armour, including a fine suit of Augsburg tilt armour of about 1580.

Alnwick Castle Northumberland

The Duke of Northumberland KG

In Alnwick

This great Border castle which has belonged since 1309 to the Percy family, successively Earls and Dukes of Northumberland, dominates the little town of Alnwick. The earliest fortifications date back to the 14th century with even earlier examples of Norman masonry, but the castle was much restored in the 1760s, when Robert Adam worked here, and again far more extensively in the 1850s by the perfectionist 4th Duke, a great admirer of the High Renaissance in Italy. He employed distinguished Italian experts to supervise the interior decoration in this magnificent style, with schools of British artisans carrying out most of the work.

The grandeur achieved is evident on the Grand Staircase, whose walls are lined with Carrara marble, in the Guard Chamber, whose Venetian marble pavement was made in Rome, and throughout the State Rooms. The carved, gilded and painted wood ceilings completely replaced Adam's designs. The walls are covered with rich damask and the great marble chimneypieces are by Roman sculptors.

The Dining Room furniture is mainly sound Victorian mahogany but there are fine examples of earlier periods elsewhere. The Guard Chamber contains a circular painted gaming table on fluted legs, mid-18th-century English

Titian (c.1487/90–1576) The Bishop of Armagnac and his Secretary; *Alnwick Castle.*

carved gilt chairs covered with silk, and Kentian gilt console tables with marble tops. French furniture includes the handsome late-17th-century floral marquetry commode enriched with ormolu in the Music Room and an even richer pair of ebony cabinets of 1683 with *pietre dure* panels in the Red Drawing Room.

In this elaborate setting, the glorious collection of paintings glows like jewels. Titian is represented by three fine works, including his magnificent *The Bishop of Armagnac and his Secretary*, which hangs in the Ante-room

Tureen from one of the two Meissen dinner services, c.1780, at Alnwick Castle.

alongside works by Tintoretto and Palma Vecchio. The Music Room contains Canaletto's painting of Northumberland House, London, since demolished, and a fine triple portrait by Dobson of three cavaliers. Van Dyck's imperious 10th Earl as Lord High Admiral of England hangs in the Guard Chamber, while the Red Drawing Room contains Turner's superb *The Temple of Aegina*. Other portraitists include Gainsborough, Reynolds, Cosway, Mignard, Dance, Grant, de Laszlo and Birley.

There are fine examples of English, Continental and Oriental porcelain. One of the two magnificent 18th-century Meissen dinner services is painted with birds and animals, including a splendid rhinoceros.

Althorp Northamptonshire

The Earl Spencer

6½ miles N W of Northampton on A428

Althorp was a dignified red-brick moated house when it was bought by Sir John Spencer in 1508. The inner courtyard was converted into the Saloon and impressive Main Staircase in 1650 for the brilliant and extravagant Robert Spencer, 2nd Earl of Sunderland, who acquired a large number of paintings for Althorp during his long and remarkable career in the service of Charles II, James II and William III. The 3rd Earl's second wife was Lady Anne Churchill, who was co-heiress to the great Duke of Marlborough, and through her the 5th Earl of Sunderland became the 3rd Duke. Anne's youngest son inherited Althorp and her grandson was created 1st Earl Spencer. The house was remodelled in 1786 for the 2nd Earl by Henry Holland, who refaced the exterior with a kind of white patent stone.

The continuing distinction of a great family over the centuries is rarely so brilliantly reflected in works of art as in the collections of the Spencer family at Althorp. The spacious well-proportioned rooms show to advantage some of the finest paintings still in private ownership. Van Dyck's superb portraits of the

2nd Earl of Bristol with the 1st Duke of Bedford, and the 1st Duke of Newcastle hang in the oak-panelled Elizabethan Picture Gallery, with Lely's 2nd Earl of Sunderland, who commissioned Lely to paint the renowned beauties at Charles II's court which also hang here, in their distinctively carved 'Sunderland' frames – named after the 2nd Earl. Elsewhere are likenesses of the Hon. John Spencer with John, his son, by Knapton and good examples by Kneller and Riley.

Reynolds was a friend of the family and one room is devoted exclusively to his and Gainsborough's family portraits. Here are Reynolds' enchanting Georgiana, Countess Spencer, with her small daughter – later to become prominent in Whig society as the Duchess of Devonshire – and Gainsborough's splendid William Poyntz, seen with gun and water spaniel, together with other outstanding portraits that cover three generations. There are also fine family portraits by Hoppner, Maratta, Kauffmann, J. S. Copley, Dance, Batoni, Grant, Archer Shee and Hayter, and the 20th-century masters include Orpen, William Nicholson, Augustus John, Birley, Gunn, Sargent and Moynihan.

Weisweiler cabinet, c.1780; Althorp.

Joshua Reynolds' portrait of Countess Spencer with her daughter, c.1759–61; Althorp.

In the magnificent Entrance Hall is the splendid collection of hunting scenes by John Wootton, while other rooms contain the vast collection of old master paintings, including a series of Rubens' portraits of the Hapsburgs and many fine examples of the 17th-century Dutch and Italian schools. The 45th volume (1974–6) of the Walpole Society, of which the 7th Earl was President, catalogues over 700 paintings.

The English and French furniture is of the finest quality. Mainly 18th century, it includes the work of Chippendale, Sheraton and William Vile and superb examples by the *ébénistes*, Saunier and Weisweiler. The fifty-four matching mahogany chairs in the Dining Room were made in 1800 by George Seddon, and the sideboards and mirrors were designed by Henry Holland. The library steps in the Long Library are especially noteworthy. The China Corridor contains excellent examples of Sèvres, 'Red' and 'Gold Anchor' Chelsea, Meissen, Nantgarw and Derby porcelain, and elsewhere are fine examples of 18th-century Chinese and Japanese ceramics.

Anglesey Abbey Cambridgeshire

The National Trust

In Lode village, 6 miles NE of Cambridge on B1102 to Mildenhall

Originally an Augustinian priory, probably founded by Henry I in 1135, Anglesey Abbey was largely destroyed after the Dissolution of the Monasteries by Henry VIII. What was left was converted into a house, which was owned for a time by Thomas Hobson, the Cambridge horse-keeper famed by the phrase 'Hobson's choice' – he offered the choice of the nearest horse or none at all – and later by Sir George Downing, founder of the Cambridge college of that name. Anglesey Abbey was largely a ruined building when it was bought in 1926 by Huttleston Broughton, 1st Lord Fairhaven. Described by Robin Fedden as 'reticent, civilized, self-sufficient', Lord Fairhaven created with his immense wealth a remarkable garden of imaginative beauty and remodelled the priory to house his distinguished and wide-ranging collections of works of art.

Hanging in the Tapestry Hall, in rooms, along corridors and on stairways are Felletin, Gobelins, Mortlake and Soho tapestries. Superb paintings include two glorious Claudes and fine works by artists as varied as Bonington, Canaletto (St Paul's with Canaletto in the foreground), Cuyp, Etty, Gainsborough, Landseer, Martin, Munnings, Pryde, Dominic and J. T. Serres, Wilson and Wootton. A unique collection of views of Windsor Castle (paintings, drawings and prints), including works by Cox, Goodwin, Marlow, Sandby, John Varley and Wilson, charts its history over 350 years. A group of miniature paintings contains works by Brooking, Crome and Constable.

The furniture, both English and Continental, is of the highest quality; among the pieces are Italian cabinets and giltwood tables; a glorious Louis XVI cylinder-top desk by Roentgen; giltwood side tables, supported by dolphins, and a carved walnut settee in the manner of Kent; an Adam-style *bonheur-du-jour* and a late-18th-century dressing-table and

J. M. Rysbrack's terracotta 'reclining goat', c.1730; Anglesey Abbey.

mirror in padouk wood; and Chinese red lacquer furniture of the late Ming period. Among the bronzes are French and Florentine mythological figures and more recent works by Leighton and Gilbert. The arms include a cup-hilt Solingen rapier traditionally said to have belonged to Prince Rupert of the Rhine.

Among other treasures are clocks, including a Regency pagoda clock, a musical clock by Bovell, and a drum-shaped Louis XV clock by Archambault. The 'reclining goat' in terracotta is by Rysbrack; there are two 18th-century Austrian bishops in the same medium as well as a 17th-century figure of Hercules. The fine porcelain includes examples from China, sometimes with ormolu mounts, from Meissen and from the Worcester and Derby factories. Carved wooden figures of various periods come from Austria, Flanders, Germany, Italy and Spain. Every item – silver, coloured book plates, embroidery, rugs, Ming pottery figures, ceremonial halberds from Venice, blue-john urns and obelisks and much else – was chosen for its individual quality and beauty.

Antony House Cornwall

The National Trust

2 miles NW of Torpoint, N of A374; 5 miles W of Plymouth via Torpoint car ferry

This silvery-grey stone mansion, redolent of dignity and charm, was built on the site of a

RIGHT *The panelled Library, Antony House, showing the portrait of Sir Alexander Carew, executed for his royalist sympathies after initially espousing the parliamentary cause.*

Tudor house by an unknown architect between 1710 and 1721 for Sir William Carew, a staunch Stuart supporter. He exchanged portraits with Sir Watkin Williams-Wynn to seal their pact to raise Wales and the south-west for the Old Pretender in 1715. Sir Watkin's portrait by Hudson is in the Dining Room. In due course the estate was inherited by the Pole family of Shute and Sir John Carew-Pole, 12th Baronet, who lives here, gave the property to the National Trust in 1961. His father, Lt-Gen. Sir Reginald Pole-Carew, was a distinguished soldier whose military trophies enhance the Inner Hall.

Antony had been important in Cornish history even before it came to the Carew family late in the 15th century, and the contents of the house reflect the family's involvement in Cornish and national affairs. Family portraits hang in the Hall, panelled in Dutch oak or pine, and on the Main Staircase. Sir John Carew and his wife were portrayed by Dahl, and other portraitists include Lely, Kneller, Northcote and Beach, a pupil of Reynolds. However, undoubtedly the most moving portrait is that of Charles I, sad and dignified at his trial at which a Carew was a judge, one of several versions by Edward Bower. Here also is a shrewd and observant Richard Carew who succeeded to the estate in 1564, painted by an unknown hand; he wrote the renowned *Survey of Cornwall*, a rhymed family history. His unfortunate grandson, Sir Alexander Carew, initially espoused the parliamentary side in the Civil War, whereat his ultra-royalist family cut his portrait out of its frame; they sewed it back again – the stitches can still clearly be seen – when he was executed by the Roundheads for reverting to the royalist cause.

Other portraits include fine examples by Reynolds – three in the Saloon and one in the well-stocked Library – by Ramsay and Gilbert Stuart, and sporting scenes involving Gilbert, Lord Coventry, by Wyck and Wootton. More sporting scenes, by Francis Sartorius, hang on the West Staircase.

Good period furniture can be found throughout the house, including Charles II chairs and Queen Anne settees in the Hall; two chairs with brilliant early-18th-century tapestry covers in the Inner Hall; Chippendale chairs and a pair of George I black marble-topped side tables in the Dining Room; a pair of Chippendale armchairs covered in *gros* and *petit point* needlework and a Queen Anne walnut table, its cabriole knees carved with Red Indian heads, in the Tapestry Room with its early-18th-century Mortlake tapestries from the 'Philosophers' series and a William and Mary seaweed marquetry table. The Saloon contains good examples of Dr Wall Worcester and Chelsea porcelain, and outside the garden door on the west side is a fine collection of Gandharan stone Buddhas acquired in India by Sir Reginald Pole-Carew.

Arbury Hall Warwickshire

Mr F. H. FitzRoy Newdegate

2½ miles s w of Nuneaton off B4102

This Elizabethan quadrangular mansion, built on the site of a former Augustinian priory, became the home of the Newdegate (original spelling) family in 1586 and the house contains paintings of that period, including an elaborate and distinguished portrait of Elizabeth I, attributed to John Bettes the younger, and one of Mary Fitton, thought to have been the 'Dark Lady' of Shakespeare's sonnets, in the style of Gower.

Sir Roger Newdigate, 5th Baronet, began the redecoration of the house, which was to take many years, in the Gothic Revival style in 1750, a year after Horace Walpole started on a similar course at Strawberry Hill. Sanderson Miller was initially responsible, to be succeeded first by Henry Keene and later by Henry Couchman of Warwick; the little chapel, completed in 1678 with an elaborate plaster-work ceiling of the period by Edward Martin, was alone left virtually untouched. George Eliot, the novelist, was brought up on the estate and the squire in *Scenes from Clerical Life* who transforms his house 'from plain red brick into the model of a Gothic manor-house' is based on Sir Roger Newdigate.

The Gothic Revival style shown in the elaborate plasterwork of the Saloon, c.1750, Arbury Hall.

The Gothic detail, copied from noted Gothic buildings, is restrained in the Long Gallery, where the original Elizabethan chimneypiece has been retained; elaborately imposing in the Saloon; grandiose in the high vaulted Dining Room with classical mythological figures standing under Gothic canopies; and almost overwhelming in the Drawing Room, especially the chimneypiece. Yet the arches, vaults and pillars have no structural significance; they are worked not in stone but in plaster, and are purely decorative.

There are good 17th- and 18th-century family portraits by, among others, Lely, Beale, Dahl, Arthur Devis (the 5th Baronet), Knapton, William Hoare, Kneller, Stuart, Hudson, Lawrence, Romney, and Mme Vigée-Lebrun. Other paintings include Reynolds' enchanting *John the Baptist when a Boy*, a gambling scene by Mercier and works by Shayer and Ibbetson.

The excellent furniture, mainly English, includes Gothic Chippendale chairs with contemporary tapestry covers in the Long Gallery; two Queen Anne walnut marquetry chairs in the Little School-Room; English and French pieces, mainly 18th century, in the Saloon, which also contains Archbishop Laud's cabinet; and in the Drawing Room late-17th-century marquetry pieces, a set of painted chairs c.1800, and fine examples of Chelsea ware, including plates decorated with exotic birds. There is Chinese export ware, a Roman sarcophagus c.AD 200 and 17th-century oak furniture in the Dining Room, where the Elizabethan portraits are hung.

In the Stables, the doorway in its middle bay probably designed by Wren, is a collection of veteran cycles and farm implements.

Ardress Co. Armagh

The National Trust

7 miles w of Portadown on Portadown–Moy road

This small, attractive, pink-washed Georgian country house stands in pleasant rural surroundings. Originally built in the mid-17th century, it was given a more sophisticated façade ten years after its acquisition in 1760 by George Ensor, an able Dublin architect.

The house's great distinction is the glorious plasterwork in the Drawing Room, for which Ensor employed the distinguished Irish stuccador, Michael Stapleton (d. 1801), who also decorated, among other Dublin buildings, the Vice-Regal Lodge, now the President of Ireland's residence. The ceiling design, painted in harmonious colours, is based on a symmetrical pattern of circles, semi-circles and segments of circles round a central plaque which contains a representation of Aurora in the Chariot of the Dawn. Similar plaques decorate the walls, festooned with husk chains. Stapleton's work is reminiscent of Robert Adam's and comparable with the best plasterwork then being produced in England.

In this elegant room and the Dining Room are good examples of English and Irish 18th-century furniture. The entertaining early-17th-century Dutch painting, showing the birth of Eve, the Temptation and the exile of Adam and Eve, in the Entrance Hall, and the two pleasant 18th-century views of the Thames, in the Parlour, are lent with the other paintings on view by Lord Mount Stewart. In the Inside Hall are examples of Waterford glass.

Period farm equipment is on display in the farmyard.

Arlington Court Devon

The National Trust

7 miles NE of Barnstaple on E side of A39

Arlington was left to the National Trust in 1949 by Miss Rosalie Chichester, whose family had lived here since 1384. The chief treasure of

William Blake's watercolour The Cycle of the Life of Man, *1821; Arlington Court.*

this restrained, late neo-classical building, c.1820, surrounded by lawns and trees, is William Blake's strange, mystical watercolour, often referred to as *The Cycle of the Life of Man*, signed and dated 1821. The house has enormous charm and contains fascinating collections – early Victorian furniture; shells, some silver-mounted and converted into snuff boxes; an impressive pewter collection; and many ship models, some made by French Napoleonic prisoners of war, and some of the heroic 'little ships' that rescued the British troops at Dunkirk in 1940. A more recent model is that of *Gipsy Moth IV*, made famous by Sir Francis Chichester when he circumnavigated the world in her in 1967.

Some of the collections are in the three airy interconnecting south rooms which in addition contain punch ladles, Chinese carvings in jade and rock crystal, French and English enamelled boxes, Russian bright enamel *niello* work and silver mugs. English porcelain, including 'Queen Charlotte' pattern Worcester, is displayed in the four white and gold *étagères* in the White Drawing Room.

On the upper stairs of the Staircase Hall are pleasant gouaches of the Bay of Naples and in the Lobby framed panels showing exotic birds made from feathers mounted on paper.

Arreton Manor Isle of Wight

Count and Countess Slade de Pomeroy

Between Newport and Sandown on A3056

This enchanting little stone house is early-17th-century, although Arreton Manor is mentioned in Domesday Book. It was bought in 1629 by Sir Thomas Bennett who probably added such features as the porch on the south side, dated 1639, although the Great Hall screen is of much earlier monastic origin. The west wing, added in 1812, is Jacobean in character.

The house contains fine panelling, c.1630, in the Entrance Hall and Dining Room. The latter room has delicately moulded pilasters with vine-leaf motifs and a chimneypiece of great merit, its overmantel flanked by carved wooden figures, one representing Mars and the other a goddess of plenty. The oak furniture is mainly Jacobean, although the heavily carved small court cupboard is probably Elizabethan.

Among the exhibits of local arts are some 19th-century sand paintings and lace-making devices, a collection of treen and of agricultural and other bygones. The attic rooms contain an extensive collection of dolls and there is also a unique collection of vintage wireless receivers spanning the period between World War I and today.

Jacobean chimneypiece in the Dining Room, Arreton Manor.

Arundel Castle West Sussex

Arundel Castle Trustees Ltd

In Arundel, between Chichester and Worthing

The great castle of Arundel, a home of the Fitzalan-Howard family, Dukes of Norfolk, stands dramatically on rising ground above the swiftly flowing Arun, the little town nestling below its walls. The 1st Earl of Arundel, whose title descended to the Fitzalans, was established here by 1138. The daughter of the 12th Earl was married in 1556 to the 4th Duke of Norfolk, who was later beheaded by Queen Elizabeth. Since the family was Roman Catholic, the tide ran strongly against its members until the Restoration, except for Thomas, the 14th Earl, who wisely kept out of politics and married a granddaughter of Bess of Hardwick; their full-length portraits by Mytens, dated 1618, are in the Drawing Room

Daniel Mytens' portrait of the Countess of Arundel, 1618; Arundel Castle.

*Carved chest from South Germany, c.1580;
Arundel Castle.*

and Van Dyck's fine painting of them together is in the Baron's Hall. The 14th Earl was a great patron of the arts and learning and was responsible with Charles I for bringing Mytens and Van Dyck to England.

The Castle itself, having suffered much in the Civil War, was in a near ruinous state by 1777, when the 10th Duke of Norfolk inherited. He planned its reconstruction, which his son carried out in the Gothic Revival manner – shown at its most successful in the Library. There was still much restoration to be done on the accession of the 15th Duke, which was undertaken by C. A. Buckler in massive Victorian Gothic style between 1875 and 1900, as illustrated by the Barons' Hall, the Dining Room and the Drawing Room. The collections now at Arundel – the early portraits, swords and armour, and the furniture – were made by the 9th Duke and his descendants.

Among the late-16th-century portraits are those of the 12th Earl of Arundel and Lord Maltravers, attributed to the elder Bettes, a Holbein disciple; one of Henry Howard, Earl of Surrey, featured against a Mannerist background, after Scrots (Stretes), which hangs at the bottom of the Grand Staircase; and one of the 13th Earl, who was accused of having a Mass celebrated on the arrival of the Spanish Armada, died in the Tower and was later

canonized. This is in the Picture Gallery, which is hung with family portraits by, among others, Lely, Lawrence and de Laszlo.

The furniture, in addition to good 18th-century English examples from Norfolk House, includes several splendid 16th- and 17th-century Continental pieces, among them a French carved chest, *c.*1560; one from South Germany, *c.*1580; a fine marquetry cabinet made in Augsburg for export to Spain, *c.*1560; a pair of Antwerp cabinets inlaid with tortoiseshell and ivory, *c.*1650; a carved ebony cabinet attributed to Jean Macé, Paris, *c.*1650; a backgammon board inlaid with bronze from South Germany, late-16th-century; a pair of inlaid cabinets from Goa, 1750; and an Indian bureau, Vizagapatam, *c.*1800. There are fine armchairs, both Venetian and English – several of the latter, made in the 1730–40s, show the influence of Kent – and two tables with remarkable early-17th-century *pietre dure* tops from Rome.

In the Armoury is an excellent collection of weapons, shields and armour, including 'Mongley', by tradition the sword of the legendary founder of the Castle; it dates from the 14th century.

Ascott Buckinghamshire

The National Trust

½ mile E of Wing, 2 miles SW of Leighton Buzzard on S side of A418

A black and white rambling Victorian house, which underwent much alteration in the 1930s, Ascott stands surrounded by fine gardens with views over the Vale of Aylesbury, a countryside with which the renowned de Rothschild family has become closely associated. This is aptly illustrated by Grant's painting in the Lobby, *Four Brothers of the Rothschild Family following Hounds* – the Rothschild staghounds were kept first at nearby Mentmore and then at Ascott until 1914. Waddesdon – the equally notable Rothschild house – is only a few miles away.

Ascott is distinguished not for its architec-

Louis XV black lacquer writing table stamped Joseph Baumhauer and BVRB; Ascott.

Famille verte horses and riders, K'ang Hsi, c.1680–1720; Ascott.

ture but for its superb collections of paintings, Chinese ceramics and 18th-century furniture, especially French, inherited or acquired by the late Anthony de Rothschild (1887–1961), who gave Ascott to the National Trust in 1961.

The particularly fine collection of 17th-century Dutch paintings includes Hobbema's *Cottages in a Wood*, Cuyp's *Dordrecht on the Maas* – a lovely scene flooded with the golden light of evening, de Jongh's *A Lady receiving a Letter*, together with works by Adriaen and Isaac van Ostade, Berchem, van der Heyden, Decker, Wouvermans, Wynants, Maes and Steen. There are several outstanding English paintings, including two impressive Gainsboroughs, especially that of the cool, appraising Duchess of Richmond, portraits by Hogarth, Reynolds and Romney, a splendid Italian scene by Turner and Stubbs' *Five Mares*. Other master works include del Sarto's *Madonna and Child with St John*, G. B. Tiepolo's *The Ascent of the Virgin* and Lotto's *A Prelate*.

Among the splendid examples of French 18th-century furniture are pieces signed by such distinguished *ébénistes* as M. G. Cramer, Franz Rübestuck, the Sauniers, Philippe-Claude Montigny and J. H. Riesener. The outstanding piece is perhaps the Louis XV black lacquer writing table in the Drawing Room bearing the stamps of Joseph Baumhauer and

'BVRB'. The fine English furniture includes a Queen Anne walnut cabinet, a William and Mary gilt gesso mirror, a Chippendale suite *c*.1760 and, in the Library, fine mahogany pieces, often crisply carved, and chairs upholstered in *gros point* and *petit point* needlework. The carpets of the 16th and 17th centuries are from Isfahan.

The great collection of Chinese ceramics and porcelain includes early pieces from the Han, T'ang and Sung dynasties, some perfect in their faultless simplicity of shape, and a wide-ranging selection of impressive K'ang Hsi porcelain, in enamels of the *famille jaune*, *famille verte* and *famille noire*, but outstanding are the rare late Ming Dynasty *san ts'ai* (three colours).

Ashdown House Oxfordshire

The National Trust

2½ miles s of Ashbury and 3½ miles N of Lambourn on B400

The 1st Lord Craven (1608–97) dedicated his life and fortune to Elizabeth, the much loved daughter of James I. Known as the Winter Queen because of the brief period during the winter of 1619–20 when her husband was King of Bohemia, Elizabeth returned to England in

1632 on her husband's death, and it is said that Lord Craven built Ashdown House, isolated high on the Berkshire Downs, for her on the Restoration of the Stuarts in 1660. Elizabeth died in 1662 and would never have seen the house completed but it remains, with its collection of portraits, as a romantic reminder of Lord Craven's devotion to her.

In the Hall and on the robust oak Staircase, which rises to an octagonal cupola on the flat roof summit, hang 23 grave, stately portraits of the Winter Queen, her family and friends, by Michel van Miereveldt and by or after Honthorst. On the top landing is a conversation piece by Dobson, one of the earliest of its kind, depicting Prince Rupert, the Winter Queen's son, with two royalists during the Civil War. Miereveldt (d. 1641) never visited England and his portraits of Elizabeth's friends and supporters date from before 1632. Honthorst's portrait of Elizabeth as Queen of Bohemia – who was called Queen of Hearts because of her vivacity and charm – is dated

Gerrit van Honthorst's portrait of Elizabeth,
Princess Royal (1618–86), at Ashdown House.

1650 and the others by him probably also date from about that time. These portraits almost certainly formed part of the Winter Queen's own collection and were bequeathed by her to the 1st Lord Craven. They were purchased by the Treasury at the Craven sale in 1968 and given to the National Trust.

Aston Hall West Midlands

The Corporation of Birmingham

2½ miles N from centre of city. Entrance for cars at Frederick Road

Aston Hall, a diaper-patterned red-brick mansion with two projecting wings, its park now surrounded by housing, was built for the Holte family 1618–37, when the influence of the Italian Renaissance was in the ascendant. There were major alterations both in the late-17th century, as a result of Civil War damage, and in the 18th. The strapwork ceilings, unusual friezes and vigorous chimneypieces of carved stone, inset with black marble 'jewels', which embellish the spacious Jacobean rooms vary in date from the 17th to the early-19th centuries. The figures of warriors in high relief in the frieze of the Great Drawing Room, which was Sir Thomas Holte's Great Dining Room or Great Chamber, are mostly believed to be original, though the panelling and ceiling are 18th-century alterations. The Great Stairs are a fine example of Jacobean craftsmanship.

Much of the furniture and paintings are from elsewhere as most of the Holte family possessions were auctioned in 1817. Noteworthy furniture pieces include two shell-back chairs, probably by Francis Cleyn, and a fine oak cupboard, dated 1690, in the Entrance Hall and an English lacquer cabinet, *c.*1700, and two early-17th-century Italian chairs covered in Turkey work in the Long Gallery, whose early-17th-century tapestries were made in Paris. Lady Holte's Drawing Room is decorated with mid-18th-century needlework hangings and a remarkable carpet worked *en suite* with the Holte arms.

Among the paintings are portraits by

Jacobean carved staircase at Aston Hall.

Beechey, Gainsborough, Soldi, Reynolds and Romney, two late-17th-century decorative landscapes in the style of Jacques Rousseau and a view of Castel Gandolfo by or after Richard Wilson.

Some changes will be made in April 1981.

Athelhampton Dorset

Sir Robert Cooke

½ mile E of Puddletown on A35, 5 miles NE of Dorchester

Before Henry VII's accession in 1485, the use of stone had been confined largely to churches because of its expense. The prosperity and stability of the Tudor period led to its increasing employment in domestic architecture and Dorset, rich in Purbeck and other stone, witnessed some of the earliest developments of domestic building in stone. Among the first was the handsome medieval mansion of Athelhampton, boldly started by Sir William Martyn in Henry VII's coronation year. Carefully and successfully restored in 1848 and 1891 and, after another period of neglect, further enhanced by the present owner and his father, Athelhampton stands amid lovely gardens, encircled by the River Piddle.

The Great Hall, with its substantially original timbered roof, contains oak furniture

31

of the 16th and 17th centuries, including a 16th-century buffet and a William and Mary love-seat covered in Flemish weave. Much of the stained glass in the windows is original. The chamber organ, *c*.1800, in the Minstrels' Gallery stands in a Gothic case, designed by James Wyatt. The large Dutch brass chandelier is dated 1756 and came from Vanbrugh's Kings Weston.

The walnut furniture in the Great Chamber, with its fine 17th-century plasterwork ceiling and oak panelling, is mainly William and Mary, including the bureau bookcase and tallboy; the display cabinet with broken pediment and the mask of Apollo is in the manner of Kent and the fine marquetry-cased harpsichord, dated 1761, was made by Kirkman for Queen Charlotte. The portrait of the daughters of the Governor of Greenwich Hospital is by Mercier. The Dining Room with its Chippendale-style mahogany furniture contains a splendid chinoiserie rococo mirror and an attractive collection of Parian figures.

LEFT *The Tudor Great Hall at Athelhampton; the timbered roof and stained glass are mostly original.*

Between the two east windows is a mirror by Thomas Johnson.

At the top of the Great Stair is an oak-panelled room containing prints by Joseph Nash of the opening of the Crystal Palace, and others of Barry's New Palace of Westminster. The great elaborately carved four-poster bed from Montacute in the State Bedroom once belonged to Lord Curzon. Wallpapers designed by Pugin for the House of Lords have been effectively used in the Screens Passage and elsewhere.

Attingham Park Shropshire

The National Trust

4 miles SE of Shrewsbury on A5

The imposing, neo-classical mansion of Attingham Park, looking south across Repton's parkland, was developed from the modest Queen Anne home of the Hill family for Noel

BELOW *'The Tiger Hunt': a detail from the 'Vue de l'Inde' wallpaper, c.1815, in the East Ante-room, Attingham Park.*

Hill, 1st Lord Berwick, by the Scottish architect, George Steuart. The 2nd Baron employed John Nash to add the Picture Gallery, then something of an innovation, which contains a large collection of 16th- and 17th-century Italian paintings, some of them copies, and portraits by Kneller and Northcote. Nash altered Steuart's Entrance Hall, marbling the walls but leaving intact the plasterwork ceiling, the scagliola columns and pilasters, and he also introduced the four grisailles by Robert Fagan, ordered by the 2nd Lord Berwick when he was in Italy. Some of the enchanting early-19th-century white and gilt Neapolitan furniture in the Drawing Room belonged to Caroline Murat, Queen of Naples – the 3rd Lord Berwick was Ambassador in Sardinia, Savoy and Naples.

The Entrance Hall was designed to stand centrally between Lord Berwick's apartments, which include the stately Dining Room, later painted Pompeian red, the restrained Octagon Room and the austere Library, and Lady Berwick's apartments. Her elegant Drawing Room with its blue silk upholstery contains Italian landscapes by Hackert and a marble figure of Venus after Canova; the remarkable 'Vue de l'Inde' printed wallpaper, *c*.1815, in the East Ante-room is by Joseph Dufour of Paris; and the Boudoir is decorated in an exceptionally delicate manner with arabesques, probably the work of the French decorative painter, Louis André Delabrière, who was active in the late-18th century. Here also is a fine chimneypiece, almost certainly supplied by the younger John Deval. By contrast, the Dining Room furniture by Gillow is boldly masculine, the backs of the chairs inlaid with a vine pattern in ormolu echoing the vine leaves of the delicate plasterwork ceiling which lends the room such distinction.

Among the family portraits are works by Cotes, Lawrence, Angelica Kauffmann, Hayter and Sickert. Attingham also contains a fine Paris dinner service by Dagoty which may have been made for the Empress Josephine.

Audley End Essex

The Department of the Environment

1 mile w of Saffron Walden on A11

A first impression of Audley End is of an unusual but compelling early Jacobean mansion. It is intriguing to discover that it is only a third of its original size and that the interior dates mainly from the late-18th century.

Started in 1603, it was built for Lord Howard de Walden, created Earl of Suffolk by James I whose Lord High Treasurer he became. Such was its size that James supposedly remarked that it was too large for a king but might do for a Lord Treasurer; soon afterwards Lord Suffolk was disgraced. After the Restoration Audley End became a royal palace and its full extent can be seen from Winstanley's engraving of 1676 on the South Staircase. In 1721 Vanbrugh advised the 7th Earl, to whom the building had been returned by the Crown, to reduce its size by two-thirds. The 1st Lord Braybrooke (1719–97), who inherited Audley End in 1762, was mainly responsible for what exists today, part of which was decorated by Robert Adam. The reorganization was completed by the 3rd Lord Braybrooke in the 1820s.

The immensely impressive Hall has at its north end a remarkably elaborate wooden screen, the work of Italian carvers *c*.1605. The stone screen and the double stone staircase with gilt iron balusters at the south end are attributed to Vanbrugh. The Hall contains a notable 15th-century pear-wood carving of a saint, a French 16th-century cabinet and faded silk heraldic banners emblazoned with the bearings of Audley End's various owners. Joseph Rose Junior, working in the 1760s, was responsible for the frieze in the Saloon; the ceiling and chimneypiece belong to the original early-17th-century house. The other first-floor rooms are early-19th-century and contain good furniture and fine paintings. There is Chinese Chippendale furniture in the Saloon and a Louis XVI writing table stamped by Montigny

RIGHT *The elaborate wooden screen, c.1605, in the Hall at Audley End.*

in the Drawing Room, now called Lord Braybrooke's Sitting Room. Adam originally decorated six ground-floor rooms, of which three remain. The Great Drawing Room and the Little Drawing Room, in which Rebecca's work is prominent, are particularly good examples of his style.

The house contains royal and family portraits by Pine (*George II*), Rebecca, Seeman, Beechey, Dobson, a number by Lely, especially the double portrait of the architect Hugh May and himself, and by Reynolds, but perhaps the finest is that of the Duchess of Norfolk, mother of the 1st Earl of Suffolk, signed and dated by Hans Eworth. Other paintings include excellent works by Van Goyen and Canaletto.

The late-18th-century Strawberry Hill Gothic Chapel contains an unusual set of Chippendale chairs in the Gothic manner and good 18th-century painted glass designed by Rebecca and executed by Peckitt of York.

At the time of writing, the contents of the house were being rearranged.

Avebury Manor Wiltshire

The Marquess of Ailesbury

In village of Avebury

This delightful Elizabethan manor house, close to the largest Megalithic Circle in Europe, was built mainly of sandstone in about 1557 on what had once been monastic land. It was partly rebuilt at the beginning of the 17th century and some of the interior redecorated in contemporary fashionable style in the 1730s, since when there has been little change. It stands amid lawns and ancient timber with the tower of the 15th-century church rising above the wall of the rose garden. It was acquired by its present owner in 1976.

Among the family portraits are those by Paul van Somer of the 1st Earl of Elgin and his wife in the Queen Anne Dining Room, that of Thomas Brudenell-Bruce, for whom the Earldom of Ailesbury was re-created in 1776, by Reynolds on the Staircase wall, and those of

Early-17th-century stumpwork box depicting Sheba's meeting with Solomon; Avebury Manor.

the 1st Marquess and his wife by Angelica Kauffmann in the panelled Elizabethan Great Parlour. Portraits of Lady Elizabeth Seymour and the 1st Earl of Elgin by Lely are in the Queen Anne Bedroom, where the Queen Anne bed is embellished with fine needlework hangings made in 1910, and an unusual stumpwork dressing box, depicting Sheba's meeting with Solomon.

The Elizabethan Little Parlour, in the oldest part of the house, contains 16th-century panelling, a harlequin set of twelve 17th-century dining chairs with their original leather coverings and studs, each slightly different in design, and pewter plates. Good panelling, a finely carved fireplace and a decorative plaster ceiling and frieze enrich the Elizabethan Bedroom. There is 16th- and 17th-century oak furniture and panelling in the Cavalier Bedroom.

Avington Park Hampshire

Mr J. B. Hickson

4 miles NE of Winchester, just S of B3047 in Itchen Abbas

Avington Park is surrounded by well-wooded parkland through which the River Itchen gently flows. Originally a monastic property, building was carried out here in Elizabethan times when the Banqueting Hall was raised on the site of the present Orangery. The house was remodelled after the Restoration by George Brydges, who hoped that Charles II would

*The Ballroom ceiling, Avington Park, with late-18th-century
gilding and a central panel perhaps by Valdrè*

reside here when in Winchester. Further changes were made after the property passed by inheritance to the Marquess of Caernarvon, later 3rd Duke of Chandos.

The walls of the Hall, which has marbled wooden columns at each end, were attractively painted towards the end of the 18th century with panels of fruit and flowers to which cupids, perhaps adapted from Bartolozzi, were added very early in the 19th century. These cupids have since been transferred on to the Hall tables. The Hall ceiling simulates an open sky with flying birds. On the walls of the elegant Library, originally a white and gold passage, are lunettes on which Pegasus, nymphs and centaurs are depicted in Pompeian style, added perhaps about 1780.

The main Staircase, with its fine handrail and balustrade representing honeysuckle, leads to the magnificent Ballroom, undoubtedly the finest room in the house; here the head of Bacchus at four different ages is featured in the plasterwork gold-enriched cornice, at the tops of the great pier-glasses and on their attendant console tables, which were made c.1760. The painting in the centre of the ceiling and those on the Ballroom doors may be the work of Valdrè who painted the arabesques at Stowe. There are also earlier subsidiary panels on the ceiling painted somewhat in the style of Verrio.

The cornice of the impressive Red Drawing Room with its gilded pelmets is graced with gilded sunflowers and cornsheaves. The walls are embellished with large panels showing birds and butterflies perched on bowls of fruit and flowers, while smaller early Victorian panels display Plantagenet, Tudor and other figures. Its furnishings include Hepplewhite and early French Empire pieces.

Bamburgh Castle Northumberland

The Lord Armstrong

On the coast 16 miles N of Alnwick, 3 miles from Seahouses

Built by the Normans on a site of great antiquity, Bamburgh Castle, high above the

sea facing eastwards to the Farne Islands, enjoys one of the finest locations in Britain. After the Union of England and Scotland under James I, the Castle fell into decay, to be rescued and partly restored in the early-18th century by Lord Crewe, the last of the Bishops Palatine of Durham, who bequeathed the Castle for charitable purposes. Towards the end of the 19th century, the trustees of the charity fell into financial difficulties, and in 1888 it was sold to the 1st Lord Armstrong, industrialist and philanthropist, who restored it with the finest craftsmanship and materials available.

The lofty Entrance Hall and several small rooms off it have been made into a museum with a fascinating miscellany, ranging from fragments of an Anglo-Saxon cross, once in the medieval chapel, to Russian muskets and helmets captured in the Crimean War, and to Central Asian armour, a gift to the 1st Lord Armstrong from the Russian ambassador. Of special interest is the so-called 'Bamburgh Beast', a small gold object, c.AD 650, which is an outstanding example of Anglo-Saxon zoomorphic art. There are also oil paintings and watercolours by T. M. Richardson, both Senior and Junior, a picture by Richard Wilson showing the 18th-century decay of the Castle, and sketches by de Wint and Annigoni – the latter's portrait of Lady Armstrong is in the Court Room. Other objects include Sèvres and

The engraved gold 'Bamburgh Beast', c.650, an oustanding example of Anglo-Saxon zoomorphic art.

blue Spode porcelain, Bohemian cut glass, Venetian mirrors and French Empire walnut chairs.

The striking Great or King's Hall, with the Cross Hall beyond, is a vast late-19th-century chamber with a 'false hammer-beam' roof and panelled wainscoting made of Siamese teak, carved at Cragside, then Lord Armstrong's seat. It contains portraits of personalities associated with Bamburgh and remarkably fine collections of arms and armour, some on loan from the Tower of London, and others from the Joicey Museum in Newcastle, of medals and decorations, Chinese jade, works by Fabergé, and English, Continental and Oriental porcelain. In the Cross Hall are Flemish tapestries and an Aubusson carpet.

Of special interest in the Faire Chamber is the late-17th- to early-18th-century Spanish furniture from the Palace of the Dukes of Osuña, as well as a river scene by Jan Breughel II. There are more well-displayed weapons in the Armoury, mainly Napoleonic, and a sumptuous Italian marriage chest in the Court Room where hang the Armstrong family portraits.

Basildon Park Berkshire

The National Trust

2½ miles NW of Pangbourne on A329 to Wallingford

Basildon Park was built between 1776 and 1783 by John Carr of York for Sir Francis Sykes, who had made a fortune in India. The overall design, two pavilions flanking a main block, is that of a Palladian villa but the original plasterwork, which still embellishes the Hall, Staircase, Dining Room and Drawing Room, is in the delicate neo-classical style made popular by Robert Adam. In 1910 the house became empty and, apart from being used by troops in both World Wars, remained so until it was acquired in a derelict state by Lord and Lady Iliffe. Since then, they have restored it with the greatest care and affection, very successfully using fittings, including the glorious scagliola chimneypieces in the Dining Room and Library, taken from now demolished Panton in Lincolnshire, another Carr house. In 1977 Lord and Lady Iliffe very generously gave the house and contents to the National Trust.

The creator of the magnificent plasterwork is not known for certain; William Roberts, son of the better known Thomas Roberts of Oxford, is the most likely candidate. It is seen at its grandest in the Hall, whose admirable carved mahogany doors with their ormolu handles and escutcheons have been returned to their original home here. The Hall's most notable furniture is the pair of painted side-tables with marble tops after the manner of Kent, *c.*1730.

The other rooms on the *piano nobile* are hung with paintings, mainly Italian and most of them late-17th and 18th century, collected by Lord and Lady Iliffe. The Octagon Drawing Room contains a series of religious paintings by Batoni, who is better known in England for his portraits of English visitors in Rome on the Grand Tour. The three above the doorways are by the Venetian Pittoni. The large painting *Rebecca at the Well* in the Green Drawing Room is by Galeotti and the two Arcadian landscapes by Orizonte. On the Great Staircase – its wrought-iron balustrade of exactly the same pattern as that at Heveningham Hall, Suffolk – are two romantic views by Bonavia, a pupil of Vernet, and a small Pannini. Two views of Venice by Marlow grace the Library.

The many fine pieces of furniture include a gilt overmantel mirror in the Adam manner in the Library; a lovely pair of carved and painted urns on pedestals, possibly by James Wyatt, in the Staircase Hall; an outstanding pair of gilt console tables and pier-glasses, *c.*1773, on which stands a pair of bronze and ormolu candelabra, probably by Thomire, in the Octagon Room. This room also houses a fine pair of tripod candle-stands in the Robert Adam manner and eight Gothic-style mahogany armchairs designed by Porden, *c.*1810. The Green Drawing Room contains two splendid marquetry commodes with marble

The Octagon Drawing Room, Basildon Park, built 1776–83.

tops, seat furniture in Louis XVI style, and two Regency armchairs with Egyptian heads supporting the arm-rests, possibly made by the royal upholsterers Morel and Seddon.

Upstairs in the Crimson Bedroom is a magnificent state bed, *c*.1829, with its original crimson damask hangings. Another remarkable bed is in the Bamboo Room; the tester and end-posts are carved and painted to resemble bamboo. In the Shell Room a collection of shells amassed by the present Lord Iliffe's mother is displayed in a decorative setting designed and executed by Mr Gordon Davies in 1978.

Bateman's East Sussex

The National Trust

½ mile S of Burwash on A265
Hawkhurst–Heathfield road

Bateman's, built in 1634 and a very characteristic example of a Jacobean country house, was the home of Rudyard Kipling from 1902 until his death in 1936 and the writer's personality pervades the house. Kipling's writing tools still lie on the 17th-century ink-stained chestnut writing table in his study, preserved as it was in the author's lifetime complete with his books, his early-18th-century walnut chair, two large globes and his spacious waste-paper basket. Elsewhere there is solid 17th-century oak furniture, Mortlake and Brussels tapestries, the Dining Room 'papered' in fine Spanish leather, several unusual 17th-century firebacks and a scattering of oriental curios, reminders of Kipling's fascination with the East. There are watercolours by Sir Edward Poynter and sketches by Sir Edward Burne-Jones, both of them Kipling's uncles; and, particularly interesting, eight plaques by Kipling's father to illustrate his son's work.

Beaulieu Palace House
Hampshire

The Lord Montagu of Beaulieu

In Beaulieu, 5 miles SE of Lyndhurst

The National Motor Museum for which Beaulieu is widely and rightly renowned stands close to the well-preserved ruins of the Cistercian Abbey, established here in 1204. The estate was acquired in 1538 by Thomas Wriothesley, later Lord Chancellor to Henry VIII and 1st Earl of Southampton. Nearly 350 years later it was given to the 1st Lord Montagu of Beaulieu, the present owner's grandfather, as a wedding present by his father, the 5th Duke of Buccleuch, whose family had inherited it via the Dukes of Montagu from the 4th Earl of Southampton. Palace House, originally the monastery's gatehouse and now the family home, took its present Victorian Gothic shape, in which parts of the early-14th-century building can still be seen, between 1870 and 1873.

Family portraits hang in the Front Hall, including that by John Collier, RA, of the 2nd Lord Montagu of Beaulieu, founder of *The Car* magazine, who helped build the road through the Khyber Pass to Afghanistan from the north-west frontier; the most distinguished is that of the present owner, recently completed by Patrick Procktor. The Lower Drawing Room, constructed like the Dining Hall from the original medieval building, contains a

ABOVE *Rudyard Kipling's Study, Bateman's.*
BELOW *Portrait of Henry Wriothesley, 3rd Earl of Southampton (1573–1624); Beaulieu Palace House.*

Clock, 1671–3, by Joseph Knibb;
Belgrave Hall.

Belgrave Hall Leicestershire

Leicestershire Museums

Off Thurcaston road, Belgrave, 2 miles N of
Leicester city centre on A6 to Loughborough

Belgrave Hall, a pleasant unpretentious red-
brick house, was built for Edmund Cradock
1709–14. Now engulfed by Leicester's suburbs,
it contains good early-18th-century furniture
and other period furnishings not original to the
house. In the Drawing Room is a Cuban
mahogany settee and set of chairs *c*.1725, with
lion masks on the cabriole legs, a red lacquer
writing bureau, an 'apron' table with carved
flap, *c*.1730, and a fine clock, 1671–3, by Joseph
Knibb. The Dining Room possesses a pretty
neo-classical marble fireplace and Chinese
Chippendale-style upright chairs.

Other notable items include an early-18th-
century cabinet with oyster-shell walnut
veneer in the First Bedroom, and two giltwood
rococo girandoles in the Music Room, which
also contains a Bland and Weiler piano, *c*.1790
and a harp, 1836, by Sebastian Erard. There are
portraits attributed to Hoare and Hudson on
the Staircase and a suitably impressive portrait
of Ambassador Burnaby in the Burnaby
Room, attributed to the Swiss painter, Emanuel Jacob Hardman.

Belle Isle Cumbria

Mr E. S. C. Curwen

On island of Lake Windermere

This singular, handsome, circular house,
enchantingly sited on the largest island in Lake
Windermere, was completed in 1778 by John
Plaw, who was later a master-builder in
Westminster and responsible for Paddington
Church. Its construction was commissioned by
a Mr English who sold it in 1791 to Isabella
Curwen, whose husband took her surname and
from whom the present owner is descended.
Much criticized by Wordsworth, whose son,
the Rev. William Wordsworth, married
Isabella's granddaughter, and described by a

cabinet displaying both Worcester and Chinese
porcelain and a series of maps of the Beaulieu
estate at various dates. Among the family
likenesses in the Portrait Gallery are versions of
the 1st and 2nd Dukes of Montagu by Hudson,
that of Lady Mary Wortley Montagu by Jervas
and Wissing's *Duke of Monmouth*. A set of
southern European ports by Antonio Joli, a
follower of Canaletto, is in the Dining Hall;
and an equally pleasing series of views of
Naples painted in oils by the same artist
embellish the private Dining Room, whose
linenfold panelling was salvaged from the
Houses of Parliament, which were destroyed
by fire in 1834.

contemporary writer as a 'Dutch Burgo-master's Palace', it nevertheless inspired Frederick Hervey, the 4th Earl of Bristol and Bishop of Derry, in planning his building at Ickworth. The discovery of Roman artefacts during the building of Belle Isle supports the theory that the island was once occupied by a Roman villa.

The slightly cramped interior is decorated in the neo-classical style of the period, as seen in the elegant Drawing Room with its marble chimneypiece and its plasterwork on ceiling and walls, and in the white and yellow Dining Room with its frieze of foxes' masks and Gothic chairs made by Gillow. There are portraits by Romney, notably that of Isabella Curwen, and a view by de Loutherbourg of the house soon after its completion.

Carved oak seat in the Hall at Belle Isle.

Belton House Lincolnshire

The Lord Brownlow

2 miles NE of Grantham on A607

'The most accomplished of all Restoration houses' according to John Cornforth, Belton, built 1685–8, perhaps to plans by William Winde for Sir John Brownlow, has an interior as gracious as its exterior is stately. Belton was inherited by Sir John's nephew, created Viscount Tyrconnel, who died without issue. His sister, Anne, Lady Cust, was his heir and outlived her husband, Speaker Cust. Her grandson was created a Baron in 1776 and his son an Earl, a title which became extinct on the death of the 3rd Earl in 1921. The exterior of the house has been little changed but James Wyatt was employed to design the Library with its barrel-vaulted ceiling and good plasterwork, while Wyatville worked on the Staircase and the elegant Red Drawing Room.

The spacious black and white marble-floored Entrance Hall is hung with Brownlow and Cust family portraits by Romney, Hoppner and Owen together with a Lely state portrait of Charles II, facing Reynolds' suitably magisterial likeness of Sir John Cust, Speaker 1761–70, with the painter's own highly professional self-portrait nearby. Other portraitists well represented here, in the State Rooms and on the sturdy walnut Staircase include Kneller, Lawrence, Wissing, Jervas (*1st Lord Tyrconnel*), Seeman, Riley (including four impressive full-length Brownlow daughters in the Saloon), Mercier, Leighton (the wife of the 3rd Earl Brownlow) and Watts. Upstairs, in James Wyatt's Library, is a portrait of King Edward VIII, with other mementos of the brief reign before his abdication; the 6th Lord Brownlow was his close friend and Lord-in-Waiting in 1936. There are also fine paintings in the Red Drawing Room by or attributed to Rembrandt, Rubens, Ruysdael, Titian and Van Dyck, while Tintoretto's moving *Entombment* is in the Chapel.

The superb plasterwork ceilings above the Staircase, whose handsome baluster rail is inlaid with brass, in the Saloon, and especially in the

Chapel, where *putti* are entangled with flowers and fir cones, are by Goudge. The magnificent wood carving surrounding portraits and added to overmantels and wall panels is intriguing; payments are recorded to Edmund Carpenter but some may be by Gibbons himself. Wyatt designed the fine ceiling with its *trompe l'œil* fluting in the Lady's Boudoir and Robert Adam the even finer fireplace.

The furniture is of high quality. In the Entrance Hall stand giltwood marble-topped tables, supported by the Brownlow grey-hounds, together with Speaker Cust's chair, chest and solid silver wine cooler 'presented by the nation' on his retirement. The pier-glasses and attendant console tables in the Saloon are in Kent's best manner. The Red Drawing Room is furnished in French Empire style and contains two notable cabinets on giltwood stands, one Italian and the other lacquered. The Saloon and Red Drawing Room boast splendid Aubusson carpets; the Brownlow arms are painted on the wooden floor of the Tyrconnel Room, one of the few known examples in England.

Upstairs, Bow, Chelsea, Plymouth and Meissen porcelain are displayed in the Ante-Library, while good examples of 18th-century Chinese wares are to be found in most rooms. In the Blue Bedroom, the bed, one of the tallest known, and the fine walnut bureau-cabinets are William and Mary. The door and wall panels in the Chinese Bedroom simulate bamboo; the enchanting hand-painted wall-paper represents a Chinese garden party.

Belvoir Castle Leicestershire

The Duke of Rutland

7 miles wsw of Grantham between A607 and A52

This wooded hill-top, dominating the Vale of Belvoir and crowned by a stronghold since the Norman Conquest, came by marriage in the Tudor period to the already distinguished Manners family, later Earls and Dukes of Rutland. The magnificent martial Regency mansion with many neo-Gothic features which we see today replaced John Webb's castle, built after the Civil War. Started by James Wyatt in 1801, the house was partly destroyed by fire in 1816; its restoration was undertaken by the Rev. Sir John Thoroton, the Duke's domestic chaplain and an amateur architect, assisted by Wyatt's three sons.

The elaborate Gothic Guardroom contains a fine collection of weapons and other military mementos of the Leicestershire Militia. The Museum of the 17th/21st Lancers is housed nearby. In Thoroton's elaborate Gothic Ball-room at the top of the Grand Staircase are ducal portraits by Closterman, Jervas, Reynolds, Hoppner and Dame Laura Knight, RA, together with show-cases containing medieval seals and coronation robes.

The Chinese Rooms, the bedroom walls hung with 18th-century Chinese hand-painted silks, lead to the florid Elizabethan Saloon, named after Elizabeth, the 5th Duchess, whose taste and enthusiasm greatly influenced the final phase of the Castle's decoration. She commissioned Matthew, James Wyatt's third son, to furnish the Saloon in the sumptuous late style of Louis XIV, starting a new fashion, and to paint the somewhat pretentious allegorical scenes on its ceiling. The white and gold panelling is from a château of Madame de Maintenon, mistress of Louis XIV; the gilded seat furniture upholstered in rose-red silk and the fine Aubusson carpet are of the same period. Matthew Wyatt sculpted the statue of the 5th Duchess.

Reynolds' fine portraits of the 4th Duke and the warrior Marquis of Granby preside over the Grand Dining Room with its Regency mahogany furniture, the table and sideboards resplendent with silver, including a fine punch bowl of 1682, and a notable side-table by Matthew Wyatt, seemingly covered with a table-cloth but actually modelled from marble.

The Picture Gallery contains some of Belvoir's greatest treasures – the Stuart bed with original Venetian velvet hangings, elaborately carved gilt chairs from the Borghese Palace in Rome, English 16th-century silver and a glorious collection of miniatures by, among others, Cosway, Isaac and Peter

LEFT *The Chinese Bedroom with 18th-century hand-painted wallpaper; Belton House.*

Nicolas Poussin Extreme Unction, *c.1630, one of a set of 'The Seven Sacraments'; Belvoir Castle.*

Oliver, Liotard, Samuel Shelley and Catherine Read. The paintings include two woodland scenes by Gainsborough, Siberechts' view of Chevely Park, delightful genre paintings by Steen and the younger Teniers, three of an outstanding set of 'The Seven Sacraments' by Nicolas Poussin (a further two are in the Chapel), bought by the 4th Duke on Reynolds' advice, *The Dutch Fleet* by the younger Van de Velde and an imperious *Henry VIII* attributed to Holbein.

The spacious Regent's Gallery, the finest apartment at Belvoir, possesses a set of Gobelins tapestries of Don Quixote's adventures, each piece bearing the Manners' peacock crest, Nollekens' series of busts of the Prince Regent, the younger Pitt, the Marquis of Granby and others, Canova's *Three Graces*, much excellent 18th-century and Regency furniture, 17th-century blue and white Chinese vases and a Derby porcelain dinner service with inset nautical scenes, 1790. The Gothic chapel contains a *Holy Family* by Murillo over the altar and Mortlake tapestries of the Acts of the Apostles. The Old Kitchen, Servants' Hall and the Beer Cellars are also open.

Beningbrough Hall
North Yorkshire

The National Trust

8 miles NW of York, 3 miles W of Shipton (A19)

This glorious Baroque red-brick house, standing in a loop of the River Ouse in the Vale of York, was completed in 1716, over 170 years after the estate was granted by Henry VIII to one John Banister, whose daughter married James Bourchier, illegitimate son of the 2nd

RIGHT *Corner of the wood-panelled State Dressing Room, Beningbrough Hall, with Oriental porcelain displayed on the stepped overmantel.*

Lord Berners. The estate remained in the Bourchier family until 1917. Although acquired by the National Trust in 1957, it was not until 1979 that the house was opened to the public on a regular basis in conjunction with the National Portrait Gallery, which has placed on display an outstanding collection of portraits of the period 1688 to 1760 by the most distinguished painters of the day, and which has also established an exhibition on the attic floor. Most of the State Rooms have been redecorated with the guidance of Mr David Mlinaric using colours found in the house and known to have been used in the 18th century.

Beningbrough was built under the supervision of William Thornton, a carpenter-architect from York, perhaps with advice from Thomas Archer. Thornton's greatest contributions are the magnificent wood carving of the cornices, friezes and overmantels of the ground floor State Rooms, especially in what is now the Drawing Room – originally two rooms, each with its own distinctive entablature – in the Saloon, and in Lady Chesterfield's Room and Dressing Room on the first floor; the 10th Earl and Countess of Chesterfield acquired the house in 1917. On Lady Chesterfield's death in 1957, the Treasury accepted the Hall and park in part payment of death duties and gave them to the Trust.

The magnificent Baroque crimson damask state bed in the State Bedroom, in the style of Daniel Marot, the bed in Lady Chesterfield's Room and the splendid walnut pier tables and pier-glasses, c.1690, in the Drawing Room came from Holme Lacy, the Chesterfield family home. Walnut furniture bequeathed by the late Lady Megaw includes a superb Queen Anne walnut bureau-bookcase in the Drawing Room and the late-17th-century walnut cabinet with doors of 'oyster veneer' in the State Bedchamber. Other furniture includes the nine dining chairs, c.1715, in the style of Giles Grendy.

A number of pieces of Oriental porcelain were given in 1975 by Miss Dorothy Bushell, and other pieces generously loaned by the Ashmolean Museum, Oxford, which fill the overmantels with stepped edges for displaying porcelain in the smaller closets, especially those in the ground floor Dressing Room and Closet which contain mainly K'ang Hsi pieces. Other noteworthy features include the remarkably delicate wood carved baluster of the Great Staircase, again the work of Thornton and his team of carvers, and the magnificent wrought-iron grills in the side walls of the Hall, attributed to the renowned blacksmith, Robert Bakewell.

Benthall Hall Shropshire

The National Trust

4 miles NE of Much Wenlock, 1 mile NW of Broseley (B4375)

This fine example of a late-16th-century house was built for the Benthalls, a family almost certainly of Anglo-Saxon origin who remained loyal to the Stuarts and the Roman Catholic faith – the Hall contains hiding places contrived for fugitive priests.

The elaborately carved oak staircase, panelling and plasterwork were added in the reigns of James I or Charles I and the house contains good furniture of these periods. The panelling in the Entrance Hall is 18th century but the heraldic overmantel dates from c.1630, the oak refectory table and large cupboard at the west end from a few years later, while the oak armchair was made c.1600 and the heavy turned oak chair, traditionally belonging to the Abbot of Neath Abbey, could be much earlier. The pewter here is late-18th-century Welsh.

The West Drawing Room has a fine plaster ceiling of c.1630, elaborate with strapwork and jewelling, and probably the work of Italians. Even more ambitious is the frieze carved with various birds and beasts. The chimneypieces here and in the Dining Room are by Thomas Pritchard who, among other achievements, designed the Coalbrookdale iron bridge. Examples of porcelain made at the nearby Caughley factory between 1775 and 1799 are on display and there is 18th-century Chinese armorial porcelain in the Dining Room.

The chimneypiece designed by Thomas Farnolls Pritchard in 1756 in the Dining Room of Benthall Hall.   49

Berkeley Castle Gloucestershire

Mr and Mrs R. J. Berkeley

Midway between Bristol and Gloucester

This ancient fortification, a little to the east of where the Severn estuary meets the Bristol Channel, was built to dominate the River Severn and the Bristol–Gloucester road. 'The giant wall and buttresses', wrote Miss Gertrude Jekyll, 'look as if they have been carved by wind and weather out of some solid rock-mass, rather than wrought by human handiwork.' Today a peaceful air envelops the Castle, but it was here that Edward II was foully murdered in

the wretched cell which can be seen off the King's Gallery, and later its walls were breached by Parliamentarians in the Civil War.

The keep was constructed in *c.*1153 and the buildings round the courtyard some thirty years later by the Berkeley family, which traces its ancestry to pre-Norman days and still lives here. Modern comforts have been introduced, but the Dining Room, the Long and Small Drawing Rooms and especially the Morning Room, once the Chapel with its timbered roof inscribed with verses from St John the Divine, remain uncompromisingly medieval.

In the magnificent Great Hall, which dates from *c.*1340, the wooden screen retains its 16th-

The Great Hall, dating from c.1340, at Berkeley Castle; the wooden screen has painted 16th-century decorations.

century painted decoration; the fine tapestries are from Oudenarde. There are also superb Brussels sets in the Morning Room and Small Drawing Room, while the walls above the Grand Stairs are hung with late-16th-century embroideries.

Family portraits include works by Kneller, Batoni, Cotes, Gainsborough, Reynolds and Hoppner, while the Dining Room contains likenesses of 20th-century Berkeleys wearing the distinctive canary-yellow coats of the Berkeley Hunt and the Old Berkeley (now the Vale of Aylesbury) Hunt. A painting of the Old Berkeley hounds, attributed to Marshall, hangs in the Picture Gallery together with a fine Stubbs, a view of 17th-century Berkeley Castle by Knyff and seascapes by or after the younger Van de Velde.

The furniture ranges broadly from the Restoration until the Regency. There are ebony pieces from the Portuguese East Indies, briefly popularized by Charles II's wife, Catherine of Braganza; late-17th-century black-painted beechwood armchairs in the Morning Room; Queen Anne hoopback chairs, one in walnut in Marot style on the Grand Stairs, and mahogany 'ladder-back' and Sheraton chairs in the Dining Room. The loveliest pieces are the early Georgian suite of gilt furniture, covered with *petit point* embroidery by the wife of the 4th Earl of Berkeley, and the accompanying pier-glasses in the Long Drawing Room, which also contains the King's Pew, formerly in the Chapel, and a superb Hispano-Moresque carpet.

Berrington Hall
Hereford and Worcester

The National Trust

3 miles N of Leominster, ½ mile W of A49

The Hon. Thomas Harley, 3rd son of the 3rd Earl of Oxford and Mortimer, who acquired the Berrington estate in 1775, was a highly successful banker and government contractor, who became Lord Mayor of London when only thirty-seven. He brought in 'Capability'

Brown to choose a site for the proposed house and to landscape the garden, including the addition of a lake, against the lovely setting of the surrounding hills and the more distant Black Mountains. Henry Holland, probably introduced to Harley by Brown, his father-in-law, was commissioned to design the house, which was completed by 1781 or soon after. John Byng, who was here in 1784, recorded that the mansion was 'just finished and furnished in all the modern elegance, commanding beautiful views, a fine piece of water … throughout a scene of elegance and refinement'.

In contrast to Berrington's austere neo-classical exterior with its large pedimented portico, supported by Ionic columns, is the elegant richly decorated interior. Robert Adam's approach to interior decoration had been universally acclaimed but by 1780 younger men were competing for commissions; while owing much to Adam, they were developing their own styles; among them was Henry Holland, whose decoration at Berrington is among his finest achievements still in existence. His Marble Hall with its trophies of arms set in roundels in panels above the fine quality Spanish mahogany doors, the pattern of the marble floor echoing that of the ceiling, and with the pair of mahogany urns on pedestals and the long-case clock, is masculine and bold. Architecturally the Staircase Hall is the outstanding feature of the interior. Christopher Hussey wrote: 'It is a brilliant exercise in spatial design, using mass and recession asymmetrically to produce dramatic visual effects.'

The paintings on the plasterwork ceilings of the ground floor are reputedly by Rebecca; those in the Drawing Room and the Boudoir are particularly harmonious, especially in the former room, where *putti* and sea-horses are in plasterwork relief. The painting in the Library, which contains a frieze inset with panels of *putti*, displays eight English men of letters, from Shakespeare to Addison, in roundels.

In the Dining Room, which does not retain its original decorative colours, are the most interesting paintings. Four large battle scenes,

Henry Holland's Marble Hall, 1778–81, at Berrington Hall.

three of them by Luny, commemorate outstanding achievements by Admiral Lord Rodney, whose son and heir inherited the estate by marrying Harley's daughter, an only child.

Notable furniture pieces are the two north Italian commodes in the Business Room and the Chippendale writing table in the Library, whose fine early-19th-century Axminster carpet was probably woven for the room.

Blair Castle Tayside

The Duke of Atholl

8 miles NW of Pitlochry on A9

Viewed from a double avenue of limes, the complex of low, white-harled buildings is dominated by the central block of the Castle, with a crenellated tower connected by a three-storeyed range to a second lower tower. Crow-stepped gables, corbelled pepperpot turrets, picked out in black with dark slate roofs, lend a pleasing romanticism to the outline of Blair Castle, home of the Earls and Dukes of Atholl for 800 years. The original Celtic line died out in the 13th century when the first building at Blair began with the erection of what is still known as Commings Tower. The Murrays of Tullibardine acquired Blair by marriage early in the 17th century. Over the next 150 years Blair had a troubled history, having been occupied by opposing forces, captured and held by Cromwell's troops for ten years. During the '45 the army of Prince Charles Edward, led by Lord George Murray, a younger son of the 1st Duke of Atholl, besieged his old home and gave it the distinction of being the last castle in the British Isles to be besieged.

In the mid-1750s Blair was remodelled by the 2nd Duke. His splendid suites of State Rooms on the first and second floor, redecorated and furbished as befitted a Highland nobleman of the first rank, mercifully escaped alteration in the 19th century when the Castle was extended and altered in accordance with contemporary taste. Dining Room and Anteroom were created from the medieval banqueting hall and magnificently decorated with rococo plasterwork by Thomas Clayton, the heavily modelled ceiling with roundels painted by Thomas Bardwell. Thomas Carter of Piccadilly was responsible for the marble fireplace – as for others in the house – above which is perhaps the most striking of all Clayton's plasterwork, a trophy of arms. In quieter contrast to this martial note are four landscape panels of local scenes by Charles Steuart, one of the earliest of Scottish landscape artists, brother of George Steuart, who was the architect of Attingham Park. The Drawing Room has a deeply coved ceiling richly ornamented with plaster and a pair of tall niches at either end of the room, with heavy broken pediments and pilasters. The Picture Staircase, with more trophies, elaborate decorated ceilings and swags, is at first sight an exercise in Baroque style, dating from the last years of the 17th century. But the apparently glowing woodwork is plaster, painted in the 19th century.

Among the many family portraits, which include works by Lely, Ramsay, Raeburn and Lawrence, is Jacob de Wett's 1st Marquess in Roman costume and, the most appealing, Zoffany's 3rd Duke with his wife and seven children and David Allan's less sophisticated portrait of the 4th Duke and his family.

Much of the furniture at Blair is English and Georgian; many pieces were ordered for the castle at the time of the 3rd and 4th Dukes: a rococo bed and chairs by William Masters, rococo giltwood mirrors by Cole, mahogany chairs by Gordon, a Kentian cabinet, sidetables by Hodson, a set of gilt seat furniture by Chipchase, Chippendale and Sheraton cabinets. Most unusual and striking are two mid-18th-century pieces made in Perth from broom wood.

David Allan The 4th Duke of Atholl and his Family; *Blair Castle.*

Blair Castle is a very large house; thirty-two rooms are open to the visitor, from the vaulted chambers on the ground floor, mainly furnished with 16th- and 17th-century pieces, to the little Tullibardine Room dedicated to the Jacobites, with an unusual drawing of Prince Charles and of his Polish mother, Clementina Sobieska and father. In contrast the splendid Tapestry Room houses a fine set of Brussels tapestries made for Charles I and sold during the Commonwealth to the 1st Duke. The plumed bed came from the Duke's suite at Holyrood.

The China Room contains a large collection of English, European and Oriental porcelain, mainly of the late-18th and early-19th centuries Finer examples of Sèvres and Meissen are displayed in the Tea Room.

Blenheim Palace Oxfordshire

The Duke of Marlborough

NW end of Woodstock, NW of Oxford

The great Baroque Palace of Blenheim, the only non-royal or non-episcopal mansion to be called a palace, was built at royal Woodstock, the gift of Queen Anne to the 1st Duke of Marlborough to commemorate his great victory of Blenheim in 1704. The Duke, impressed by a model of Castle Howard, chose Vanbrugh as his architect, who was supported throughout by Hawksmoor. The Duchess of Marlborough wanted a modest country house but Vanbrugh insisted that it ought to be considered 'as a Monument of the Queen's glory'. Not surprisingly Vanbrugh and the Duchess clashed continuously, until Vanbrugh resigned in fury in 1716. Hawksmoor was called back to complete the task, c.1722.

Vanbrugh's masterpiece is romantic in feeling but neo-classical in design. The finest talents of the day were employed in its embellishment. Thornhill painted the ceiling of the majestic Roman Great Hall, while Gibbons carved the capitals, the mouldings of the cornice, and the arms of Queen Anne over the great arch leading to the Saloon. Here are classical statuary and a bronze bust of the 9th Duke by Epstein and, in the surrounding stone corridors, cabinets of Meissen, Sèvres and K'ang Hsi porcelain. There is a superb and highly complex brass lock on the entrance door.

Laguerre was responsible for the murals and painted oval ceiling of the Saloon. The marble doorways were designed by Hawksmoor and carved by Gibbons; the double-headed eagle in the *tympanum* commemorates the creation of the Duke as a Prince of the Holy Roman Empire. On each side of the Saloon is a suite of three State Rooms. The Green and Red Drawing Rooms, with ceilings by Hawksmoor, contain fine portraits. In the former are two outstanding Knellers, both of Marlborough's Duchess, Sarah; Reynolds' engaging portrait of the 4th Duchess with her baby, and over the chimneypiece the 4th Duke by Romney; in the Red Drawing Room is one of Reynolds' finest achievements: the 4th Duke and his family, facing Sargent's 9th Duke and family. The 9th Duchess's dress was copied by Sargent from Van Dyck's portrait of Mrs Killigrew which hangs in this same room. Hawksmoor also designed the ceiling of the Green Writing Room. Here is Kneller's most

famous likeness of Marlborough. Chambers, who did much work at Blenheim for the 4th Duke (1758–1817), designed the chimneypiece and the mahogany doors in the Red Dining Room. The magnificent tapestries, depicting Marlborough's campaigns, here and in the State Rooms beyond the Saloon were woven in Brussels by Judocus de Vos.

In the First State Room hangs the portrait of the 9th Duchess by Duran; Mignard's Louis XIV is in the Second, and Seeman's 1st Duke with his chief engineer in the Third, which Sarah considered 'as like him as ever I saw'. The gilded woodwork in all three was executed by French craftsmen in the 1890s for the 9th Duke when, as he later admitted, he was 'young and uninformed'. In the Third State Room is splendid Boulle furniture, together with a delectable Savonnerie carpet; and the other five State Rooms contain fine examples of French furniture signed by such *ébénistes* as Chevalier, Heurtaut, Migeon, Rousseau and Wolff. English makers are represented by the pier-glasses and giltwood side-tables of Ince and Mayhew and of James Moore, who was employed by Sarah to supervise the building work on Vanbrugh's resignation. Other treasures in these rooms include a clock by Gosselin, many bronzes, among them examples by Coysevox, blue-john candelabra by Matthew Boulton, a rococo inkstand by de Lamerie, late-17th-century porcelain from China and Japan and the 10th Duke's Italian cradle.

The Long Library, running the full length of the west front and originally intended as a picture gallery, was one of the last rooms to be completed; Hawksmoor directed its decoration, including the design of the great marble doorway. The splendid plasterwork was executed by Isaac Mansfield. The statue of Queen Anne and the bust of the 1st Duke, which stands on a pedestal by Chambers, were commissioned by Sarah from Rysbrack, who was also responsible (with Kent) for the massive monument to the 1st Duke and Duchess and their two infant sons in the Chapel.

Winston Churchill was born in a small room

Brussels tapestry illustrating the Battle of Blenheim (1704) in the Green Writing Room, Blenheim Palace.

lying between the Library and the Great Hall, a bedroom originally allotted to Marlborough's domestic chaplain. The Winston Churchill Exhibition contains many mementos of the great man, among them paintings and writings, while recordings of the unforgettable voice repeat some of his greatest speeches.

Blickling Hall Norfolk

The National Trust

1½ miles NW of Aylsham on N side of B1354

The manor of Blickling is recorded in Domesday Book. Its owners have included Sir John Fastolf and Geoffrey Boleyn, father of Anne Boleyn, the luckless wife of Henry VIII. A woodcarving of Anne can be seen in a niche on the remarkable 18th-century Staircase. The present red-brick mansion was built 1616–24 by Robert Lyminge, the architect of Hatfield, for Sir Henry Hobart, 1st Baronet, James I's Lord Chief Justice. After the death of his direct descendant, the 2nd Earl of Buckinghamshire, in 1793, Blickling passed through the female line to the Marquesses of Lothian. The 11th Marquess was largely responsible in the late 1930s for the National Trust's 'Country House Scheme' whereby an owner can endow and transfer a house and its contents to the Trust, but may remain in occupation, subject to providing public access. As a result Blickling was the first great house to come to the National Trust under this scheme on Lord Lothian's death in 1940 when British Ambassador in Washington.

Blickling's welcoming exterior retains its Jacobean character but the interior was extensively redesigned in the 18th century by Thomas Ivory and William, his son, for the 2nd Earl, who was Ambassador to Russia. This is commemorated by the magnificent tapestry woven in St Petersburg, given him by the Empress Catherine, of Peter the Great at his triumph over the Swedes at Poltava in 1709; it hangs in the Peter the Great Room together with Gainsborough's fine portraits of the 2nd Earl and his wife, and the equestrian portrait of George II, the figure painted by Jervas and the horse by Wootton.

The State Bedroom contains a crimson upholstered bed with hangings made from a

canopy with the royal insignia of George II which the 2nd Earl acquired on that monarch's death. Here also is Mytens' shrewd portrait of Sir Henry Hobart, 1st Baronet. Another historically interesting portrait, perhaps by Dahl, in the South Drawing Room is that of Henrietta Howard (1681–1767), Countess of Suffolk and daughter of the 4th Hobart Baronet, reputed mistress of George II and beloved friend of Pope and Horace Walpole. There is a fine view of Chelsea by Canaletto and another of Blackfriars Bridge in the manner of Samuel Scott in the Brown Drawing Room. Other tapestries include an 18th-century Flemish set of Teniers' designs in the Ante-room and a 17th-century set of Mortlake tapestries, depicting the life of Abraham, in the Upstairs Ante-room.

The Long Gallery is outstanding for its elaborately intricate Jacobean plasterwork ceiling, its panels containing Emblems, Virtues

Canaletto Chelsea from the Thames, *1751; Blickling Hall.*

and heraldic achievements. The bulk of the large library was collected early in the 18th century by Sir Richard Ellys of Nocton and contains a wide range of the classics, rare Bibles, atlases and an important contemporary collection of pamphlets. The bookcases and painted designs above them are by John Hungerford Pollen, a follower of Ruskin.

There are remarkable 17th-century or earlier chimneypieces in the Dining Room, the South Drawing Room and in the Brown Drawing Room. Everywhere there is fine period furniture, much of it English. In the enchanting Chinese Bedroom and Dressing Room with its 18th-century Chinese wallpaper are two Chinese hand-carved pagodas. The late-18th-century Print Room is a nostalgic reminder of the Grand Tour.

Bodrhyddan Hall Clwyd

Colonel The Lord Langford

4 miles SE of Rhyl, near Rhuddlan

This mellow red-brick mansion, secluded in well laid out grounds and built at the end of the 17th century on Tudor foundations, was further expanded by the addition of the west wing by Nesfield in the 1870s. The Rowley-Conwy family, which own it, has been established in this part of North Wales for at least 700 years. The Conwys have held the appointment of Hereditary Constables of Rhuddlan Castle since 1399. The present owner inherited the Irish barony of Langford from a cousin in 1953.

The Front Hall contains a fascinating miscellany of Saracen, Augsburg (1485–1500) and Cromwellian armour, oriental flintlocks, family naval and regimental swords and Life Guards' cuirasses and helmets. Here also is the Charter of nearby Rhuddlan with its Castle, granted in 1284 by Edward I. Off the Front Hall in a little room known as Herbert's Room is a small but interesting collection of Egyptian antiquities, including the mummified body of a priest, *c.*1200 BC, which was unexpectedly found recently in one of the two mummy cases

standing one each side of the front door. The Great Hall contains excellent portraits, notably those of the Duc d'Anjou and the Duc de Berry by de Troy, 1696, and two by Hudson, one attributed to Dahl, and an enamel altar set from Spain, looted by the French and captured after Waterloo.

In the cheerful White Drawing Room upstairs, redecorated to designs by the late Herman Schrijver, is a collection of 18th-century Chinese export wares and more family weapons, including a sword presented by Lloyd's Patriotic Fund in 1804. The small panels around the fireplaces include religious scenes, said to have been salvaged from the chapel of a Spanish Armada ship wrecked off Anglesey. In the Big Dining Room hangs an impressive portrait of Frances, Lady Stapleton, with her infant sons, dressed in black with her widow's veil over her white 'tower' head-dress; there are other good family portraits by Vanderbank, Hudson and Ramsay. The Little Dining Room contains Arthur Devis' *Jonathan Shipley (1714–88), c.*1770, Bishop of St Asaph, whose son, William, Dean of St Asaph, inherited Bodrhyddan by marriage. There are other portraits here by Wheatley, *c.*1767, of the 2nd Viscount Langford, and one of the Baroness Langford (1775–1860), by Edouard Dubuffe, 1850.

Bolling Hall West Yorkshire

Bradford Metropolitan Council

Bowling Hall Road, Bradford

The manor of Bolling is mentioned in Domesday Book and by 1316 a William Bolling is described as lord of the manor. By the mid-15th century, the Bolling family was of considerable local importance; a Bolling descendant settled in Virginia in 1660 and married a grand-daughter of the Indian Princess Pocahontas. The estate passed by marriage sometime after 1497 to the Tempest family, who sold it in 1649. Subsequently the Hall was acquired by the Lindleys and in due course descended to the Wood family of

glass panes, and good pieces of 17th-century oak furniture, including two court cupboards. The elaborately carved oak chimneypiece and plasterwork ceiling in the 'Ghost Room' are early 17th century but the frieze is Victorian. The Couch Room has recently been renovated in mid-18th-century style, the walls being decorated with damask hangings. This room contains the recently restored couch bed made in 1769 by Thomas Chippendale for Harewood House. Carr's fine plasterwork ceiling in the Drawing Room shows his debt to Robert Adam; Carr was also responsible for the Dining Room frieze. The Drawing Room contains fine 18th-century furniture including a Chippendale sofa of *c*.1773. The Dining Room has recently been restored in early-19th-century style. It contains furniture of the 18th and early-19th centuries, including a mahogany extending dining table of *c*.1805 made by Thomas Butler of London.

The couch bed made in 1769 by Thomas Chippendale for Harewood House and now in Bolling Hall.

Barnsley. Portraits of both these families are on loan from Lord Halifax. Eventually, in a state of disrepair, the Hall was given in 1912 to the city of Bradford, which has converted it into a period house and museum of local history, which nevertheless retains something of a domestic atmosphere.

The tower is probably 15th century and the rest of the Hall was built in the 16th and 17th centuries; the east wing was remodelled in 1779–80 by John Carr of York. Rooms of particular interest are the Housebody, the 'Ghost Room', the Couch Room, the Drawing Room and the Dining Room. The Housebody, a word formerly used in the West Riding to describe the main living room, contains a large window with twenty-four heraldic stained

Boughton House
Northamptonshire

The Duke of Buccleuch and Queensberry

3 miles N of Kettering on A43

Originally a monastic building, Boughton was transformed by an unknown architect into the likeness of a great French château, *c*.1687–99, for Ralph, 3rd Lord Montagu, created a Duke in 1705, who as British Ambassador in Paris became a keen admirer of French architecture and culture. He employed the Huguenot Louis Chéron to execute the not always distinguished ceiling paintings. Because Boughton was virtually uninhabited between 1770 and 1910, its original contents, which are superb, and its distinctive French character have been remarkably retained.

The house has a splendid collection of French furniture, much of it collected by the 1st Duke's grandson, Lord Monthermer; when he died this great property passed to the 3rd Duke of Buccleuch. Louis XIV gave the Boulle writing table in the Rainbow Room and the little bureau by Pierre Golle, bordered with crushed mica, in the Low Pavilion Ante-room to Duke Ralph, whose oval portrait by Dahl presides over the latter room.

Here also is a splendid pair of Gerreit Jensen pier-glasses and matching chests of drawers, each of the same design but with pewter and brass reversed. Elsewhere on the ground floor and in the handsome first-floor State Rooms are signed pieces by distinguished *ébénistes*, among them Martin Carlin and Joseph Baumhauer (tables inlaid with Sèvres plaques), J. P. Latz, André Criaer, Levasseur, Roussel, and Mondon; Boulle marriage caskets stand in the Great Hall and the Fourth State Room. In addition there are important English pieces by Matthias Lock, Langlois, by and after Kent, James Moore, Gerreit Jensen, and Indo-Portuguese ebony pieces, possibly given by Catherine of Braganza, wife of Charles II.

The paintings are magnificent. The portraits, ranging from Gheeraerts' *Queen Elizabeth* to Batoni's excellent *Lord Monthermer*, are mainly in the Great Hall and the Audit Room Gallery; they include works by Lely, Closterman, Kneller, Jervas, Van Loo, Hudson, Beechey and Gainsborough. Among other notable paintings are an early *Adoration* by El Greco, a harvest scene by the younger Teniers, portraits by Annibale Carracci and Frans Pourbus the Elder, religious paintings by Van Dyck, Murillo, Dolci, Solimena, a magnificent cartoon, *The Vision of Ezekiel*, from Raphael's workshop and fine views by Zuccarelli, Marlow, Samuel Scott, the younger Van de Velde, Wootton and Cuyp (notables in a rowing boat with a trumpeter announcing their approach to an anchored ship). Of particular interest is the set of forty sketches in grisaille by Van Dyck of his famous contemporaries, thirty-seven of which once belonged to Lely.

The tapestries both from Paris and Mortlake, whose factory Lord Montagu acquired and managed, 1674–91, are of fine quality, especially the set of four from Mortlake depicting 'The Elements' which hang in the Great Hall. There are fine carpets from Isfahan and three late-16th-century pink carpets, among the earliest known to have been made in England. The ceramics include two Meissen swans, designed by Kändler and made for Madame de Pompadour, mounted in ormolu, and examples of Sèvres, Vincennes, Derby, Chelsea Derby, Ch'ien Lung and late-17th-century Kakiemon.

Writing table, c.1768, by Martin Carlin; Broughton House.

Boughton Monchelsea Place

Kent

Mr M. B. Winch

5 miles s of Maidstone off A229 at Linton

The present restrained Elizabethan house, reached through woodland, is marvellously sited overlooking the spreading Weald of Kent. It was completed in about 1575 by Robert Rudston, a Lord Mayor of London, who had acquired it in 1551. Alterations were made towards the end of both the 17th and 18th centuries, mainly to the interior. It remained with the descendants of Robert Rudston until acquired from them by the Winch family in 1902. Today it is an unpretentious home with good furniture, interesting features and an agreeable air.

In 1790 slender columns were introduced to give a Gothic character both to the handsome Red Dining Room, with its mid-18th-century giltwood oval mirrors and Regency mahogany chairs, and to the Hall with its parquet floor and crested mahogany hall chairs. A shield above the entrance to the Staircase proclaims its presence there 'in honour of the Reform Bill by which the ancient liberties of England, regained at Runnymede in 1215 and confirmed in 1688, were rescued from corruption (and it may be hoped perpetuated) in 1832'. The handsome Staircase beyond, with twisted balusters, was installed in 1690.

The Drawing Room contains 17th- and 18th-century furniture, both English and French; there is a good French marquetry two-drawer chest, enriched with ormolu, and a fine mid-18th-century giltwood mirror above the fireplace. Elsewhere is a late-15th-century Flemish dower chest, three late-17th-century Mortlake tapestries, and a collection of late-19th- and early-20th-century dresses, fans and sewing machines. Nineteenth-century family carriages and penny farthing bicycles are in the coach house.

Bowhill Borders

The Duke of Buccleuch and Queensberry

3 miles w of Selkirk off A708

Large, rambling and somewhat dour, Bowhill gives little hint of the richness within. This is the preferred home of one of the greatest Border families, heirs to two dukedoms and the possessions though not the title of a third. The Scotts of Buccleuch were an old Border family with roots deep in national history when Anne, sole heiress to the last Earl of Buccleuch, married James, Duke of Monmouth, natural and favourite son of Charles II. They were created Duke and Duchess of Buccleuch and many Monmouth relics are at Bowhill and at Drumlanrig. Henry, 3rd Duke of Buccleuch, married the heiress of the 2nd Duke of Montagu and inherited in 1810 the Queensberry dukedom from his Douglas cousin, the

notorious 'Old Q'. Treasures from Dalkeith Palace – the home of Duchess Anne in her widowhood – and from Montagu House in London enrich a collection remarkable by any standards.

The house grew from a modest 18th-century house from 1812 until about 1876 when the building was completed so that it now forms a single range over 400 feet long, looking out to the gentle moors and hills of the Ettrick and Yarrow valleys. The Gallery Hall through which the visitor enters gives some idea of the quality of Bowhill's contents. It contains three Mortlake tapestries woven in 1670 with designs taken from the Mantegna cartoons *The Triumphs of Julius Caesar* at Hampton Court. Portraits, modestly attributed to Van Dyck, line the lower level. The furniture is French and includes a Louis XIV mirror given to the Duke of Monmouth by Charles II, signed chairs of the same period, a Boulle bracket clock by Melot, dated 1710, and a *bureau plat* stamped Dubois and Genty. The wealth of French furniture is remarkable. The quality may be judged from a few examples: a parquetry commode by Dubois 1745–6, a Louis XVI ebonized table by Levasseur. Examples of earlier periods are fewer in number but not less outstanding in quality, including a coromandel desk by Gerreit Jensen in the Morning Room, which is fittingly hung with Chinese hand-painted wallpaper of about the same date.

It is, however, the paintings that dominate the house and dazzle the visitor. In the room dedicated to Monmouth is his full-length portrait by Lely and an unusually sympathetic Kneller of Duchess Anne and her two sons. (Monmouth's cradle is shown here, and his richly decorated saddle and trappings, besides the shirt in which he was executed in 1683.) The many Buccleuch family portraits depict the unfortunate Duke's descendants, who led happier and gentler lives, in a series of works of superb quality; a Gainsborough of the 3rd Duke, of his father-in-law and mother, and half a dozen of Reynolds' best paintings, including the 3rd Duchess with her daughter and outstanding child portraits of two more of her family – *The Pink Boy*, Charles, later the 4th

Reynolds' portrait Winter, *1777, of Caroline Montagu; Bowhill.*

Duke, in cavalier costume, and a wholly entrancing portrait of his sister Caroline as *Winter* dated 1777. The little girl is said to have entered the room where Reynolds was working and he insisted on painting her exactly as she is shown in the picture, her cheeks scarlet from the cold, hands tucked in a scarlet muff and wearing a large black and white hat.

Family portraits are hung all round the comfortable Library dominated by a huge marble fireplace from Dalkeith Palace that bears Duchess Anne's monogram. Here are to be seen works by Kneller, Lely, Bardwell and Lawrence. Among these a portrait by Mengs stands out, as does a set by Beechey. The Bowhill paintings are, however, far from confined to family portraits. One of Canaletto's finest English works hangs in the Dining Room, *View of Whitehall from beside Montagu House*. Eighteenth-century Italian *vedute* include works by Guardi, Joli, Marieschi and Pannini, all shown together in the Italian Room. Dutch and French landscapes are concentrated in the Drawing Room. Of two Claudes, *The Judgement of Paris*, dated 1633, is the earliest of his mythological scenes. A pair of

Vernet landscapes are dated 1746. An outstanding Ruysdael, represents the best in Dutch 17th-century painting. Native Scottish art is well represented in the collection of works by Sir David Wilkie, notably his portrait of George IV painted shortly before the king's death, and by a Raeburn of Henry Scott, Lord Montagu of Boughton. The 4th Duke was the friend and patron of Sir Walter Scott, whose well-known portrait also by Raeburn dominates the Study.

The porcelain at Bowhill is magnificent and is especially notable for the amount of Sèvres and Meissen. A dessert service displayed in Boulle cabinets in the Drawing Room was made in the German factory for Mme Du Barry in 1771. Long corridors are lined with cases which deserve close attention. Early Meissen tea-sets and beakers, examples of Chelsea, Worcester and other English factory wares, are shown in such a way that they may almost be taken for granted. Such lack of ostentation amid so many treasures is perhaps the key to Bowhill's charm.

Braemar Castle Grampian

Captain A. A. Farquharson of Invercauld

3 miles from Braemar on A93

The strath of the River Dee runs westward from Aberdeen to the Grampian watershed above Braemar. Here at a strategically important site commanding the vulnerable southern approach to the glen, the Earl of Mar built Braemar Castle *c*.1628. Sixty years later John the Black, Colonel John Farquharson of a neighbouring and unfriendly clan, took advantage of the revolt of Graham of Claverhouse (Bonnie Dundee of song and legend) against James II to burn down the Castle.

In 1732 the Farquharsons bought the ruined stronghold and owned it until after the '45 when the Hanoverian government leased the property. The Castle was rebuilt as a garrison post, the architect being John Adam, elder brother of Robert. The keep was heightened, the conical roof replaced by a flat battlement

top and a low curtain wall laid out round the Castle like a star. Braemar's defences were never tested and in 1807 the Farquharsons of Invercauld regained the property.

The Castle is endearingly small, the rooms modestly furnished with late Georgian and Victorian pieces. The Drawing Room contains some good Dutch marquetry and a Boulle-type writing table. A charming watercolour of Queen Victoria commemorates her visit when she attended the Braemar Games. A more fanciful gouache and watercolour depicts the Castle as the background to the first Braemar Games held in the neighbouring meadow in 1834. The painter was George Campion, a minor follower of Sir David Wilkie. An equally romantic view of the Castle was painted by Gustave Doré during a visit in 1873.

Bramall Hall Cheshire

Metropolitan Borough of Stockport

2 miles s of Stockport centre off A5102

This picturesque oak-timber-framed house is one of the four best of its kind in England. It was probably built in the 15th century and added to and altered at the end of the 16th century, when the original Great Hall was divided to make the Withdrawing Room above. The ancient, highly respected Cheshire family of Davenport, to whom the Bramall estate came through marriage late in the 14th century, remained here for some 500 years until 1883, when the Hall was sold to Captain T. M. C. Nevill, who made a number of alterations. Bramall Hall's life as a country house ceased in 1938 when it was acquired by the Hazel Grove and Bramhall UDC. It is now in the care of the Metropolitan Borough of Stockport which has restored the medieval wall paintings on the north and east walls of the Ballroom.

Fine craftsmanship is evident throughout the house and especially in the Withdrawing Room with its oak panelling and its fine plasterwork ceiling with pendants and frieze. The Chapel Room is also handsome but the

ornately carved fireplace and timber raftered ceiling were installed by Nevill late in the 19th century.

The rare medieval wall paintings in the Ballroom were discovered by Nevill under panelling and plaster. They show a man in contemporary costume with a lute, and a woman holding a sheet of music; a winged character on a white horse which has the head of a cock; a demon charming sea horses with his lute; and other fantasies. Another medieval painting has been found in the Chapel; the 'Ten Commandments' were probably added in the 16th century. An elaborate 15th-century roof with cambered beams and arched braces runs the whole length of the south wing and can be seen in the Ballroom.

The family portraits are on loan from Mr D. J. Davenport Handley of Clipsham Hall.

Bramham Park West Yorkshire

Mr and Mrs George Lane Fox

5 miles s of Wetherby on A1

The approach to Bramham Park from the east reveals a dignified limestone mansion linked by Palladian-type colonnades to end-pavilions. It was designed by Robert Benson and built between 1703 and 1710; William Thornton, the architect of Beningbrough, is known to have advised on the interior design. Benson, son of a Yorkshire attorney who prospered under both King and Cromwell, was a politician, courtier and ambassador; he became Lord Bingley in 1713. Benson's only daughter married George Fox, a member of a Worcestershire family, who was created Lord Bingley in 1762. The family continued here in unbroken succession until 1947 when another George, Lord Bingley, died leaving four daughters but no son. The husband of the eldest daughter changed his name to Lane Fox; their son, his wife and family now live here.

Charming watercolours by Ziegler show the modifications made in the 1800s before a fire seriously damaged the house in 1828; these modifications were removed when restoration

Agasse Leopards at Exeter Zoo; *Bramham Park.*

18th-century Imari vase; Bramham Park.

started in 1906. The thirty-foot-cube Entrance Hall remains in its original state apart from the ceiling. Queen Anne's portrait and bust here were presented by the Queen to the original owner; the splendid full-length painting of the Duke of Cumberland is by Reynolds, the battle scenes by 'Le Bourgoignon'. The Library contains pictures by J. N. Sartorius, Cooper Henderson and Agasse's portrait of Lord Rivers coursing. Agasse's fine *Leopards at Exeter Zoo* is in the East Room; the gilt plates and loving cups belonged to Robert Benson and the gilt service was presented to George Lane Fox, Master of the Bramham Moor Foxhounds for forty-eight years. The trumpets and banners in the North Room were used at the proclamation of King Edward VIII in 1936.

The Gallery, originally three rooms, contains Meissen porcelain and 18th- and 19th-century Japanese Imari ceramics, some pieces with false Chinese symbols. The splendid central bureau may have been made for King Louis XV. In Mrs Lane Fox's Sitting Room is a portrait attributed to Pourbus the Younger, one of Jordaens, landscapes by Vogelsang and a scene by Wootton.

The gardens are so well preserved that John Wood's plan of about 1725 would serve as an excellent guide today.

Breamore House Hampshire

Sir Westrow Hulse, Bt

3 miles N of Fordingbridge off A338 to Salisbury

Despite a fire in 1856, the interior of this impressive, welcoming, red-brick Elizabethan mansion, completed in 1583, is largely unchanged. In 1748 it was acquired by Sir Edward Hulse, 1st Baronet, whose father had been physician to William III. Fine stone-carved Renaissance fireplaces and overmantels stand in the spacious Dining Room and Great Hall and the house contains notable paintings and good furniture.

RIGHT *Van Dyck's double portrait of the 2nd Earl of Bristol with the 1st Duke of Bedford, c.1633; Althorp*

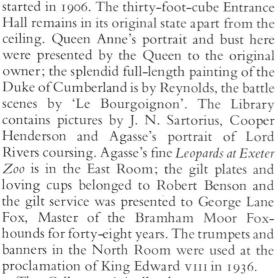

One of the earliest representations of cricket,
Thomas Hudson's mid-18th-century portrait
Boy with the Bat; *Breamore House.*

The paintings in the Dining Room are, appropriately, mainly of dead game, four by Peter Andreas Rysbrack and one by Jan Fyt. The Great Hall contains a splendid village scene, *The Coming of the Storm*, by the younger Teniers, and works by or after Johnson, Coello and Gheeraerts. Elsewhere are portraits by Riley, Cotes, Simon Verelst, Beach and Hudson, in particular the latter's portrait of a boy with a cricket bat which hangs in the West Drawing Room. The Inner Hall and Staircase contain 17th-century Dutch genre paintings, a scene by de Loutherbourg, an unfinished sketch by J. Lucas of the 1st Duke of Wellington, and twelve battle scenes by Beaufort, a war artist with Napoleon.

The furniture includes Tudor oak refectory tables with carved supports, perhaps of monastic origin, Charles II caned long-back chairs, a fine collection of Dutch marquetry furniture, two elegant rococo Chippendale gilt mirrors, early mahogany Queen Anne chairs and an intriguing Mexican table with alabaster top and silver plaques, seized by the enterpris-ing Admiral Westrow from the Spanish fleet together with fourteen paintings of Mexico's inhabitants, white and Indian, said to be by a son of Murillo, and a glorious Mexican Indian feather fan in the upstairs Alcove.

Other treasures include Tudor and Sheraton beds, several excellent Brussels and Flemish tapestries, especially those in the Great Hall made to Teniers' designs, and the magnificent English pile carpet, 1614, on the Staircase wall.

Broadlands Hampshire

The Lord Romsey

Off A31, Romsey Bypass

After the suppression of the monasteries, 1536–9, the manor of Romsey, once owned by Romsey Abbey, passed through various hands, until acquired in 1736 by Henry Temple, 1st Viscount Palmerston. He commissioned Kent to produce the gentle slope down to the River Test, which involved changing its course. In 1767–8 'Capability' Brown was engaged by the 2nd Viscount to carry out further landscaping and to transform the earlier manor house into the present gracious neo-classical mansion. Afterwards Henry Holland, Brown's son-in-law, added the east front portico and Sculpture Hall in 1788, and undertook the decoration of the main State Rooms in the style of Robert Adam, who may have supervised the work; Angelica Kauffmann helped design the Saloon and added the oval paintings to the Drawing Room ceiling. Broadlands was the home of the 3rd Viscount Palmerston, Prime Minister to Queen Victoria, and then passed by inheritance to Lord Mount Temple of Lee. On his death in 1939, the estate was inherited by the Mountbatten family through his elder daughter, Edwina, the wife of Lord Louis Mountbatten, later Earl Mountbatten of Burma, who was assassinated in Ireland in 1979. The present Countess Mountbatten, his elder daughter, is married to Lord Brabourne and their eldest son, Lord Ramsey, now lives in the house.

The octagonal domed Entrance Hall and the Doric screened Sculpture Hall beyond contain

LEFT *The soaring Great Hall at Castle Howard, designed by Vanbrugh 1699–1726.*

The Sculpture Hall, Broadlands, added by Henry Holland in 1788 to house the Greek and Roman works and 18th-century pieces acquired by the 2nd Lord Palmerston.

fascinating Greek and Roman sculptural works and contemporary 18th-century pieces, mostly acquired in Rome in 1765 by the 2nd Lord Palmerston while on the Grand Tour. Four magnificent Van Dyck portraits embellish the Dining Room; here also is a delightful likeness of Emma Hamilton by Lawrence, in an earlier floral garland by Monnoyer. Above the chimneypiece is a genre scene of an itinerant musician by the 17th-century Flemish artist van Tillborch. The four marble-topped side-tables are by Holland, while the gold-painted radiator grills are designed by Rex Whistler.

The magnificently decorated Saloon with 18th-century period seat furniture contains some fine porcelain, mainly Vincennes and Sèvres, including Marie Antoinette's basin and ewer, but there are also Wedgewood black and white urns, early oriental Lowestoft and Chelsea 'Red Anchor' tureens, and, in the two alcoves, Vienna and Meissen pieces, arranged by the late King Gustav of Sweden, Lord Mountbatten's brother-in-law and an acknowledged expert on porcelain. Family portraits mainly of the Palmerston family hang in the Drawing Room and include works by Reynolds, Raeburn, Romney, Lawrence and Hoppner. The blue silk curtains with white neo-classical motifs were woven after World War II to exactly the same pattern as the 18th-century originals.

In addition to the Wedgwood collection in

the Wedgwood Room, started by the 2nd Lord Palmerston, there are four Lely portraits of 'court beauties', including Barbara Villiers and Lady Annabella Howe. In the Library is Dahl's portrait of the 1st Lord Palmerston's wife and Kauffmann's 2nd Viscount. Here also is the Garter Star worn by Wellington at Waterloo, and a miniature model of King Theebaw's throne, given to Lord Mountbatten by the people of Burma. There is also an interesting collection of swords and daggers on show in the Oak Room.

The portraits on the North Stairs are of Lord Mountbatten's ancestors and of European and Russian royalty. Here also are his polo trophies. The Portico Bedroom is decorated with chintz curtains and chair-covers, incorporating the delicately traced profiles of Queen Victoria and Prince Albert, originally ordered for the royal yacht in 1854. The present Queen uses this bedroom with the Chinese Room as a dressing room when at Broadlands. The family portraits in the Green Room are by de Laszlo. The Palmerston Room contains an unfinished oval portrait by Landseer of Lord Melbourne and likenesses of the late Lady Mountbatten's grandparents.

The Ships Passage displays models of the various ships on which Lord Mountbatten served. There is also a fascinating exhibition, encompassing his remarkable career, which should not be missed.

Brodick Castle Isle of Arran

The National Trust for Scotland

1½ miles N of Brodick pierhead

Since the 13th century, when Viking long ships threatened the Western Isles, there has been a castle at Brodick overlooking the sweep of the bay below. In 1503 the Castle and much of the island was granted by James IV to his cousin, Baron Hamilton, who also was given an earldom and was the ancestor of the Dukes of Hamilton. He enlarged and rebuilt Brodick Castle c.1558. It was captured and occupied by Cromwellian troops and further rebuilt and

fortified during the Commonwealth. Brodick remained a Hamilton seat and in 1844 the Marquess of Douglas and Clydesdale and his bride, Princess Marie of Baden, decided to make it their home. They commissioned Gillespie Graham, an architect with a sensitive approach to traditional styles, to reconstruct and enlarge the Castle. The result is 'a building such as only Scotland can show, making its effect, like its 17th-century prototype, by height and stark simplicity which belies and then enhances the richness within'. For Brodick is a treasure house.

The Marquess (later the 11th Duke of Hamilton) was the son of the younger daughter of William Beckford, from whom she inherited what was left of his fabulous collection after the Fonthill sale. Although further diminished by the Hamilton Palace sale of 1862, Beckford's legacy is still astonishing, and much can be seen at Brodick. Turner's watercolour of Fonthill and an ebony cabinet (also seen in a sketch of the great collector on his deathbed) underlines the evidence of Beckford's eclectic and sometimes exotic taste seen throughout the house: *objets d'art*, porcelain, ivories, silver, furniture and paintings – among which are a religious panel by Teniers, a sea scene by Copley Fielding, a Fragonard portrait and two small pastorals by Watteau: Hamilton paintings include a rare portrait by

Venetian Blackamoor stool, part of William Beckford's Fonthill collection now at Brodick Castle.

David Scougall of Anne, Duchess of Hamilton in her own right, Gainsborough landscape sketches and a portrait of the Duc d'Alençon by Clouet, once in Charles I's collection and bearing the royal cypher.

Later Dukes had sporting tastes, and Brodick boasts an outstanding collection of trophies and sporting pictures, including works by Thomas Bardwell, Ben Marshall, the Alkens, Rowlandson and J. F. Herring, notably his painting of

The interior porch in the Oak Room, Broughton Castle; the elaborate carving is 16th century.

the 1845 Derby, *The Dirtiest Derby in History*.

The Drawing Room contains the most notable furniture, largely from the 18th and 19th centuries, French and Italian. A fine pair of neo-classical commodes beneath large Venetian giltwood mirrors are probably from Piedmont, *c*.1780. The gilt settees, love-seats, chairs and *chaise longue* are Louis-Philippe, dating from the 1830s. The Boudoir and Bedroom of the Duchess of Montrose (who inherited Brodick from her father, the 12th Duke of Hamilton) are furnished simply with 18th-century pieces, mainly English, notably a Hepplewhite four-poster and a Chippendale chest.

Examples of silver from both the Beckford and Hamilton inheritances and of fine porcelain – Chelsea, Meissen, Sèvres – are changed from time to time. But the splendid pair of Ch'ien Lung goose tureens in the Drawing Room, mounted on Dutch silver bases made to represent waves, remain undisturbed, immutably dignified and serene.

Broughton Castle Oxfordshire

The Lord Saye and Sele

$2\frac{1}{2}$ miles s w of Banbury on B4035

Described by Nikolaus Pevsner as 'the finest and most complete medieval house in the county', Broughton Castle, originally built at the very start of the 14th century as a fortified manor house, stands serene amid lawns, surrounded by the placid waters of its wide moat. It came in 1451 to Sir William Fiennes, 2nd Lord Saye and Sele, by marriage with a descendant of William of Wykeham, founder of Winchester College and New College, Oxford. During the second half of the 16th century, the ancient house was converted into a splendid Tudor mansion, a third floor added as well as a west wing, but the basic medieval structure remains. The Chapel, built *c*.1331, is, moreover, a rare example of an unaltered medieval private chapel. Broughton escaped restoration in the Victorian era because the family was almost ruined by the riotous extravagance of the 15th Baron, making necessary the sale of the Castle's contents, even including the swans on the moat.

Off the groined 14th-century corridor to the Great Hall is the vaulted Dining Room with fine linenfold panelling, *c*.1540. The superb Great Hall is also 14th century but with broad 16th-century windows and a Tudor plaster ceiling perhaps remodelled by Sanderson Miller in the 1760s when the bold pendants were added. It is decorated with arms, armour and several family portraits, including that of William Fiennes, created 1st Viscount Saye and Sele by James I in 1624; nicknamed 'Old Subtlety', he opposed Charles I's autocracy and made Broughton a centre of opposition. Another portrait of 'Old Subtlety', who disapproved of Charles I's execution and went into retirement until pardoned by Charles II at the Restoration, hangs in the Gallery. He was responsible with others for the establishment of the Providence Island Company in 1630 and later founded with Lord Brooke a Puritan settlement called Saybrook at the mouth of the Connecticut River in New England.

Queen Anne's Room rejoices in a large Renaissance chimneypiece with classical features, made *c*.1551 or earlier, and a fine bow-fronted marquetry chest of drawers. Even more interesting is the Star Chamber's chimneypiece; its central lively plasterwork feature shows Dryads dancing round a sacred oak, perhaps the work of Italian plasterers, and is reminiscent in style and subject of Francis I's Gallery at Fontainebleau. The Gallery, remodelled in the 18th century and recently redecorated by the late John Fowler, contains marble busts, one at each end, of Inigo Jones and Ben Jonson by Rysbrack, lively family portraits, good furniture and late-18th-century English and Chinese porcelain. The White Room has an elaborate plaster ceiling, dated 1559, some fine glass in a breakfront cabinet and Charles II's pardon of the 1st Viscount.

The Oak Room is glorious with late-16th-century oak carving, including the interior porch crowned with its elaborate cartouche, which bears a Latin inscription, meaning 'there is no pleasure in the memory of the past',

perhaps to emphasize 'Old Subtlety's' loyalty to Charles II at the Restoration. Above the fireplace is a seascape by Joannes Peeters, showing Charles II leaving Holland for England. The portrait of Mrs Nathaniel Fiennes by Lely hangs above some fine porcelain made in Paris, *c*.1795, by Guerhard and Dahl.

Smaller rooms at the top of the West Staircase enjoy fine views and include the Council Chamber where opposition to Charles I was plotted.

Browsholme Hall Lancashire

The Parker family

Near Clitheroe, off B6243, signposted Bashall Eaves – Whitewell

The Parker family lived here long before the dignified Tudor stone house was erected in 1507. In 1604 the house was re-fronted with dressed red sandstone. Further additions were made in the 18th century and Wyatville worked here during the Regency, when over £100,000 was spent on landscaping the gardens.

The Tudor Hall, part of the original Great Hall, contains a fascinating miscellany collected by generations of Parkers. Armour and weapons from the Neolithic period to the Civil War hang on or lean against the whitewashed walls wherever there is room – helmets, shields, crossbow, spears, swords, the buckskin coat and jackboots of a Civil War royalist – mainly collected in the 1800s. The carved fire surround of different periods is flanked each side by a turned or bobbin armchair, *c*.1600. There are two court cupboards, one of 1590, the other dated 1704; on the former is a glazed case containing thirty-three miniature figures of monks and nuns, supposedly recording the various religious orders restored by James II, the abbess wearing the red of a 'scarlet woman'. Two Charles II oak chests and a family manuscript cupboard, *c*.1681, support a fine 13th-century reredos; shelves on both sides hold Roman pots, and medieval and Charles I tankards.

The living rooms, some with fine oak panelling and splendid chimneypieces, as in the Breakfast Parlour and Ante-room, contain good period furniture with an emphasis on comfort, although more formal in the Drawing Room with its ceiling and decorations by Wyatville, mahogany doors by Gillow of Lancaster and marble chimneypiece carved by Canova. Here are fascinating Jacobite relics and portraits mainly of the Parker family, by or attributed to Lely, Kneller, Northcote, Batoni and Reynolds.

There are two portraits by Arthur Devis in the Breakfast Parlour and more portraits in the Dining Room, which contains a tea and chocolate set, painted in China, given to the family in 1778.

The bedrooms are mainly furnished with sound 17th- and 18th-century furniture; a remarkable red walnut 'guest chair', *c.*1720, stands in the Velvet Room.

Brympton D'Evercy Somerset

Mr Charles E. B. Clive-Ponsonby-Fane

2 miles w of Yeovil, A3088

The setting of Brympton D'Evercy with its church, Chantry House and outbuildings is one of the loveliest in England. Christopher Hussey wrote that there was 'none that summarizes so exquisitely English country life'. These ancient buildings of golden Ham Hill stone dream amid spreading gardens to which a flourishing vineyard has been added. The Elizabethan Hall, facing west, contains a variety of Tudor carved panelling – its massive chimneypiece enclosing an alabaster panel on which Neptune is depicted. A modern tapestry in dark brown and beige shows the estate as illustrated in Knyff's view of *c.*1700.

The south range, built shortly before 1697, contains the State Rooms. In the Drawing Room are Riley's portrait of the Duke of Monmouth, one of the 10th Earl of Westmorland and an engaging sketch of his daughter, both by Lawrence, and two views of classical ruins by Pannini. In the Oak Room is a small collection of watercolours, including five each by John Varley and Edward Lear. Another Lawrence portrait hangs in the Dining Room. The Felix Room contains Victorian costumes. The furniture includes good English 18th- and early-19th-century pieces, and an interesting variety of porcelain. The Chantry House contains a collection of illustrations of Brympton D'Evercy. There is also a museum devoted to coopering and to cider making.

Bryn Bras Castle Gwynedd

Mrs M. Gray-Parry and Mr R. D. Gray-Williams

At Llanrug, 4½ miles E of Caernarvon

The ancient site of Bryn Bras was important for control of the route overland through the Pass of Llanberis to Caernarfon, probably already in use in Roman times. The Castle, standing in its romantic garden, was erected 1830–5 for Thomas Williams and his wife, Lauretta Panton, both descended from distinguished Welsh antiquarians. After Williams' death in 1874, the Castle passed through many hands until 1965 when it was acquired by the present owners, who are lovingly restoring one of the most picturesque sites in North Wales.

Bryn Bras was started in a fantasy style, perhaps by John Provis who worked on Telford's Menai Suspension Bridge, but this element was later subdued by solider construction probably introduced after the owners' occupation in 1833. Many decorative features, both external and internal, derive from nearby Penrhyn Castle, which was built concurrently (1827–37) by Thomas Hopper in his neo-Norman style or, more likely, from Hopper himself, as seen in the Entrance Hall ceiling, in the painted slate fireplaces and in the Circular Room.

There is interesting furniture by local craftsmen, including two Eisteddfod chairs, and an early Victorian sideboard elaborately carved with Biblical themes. There are unusual wood carvings on the Library walls and a painting by Bernard Gribble of Henry VIII leaving for the Field of the Cloth of Gold.

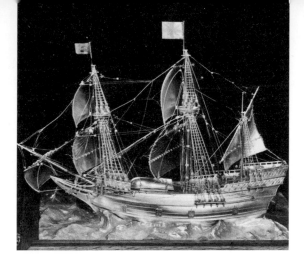

Silver model of the Golden Hind; *Buckland Abbey.*

Buckland Abbey Devon

The National Trust, administered by Plymouth Corporation

11 miles N of Plymouth between Tavistock–Plymouth road (A386) and River Tavy

Buckland Abbey, a Cistercian foundation, was sold to the Grenvilles in 1541 after the Dissolution of the Monasteries and converted by Sir Richard Grenville of the *Revenge* into a country house. When he sold the property, it was bought in 1581 by his rival Sir Francis Drake. Buckland eventually came to the Trust in 1948 and is now managed as a museum by the Plymouth Corporation.

The Great Hall is impressive, with its plaster ceiling of strapwork and pendants, its carved oak panelling and pediment inlaid with holly and box wood. There is a splendid frieze on its west side symbolizing Grenville's return to Buckland from campaigning; the plaster frieze over the fireplace is dated 1576. The most important item in the Hall is Drake's drum. Adjoining the Hall is the small Chapel containing an outstanding collection of silver, mainly ecclesiastical, some bearing the long discontinued Plymouth hallmark.

The Drake Gallery contains many mementos and documents of this famous sailor, including Drake documents of the Armada year, his lodestone and a modern model of the *Golden Hind* in which he sailed round the world in under three years. In the adjoining Drake's

Drawing Room is the fine portrait of Sir John Hawkins by Custodis, one of Queen Elizabeth I supposedly by Zuccaro and one of Drake himself attributed to Gheeraerts.

There is a Folk Gallery devoted to traditional Devon crafts, a Naval Gallery containing ship models from sail to steam, mainly from the Harmsworth Collection, marine paintings on the Upper Staircase and a small interesting collection of wheeled transport in the Tithe Barn.

Burghley House Northamptonshire

The Marquess of Exeter KCMG

1 mile SE of Stamford, B1443

Burghley House, one of the great Elizabethan 'prodigy houses', was built 1556–87 for the immensely wealthy William Cecil, 1st Lord Burghley, who by intelligence and intrigue became the most powerful of all Queen Elizabeth I's ministers: he was made Secretary of State in 1558, Baron of Burghley in 1571 and Lord High Treasurer in 1572. His direct descendants still live here. The present Marquess of Exeter was, as Lord Burghley, a distinguished athlete, winning an Olympic gold medal in the 400 metres hurdles at Amsterdam in 1928.

The exterior of the great house has been little changed but the 5th Earl of Exeter, devoted to architecture and the arts, created the glorious Baroque suite of State Apartments or 'George Rooms' on the first floor, 1681–1700. The State Bedroom or 2nd George Room was used by Queen Victoria and Prince Albert in 1844. Verrio was appointed to paint four of their ceilings and to transform the walls and ceiling of the Saloon, or Heaven Room, into a vast mythological scene in which the Olympian deities are crowding to inspect Venus and Mars, trapped by Vulcan, undoubtedly this artist's finest achievement. His self-portrait can be seen close by Cyclops' forge. Verrio also started on the Grand Staircase ceiling before he was sent packing because of his continuing truculence: its walls were eventually painted in

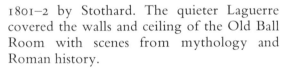

Thomas Lawrence's portrait of the 1st Marquess of Exeter with his 'cottage' Countess; Burghley House.

Jan Van Eyck (c.1385–1441) Self-portrait *in the Pagoda Room at Burghley House.*

1801–2 by Stothard. The quieter Laguerre covered the walls and ceiling of the Old Ball Room with scenes from mythology and Roman history.

Burghley contains a large number and range of fine paintings. Family portraits hang in the Billiard Room together with portraits of members of the 5th Earl's 'Little Bedlam Club', which included Verrio. Kneller's paintings of him and of the 5th Earl and his two wives hang close by Kneller's self-portrait. Here too are portraits by Gainsborough and Lely and a notable Lawrence of the 10th Earl and 1st Marquess with his family – his 'cottage' Countess was unaware of her husband's rank when she married him. In the Pagoda Room hangs a portrait of William Cecil himself, near one of the aged Queen Elizabeth, both attributed to Gheeraerts; together with portraits of 'Capability' Brown, who worked at Burghley as architect and landscapist, Angelica

Kauffman attributed to Dance, the 1st Earl of Exeter by Johnson, Lady Anne Cecil by Van Dyck and Van Eyck's revealing self-portrait.

The remarkably comprehensive collection of works by Italian masters, mainly 17th-century, includes Giordano, Reni, Maratta, Agostino and Ludovico Carracci and Dolci. In the Ante-Chapel and Chapel are three fine paintings attributed to Veronese, one of them the altarpiece. Among other paintings in Burghley's vast and rich collection are four by Jan Breughel and Zuccarelli's *Flight into Egypt*.

The house is also rich in English, French and Italian furniture, including six handsome mahogany commodes enriched with ormolu by Chippendale, who also created the fine gilt rococo mirror and console table in the Brown Drawing Room. The 4th George Room contains two splendid marquetry cabinets, with matching corner cupboards by Chippendale to Adam's design. Fine Soho tapestries hang in Queen Elizabeth I's Room where the four-poster bed and seat furniture are still covered with their original material. Rich wood carving, confidently attributed to Gibbons, fine panelling, chimneypieces, Chinese ceramics and snuff-bottles, bronzes and an immense Queen Anne wine cooler – reputedly the largest in the world – are more of Burghley's treasures.

Burton Agnes Hall Humberside

The Trustees of Burton Agnes Hall Preservation Trust Ltd

In Burton Agnes village, 6 miles s w of Bridlington on A166

The highly satisfying warm red-brick Gatehouse, its well-proportioned angle turrets capped by domes, is a worthy introduction to Burton Agnes Hall, built of the same material. Its architect, Robert Smythson, who designed the Hall between 1601 and 1610, also created Hardwick and Longleat. The house passed in 1654 to the Boynton family, who still live here.

The interior is remarkable for its extraordinarily exuberant carving and for its fine collection of paintings. The frieze of the handsome oak screen in the Great Hall contains figurines of the Twelve Tribes of Israel: above are three plasterwork tiers, crowded with biblical, mythological and allegorical figures, some of them standing along the top of the screen. The lower half of the overmantel, rising above the intricately patterned chimneypiece, tells the story of the Wise and Foolish Virgins; the upper half incorporates the arms of members of the Boynton and Tempest families. There is excellent wainscot panelling above which are full-length portraits of the 6th Baronet and his wife by Cotes together with other family paintings.

The Inner Hall with its handsome Nonsuch chest, Gheeraerts' painting of the three Miss Griffiths and a bronze by Epstein leads to the Drawing Room. Here there is fine gilded panelling and, above the fireplace, a fantastic carving of the Dance of Death, personified by

the central skeleton which is separating the Damned from the Saved. A china cupboard contains good examples of 18th-century English and Continental porcelain.

Eighteenth-century Chinese lacquer screens hang on the walls of the small Chinese Room together with a portrait of the 5th Baronet by Mercier. Some of the paintings in the house are in the little Garden Gallery, including two seascapes by Boudin, examples by Renoir, Pissarro, Manet, Gauguin, Vuillard and Utrillo, together with works by Sickert and Augustus John, who is also represented by a masterly group of drawings. In the Dining Room, with its carved Elizabethan chimneypiece, are portraits by Kneller, Cotes and Reynolds, landscapes by Gainsborough and Marlow and several silver racing trophies.

How well fine quality late-18th-century furniture can live with 20th-century paintings, including works by Matisse, Rouault and Vlaminck, can be seen in the airy Upper Drawing Room. The splendid recently restored Long Gallery with its elaborate plaster-

Camille Pissarro Woman Shelling Peas, *c.1897; Burton Agnes Hall.*

Paul Gauguin Head of a Tahitian Woman;
Burton Agnes Hall.

work ceiling contains mainly mid-20th-century French Expressionist paintings but earlier masters, including Corot, Courbet and Derain, are also represented. Vlaminck's excellent *The Village, Evening* embellishes the Library together with more Expressionist paintings and two by Duncan Grant.

Burton Constable Humberside

Mr J. Chichester-Constable

At Burton Constable, $1\frac{1}{2}$ miles N of Sproatley, $7\frac{1}{4}$ miles NE of Hull (A165)

The Constable family acquired Burton manor early in the 12th century but they did not live here until 1600 when this impressive Elizabethan mansion, remodelled in the 18th century, was built. A view of the east front of the house, *c*.1700, hangs in the Great Hall.

Cuthbert Constable, advised by 'Capability' Brown, converted a series of bedrooms into the impressive Long Gallery, *c*.1740, although the 'Jacobean' ceiling design was only completed in the 1830s and the frieze with its mermen and squids is a fascinating piece of 18th-century antiquarianism. The Bartoli brothers made the scagliola marble chimneypiece. The furniture here includes the original late Stuart long-back chairs, made in Hull *c*.1690, which were added to in 1840. Among the family portraits hanging here is one, *c*.1770, by the Swiss pastellist Liotard, of Cuthbert's son William, a scientist and Fellow of the Royal Society, shown wearing the clothes of his friend, J. J. Rousseau. William's 18th-century scientific equipment is in the Museum Room, where there is also a delightfully decorated Dolls' Museum.

It was William Constable who remodelled the house *c*.1750–70, and added a third storey. He commissioned plans from Robert Adam, 'Capability' Brown, James Wyatt, Thomas Lightoler and Atkinson and Carr of York, some of which are displayed in the Muniment Room. Lightoler designed the Great Hall using, according to Christopher Hussey, 'renaissance and classical elements to produce a Gothic effect with rococo details'. The rococo carved wood chimneypiece is an unusual feature. Lightoler was also responsible for the Staircase Hall and its fine cantilever staircase with 'tulip' lights on its rail and, most successful of all his work here, for the glorious Dining Room whose fine plasterwork is by Collins.

Atkinson designed the Billiard Room, now the Chapel, with plasterwork by Cortese and chairs in the Chippendale manner. He also designed the Blue Drawing Room, which contains 17th- and 18th-century Dutch and Flemish paintings and fine embroidery by members of the family.

The execution of Wyatt's designs, 1775–6, for the Ballroom or Great Drawing Room with elegant plasterwork by Cortese marked the end of William Constable's plans for remodelling the interior. Little has changed since.

The Stables contain a comprehensive carriage collection, a vintage car museum and one devoted to agricultural machinery.

Buscot Park Oxfordshire

The National Trust

2 miles SE of Lechlade on A417

This restrained mansion in the Adam style was built to his own designs by Edward Loveden Townsend in about 1780, to which a pretentious porch and a vast wing were added in the mid-19th century by Robert Campbell, an Australian tycoon. Campbell industrialized the estate to produce sugar beet and alcohol, laying down six miles of narrow gauge railway track to convey the beet from field to factory. When this enterprise collapsed, Buscot was acquired by Alexander Henderson, later created Lord Faringdon of Buscot, a successful financier and connoisseur, who collected an important group of paintings and notable pieces of furniture. His grandson, Gavin Henderson, who succeeded as 2nd Baron Faringdon in 1934, employed the architect Geddes Hyslop to remove Campbell's additions and to design the two balancing pavilions that now stand west and east of the house. In 1948 the house was acquired by the late Ernest Cook and given to the National Trust. The works of art were transferred in 1962 to the Faringdon Collection Trustees to ensure their permanent retention at Buscot.

The Italian paintings are mainly in the Drawing Room and the Staircase Hall, and include distinguished works by Palma Vecchio (a moving *Marriage of St Catherine*, thought to be part of a larger canvas), Palma Giovane, Salvator Rosa, and *The Rest on the Flight into Egypt* attributed to Previtali. Also in the Staircase Hall is Murillo's splendid *Faith presenting the Eucharist*, looted from a Spanish church by the French in the Peninsular War. The English works in the Sitting Room are nearly all 18th century, among them portraits by Reynolds, Cotes, Kauffmann and Lawrence, two of Reynolds' genre paintings and views by Gainsborough, Ibbetson and Richard Wilson. The 1st Lord Faringdon also collected paintings of his own time. In the Saloon is Burne-Jones' *The Legend of the Briar Rose*, a fine example of his escape into the medieval past

Rembrandt (1606–69) Portrait of Clement de Jongh; Buscot Park.

from Victorian reality; further fine paintings and drawings by Victorian artists including Landseer, Millais, D. G. Rossetti, Leighton, Watts and Ford Madox Brown are in the downstairs Billiard Room. This tradition of collecting contemporary works of art continues and the small well-chosen collection of 20th-century English paintings includes works by Ravilious, Hitchens, the late Graham Sutherland and Lord Methuen.

Perhaps, however, the outstanding painting at Buscot is Rembrandt's portrait of Clement de Jongh in the Music Room, which also contains fine portraits by Rubens and Jordaens and an enchanting *Temptation* by Roelandt Savery. At the end of the Staircase Hall are three Rembrandt drawings and others by or attributed to Lely, Ludovico Carracci, Maratta and Guercino.

The furniture is admirable and mainly English of the late-18th and early-19th-century. In the Hall are rare examples of Hope's Regency Egyptian style. The Sitting Room and Music Room also contain Regency furniture. In the Drawing Room is a delightful collection of late-18th-century rosewood and satinwood furniture painted with a peacock feather decoration; in the Saloon the set of giltwood chairs and settee, still covered with original silk, are Empire, stamped by the *ébéniste*, Pierre Antoine Bellangé. An elaborate 'Chinese Chippendale' style overmantel and the girandoles on either side in the Dining Room exemplify the high rococo style associated with Thomas Johnson. The plaster-work ceilings in the ground floor rooms are mainly late-18th century.

Excellent examples of Oriental ceramics, mainly Chinese, embellish most rooms, together with bronzes, blue-john vases, Renaissance ivories and, in the Hall, Sèvres *bleu céleste* shell-shaped dishes mounted on ormolu bases.

Cadhay Devonshire

Mr Oliver William-Powlett

½ mile from Fairmile on Honiton–Exeter road, A30

'John Haydon esquire, sometime bencher of Lincoln's Inn, builded at Cadhay a fair new house and enlarged his demesnes' according to Risdon in his *Survey of Devon, 1620*. Haydon, a successful lawyer, acquired the estate by marriage in 1527. He did not start on his 'fair new house', perhaps the finest Tudor manor in Devon, until the suppression of the College of Priests in Ottery St Mary in 1545, as a result of which building stone became easily available. The primary material used, however, is Salcombe sandstone with stone dressings from the nearby Beer quarry.

The house, built round a quadrangular courtyard – the Court of the Sovereigns –

Regency Egyptian style sofa, c.1805, by Thomas Hope; Buscot Park.

underwent a number of changes after the Haydon family disposed of the property in the mid-18th century. The original Great Hall was divided horizontally to give two rooms. Made into several dwellings in the 19th century, the property was well restored by Mr W. C. Dampier Whetham who acquired it in 1910. Since 1924 it has been occupied by the William-Powlett family.

The most interesting interior features are the Tudor fireplaces, especially that in the Dining Room, originally the Great Hall, with its traceried heraldic frieze, and the barrel-vaulted ceiling of the Roof Chamber above, although it is without its hammerbeams, which were cut away in the 19th century. There is some agreeable period furniture and pewterware.

Callaly Castle Northumberland

Major A.S.C. Browne

2 miles w of Whittingham, 8 miles n of Rothbury

Standing in parkland, remote in the spacious Northumbrian countryside, Callaly Castle is a late Stuart classical mansion, incorporating a 14th-century pele tower, with 18th- and 19th-century additions. It was acquired in 1877 by the grandfather of the present owner, members of an ancient Northumbrian family and direct descendants, through the female line, of the Claverings to whom, until then, it had belonged for nearly 650 years. It is a family home in which the furniture and paintings have not been purchased as collectors' pieces, but acquired through inheritance, marriage or because the design or associations of each item appealed. There is no attempt to impress the visitor and the very considerable charm of the interior and its contents lies not only in their often impressive quality but also in the unself-conscious way in which they are laid out.

The entrancing 1757 Drawing Room contains remarkable plasterwork on ceilings and walls, in which there are medallion portraits – the work of Italian stuccoists. The two galleries, one at each end, supported on Roman Doric pillars, have chinoiserie balustrades.

Greek marble horse head found at Ephesus in 1841; Callaly Castle.

There are three tables, consisting of Chippendale-style mahogany frames, surmounted by fine Italian scagliola tops, one of them with a design of playing cards, an open music book and an envelope addressed to Lady Dorothy Marsh, signed by Laurentius Bon Ucelli; the unusual 19th-century gilt bedstead is also Italian. The Aubusson carpet is of the Louis Philippe period.

Elsewhere is sound George III and Regency furniture in addition to the set of James II chairs with matching stools in the Ballroom, which also contains four Gobelins tapestries, signed by Audran, 1787, and two 17th-century Brussels tapestries. The portraits include one of Princess Mary Stuart, aged fifteen, later the wife of William III, painted in Holland by J. D. Hennin in 1677. Equestrian and sporting paintings are much in evidence, among them works by Seymour, J. N. Sartorius and George Morland. Other paintings include works by or attributed to Hayman, Hogarth (*The Fairies Dancing*), Wheatley and Jan Wyck (*William III at the Battle of the Boyne*).

The Museum contains game trophies, much Victoriana and a splendid Greek marble horse's head found at Ephesus in 1841.

Cannon Hall South Yorkshire

The Barnsley Metropolitan Borough Council

Near Cawthorne, 4 miles s of Barnsley on A635

This handsome late-18th-century house, standing on high ground which looks south over

The Victorian Gothic Venetian Drawing Room by J.F. Bentley; Carlton Towers.

parkland towards Cawthorne village, is typical of the lesser country mansions of its period. The property had been acquired by John Spencer at about the time of Charles II's restoration in 1660, but the present sandstone building was designed for his great-grandson by John Carr of York in 1764, who employed local craftsmen whenever possible. It was his plasterer, James Henderson, who executed the fine Dining Room and Library ceilings. A north-east wing, which included a ballroom, was added about 1890 by Sir Walter Spencer Stanhope, the panelling made by the estate carpenters. The Ballroom fireplace contains small paintings by Roddam Spencer Stanhope, who was associated with the Pre-Raphaelite circle. In 1951 the property was acquired by the Barnsley authorities who have imaginatively converted it into a Country House Museum; the Museum of the 13th/18th Royal Hussars (Queen Mary's Own) is also housed here.

Good furniture, glass and picture collections have been built up since 1951 by local grants, with help from the government fund administered by the Victoria and Albert Museum and general assistance from the National Art Collection Fund as well as from private sources. The furniture ranges from the 17th century to the Regency period. There are examples of 17th-century oak furniture, a fine set of late-17th-century Dutch chairs with elegant carved back and cabriole knees, a rococo side-table of 1745 and representative pieces of Chippendale, Sheraton and Hepplewhite, especially the breakfront library bookcase, c.1785. The pedestals and wine coolers, embellished with ormolu decoration, are especially pleasing. The fine barometer c.1720 by John Hallifax was made locally.

The glass collection includes examples from Rome and Syria of the 1st and 2nd centuries AD and modern pieces from France, Sweden and Finland. Among the engraved glass is a goblet bearing a likeness of Byron and fine examples from Bohemia. Barnsley has long been a glass manufacturing district.

The small collection of paintings and drawings includes 17th-century portraits by Lely, Wright and Huysmans, and 18th-century portraits by Highmore and Mercier together with an Italian landscape by Wootton. Among the drawings are examples by Ruskin, Cosway, Birket Foster, Walter Greaves and Sickert. Hitchens and Sandra Blow are among the few contemporary artists whose works are exhibited. Also here is the William Harvey Collection, formerly the National Loan Collection, of Dutch and Flemish paintings.

Carlton Towers North Yorkshire

The Duke of Norfolk

6 miles s of Selby, 1½ miles N of Snaith

Carlton Towers has passed by inheritance ever since the Norman Conquest and became the property of the Stapleton family in 1301. They became heirs to the Barony of Beaumont late in the 15th century and have remained staunchly Roman Catholic except for a brief period after the Beaumont title was successfully revived, having been dormant for three centuries, for Miles Stapleton in 1840. He became the 8th Baron and joined the Church of England as a protest against the restoration of the English Catholic hierarchy; his son reverted to the Old Faith in 1869. The present Baron (12th) inherited the title and Carlton Towers from his mother who was Baroness Beaumont in her own right; he is also the 17th Duke of Norfolk.

The three-storeyed block is of Jacobean origin, c.1614. The south front was added c.1777, designed by Thomas Atkinson of York, but the extraordinary high-Victorian Gothic appearance of Carlton Towers, created between 1873 and 1875, is due to the eccentric 9th Lord Beaumont (1848–92) and his capricious architect, Edward Pugin, son of the more renowned A. W. Pugin. Both became bankrupts; the intended grandiose east wing and chapel were never started.

Pugin got no further than the general design of the Outer Hall before he quarrelled with Lord Beaumont who replaced him with the scholarly J. F. Bentley, who had worked under Henry Clutton, once the partner of Burges.

and firedogs by Longden and Co. of Sheffield.

The paintings in the Picture gallery are mainly 17th- and 18th-century Italian, some previously belonging to Cardinal Fesch, Napoleon's uncle, and to the Cardinal of York, younger brother of the Young Pretender. The family portraits in the Dining Room and the Bow Drawing Room are more recent.

Castle Ashby Northamptonshire

The Marquess of Northampton

6 miles E of Northampton, 1½ miles N of A428

A stronghold already existed here, in the green heart of England, in the 12th century though no traces of it now remain. The property was acquired early in the 16th century by the Compton family and the 1st Lord Compton, whose son was created Earl of Northampton in 1618, started to build a handsome Elizabethan mansion in 1574. A graceful screen, attributed to Inigo Jones, was added in 1635 to enclose the open courtyard on the south side, its upper storey forming the Long Gallery. Fire damaged the east wing in the Civil War but after its restoration in the 1670s only minor alterations were made to the house until the 1880s, when the 4th Marquess commissioned Sir Thomas Jackson to redecorate the Chapel, the Long Gallery and the Big Hall.

Castle Ashby is renowned for its collection of superb paintings and fine furniture and although, at the time of writing, Lord Northampton is making Compton Wynyates his home, to which a number of items are being transferred, Castle Ashby still contains many impressive treasures.

Distinguished 17th- and 18th-century portraits include Johnson's 2nd Earl of Northampton, Dobson's 3rd Earl in cavalier costume – he fought for the king in the Civil War – Kneller, Reynolds (*Mrs Drummond Smith*), Ramsay, Philips, Raeburn, Dance, Lawrence, West, Copley and Hoppner. Other outstanding paintings include Bordone's *Rest on the Flight into Egypt*, *Cattle by a Mountainous Stream* by de

Newel post on the stairs at Carlton Towers where all the Victorian wood-carving is by J. Erskine Knox.

Bentley gave the Outer Hall an ecclesiastical character in time for its temporary use as a chapel by Cardinal Manning, who celebrated Mass here in 1876. He designed not only the decor but much of the furniture, curtains, wall coverings and the excellent chandeliers in the Inner Hall, the Venetian Drawing Room with its impressive moulded plasterwork stamped and gilded to resemble leather, the Card Room, and the Picture Gallery, all of them impressively Victorian Gothic. Of the rooms open to the public, only the Dining Room with its Corinthian column screen and the Bow Drawing Room are 18th-century in character. The fine wood panelling and carving throughout are by J. Erskine Knox, the fireplace tiles are by de Morgan and the fine metal chandeliers

Loutherbourg and two watercolours – of Staffa and of Stonehenge – by Copley Fielding. The large canvas in the Dining Room, celebrating the naval battle off Martinique when Admiral Rodney, brother-in-law of the 7th Earl, defeated the French, is suitably set off by its fine gilded Chippendale-style frame. Dutch 16th-century paintings in the passage leading to the Grand Staircase include works by Van Ostade and Dou and an allegorical scene by Dossi.

Three splendid 17th-century Flemish tapestries, with designs after Teniers, hang in the Dutch Wedding Room and elsewhere are Mortlake tapestries of the same period. The handsome furniture includes six Venetian carved oak chairs, *c.*1680, with velvet-covered backs and seats, two remarkable Chinese lacquer chests on gilded English stands, *c.*1730,

William Dobson's portrait of the 3rd Earl of Northampton, c.1644; Castle Ashby.

in the Big Hall, fine William and Mary walnut chairs in the Dutch Wedding Room, a splendid pair of oval carved and gilded mirrors, *c.*1760, and two James II walnut caned chairs in King William's Dining Room.

A handsome Adam-type marble chimney-piece graces the Long Gallery, where there is an important collection of Etruscan red and black vases and excellent Chinese export wares, as well as an impressive Italian *cassone*, Charles II wig boxes and needlework gilt firescreens.

Castle (Castell) Coch
South Glamorgan

The Welsh Office

6 miles N of Cardiff on Pontypridd road, by village of Tongwynlais

Castle or Castell Coch, a 13th-century fortress on a spectacular wooded site above the Taff Vale, was in ruins when William Burges, the designer of Cardiff Castle, was invited by the 3rd Marquess of Bute to submit plans for its rebuilding. Burges accordingly prepared an elaborate set of drawings, now in the Art Department of the National Museum of Wales, showing his conclusions about its original appearance and his recommendations for its reconstruction, working very much on the principles of Eugène Viollet-le-Duc, the French neo-Gothicist who rebuilt among other places the town and castle at Carcassonne. Burges died in 1881 before the interior decorations were fully under way: his successor, William Frame, toned down some of Burges' more flamboyant schemes but the results still represent a Victorian medieval fantasy.

The walls above the green panelled octagonal Drawing Room are painted with scenes from Aesop's fables; the eight ribs of the painted ceiling, radiating out from the apex, are decorated with butterflies. The arch round the door is a young tree, its foliage alive with lizards and butterflies.

The Lives of the Saints embellish the two end walls of the Banqueting Room. The Lady's

William Burges' neo-Gothic fantasy at Castell Coch, shown in the Lady's Bedroom (below) with its painted bed embellished with crystal and its wash-basin (above) with porcelain hot and cold water towers.

Bedroom in the Keep Tower with its great painted bed, adorned with crystal, and its remarkable wash-basin with porcelain 'towers' for hot and cold water, epitomizes Burges' romantic, comfortless dream.

Castle Coole Co. Fermanagh

The National Trust

1½ miles SE of Enniskillen on A4

Screened by a wooded ridge from spreading Enniskillen, the austere yet immensely satisfying neo-classical building of Castle Coole, built at vast expense of Portland stone brought from Dorset, stands above the placid waters of its lough. It was commissioned by Armar Lowry Corry, MP, created in turn Baron, Viscount and in 1797 Earl of Belmore; his father

RIGHT *The elliptical Saloon at Castle Coole, designed by James Wyatt; the plasterwork is by Joseph Rose Jr.*

inherited the estate through marriage to Śarah Corry, whose grandfather, a Belfast merchant who had emigrated there *c*.1640 from Dumfriesshire, acquired it in the 1650s. The plans were drawn by James Wyatt, who never visited Enniskillen, and the work was supervised by Alexander Stewart, a local builder-architect. Nevertheless, Castle Coole is one of Wyatt's outstanding creations. The contents, unless otherwise indicated, belong to the present Lord Belmore.

The austerity of the exterior is re-echoed in the stone-floored Entrance Hall with its screen of purple scagliola columns. The marble chimneypieces here and those elsewhere on the ground floor were carved by Westmacott. Dominic Bartoli was responsible for the scagliola work in the house.

Beyond the Hall screen, reached through gently curving mahogany double doors of remarkable quality, like the joinery throughout, is the elliptical Saloon which stands between the Drawing and Dining Rooms; the curve of its walls is broken by niches, mirrors and grey mottled Corinthian scagliola pilasters. The creation of the magnificent plasterwork here and elsewhere was directed by Joseph Rose Jr, who twice visited Castle Coole, and carried out by his staff, who crossed the Irish Sea in fear of being press-ganged into the Navy. Much of the Saloon's rich gilt furniture in the Regency manner was supplied at great cost some twenty years after the completion of the house by John Preston of Dublin.

By contrast the superb sideboard, flanking urns and the sarcophagus wine cooler in the Dining Room, which shows Wyatt's restrained elegance at its best, were made for under £50 by the joiners building the house.

Wyatt's schemes for the Drawing Room, with its 'country house' family portraits, and the Library were later discarded for richer, heavier furnishings, although the Library bookshelves are his. An unusual feature is the first-floor Lobby, hung with Corry portraits, which is reached up a gracious stairway and lit by a domed skylight. The Lobby opens into the State Bedroom, which was elaborately furnished to receive George IV who preferred, however, to remain in Dublin. In the Dressing Room are four classical landscapes by Cassas and an unfinished portrait by Lawrence.

Castle Drogo Devon

The National Trust

1 mile W of Drewsteignton, 2 miles NE of Chagford and 1 mile S of A30 (turn off at Crockernwell)

Sir Edwin Lutyens' magnificently sited bold granite castle, built between 1911 and 1930 for the Drewe family, is perhaps the last great country house to have been erected in Britain. There are Chinese Chippendale chairs and a pair of George II giltwood mirrors in the Drawing Room, mahogany panelling in the Dining Room, tapestries in the Library and in the Hall with its Persian rugs and Spanish furniture, but the principal interest of the house is architectural.

Lutyens' drawings showing the evolution of the Castle are displayed in the Gun Room. They, together with the contents of the house, belong to Mr Anthony Drewe who gave the property to the National Trust in 1974.

Castle Fraser Grampian

The National Trust for Scotland

3 miles S of Kemnay off B993, 16 miles W of Aberdeen

The native Scottish style of castellated tower-house was born out of defensive necessity and the building materials available in a country rich in stone and chronically short of wood. By the late-16th or early-17th century, when military requirements no longer dominated, these castle dwellings developed a splendour unique in western Europe. Nowhere is this better exemplified than in the group known as the 'castles of Mar', situated in part of the ancient Celtic province of Mar, which included the lower valleys of the Dee and the Don and

Miss Elyza's mid-19th-century 'worked room' at Castle Fraser.

the rolling uplands between the rivers.

Here stands Castle Fraser, perhaps the largest and the noblest of the group, begun about 1575 by Michael Fraser, chief of his clan, and completed by his son. The stone tower and corner circular tower, with low attendant wings forming an enclosed courtyard, have changed little externally since that time. The interior speaks less of the 17th than of the late-18th and early-19th centuries. However, the High Hall on the first floor of the tower block retains its barrel-vaulted ceiling and is furnished mainly with 17th-century oak pieces, including a set of carved chairs, known as the Inverallochy chairs, originally in another Fraser house. Portraits include a Raeburn copy of General Alexander Mackenzie and his brother-in-law, the 1st Lord Seaforth, wearing the dramatic feather bonnet of the Seaforth Highlanders.

The more intimate Dining Room next door has painted wood panelling and is furnished with agreeable 19th-century English pieces. It contains family portraits, among them Colonel Charles Fraser Mackenzie and his wife. The Colonel had a distinguished military career as did many of the Mackenzies, both in the Napoleonic Wars and later in Canada. He lost a leg at the siege of Burgos and was shot through his hat (which is displayed beside the portrait).

His son, another Charles, inherited the estate from a formidable maiden aunt, Miss Elyza Fraser, whose personality still dominates her little bedroom, unchanged since her death. Known as the 'worked room', the bed-hangings, curtains and seat covers were embroidered by her in wool and silk on moreen, a kind of worsted woollen fabric. The colours are remarkably well preserved, due to the vegetable dyes used by Miss Elyza.

The note of calm domesticity, somewhat at odds with Castle Fraser's external appearance, is struck again in the Victorian Smoking Room, with its delightful smoker's companion and a series of topographical watercolours by James Giles. More exotic is the early-19th-century glass painting – a portrait of Charles I which was made in China.

Castle House Essex

The Sir Alfred Munnings Art Museum

At Dedham, 7 miles NE of Colchester, 2 miles E of A12

This pleasant, spacious house on the outskirts of Dedham village was the home of the distinguished painter, Sir Alfred Munnings RA, from 1920 until his death in 1959. A valiant traditionalist quite out of sympathy with contemporary experimental schools of paint-

ing, he was elected RA in 1925 and became President of the Royal Academy, 1944–9. His dazzlingly accomplished paintings of the countryside, hunting, the race course and gypsies and his portraits won not only popular acclaim but the admiration, reluctant on occasion, of his professional colleagues. Castle House contains a splendid cross-section of his work over more than fifty years.

Castle Howard North Yorkshire

Mr George Howard

15 miles NE of York, 3 miles off A64 and 6 miles W of Malton

Charles Howard, 3rd Earl of Carlisle, descended from the 4th Duke of Norfolk, had not only intelligence and wealth when, in 1700, he accepted the bold ideas of John Vanbrugh for a new residence on his North Riding estate to replace his burnt-out castle, but also great discernment and taste. For Captain, later Sir John Vanbrugh, soldier, playwright, and fellow member of the Kit-Cat Club, Castle Howard was his first incursion into architec-

Alfred Munnings' Sketch of a Start at Newmarket, *1951; Castle House.*

The Music Room, Castle Howard.

ture. Fortunately he had Nicholas Hawksmoor, scholarly, tactful and with twenty years of practical experience under Wren, to translate his inspiration into architectural reality.

When the 4th Earl succeeded in 1738, only the central block and the east wing of this magnificent Baroque mansion had been built: the west block was completed some twenty years later in Palladian style. While Vanbrugh's original plan is somewhat out of balance, the satisfying splendour of the main design remains: 'I have seen gigantic palaces before,' wrote Horace Walpole, 'but never a sublime one.'

The interior is equally remarkable, especially the stone paved Great Hall whose pilasters soar upwards into arches, through which further vistas of stairs and wrought-iron balustrades are visible, and on to the dome above. The Italian stuccoists, Bagutti and Plura, created the delightful chimneypiece, whose marble surround and that of the shrine opposite is of scagliola, one of the earliest recorded uses of this material in English architecture. The walls and the dome were covered with enchanting frescoes by Pellegrini. The dome and the High Saloon, which contained similar splendours, were destroyed by fire in 1940; happily the dome has been rebuilt and Pellegrini's Phaeton with his chariot have been re-created by the Canadian artist, Scott Medd.

The contents of Castle Howard are superb. On the Grand Staircase hang Soho tapestries woven by Vanderbank after the younger Teniers; nearby are Roman, Greek and Egyptian antiquities. Meissen, Crown Derby and Chelsea (the Sir Hans Sloane service) porcelain is on the China Landing. In the Antique Passage is a marble bust by Bernini, a Graeco-Roman figure of Ceres, and marble-topped tables in many designs, some by Kent and Batty Langley.

Both the Music and the Tapestry Rooms are embellished with carved pinewood friezes, door surrounds and swags by Nadauld and Carpenter. The paintings in the former include Wheatley's portrait of the 5th Earl and family in Dublin, two racing scenes by Wootton and Gainsborough's *Girl with a Pig*, bought by Reynolds for 100 guineas. The Tapestry Room contains fine portraits by Reynolds, Gainsborough and Romney. In the Orleans Room is Rubens' *Herodias and Salome with the Head of John the Baptist* and other master paintings, mainly of the 17th and 18th centuries, including Feti's *The Music Master*, three landscapes by Gaspard Poussin and others from the Duke of Orleans' collection.

Outstanding works in the Long Gallery are Holbein's portraits of Henry VIII and the 3rd Duke of Norfolk. The family portraits here include works by Van Dyck, Lely, Kneller, Hoppner and Lawrence and a version of Scrots' *Henry Howard, Earl of Surrey*. Among other treasures are fine oriental rugs, richly decorated classical bronzes, Italian cabinets, 16th- and 17th-century Italian religious paintings and a fine English inlaid commode, *c.*1780, by Fuhrlohg.

Castle Ward Co. Down

The National Trust

7 miles NE of Downpatrick, off A2 to Strangford

Castle Ward, one of the most attractive and intriguing National Trust properties in Northern Ireland, was built on a superb site overlooking Strangford Lough in the 1760s by an unknown architect for Bernard Ward, 1st Lord and later 1st Viscount Bangor. It is remarkable for having two fronts in contrasting styles. Ward favoured the classical manner as exemplified by the south-west façade; his

whimsical wife, daughter of the 1st Earl of Darnley, preferred the then fashionable Gothic taste for the north-east side, perhaps used here for the first time in Ireland. The interior was likewise divided. Few of the present furnishings, apart from the family portraits, are original to the 18th-century house – the original contents were dispersed in 1827 – but they are good examples of that period.

There is a sparkling lustre about the interior which is immediately compelling. The Entrance Hall is richly embellished with pleasing Dublin plasterwork panels, some of which contain paintings, interspersed with swags which include musical instruments; there are also plaster trophies on the entablature above the screen of yellow scagliola Doric columns. The coat of arms of the 3rd Viscount Bangor, who succeeded in 1827, is to be seen above the broken pedimented doorway into the Saloon which is flanked by elegant rosewood marble-topped commodes on which stand good examples of *famille rose* and Imari ceramics.

The handsome Dining Room contains mid-18th-century country-made dining chairs with splats and cresting in the Chippendale style and silver of the same period. Over the fireplace is a painting, attributed to Thomas Robinson, a pupil of Romney, showing Lord Castlereagh and the Hon. Edward Ward, son of the 1st Viscount Bangor, at the Bishop of Dromore's Palace.

The doors, panelling, chimneypiece and unusual plasterwork ceiling in the Saloon are in the Gothic manner. The furniture includes a late-17th-century japanned cabinet on an ebonized stand and an Italian cabinet of the same period veneered with tortoiseshell, ivory and ebony, with a 1760 chinoiserie lacquered long-case clock close by. Here are important family portraits, including works by Batoni, Cotes and Romney. In the Gothic overmantel is a painting of Prince George of Denmark and Lady Mordaunt in the guise of Vertumnus and Pomona.

The Gothic style is at its most inflated in Lady Bangor's Boudoir, whose ceiling is fan-vaulted with ribbed and quatrefoil plaster decorations. Auguste Edouart was responsible

RIGHT *The State Drawing Room, Chatsworth, with Mortlake tapestries, c.1635, and ceiling paintings by Laguerre.*

for the silhouette picture, dated 1833. The Library with book presses of curved and figured mahogany contains a view of Old Castle Ward, 1785, by William Ashford (another of his paintings is in the Morning Room); the other scenes are attributed to Jonathan Fisher, another Irish painter.

The well-proportioned Staircase Hall is enriched by a broad band of Vitruvian scroll ornament, taken perhaps from Abraham Swan's *Collection of Designs*, 1757; the staircase itself has fine wrought-iron balusters, a mahogany rail inlaid with ebony and satinwood stringing and carved parcel-gilt newels. A charming set of seven oval portraits of Lady Mordaunt (d. 1679) and six of her children hangs over the door leading to the Hall.

The Laundry in the courtyard, fitted out in mid-Victorian style, contains finely laundered period clothes, table and bed linen.

The mid-Victorian Laundry at Castle Ward.

Cawdor Castle Highlands

The Earl of Cawdor

5 miles s of Nairn on B9090

> 'This Castle hath a pleasant seat. The air Nimbly and sweetly recommends itself Unto our gentle senses.'

So said the doomed King Duncan of Macbeth's abode. Though he was not speaking of Cawdor, Shakespeare's description aptly fits the Castle today. Despite inevitable and overpowering associations with medieval tragedy, distant horrors are no more than faint shadows and Cawdor Castle is now an urbane castle home, set above a deep rushing stream set off by wooded parklands and an exceptionally beautiful garden.

The history of the Cawdors stretches back beyond the recorded past; the first written

LEFT *Carved gilt-framed mirror, 1772, by Robert Adam above a commode and torchères, 1772, by John Cobb; Corsham Court.*

93

The Old Kitchen, Cawdor Castle, which was in active use from 1640 to 1938 and contains numerous utensils and kitchen equipment from the past, including an 18th-century spit, a 19th-century cooking range, ice-box, flat irons and butter-hands.

evidence dates no earlier than the 13th century with a charter of the Thanage to Donald Calder. The 8th Thane died in 1498 leaving a posthumous daughter who was promptly abducted by Argyll Campbells and married off at the age of twelve to a younger son of the Chief. From this surprisingly happy union the Campbells of Cawdor are descended. Between 1663 and 1676 the 15th Thane, Sir Hugh, greatly enlarged and embellished the medieval keep. His arms and those of his wife, Lady Henrietta Stuart, are to be found on exterior walls and interior stonework. Later generations made further additions that blended happily with the older buildings so that the house today is an assured and agreeable amalgam of some 600 years of building.

Unbroken occupancy of so long a span by a single family leaves indelible traces upon a house. There are no spectacular treasures here, rather the gradual accretions of generations of Cawdors, a family that produced a fair share of talent and an uncommon number of men of courage while 'making no undue stir in the world'. Perhaps the most notable things at Cawdor are the tapestries, among them a set of late-17th-century Arras hangings depicting the story of Noah that were ordered for the house and brought from Flanders via Leith and Findhorn at a total cost of £483. An Antwerp set of the 'Liberal Arts' is of the same period, and a highly unusual set in the Dining Room illustrating the adventures of Don Quixote dates from *c.*1680. They were once thought to be of Spanish origin, but their 'grotesque' style suggests they may have been made at the Hatton Garden workshop.

A curious stone fireplace in the same room is *c.*1670 but bears the date 1510. An elaborate one in the Blue Room bears the arms of Sir Hugh and Lady Henrietta. An Italian Baroque bed with velvet hangings dates from their time. A set of black 'Russia' leather chairs was bought in 1722 for 7s 6d apiece, a sum thought vastly high at the time. A roll-top George II desk and a Gothic-style yew chair of 1760 should also be noted.

In so old a house it is refreshing to find 20th-century paintings amid the pictures. An early Stanley Spencer, watercolours by John Piper and a Dali drawing of Macbeth hang harmoniously in the same room as an early Claude landscape and a fine still-life by Bogdani. There are many family portraits, the most striking a pair of sparkling Lawrence sketches of the 1st Earl and his wife and a full-length Reynolds. The little 17th-century portrait of Lady Alice Egerton, one of the players in the first performance of Milton's *Comus*, has all the characteristic quality of Soest's work.

Chalcot House Wiltshire

Mrs Anthony Rudd

2 miles w of Westbury on A3098 to Frome

This enchanting small manor house of brick with stone dressings, built high on a hillside with distant views over Wiltshire, is of medieval origin, but was embellished by a neoclassical front *c.*1680. Subsequently there were alterations and additions in the 18th century and by St Aubyn in the 19th. The present owner, who acquired what was then a decaying property in 1971, has restored the house with scrupulous care, demolishing many of the Victorian additions and introducing circular skylights over the Hall and Staircase. The white and gold Ballroom with its original plasterwork has also been renovated. This restoration won a European Architectural Heritage Year Award in 1975 for owner and architect.

The 18th- and early-19th-century furniture is of good quality. The walls of the Victorian Dining Room have been appropriately covered with a William Morris paper design, on which hang family portraits. The owner's adventurous good taste is shown to advantage by Chalcot's small but growing collection of post World War II paintings by, among others, David Inshaw and Ewan Uglow. A tapestry showing Chalcot by Polly Hope covers one of the walls of the Drawing Room.

There are several fascinating small collections, including one of Carolingia (Queen Caroline, consort of George IV) and another of the Boer War.

Nearby was a Romano-British settlement and the recent work at Chalcot revealed many finds, including a large number of coins dating to the third century A D.

Charlecote Park Warwickshire

The National Trust

4 miles E of Stratford-upon-Avon on N side of B4086

Charlecote was owned by the de Lucy family from the 13th century until given to the National Trust in 1945 by Sir Montgomerie Fairfax-Lucy, whose descendants are still in residence. Charlecote Park is perhaps best known for its associations with Shakespeare when young: he is traditionally said to have been caught poaching in the park and was punished accordingly by Sir Thomas Lucy, whom the poet eternally pilloried as Mr Justice Shallow in *Henry IV, Part Two* and *Merry Wives of Windsor*.

The Elizabethan house was heavily restored in the 'Elizabethan Revival' style, popular *c.*1825–50, by George Hammond Lucy and his heiress wife, energetically aided by Willement. Lucy also bought extensively at William Beckford's 1823 sale, where he acquired the great marble table, the top once in the Borghese Palace and supported by the Gothic frame designed for Beckford, now standing in the Great Hall. The walls here are decorated with antlers' heads, weapons, and Lucy portraits by, among others, Jonathan Richardson, Kneller and Gainsborough (the bachelor *George Lucy*); Larkin almost certainly portrayed the 3rd Sir Thomas Lucy and Lord Herbert of Cherbury. The largest painting in the Hall, that of the 3rd Sir Thomas with his family, perhaps after Johnson, is over the mantelshelf, on which stands the bust of Queen Elizabeth I, who once stayed at Charlecote, copied from her tomb effigy in Westminster Abbey. Shakespeare's bust faces the entrance: busts of George Hammond Lucy and his wife in Carrara marble by Behnes, 1830, are by the windows which contain

ABOVE *Silver-gilt font-shaped wine cup, 1524; Charlecote Park.*

LEFT *The 'Charlecote Buffet', an oak sideboard, 1858, carved by J. M. Willcox.*

armorial glass, some of it 16th century.

Willement redesigned the Library and the Dining Room with their rich, somewhat 'busy' wallpapers, as well as the 1833 bookcases, the 'strapwork' chintz covers on the seat furniture, the fire-grate and door-stops in the Library. The Dining Room contains the enormous 'Charlecote buffet' with its central carving of a whippet, made in Warwick. Of special interest is the very rare Tudor silver-gilt wine cup, 1524. Its delicate engravings show a hedgehog, a coursing hound and a monkey.

The Ebony Bedroom contains Beckford's ebony bed, made from a 17th-century East India settee, a Japanese lacquer cabinet and marquetry furniture. Two Chinese Chippendale rococo pier-glasses are in the Drawing Room with more Beckford furniture and Batoni's portrait of George Lucy, dated 1758. Also fascinating are the Great Kitchen, the Brewhouse, the Museum in the Gatehouse and the splendid carriages in the Coach-house.

Chartwell Kent

The National Trust

2 miles s of Westerham off B2026

In 1922 Sir Winston Churchill acquired this then ivy-clad Victorian mansion set high in wooded hills, yet only twenty-five miles from Westminster, because of the magnificent view southwards over the Weald of Kent. He

John Sargent's charcoal drawing, 1929, of Sir Winston Churchill as Chancellor of the Exchequer; Chartwell.

commissioned Philip Tilden, a successful architect, to modernize it, which he did with greater emphasis on comfort and manageability than on style. Here the Churchill family lived for over forty years. In 1945 an anonymous group of friends bought Chartwell and gave it to the National Trust for preservation, while Churchill retained a life tenancy.

Chartwell remains very much as it was in Churchill's lifetime. Its contents are remarkable not in themselves but as a reflection of the great man's tastes and the deep affection in which he was so widely held. He was devoted to his family and among portraits of Lady Churchill, of his children, his father Lord Randolph, and himself are works by Lavery, Sargent and William Nicholson, together with many photographs, including those of his friends.

Perhaps Chartwell's most distinguished painting is Monet's *London Bridge* in the Drawing Room, but Churchill's own works hanging in the house and in the Studio show

the considerable ability which he attained in this field, recognized by his election as Honorary Academician Extraordinary by the Royal Academy in 1948. He once said, 'If it weren't for painting I couldn't live; I couldn't bear the strain of things.' There are also several paintings by his daughter, Sarah.

In the Ante-room are displayed many gifts from all over the world and war-time souvenirs such as a facsimile of the letter sent by Roosevelt to 'A certain Naval Person' in 1941. Churchill's life from childhood to old age is surveyed photographically in the Museum Room where handsome gifts from governments and heads of states are shown. The Uniform Room contains his uniforms, robes and the insignia of the many orders to which he belonged.

In the Dining Room is a gift which probably meant as much to Lady Churchill and himself as any they received. It is the 'Golden Rose Book', the golden wedding present given in 1958 by their children; it contains watercolours by outstanding contemporary painters, including Ivon Hitchens, John Nash and Matthew Smith, of twenty-nine of the thirty-two yellow and golden species of roses planted in the garden at Chartwell on that occasion.

Chastleton House Oxfordshire

Mrs A. Clutton-Brock

4 miles SE of Moreton-in-March and 5 miles NW of Chipping Norton

In 1603 the Chastleton estate was bought by Walter Jones, a successful Witney wool merchant, for £4,000 from Robert Catesby, later notorious for his involvement in the Gunpowder Plot. Jones erected this impressive early Jacobean mansion which has remained virtually unchanged since his death in 1632; Chastleton is notable both for this and for its fine woodwork.

The carved oak screen between the Entrance and the Great Hall is an excellent example of this period. Even more elaborate is the panelling in the first-floor Great Chamber,

Early Jacobean carved oak screen in the Hall at Chastleton House.

which is carved with pilasters and arches; in its frieze are twenty-four paintings of prophets and sibyls. There are boldly carved and painted stone chimneypieces both in the Great Chamber, which contains the arms of Walter Jones and his wife, Eleanor Pope, and in the Middle Chamber. The plasterwork ceilings of the bedroom known as the State or Fettiplace Room, of the Long Gallery and especially of the Great Chamber are intricately designed.

Family portraits, two by Hudson but mostly by unknown hands, hang above the panelling in the Great Hall and in the Middle Chamber; there are more on the walls of the impressive oak staircase with its original balusters and obelisk mounted newel posts. Noteworthy furniture includes the eighteen-foot-long refectory table in the Great Hall, which has remained in position since it was first brought here, several walnut and cane long-back late Stuart chairs and two lacquer cabinets. The books in the Library are mainly 18th century. The Great Hall has Cromwellian armour.

Chatsworth Derbyshire

The Trustees of the Chatsworth Settlement

Off A263, ½ mile E of Edensor between Bakewell and Chesterfield

Chatsworth, built in magnificent surroundings in the heart of the Peak District, is always ranked extremely high among England's very finest houses. It was the ambitious Bess of Hardwick who persuaded Sir William Cavendish, the second of her four husbands and the only one by whom she had a family, to acquire the estate and to build an imposing manor house on the terrace above the River Derwent in the 1550s. Their second son became the 1st Earl of Devonshire. It was the 4th Earl – he became the 1st Duke in 1694 – who decided to rebuild the south front; he was then led by impulse and enthusiasm to rebuild all four wings on the foundations of the previous house.

Although devoted to music and the arts, the

1st Duke was also violent and quarrelsome; he was fined £30,000 for tweaking the nose of a Colonel Colepeper. His choice of Talman, equally quarrelsome, as architect inevitably led to trouble. Talman carried out his noble Baroque design for the south front and had perhaps started on the west front when he was dismissed. The north front may have been designed by Thomas Archer with help from the Duke himself. Improvements to lighten the great house were made by Wyatville for the 6th Duke but its Baroque character remains.

Chatsworth's splendour is illustrated by the richness of its decorative painting. Laguerre, helped by Ricard, was responsible for the resplendent Painted Hall's ceiling and walls, for those in the Chapel and for the ceilings of the State Rooms, except for the State Dining Room, which was painted by Verrio, then working at Burghley. Verrio's canvas *Doubting Thomas* is set high in the Chapel's superb marble and alabaster altarpiece, sculpted by Cibber. Verrio and Cibber are also represented in their respective roles in the decoration at the head of the Great Staircase, joined by Samuel Watson, a Derbyshire carver in wood, stone and marble, who made his career at Chatsworth. A third decorative painter was James Thornhill, whose achievements in the Sabine Room and on the West Staircase are as accomplished as the rest of the decorative painting at Chatsworth.

The paintings are outstanding. Fine portraits include those by Van Dyck, Lely, Honthorst, Wissing, Kneller, Zoffany, Hudson, Knapton (*The 3rd Earl of Burlington*), Reynolds (*Georgiana, Duchess of Devonshire and her Daughter*), Beale, Hayter, Millais, Watts, Sargent, de Laszlo and Lucien Freud. The list of great artists seems endless. There are excellent works by Veronese, Giordano, Bordone, Domenichino, Gaspard Poussin, Ricci, Murillo, Van Goyen, Berchem, Monnoyer and Landseer. Rembrandt's superb *Portrait of an Oriental* and two likenesses by Hals are in the Sculpture Gallery, where works by Canova, Thorvaldsen and other 19th-century sculptors are displayed.

ABOVE *Rembrandt* Portrait of an Old Man, *1651; Chatsworth.*

BELOW *Gilt-framed table by William Kent; Chatsworth.*

Excellent examples of Mortlake tapestries, 1635–45, are in the South Sketch Gallery and especially in the State Drawing Room. Samuel Watson carried out most of the carvings in the Grotto, on the Chapel altarpiece and, together with Lobb, Young and Davis of London, in the State Rooms: Gibbons' work is represented only on Kent's gilt-framed table on the Oak Staircase Landing. There are particularly fine

Mid-16th-century and early-17th-century panelling enriched with gilding and carving at Chavenage.

examples of Kent's work at Chatsworth because the 4th Duke inherited the estates and possessions of his wife's father, the Earl of Burlington, who was a disciple of Palladio and patron of Kent. The furniture includes handsome late Stuart chairs, early-17th-century Italian inlaid mosaic cabinets, a splendid French writing desk with ormolu mounts by Roentgen, c.1780, candelabra stands and other pieces by Boulle, English and Coromandel lacquer chests, chairs by Chippendale and solid 19th-century library furniture.

There are items to delight everywhere – the Dutch silver chandelier in the State Dressing Room; two Egyptian commemorative tablets, c.5,000 years old, and a torso of Athena found in Tyre in the West Sub-Corridor; Tijou's gilt-iron balustrade on the Great Stairs; the magnificent George II state bed; a two-manual Shudi and Broadwood harpsichord, 1782, in the State Music Room; an English needlework carpet, c.1710, in the State Drawing Room; Delft blue and white tulip vases in the South

Sketch Gallery; a fine marble chimneypiece by the younger Westmacott in the Dining Room and much fine porcelain from Sèvres, Meissen and the Orient.

Chavenage Gloucestershire

Mr David Lowsley-Williams

2 miles N of Tetbury, 1 mile off A434

The Chavenage estate was originally monastic property; after the Suppression of the Monasteries, c.1539, it was acquired in 1553 by the Stephens family, who were successful wool merchants and sheep farmers. The fine E-shaped Elizabethan mansion, which was built c.1576, incorporates material which had once formed part of the prior's house, such as the 15th-century window over the main porch. There are signs of later building alterations, the last being the bow window added early in this century to the Dining Room. Its overall character remains Elizabethan.

The impressive Hall, which is two storeys high, is lit by two tall mullioned and transomed windows, which contain medieval stained glass. Its fine stone chimneypiece bears the arms of the son of the Edward Stephens who originally acquired the house; it is embellished with swags of fruit, wreaths of bay leaves and black marble inlay. The panelling of the Dining Room enriched with gilding and carving, is dated 1627.

The Stephens family was firmly Parliamentarian; both Cromwell and Ireton stayed here and their bedrooms in the south-east wing are hung with contemporary Mortlake tapestries.

Chawton Cottage Hampshire

The Jane Austen Memorial Trust

1 mile sw of Alton off Alton bypass

In 1809 Jane Austen, with her sister, their widowed mother and a family friend, moved from Southampton into this small, late-17th-century country house on the Chawton estate, which had been bequeathed to Jane's third brother.

Only a few pieces of family furniture remain, including her father's Hepplewhite bureau bookcase and two chairs, and Jane's work-table japanned with Canton lacquer – at which she worked on *Mansfield Park*, *Emma* and *Persuasion* – but the early-19th-century wallpaper gives a strong period atmosphere and the many mementos will interest all Jane Austen admirers. These mementos include examples of Jane's excellent needlework, among them the patchwork quilt on which her mother also worked, photostat copies of family letters, family likenesses, printers' proofs of Hugh Thomson's delightful illustrations for Macmillan's edition of *Pride and Prejudice*, documents and other relics of Jane's two Admiral brothers, and the verses she wrote in July 1817, three days before her death.

The wash house at the rear of the building still contains the donkey cart in which Jane used to ride through the countryside, as well as old kitchen utensils.

Patchwork quilt worked by Jane Austen and her mother; Chawton Cottage.

Chicheley Hall Buckinghamshire

The Trustees of the Hon. Nicholas Beatty

2 miles E of Newport Pagnell on A422 to Bedford

A Baroque red-brick building with stone dressings, its entrance front decorated with Corinthian pilasters and its windows with stone surrounds, Chicheley Hall was built in 1719–23 by Francis Smith of Warwick for Sir John Chester, 4th Baronet; the earlier house had been sacked by the Parliamentarians in the Civil War. The marble floored Hall is by Henry Flitcroft in sober neo-Palladian style; the ceiling painting from Ovid is by Kent. The house was acquired in 1952 by the 2nd Earl Beatty, son of the great naval commander of World War I, and Chicheley contains many mementos of the Admiral's career. His portrait by Sargent hangs in Lord Beatty's Study beneath a portrait of Nelson by L. F. Abbott.

On the Hall chimneypiece, together with

The Drawing Room, Chicheley Hall, with walnut panelling lightly enriched with gilt.

two Chinese armorial bowls, is the bronze lion which Admiral Beatty placed on the desk facing the German Commander when the German fleet surrendered to him in 1918. Also in the Hall are two Adam gilt *torchères* with rams' heads, the emblem of the Chester family who owned Chicheley for over 300 years, together with two Italian walnut side-tables supported by eagles with snakes in their beaks. Beyond the scagliola screen of Tuscan pillars is the graceful Main Staircase, its oak handrail and stair-ends inlaid with bands of walnut, its balusters in groups of three different designs.

A striking feature of the house is the panelling, especially in the Sitting Room and Dining Room, whose mouldings, panel surrounds, architraves, cornices and garlands of fruit and flowers above the chimneypiece are of walnut, lightly and effectively enriched with gilt. The former room contains sporting paintings by John Ferneley Sr and Herring,

whose coaching scene hangs over the finely carved marble chimneypiece made for the house. Both rooms contain fine gilt framed mirrors, especially the set of four in the Drawing Room, in which a collection of Stuart mother-of-pearl tankards, plates and candlesticks are displayed, together with Hudson's portrait of Sir John Chester, who built the house.

In Lord Beatty's Study are seascapes by, among others, Serres and Buttersworth and decorations awarded to Admiral Beatty. The Dining Room with fine gilt framed oval mirrors contains portraits by Cornelius Johnson. Naval scenes by W. L. Wyllie hang on the Back Staircase which leads to Sir John Chester's Library where the finely carved panelling conceals shelves behind, and to the Jacobean Room and Dressing Room, both of which contain fragments of the long demolished 16th-century house at Chicheley.

Chiddingstone Castle Kent

The Executors of the late Mr Denys E. Bower

In Chiddingstone village, 5 miles E of Edenbridge

The conversion of the earlier red-brick Carolean mansion into the present romantic Gothic Revival castle was started during the Regency and completed in the 1830s. It contains fascinating and important collections of ancient Egyptian artefacts and Stuart relics, an outstanding collection of Buddhist and Japanese objects, and good furniture, mainly English, all assembled by the late Mr Denys E. Bower.

In the Buddha Room stand images of various periods of the Buddha from India, Ceylon, Tibet, Burma, Siam, China and Japan; the three over the fireplace, especially that in blue glaze, show the remote but firm influence of the so-called Graeco-Buddhist work of Gandhara. The Tibetan shrine of gilt copper enriched with semi-precious stones is 18th century; other intriguing and delightful items include three temple trumpets in copper and brass, two straight and the third curved; a Lama's teapot, the handle shaped like a wolf; incense burners and Tibetan charm boxes.

The Great Hall includes late Stuart chairs, a 17th-century Flemish tapestry and Chinese and Japanese ceramics. The Stuart collection includes letters and documents starting with Mary Queen of Scots, and ending with Cardinal York, the younger brother of Bonnie Prince Charlie and the last of the direct Stuart line; a letter from the Duke of Monmouth begs for an extra day to prepare for death 'so that I may goe out of this World as a Christian ought'; there are also Stuart portraits, engraved glass and other mementos.

Three rooms contain Japanese armour, weapons, netsuke, theatre masks, lacquer work, remarkable models of fish, insects, etc. in metalwork and three clay figures from tombs, *c.* AD 400–600.

Some of the great variety of Egyptian objects date from the fourth millennium BC; others cover the intervening centuries down to Roman times and include a fine grey marble bowl from the Old Kingdom, Babylonian and Abyssinian clay tablets and cylinder seals and a little wooden model of a funeral boat, powered by two oarsmen, in which a small, lonely figure of a 12th Dynasty king sits under an awning.

Blue-glaze Buddha (left) and a model of an Egyptian 12th Dynasty funeral boat (below) at Chiddingstone Castle.

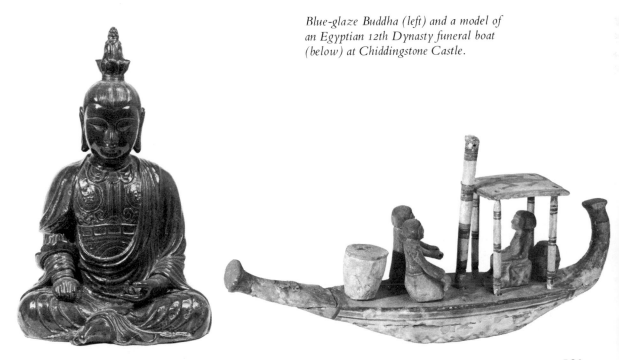

Chillington Hall Staffordshire

Mr P. R. de L. Giffard

4 miles sw of A5 at Gailey, 8 miles NW of Wolverhampton

This dignified red-brick mansion was started by Peter Giffard in 1724, but the Giffard family, of Norman origin, established itself at Chillington about 1178; for the following 800 years, Chillington has descended in a direct male line.

The Tudor house was visited by Queen Elizabeth I in 1575 and considered as a place of detention for Mary Queen of Scots, but was found not to be sufficiently secure. In 1724 Peter Giffard demolished part of the Tudor mansion and commissioned Francis Smith of Warwick to raise the south side of three storeys. Soane in 1786–9 built the east front with the massive four-columned pedimented portico in front of the Entrance Hall with its Ionic screen and two chimneypieces.

The 1724 Staircase Hall is admirable. Each three-balustered tread is embellished with the carved panther of the Giffard crest. The walls are decorated with Baroque plasterwork panels enclosing busts and whole figures, possibly by Vassalli. The heraldic stained glass of c.1830 is by John Freeth. The Morning Room also boasts a fine plasterwork ceiling, an allegorical figure at its centre, again perhaps Vassalli's work. The Dining Room's delicate frieze dates from Soane's period: its furniture is late Regency. In it are two portraits by Batoni of Peter Giffard's son and grandson, both christened Thomas, painted while in Rome; here also is Hewetson's marble bust of the younger Thomas.

Architecturally the most fascinating room is Soane's Saloon, which has taken the place of the Tudor Great Hall; its coved oval ceiling leads up to an oval lantern. The chimneypiece bears the Giffard family arms.

The handsome domed state bed with splendid furnishings was installed in the State Bedroom in 1788 on the occasion of the younger Thomas' marriage to Lady Charlotte Courtenay. 'Capability' Brown landscaped the beautiful park in the 1770s and, in collaboration with James Paine, formed the great lake of seventy-five acres.

The chimneypiece bearing the Giffard family arms in the Saloon, Chillington Hall.

Chirk Castle Clwyd

Administered by the National Trust for the Secretary of State for Wales

2 miles from Chirk on A5, 7 miles SE of Llangollen

Chirk Castle, magnificently sited on a wooded ridge amid spreading parkland, was built as a great Border castle on the Welsh Marches for Edward I and completed by 1310. After passing through the hands of the Crown and of many distinguished families, it was acquired in 1595 by Sir Thomas Myddelton, whose descendants still live here. The main alterations to the interior of the castle, which retains much of its original character, were made on the arrival of the Myddelton family, again after the Civil War and in the second half of the 18th century, and lastly in 1845–7, when Pugin designed the present neo-Tudor Entrance Hall with its panelling, its heavy chimneypiece and fine brass andirons, c.1615; the weapons and armour displayed here are mainly from the Civil War.

The Staircase Hall is 18th century and the handsome staircase with its elegant gilt-enriched balustrade is in the Robert Adam manner, as is the ceiling both here and in the State Rooms, with the possible exception of the Dining Room which is decorated in a style closer in feeling to that of James Wyatt. On the staircase hang historical documents, including the Baronet's patent granted by Charles II to the son of the 2nd Sir Thomas Myddelton. Paintings on the Staircase Hall landing include one by an unknown hand of Anna Maria, Countess of Shrewsbury (d. 1702), one of Roland Jones, the Welsh Bard, aged ninety, which is one of Richard Wilson's few portraits, two scenes by Tillemans, one of them of Llangollen and the Dee Bridge, and a stag hunt with the Castle as background by Wootton. In the Dining Room is a carved marble fireplace, with a handsome Régence Boulle wall bracket clock above it by Charles Balthazar of Paris, an Adam style mahogany sideboard and an impressive brass and crystal chandelier, *c*.1775.

The magnificent Saloon, its fifteen ceiling panels painted with mythological scenes, contains good furniture in the Chippendale manner, pier-glasses surmounted by roundels painted by Kauffmann, a set of four late-17th-century Mortlake tapestries with scenes from the story of Cadmus, a fine Burkat Shudi harpsichord, *c*.1742, and portraits by or attributed to Kneller, Wright, Dahl and Van der Mijn. The superb Drawing Room contains more good furniture, both English and French, a fine panel of needlework, 1704, and portraits by Kneller, Ramsay and Dahl.

The superb Long Gallery with its fine panelling, carving and friezes celebrates the period of Charles II, whose portrait in the middle of the east wall presides over a magnificent Dutch ebony and tortoiseshell cabinet with silver enrichments, given by the monarch to the 2nd Sir Thomas Myddelton (d. 1666). The length of the Gallery on both sides is hung with Royalist and Parliamentarian portraits, interspersed with Charles II silver

Dutch ebony and tortoiseshell cabinet given in 1666 by Charles II, whose portrait features above, to Sir Thomas Myddelton; Chirk Castle.

sconces. The south wing includes the Tudor block with Chapel, a bedroom once slept in by Charles I, the fascinating late-18th-century Servants' Hall and the much older dungeons.

Chiswick House Middlesex

The Department of the Environment

1 mile w of Hammersmith in Burlington Lane, Chiswick, London w4

Chiswick House was raised between 1725 and 1729 by the 3rd Earl of Burlington, the high priest of the early-18th-century Palladian Revival, with the assistance of William Kent.

View of the Gallery, Chiswick House; the interior decorations are by William Kent.

This building of remarkable beauty is mainly based on the work of Palladio but partly also on that of Scamozzi and the ancient Romans. The influence of Palladio's Villa Capra, near Vicenza, is evident, but instead of having four entrances, Chiswick House has only one because of the much cooler English climate. It was built after part of the old Jacobean mansion, now long since disappeared, was destroyed by fire in 1725. It was never intended as a home, and the ground floor held the Earl's books while the *piano nobile*, surrounded by his works of art, was where he entertained. The interior was decorated by William Kent, often using Inigo Jones as a model. Everywhere is rich decorative invention of the greatest skill.

The tall octagonal Domed Saloon, with its pedimented doorways in four of the sides, is at the centre. Classical busts stand on brackets. Between each pair of doorways hangs a large painting in a heavy gilt frame, four of these historical and four allegorical or classical. The dome is decorated in ancient Roman style with recessed octagonal coffers which decrease in size as they near the summit. Kent's ceilings are even more elaborate in the Red Velvet Room and the Blue Velvet Room, each so called from the original wall covering. Equally notable are the carved chimneypieces of marble and gilded plaster. Antique statues stand in niches, porphyry vases flank the windows, doorways are surmounted by roundels and supported by cherubs.

The surrounding gardens by Kent mark the first step away from the rigid design of the age of Wren towards the landscape garden.

Clandon Park Surrey

The National Trust

3 miles E of Guildford, off the A246
Leatherhead–Guildford road

Undoubtedly one of the grandest English interiors of the 18th century, the two-storey Entrance Hall of Clandon Park, painted in shades of grey and white to blend with the two exquisite marble chimneypieces by Rysbrack, is in its cool majesty the crowning achievement of the Venetian architect, Giacomo Leoni, to whose plans this red-brick mansion was erected for the 2nd Lord Onslow in about 1730. Its style is partly Baroque and partly Palladian. The magnificent plasterwork of the Baroque ceiling is confidently attributed to the Italian plasterers, Bagutti and Artari, who were probably also responsible for the plasterwork ceilings in the ground floor state rooms and the stucco overmantel in the Saloon.

These rooms, one of which, the Palladio Room, is hung with 18th-century French wallpaper, contain furniture from the Onslow family, later Earls of Onslow, who owned Clandon for over two centuries, and from the very fine collection bequeathed to the Trust in 1969 by Mrs Hannah Gubbay. In this collection are a pair of William and Mary pierglasses in gilt and red *verre églomisé* frames; a pair of George III commodes in the style of Pierre Langlois; a satinwood commode of the same period with amboyna panels, and Queen Anne chairs, covered in fine needlework and in contemporary Soho tapestry. Upstairs the furniture in the Prince Regent's Room is mainly Chinese Chippendale.

In the State Dining Room, which was on the upper floor, stands early-18th-century needlework furniture, while the Blue China Room has been adapted to show most of Mrs Gubbay's large and comprehensive collection of English and European porcelain, mostly of

'Parrot Eating a Nut',
Bow, c.1760; Clandon Park.

*Nymphenburg figure of Octavio
by Bustelli, c.1760; Clandon Park.*

*The Hunting Room, Clandon Park; a Soho tapestry, c.1740, is on the right
and the overmantel mirror contains a conversation piece by Daniel Gardner.*

an ornate character; there are fine examples of Bow, Chelsea, Derby and Liverpool, and of Meissen, Höchst, Frankenthal, Nymphenburg and Sèvres. There is a Meissen monkey band from Kändler models and a group of 18th-century Staffordshire pottery figures. Mrs Gubbay's exotic collection of Oriental ceramic birds is scattered among the State Rooms, including the Hunting Room, which also contains panels of Soho tapestry, c.1740, and an oval conversation piece, oil on canvas, by Daniel Gardner in the overmantel mirror. This painting, like most others, depicts members of the Onslow family, three of whom became Speakers of the House of Commons. Another portrays Arthur Onslow as Speaker, seated in the Speaker's Chair in the Chamber, with Sir Robert Walpole recognizable on the government benches. It was painted by Thornhill in

1730 with the assistance of his son-in-law, Hogarth. There are large paintings of birds and fish by Francis Barlow and a series by Ferneley portraying horses in the stud of the 3rd Lord Gardner, a relation by marriage of the Onslows.

Claverton Manor Avon

The American Museum in Britain

2½ miles from Bath Station via Bathwick Hill

Claverton, a neo-classical country house of Bath stone designed in 1820 by Wyatville, proves an ideal setting for the American Museum in Britain, started here in 1961. Founded to increase Anglo-American understanding, the Museum shows how a distinctive

ABOVE *Shaker cherrywood sewing chair and round stand, 1815–20, from New Lebanon, New York; Claverton Manor.*
RIGHT *Philadelphia bonnet-top mahogany highboy, c.1770; Claverton Manor.*

American art came into being between the late-17th century and the middle of the 19th. Rooms within rooms illustrate various periods and influences, which were at first mainly British. After Independence, mercantile contacts developed with Europe and the Far East and, through overland expansion west and southwards, with colonial Spanish and American Indian cultures. In addition there was the distinctive Shaker craftsmanship and the

Doorcase in the Chinese Room, Claydon House, with its intricate chinoiserie wood-carving by Lightfoot.

colourful peasant designs of the Pennsylvania-Germans.

Chippendale's influence remained strong on the Eastern Seaboard as is shown by the furniture in the Perley and Deming Parlors, including the bonnet-top mahogany highboy, *c.*1770, and the mahogany chairs and block-front desk, while Hepplewhite and Sheraton designs are noticeable in the later Deer Park Parlor. Impressive examples of Greek Revival furniture by the celebrated Duncan Phyfe and by Ephraim Haines are in the Greek Revival Room. Fine textiles, silver, pewterware as well as pioneer artefacts are well represented and much else besides in a warmly welcoming atmosphere.

Claydon House Buckinghamshire

The National Trust

At Middle Claydon, 3½ miles s w of Winslow, 13 miles N w of Aylesbury

The restrained classical exterior, added in the mid-18th century to the older red-brick manor house by the attractive yet thriftless 2nd Earl Verney, does not prepare the visitor for the astonishing rococo virtuosity of the woodwork within. Richly inventive, it is seen at its most fantastic in the chinoiserie of the first floor Chinese Room with its Chinese tea-party – a vision of Cathay unparalleled elsewhere in England. It is the only known achievement of a Mr Lightfoot, who appears to have acted as both carver and amateur architect of this house until the appearance of Sir Thomas Robinson, who replaced him. Lightfoot's work is also to be seen in the Pink Parlour and North Hall on the ground floor, in the upper Gothic Room and in the carved wood ceiling of the main staircase. The beautifully contrived doorways in the North Hall and the Saloon and the superlative joinery of the mahogany staircase, inlaid in elaborate patterns with holly, ebony and ivory, are also by his team of craftsmen. The delicate ironwork balustrades with trembling ears of wheat are outstanding.

The plaster ceiling of the Saloon is the work

Detail of the Chinese tea-party, part of Lightfoot's richly inventive wood-carving at Claydon House.

of the plasterer Joseph Rose Jr, often employed by Robert Adam. Other fascinating items are letters from, among others, Charles I and Cromwell, a complete set of Javanese gamelan gongs, and mementos of Florence Nightingale, who lived here for many years with her elder sister, Parthenope, who married Sir Harry Verney in 1858.

Clouds Hill Dorset

The National Trust

9 miles E of Dorchester on B3390 and 1 mile N of Bovington Camp

This tiny cottage, home of the famous Lawrence of Arabia who described it as 'an earthly paradise and I am staying here until I feel qualified for it', stands isolated among woods some 300 yards from the site of his fatal motorcycle crash in 1935. It consists merely of the Book Room, the Music Room above it and the tiny Bunk Room in which one of his Arab jellabas and the glass domes which covered his food are displayed.

The contents are of the simplest, his personality all pervasive. Downstairs are three of Eric Kennington's illustrations from *Seven Pillars of Wisdom*, and photographs both of and by Lawrence, and of paintings, sculptures and drawings of Lawrence by Kennington, Augustus John and William Roberts. The wrought-iron fender with stainless-steel top was made locally to his design, as was that in the Music Room where Lawrence's bust by Kennington stands over the fireplace looking towards his gramophone.

Cobham Hall Kent

Westwood Educational Trust Ltd

4 miles W of Rochester on Watling Street and Rochester Way (B2009) off A2

The ancient manor of Cobham Hall was transformed into a splendid Elizabethan mansion by the addition of two Tudor wings with octagonal lead-capped turrets at each of their ends; the porch of the northern wing is of Caen stone exported from France with special licence from the French king. Further changes were made by Webb, 1662–70, and between 1768 and 1830 by Chambers, James Wyatt and the Reptons; Bernasconi was employed, 1800–9, to make the Gothic plasterwork mouldings. Now an independent public school for girls, it stands peacefully in gardens and park landscaped by Humphry Repton.

Wyatt was responsible, 1802–9, for the somewhat characterless Gothic Entrance Hall, including presumably the faked coat of arms of Elizabeth I above the doorway, for the Gothic screen in the Inner Hall and for the reconstructed Long Gallery, which contains two splendid fireplaces and overmantels, probably by Giles de Witt; one of them is dated 1599.

The State Dressing Room has excellent hand-painted Chinese wallpaper and a Wedgwood blue and white ceiling by Wyatt. George Repton designed the Library, built

1817–20. The Vestibule, until 1802 the Entrance Hall and now the headmistress's study, was created by Wyatt in 1773–4 with ceiling plasterwork in the Adam manner; a glorious white marble chimneypiece has a niche on each side sheltering a pair of lovers.

The impressive Gilt Hall rising through two storeys has a gilded plaster ceiling, 1672, with later neo-classical additions by Chambers, including the musical trophies in gilt frames and the two Galleries, one of which contains a fine two-manual organ by Snetzler, built in 1779 and still in use. The magnificent chimneypiece is by the elder Westmacott and the red damask seat furniture by Wyatt. Giles de Witt was responsible for the fireplace, dated 1587, in the Dining Room with a near naked figure of Pomona in the centre of the over-mantel, supported on each side by enormous baskets of fruit. Opposite, beneath the window, is an elaborate wine cooler. The adjoining Chapel, which was never consecrated and is now a dining room, was 'gothicized' by Wyatt in 1812. The gilded Darnley state coach. *c*.1715, is a fine example of its kind.

Antonio Mor Mary I, 1554; *Compton Wynyates.*

Compton Wynyates
Warwickshire

The Marquess of Northampton

10 miles w of Banbury, just off Shipton road (B4035)

The Compton family, ennobled in 1566 and later created Earls and Marquesses of North-ampton, were already here in 1204. The present building, romantically sited in its green hollow and surrounded by wooded slopes where vines once flourished, was built early in the 16th century of rose-red bricks, rarely used at that time outside East Anglia because of their expense. Much of the material came from Fulbroke Castle near Warwick, given by Henry VIII to William Compton. The house suffered in the Civil War; the battlements were destroyed and the moat filled in by order of the Parliamentarians. Alterations and additions were made early in the 18th century and again

by Sir Digby Wyatt in the mid–19th century. Its complete contents were sold in 1744 to pay off debts. Lord Northampton has recently decided to bring here, from Castle Ashby, Antonio Mor's magnificent portrait of Queen Mary Tudor and some of the fine 17th-century Dutch paintings.

Across the internal courtyard is the entrance to the screens passage and the Big Hall whose oriel window and ceiling were brought here in 1512. The pair of panel paintings of the 1st Earl of Shrewsbury and his second wife must be among the earliest known English portraits. The large *Mystic Marriage of St Catherine* by Marco Palmezzano of Forli, 1537, hangs over the much later fireplace. The large early–16th-century tapestry of cupids picking grapes and at play is North Italian. Between the screen doors is a carved panel of English and French knights at the Battle of Tournai, 1521.

The panelled Dining Room with plaster ceiling, *c*.1620, contains 17th-century family portraits. On the Main Staircase, designed *c.*1860 by Wyatt, hangs an early-16th-century altarpiece of the Virgin and Child enthroned with Saints, attributed to Battista Bertucci of Faenza, and a little Pater of a couple dancing by a stream. The splendid panelled Drawing Room has a William and Mary seaweed marquetry table, several fine Italian paintings, including a pastoral scene attributed to Giorgione, a crucifixion by Matteo Balducci and a delightful needlework picture, *c.*1590, showing Orpheus charming the beasts, among them a camel. The adjoining Chapel Drawing Room, looking down into the Chapel, possesses an enchanting Florentine Nativity by the Master of the Lively Child in which angels hold up a length of plainsong for all to join in. The Chapel screen incorporates two panels, carved on each side, one of which illustrates the Seven Deadly Sins being welcomed at the entrance to Hell.

Henry VIII's Room possesses a strapwork ceiling, *c.*1630, and a four-poster bed with an excellent carved headboard. The Tudor panelling in the Council Chamber is genuine, and the Elizabethan Sheldon tapestry was one of the first to be made in England. The Priest's Room above displays a fine Italian carving over one of its three doors.

Constable Burton North Yorkshire

Mr M. C. A. Wyvill

On A684 between Leyburn (3 miles) and Bedale

John Carr of York, instructed by Sir Marmaduke Wyvill, the 5th Baronet, in 1762 to carry out alterations to his residence, reduced it by mistake to its foundations, and for an extra £10,000 built in its place this delightful restrained Palladian villa. A print of the original house hangs in the Outer Hall.

The main rooms are well proportioned, with the Drawing Room plaster ceiling reflecting the influence of Adam, and contain fine marble chimneypieces, especially in the Drawing Room. There is good furniture, including a library table by Gillow, based on a design in Chippendale's *Director*, and a mid-

18th-century Dutch marquetry bureau bookcase in the Drawing Room; window seats after Chippendale, four Louis XV armchairs (*fauteuils*) and George III mahogany pieces in the Morning Room. The Dining Room table and chairs are by Gillow and two display cabinets attributed to Linnell are in the Inner Hall with its splendid cantilevered stone staircase and pretty wrought-iron balustrade.

The portraits, some of them family, include works by Kneller, Mercier, Soldi and Hoppner. The other paintings are mainly Dutch and Italian by, among others, Hondecoeter, Van Mieris, Snyders, Weenix and Castiglione.

Corsham Court Wiltshire

The Lord Methuen

In Corsham, 4 miles w of Chippenham off the Bath road (A4)

Corsham Court, originally stone built in 1582 near the site of a much older manor house, was acquired in 1745 by Paul Methuen, an eminent clothier of Bradford-on-Avon. He commissioned 'Capability' Brown to enlarge and modify the building, having in mind that he was to inherit the splendid collection of paintings and objects of art of his cousin, Sir Paul Methuen (1672–1757), a distinguished diplomat who had helped his father negotiate the political and commercial treaties in 1703 with Portugal, England's oldest European ally. A second collection of Italian master paintings and *pietre dure* cabinets came by inheritance to Corsham through the Rev. John Sanford (1777–1855). Additional modifications were made to Corsham in 1800 by Nash, whose work was largely superseded in the 1840s by Bellamy.

'Capability' Brown designed the Cabinet Room, the State Bedroom, the Octagon Room and the glorious triple-cube Picture Gallery, *c.*1760, to display Sir Paul's paintings. His bold plasterwork ceiling (with medallions containing *putti*), which had originally been offered to but not used by William Constable of Burton Constable near Hull, was executed by Stock-

*The triple-cube Picture Gallery designed by 'Capability' Brown, c.1760,
to house Sir Paul Methuen's paintings at Corsham Court.*

ing, a stuccoist as eminent in the south-west as
members of the Rose family. The carpet, made
in 1959 by the Royal Tapestry and Carpet
Factory, Madrid, was designed to echo Brown's
ceiling. The paintings in the Picture Gallery, its
walls covered with crimson damask, are
displayed in groups to achieve a harmonious
balance with the room's architectural design
and the placing of the magnificent seat
furniture, attributed to Chippendale; even the
two lines of nailing on the seats match the
pattern of the fillet edging the wall coverings.
The *Wolf and Fox Hunt* by Rubens, hanging
above Scheemakers' white marble chimneypiece, is in a splendid frame designed by Adam
who also designed the set of four fine pier-
glasses and marble-topped console tables against
the opposite wall. The paintings here are mainly
16th- and 17th-century Italian, including fine
examples by Annibale Carracci, Caravaggio,

Dolci, Reni, Strozzi and Rosa, but there are also
Ribera's *A Physician's Consultation*, three
exceptionally fine Van Dycks, including *The
Betrayal of Christ*, and Dobson's *Head of a
Cavalier*.

The Cabinet Room contains three Italian
cabinets of *pietre dure*, and more Italian pictures
among which Lippi's *Annunciation* is outstandingly lovely. The pier-glass is by Adam, the
marquetry commode beneath it and the two
torchères by John Cobb, c.1722. Over the
north doorway is an enchanting plaque, *The
Madonna in Contemplation*, by della Robbia.

Rosa's *Wooded Landscape* is above the
fireplace in the State Bedroom whose furniture
is in the Chippendale manner; the pair of
delightful rococo carved oval mirrors with
squirrels and the mirrors and elaborate console
table in the Octagon Room are similar to a design by Thomas Johnson of 1761. The Octagon

Room also contains a wide-ranging collection of English and European paintings by, among others, Claude, Zuccaro, del Sarto, the younger Teniers, Wouvermans, Hoare, Ibbetson, Monamy and Riley. Also noteworthy are a marble carving of the sleeping Cupid on a lionskin attributed to the young Michelangelo and fragments of two Indian shrine carvings.

In the Hall and corridors are family portraits and statuary from the 17th century onwards; Dobson, Johnson and Lely are represented together with two large decorative works executed jointly by Gerard de Lairesse and Adam Pijnacker. Also on display are fine Sung, Ming and K'ang Hsi ceramics and 12th-century Persian glass bottles. The Music Room contains a fine Regency mahogany horseshoe-shaped wine table with a movable coaster. There are more fine family portraits in the Dining Room by Kneller, Reynolds, especially his two delightful renderings of Paul Methuen's children, and by Romney. The high-backed walnut carved chairs are William and Mary, the Gothic sideboard by Nash, *c*.1800, the glass Venetian and the dessert service from Limoges.

Cotehele Cornwall

The National Trust

On w side of River Tamar, 8 miles sw of Tavistock and w of Calstock

This romantic grey granite house, secluded in woods high above the Tamar's west bank, is mainly Tudor, but it probably enfolds part of the original fortified manor house which was already there when William Edgcumbe acquired the property through marriage in 1353. Cotehele remains one of the least spoilt of the few surviving late medieval buildings; virtually nothing has been changed since the north-west tower was added in 1627. The Edgcumbes lived here until late in the 17th century when they moved to Mount Edgcumbe, near Plymouth.

The soaring Hall with its elaborate medieval roof supports and its vast Tudor open fireplace contains a collection of arms and armour, both English and foreign, ranging from Tudor to Napoleonic days. The fine refectory table on four baluster legs is late-16th-century, the pewterware displayed on it mainly 18th-century. Here also are a renowned Charles I chair-table, dated 1627, two notable oak

Part of Soho tapestry, c.1700, showing amorini at the wine press, in the Punch Room at Cotehele.

armchairs with carved backs, *c*.1650, and unusual George II folding chairs. The banners belonged to the Royal Middlesex Militia.

Cotehele's rooms are hung with splendid tapestries mainly of the 17th century; that in the Dining Room shows Venus at her toilet. In the Punch Room hangs a set appropriately showing *amorini* vigorously at work at the wine press. The White Room at the foot of the Tower possesses three Mortlake tapestries, *c*.1700, while others, depicting episodes from the story of Hero and Leander, hang in King Charles' Room, which also contains Flemish pieces, as do Queen Anne's Room, the South and the Red Rooms; the last two bedrooms display Brussels work as well.

The other rooms contain an important collection of Jacobean and Stuart furniture together with some earlier and later pieces. Of special interest is the Cotehele tester, an early-16th-century oak bedhead, with a Welsh inscription, in the Staircase Lobby; two of its eight panels are probably of a different period. Other pieces of note include Charles II walnut armchairs, a mahogany fourposter bed probably from Goa, a Charles II stumpwork looking-glass, an Italian upright walnut cabinet *c*.1600, and a Spanish *escritoire* inlaid with various woods of about the same date. A very rare curiosity is the steel speculum or mirror of *c*.1625 in King Charles' Room, in use before looking-glasses became widespread.

The Chapel contains the earliest working clock in England, unaltered and in its original position – it was installed by Sir Richard Edgcumbe *c*.1488. Three centuries later, in 1789, George III and Queen Charlotte took breakfast in the Old Drawing Room and the cushions upon which they sat record the event in writing upon the undersides.

Coughton Court Warwickshire

The National Trust

2 miles N of Alcester on A435 road to Redditch

The magnificent Tudor gatehouse of Coughton, flanked by late-18th-century Gothic

wings, was erected *c*.1509 by Sir George Throckmorton, in whose family it remained until 1946 when Sir Robert Throckmorton, the 11th Baronet, gave the property to the National Trust. Always staunch Catholics, members of the family suffered persecution, fines and imprisonment for the active support of their faith. Here the wives and friends of the conspirators anxiously awaited the outcome of the Gunpowder Plot of 1605, to scatter quickly on hearing of its failure.

Coughton, damaged and ransacked by the parliamentary forces in the Civil War, underwent alterations in the 1780s and again in the 1830s and in 1910; on this last occasion the chapel was converted into a large Saloon. Not surprisingly, there are secret passages and hiding rooms in the gatehouse and elsewhere.

The Drawing Room above the gatehouse entrance contains two splendid portraits painted in 1729 – that of the 4th Baronet faces the one of Anne Throckmorton, daughter of the 2nd Baronet and a Dominican nun, both by Nicholas de Largillière. There are also fine

Nicholas de Largillière Anne Throckmorton as a Dominican Nun, *c.1729; Coughton Court.*

miniatures of the Acton family, together with six Dutch inlaid and walnut veneered chairs of the William and Mary period, a double Chippendale chair convertible into library steps, and a Chinese Chippendale table. In the Little Drawing Room is an unusual Rockingham service of plates decorated with the counties of England, a Worcester dessert service and portraits by Johnson and Lely. The Tower Room contains a painted canvas known as 'The Tabula Eliensis', dated 1596, showing details of the garrison quartered on Ely Abbey by William the Conqueror, together with the arms of the Catholic gentry imprisoned for their faith by Queen Elizabeth I.

There is excellent panelling dating from the reign of Henry VIII and Charles I and a fine chimneypiece of Renaissance character made from oak, marble and polished black slate in the Dining Room. On the table laid for dinner is Georgian silver. In a little closet beyond is a Nottingham alabaster relief of the Nativity. The Tapestry Dressing Room possesses six gouache drawings of dockyards and views around Castellamare attributed to the Swiss artist Ducros (1748–1810). Displayed in a case in the Tribune is the chemise worn by Mary Queen of Scots at her execution, and Jacobite relics. The Saloon contains a rosewood Mass Cabinet, more family portraits and the 'Throckmorton Coat', 1811, made for a wager from wool cut from a sheep at sunrise and completed as a coat by sunset.

Cragside Northumberland

The National Trust

½ mile E of Rothbury, 28 miles N of Newcastle-upon-Tyne

Cragside is built on a hillside above the River Coquet, a dramatic site for a country house which posed difficulties in building that were just the type of challenge to which William Armstrong vigorously responded. Born in 1810, the son of a prosperous merchant, he was destined for the law but he soon became intrigued with hydraulics. In collaboration with the contractor, Henry Watson, he produced a hydro-electric machine for which he·was elected a Fellow of the Royal Society while still a solicitor. He later invented the world's first efficient hydraulic crane for Newcastle's docks and established the firm of W. G. Armstrong and Co. at Elswick, on the River Tyne. From hydraulics he turned his attention to armaments – in response to Britain's inefficient weaponry in the Crimean War – which in turn led to the design and construction of ironclad warships. He was made a peer in 1887, by which time his pre-eminence in these fields was only rivalled by Krupp's. Dying childless in 1900, the peerage lapsed, but in 1903 his great-nephew and heir, William Watson-Armstrong, was made Lord Armstrong of the second creation. In 1977 Cragside passed to the Treasury in part payment of death duties and was transferred to the National Trust through the National Heritage Fund.

Armstrong first built a lodge at Cragside in 1864 close to the river that he loved to fish and then, in 1869, he called in Norman Shaw, equally adventurous and determined as an architect, and together they converted the lodge over the next sixteen years into a large country house. All Armstrong's inventiveness was happily brought to bear in making this highly picturesque mansion as practical as possible. A dam was built to ensure a constant water supply for the house and to operate a kitchen spit, central heating and hydraulic lifts. Additional water was harnessed to drive turbines for electric light and Cragside became the first house in the world to be lit by electricity in this way. A more extensive scheme using Joseph Swan's newly invented incandescent lamps was installed in 1880. Visiting war lords coming to purchase battleships and guns were immensely impressed. The Japanese prints in the Japanese Room and the Japanese ceramics in the Library and elsewhere testify to this.

The furniture is contemporary with the house, a mixture of the Arts and Crafts and neo-Georgian movements. In the Library, Cragside's main living room, the ebonized mahogany cane and leather chairs were made

The Library at Cragside, with furniture by Gillow and Co. and walls hung with Pre-Raphaelite paintings.

by Gillow, whose name is also stamped on the sturdy square leather-topped writing table and on the comfortable red leather settees. The four black corner chairs with gold-painted flower-pieces on the back and gilt leather seats were very probably designed by Shaw. James Forsyth carved the ceiling bosses and the light oak panelling; he also made the surround to the fireplace of Egyptian onyx in a frame of red marble.

The stained glass in the bay window was designed by Rossetti and made by Morris and Co. Morris-designed wallpaper was also used in several of the bedrooms. The principal feature of the Dining Room is the wide Gothic arch and its elaborate frieze above the fireplace with its cosy inglenook. The fireplace itself is framed by shafts of Derbyshire russet marble. The sideboard and heavy oak settles were probably designed by Shaw and made by Forsyth.

The Main Staircase is notable for its bulbous 'Queen Anne' balusters and the lions rampant carrying electric light fittings on the newel posts. Shaw made great use of tiles on the stairs to the Picture Gallery, and in the passages. These are of Spanish origin. The Drawing Room, lit from above, is perhaps the most impressive room, with its double-storey chimneypiece above the inglenook, which was designed by W. R. Lethaby, then Shaw's chief assistant, and beautifully carved in early Renaissance style by the celebrated firm of Farmer and Brindley.

The paintings acquired by Lord Armstrong reflect the tastes of the second half of the 19th century, although the more important works, which originally hung in the Drawing Room and Library, were sold in 1910 and have now been replaced by Pre-Raphaelite works generously loaned by the de Morgan Foundation. The Drawing Room also has magnificent pottery by William de Morgan himself. Paintings by H. H. Emmerson, a local artist much admired by Lord Armstrong, are in the Dining Room, including one of him sitting with his dogs beside the fireplace. Most of the Watson-Armstrong portraits are in the Gallery, together with two typical genre works by Emmerson; a beautiful book of his watercolours, presented to the Armstrongs by the people of Rothbury to commemorate the Royal visit in 1884, is in the Watercolour Gallery together with paintings by T. M. Richardson Sr, Clarkson Stanfield and others.

Craigievar Castle Grampian

The National Trust for Scotland

6 miles s of Alford on A980, 16 miles w of Aberdeen

Craigievar stands like a castle in a fairy tale, a high tower crowned with turrets rising straight and tall on a steep and lonely hillside. It has, more coldly, been described as a 'monstrous rocket stuck into the ground and only requiring a match to be put to the weather cock'. It strikingly illustrates characteristic Scottish traits: family pride, romanticism combined with sound commercial sense and a capacity for hard work. The builder was William Forbes, younger son of the laird of nearby Corse and brother of Patrick, Bishop of Aberdeen who had 'made a goodlie pile merchandizing at Danzick' and was thereafter somewhat slightingly known as Dantzig Willie. He bought the property in 1610 and completed the building of his castle in 1626, the year before he died. Externally it has not been changed, except that the surrounding low service buildings have gone.

Internally Craigievar perfectly expresses the spirit and the tastes of that brief period of peace and prosperity between the accession of James VI to the throne of England and the outbreak of the Civil War in the reign of his son and successor. Craigievar is on a modest scale the Scottish equivalent of Elizabethan prodigy houses. The internal arrangement of tower-houses has been neatly described as that of 'a medieval manor house set upright', with a great hall on the first floor, service chambers below and living rooms and bedrooms above. Craigievar is six storeys high, the only access by narrow spiral staircases.

Craigievar's internal decoration is as exceptional as its external appearance. The Great Hall is one of the most remarkable rooms in Scotland, medieval in design, with a wooden screen and miniature musicians' gallery above it, and a quadripartite vaulted ceiling. The decoration is wholly Renaissance, the ceiling being completely covered in elaborate plasterwork with large decorative pendants; above the massive stone fireplace is a huge armorial achievement of the royal arms of Great Britain and Ireland flanked by caryatids, the finest of its kind in the country. The woodwork of the screen is carved with classical arcading and topped by a balustrade, but all on a small scale and executed with considerable artistry. Other rooms are similarly decorated in a more restrained style, including the Ladies Withdrawing Room, panelled in Memel pine. Some of the plasterwork dates from as late as 1668, the time of the 2nd Baronet, Red Sir John, whose portrait hangs in the house, together with two rare, authentic works by Jamesone. The most notable paintings at Craigievar are two early Raeburns of the 5th Baronet and his wife Sarah Sempill. The 1788 receipt, 16 gns for the paintings and £3 9s 6d for the frames, hangs beside the pictures.

Some of the furniture is unique, having been made on the estate from local timber and some of it actually constructed within the Castle – it would be impossible to carry anything but small pieces up the steep and narrow spiral staircase. What was made for Craigievar has remained and will remain there as long as the Castle stands. Dantzig Willie, his son and then nineteen successive Forbes and Forbes-Sempill baronets would feel perfectly at home in this 17th-century home.

16th-century painted figures decorating the ceiling beams of the Nine Muses Room, Crathes Castle.

Crathes Castle Grampian

The National Trust for Scotland

3 miles E of Banchory on A93, 15 miles W of Aberdeen

In the High Hall of Crathes hangs its most treasured heirloom: a semi-circular ivory horn banded with gilt and set with cabuchon rubies, carbuncles and rock crystals. The 'Horn of Leys' traditionally symbolized authority over the nearby royal forest of Drum, granted by King Robert I in 1323 to Alexander Burnet of Leys (pronounced 'Lays'). Half a century earlier his forebears had come to Scotland from Huntingdonshire in the train of King David I and the family had faithfully served the Crown ever since then. Over 600 years later, Major-General Sir James Burnett of Leys gave Crathes

to the National Trust for Scotland. Such continuity of family possession has set its inevitable mark upon the Castle and its contents.

The present house was begun about 1553 but was still incomplete by 1578; only *c*.1596 was Alexander Burnet able to live there and to inscribe his arms and those of his wife, Katherine Gordon, about the house, notably on their splendidly carved four-poster bed and two chairs of state. Alexander was a cultured man and his taste is evident in those parts created under his direction, above all the painted ceilings for which the Castle is famous. Brilliantly coloured figures, formalized designs, devices or emblems dear to 16th-century taste decorate the ceiling beams; the joists between are covered with suitably improving inscriptions. The Room of the Nine Nobles could equally be named the 'Room of the Nine Worthies'; the figures represented are three classical heroes, three from the Old Testament and three Christian kings, Arthur, Charlemagne and the Crusader Godfrey de Bouillon, King of Jerusalem. The Nine Muses Room celebrates the Seven Virtues as well. The designs, naïve and sometimes crude, but always vigorous and lively, have variously been ascribed as Scandinavian, Netherlandish or Tyrolean. The fashion was short-lived and many ceilings were covered over and only later revealed, which accounts for the good condition of those that survive.

The Long Gallery at the top of the tower-house has a different point of interest. The ceiling is panelled with oak planks of exceptional width, unique in Scotland, and enriched with painted coats of arms.

Although the principal attraction of Crathes lies in its ceilings and family relics, the furniture is not without interest. Much is early-17th century and Scottish, including some children's chairs and a fine Jacobean cradle. There are

Detail of wood-carving showing the arms of Alexander Burnet and his wife Katherine Gordon; Crathes Castle.

family portraits, mostly of the anonymous Scottish school of the 17th century, some being ascribed to Jamesone. The Burnets were quiet men, taking little part in national affairs. The most distinguished member of the family was Gilbert Burnet, Bishop of Salisbury from 1689, who held court appointments under Charles I. His portrait, attributed to Lely, reminds the visitor of the link between the house of a Deeside laird and Restoration England.

Croft Castle Hereford and Worcester

The National Trust

5 miles NW of Leominster just N of B4362, signposted from Ludlow road (A49)

From Croft Ambrey, an iron-age hill fort which dates back to the 4th century BC and from which there are splendid views, a footpath leads through woods to Croft Castle. The Croft family are known to have been established here as a family of substance in the 11th century but the walls and towers of the present Castle are probably of the 14th or 15th century. John Leland, the King's Antiquary in the reign of Henry VIII, described it as 'sett on the browe of a hill, somewhat rokky, dychid and waulled castle like'. Camden's *Britannia* refers to the 'famous and very Knightly family of the Crofts'. The family was active for Charles I in the Civil War, when the Castle was plundered, and Sir Herbert Croft was given a baronetcy in 1671.

In the 18th century, the family fell on hard times and the Croft estate was sold, to be owned consecutively by the Knights and Johnes families, for whom Pritchard, the Shrewsbury architect, carried out improvements, some of them in the Gothic taste. There is Gothic detail in the mid-18th-century ceiling of the Blue Room, in the carved quatrefoil frieze of the Library, in the Library Ante-room's 'chimney-frame', in the 'Gothic' Bay Room with its watercolours by Varley, Buckler and John 'Warwick' Smith, and above all on the enchanting 'Gothic' Staircase. There is also a notable collection of Gothic furniture

Combined writing table and filing cabinet by Seddon, known as 'the Croft', in the Library, Croft Castle.

Culzean Castle Strathclyde

The National Trust for Scotland

12 miles s w of Ayr off A719

The national preference for living in castles had long outlived the necessity for a secure defensive home when, about 1777, Robert Adam was called in to transform the 16th-century Castle of the Kennedys of Culzean (pronounced Killane) by David, 10th Earl of Cassillis. The Kennedys came from an old family settled in the ancient province of Carrick by the 10th century and could boast of a long pedigree with descent from the royal house through marriage to a daughter of Robert II. They had subsequently played their part in national events; one fought in the 100 Years War for the French, another led his Scots contingent under Joan of Arc at the siege of Orleans, and the 1st Earl of Cassillis fell at Flodden in 1513. In the early 18th century the 8th Earl died without heirs and there was a protracted legal dispute before the title was settled on Sir Thomas Kennedy of Culzean who had inherited that property in 1744. He set about improving the Castle, which was basically a traditional defensive tower-house with surrounding walls built on a medieval site. Sir Thomas died unmarried and was succeeded by his brother David. These bachelor brothers were in essentials the creators of the Castle we see today.

Adam's solutions to his client's requirements were brilliantly successful and Culzean is one of his finest achievements. He created a romantic castle, with a strong Italian flavour, taking full advantage of the site, which is magnificent and probably without parallel in Western Europe. Culzean stands on a bluff above cliffs falling sheer to the rocky shore and looks straight across twenty miles of the open waters of the Firth of Clyde to the hills of Arran.

His internal designs were equal to the challenge, above all in his Saloon on the first floor of the round tower which thrusts out from the centre of the house towards the cliff edge. Of his many fine rooms, this one is unique in the contrast of ordered elegance

which, together with most of the contents, belongs to Lord Croft. His father, the 1st Baron, inherited the Castle, the family paintings and heirlooms from his cousin, the 11th Baronet, whose Trustees had bought the Castle back into the family in 1923. Because of death duties, the Ministry of Works acquired the property and gave a grant for repairs. The National Trust took over the freehold in 1957 and the Croft family with public help gave the endowment to preserve the property for posterity.

In addition to the Gothic furniture, there are good 17th-century oak pieces, William and Mary walnut furniture and chairs with incised gesso frames, a Queen Anne side-table, four Irish 'Chinese' Chippendale chairs, a combined writing table and filing cabinet by Seddon, known as 'the Croft', and made for the 5th Baronet, and Sheraton-style tub chairs. There are portraits by Gainsborough, Hanneman, Lawrence, George Richmond and de Laszlo and others attributed to Beechey and A. W. Devis.

Pier-glass and table designed by Robert Adam, c.1777, for Culzean Castle, which he was asked to transform by David, 10th Earl of Cassillis.

within and the wild scenery of sky, sea and mountains that can be seen from the floor-to-ceiling windows. The colour scheme of the delicately moulded ceiling echoes the tones of the carpet, woven to Adam's design in the nearby town of Maybole. Mirror, fireplace, sconces and one set of chairs are also Adam. Behind this triumphant and formal room, almost bare of furniture, lies a second major achievement; the two-storeyed oval staircase. Contrived to fit the space left by an enclosed courtyard, his solution produced out of necessity one of his finest creations. The staircase forms the pivot round which Adam created a circuit of living and reception rooms and service ante-rooms. Much of the redecoration has been carried out since the National Trust for Scotland undertook an extensive programme in 1972. The interiors now are as crisp and fresh as when Adam's team, including Zucchi and Paul Henderson of Edinburgh, worked at Culzean.

These rooms include the First Drawing Room hung with specially woven *bleu céleste* brocade and silk damask curtains. Girandoles and china cupboard are again Adam-designed, as is the overmantel mirror – with the difference that the latter was made in 1977. The adjacent Picture Room has chimneypiece, overmantel mirror, sconces and *torchères* by Adam, while a table and set of Hepplewhite chairs are part of the original furnishings.

Much of the essential furniture of the Castle came to the Trust in 1945 when the 5th Marquess of Ailsa and the Kennedy family gave Culzean and its estate. The inevitable gaps have been filled with loans, gifts and benefactions from both the family and other sources. Great care was taken to maintain the highest standards, and today Culzean is furnished with pieces perfectly appropriate to the period and quality of the house. Furniture made for the house includes a set of George III hall chairs.

There is an agreeable mixture of 18th-century English, Dutch and French furniture; the last is well represented by Louis XVI *fauteuils* covered in Beauvais tapestry in the Saloon. There are some splendid George III pieces, including a beautiful pair of satinwood commodes by Elliott, the king's cabinet maker. There are six George II chairs, which have the additional interest that their covers were worked by Wellington's mother, the Countess of Mornington, and a fine wardrobe in the style associated with Grendy. Several clocks are of the highest quality, including one by Worgan of Bristol and a French marble-mounted example by Lepaute, Napoleon's clockmaker. The most important is the walnut long-case clock with movement by Graham. But of all the fine pieces, perhaps best of all is the exquisite little fruitwood spinning wheel of the last quarter of the 18th century, perfect in design and finish. In a very different style, but an outstanding example of the design and craftsmanship of its period, is the fitted dressing case given to his bride by the 3rd Marquess of Ailsa in 1870. In practical contrast is the sturdy pram dinghy model, made at the family's shipyard and fitted as a cradle.

The Kennedy links with the sea are well represented in many good seascapes by the younger Van de Velde, Luny and the less well-known Charles Brooking. There are some good 17th-century Dutch genre pictures and a delightful painting by Deschamps. Family portraits are well in evidence and include a large, stiff portrait by Gavin Hamilton of a Kennedy daughter who became Countess of Eglinton. The full-length by Mossman of the 9th Earl is a lively example of his style and also shows the Earl's remarkable likeness to his brother, who was depicted by Batoni. Ben Marshall painted the 1st Marquess on horse-back; the paintings of his parents, Captain and Mrs Archibald Kennedy, are by Mather Brown. Captain Kennedy, who had settled in America and married a New York lady, inherited the title after the death of the 10th Earl. The pride of the collection is, however, indubitably the two large views of Culzean by Naysmith.

One last feature of Culzean must not be overlooked. In 1945, as an expression of Scotland's gratitude to her US ally, General Eisenhower was asked to accept the tenure of a guest apartment at Culzean for life. He often came to stay at the Castle and a presentation room, which includes his desk and a Presidential standard, has been set up to illustrate his character and achievements.

Dalemain Cumbria

Mr and Mrs Bryce McCosh

3 miles W of Penrith on A592

This small distinguished house, north of Ullswater, was purchased by Sir Edward Hasell in 1679 and is still inhabited by his descendants. Its oldest part is the early-12th-century pele tower, now containing the Westmorland and Cumberland Yeomanry Museum. The restrained neo-classical entrance front was completed c.1750.

The Entrance Hall, with its stone floor inset with black lozenges, its fine cantilever staircase with graceful balusters rising through two storeys, contains good portraits by or after Van Dyck and Kneller. In the small Chinese Drawing Room, its hand-painted Chinese wallpaper enlivened with additional figures of birds and insects added on cut-out paper, are entertaining portraits by Arthur Devis and Zoffany; here also is a splendid walnut chest of drawers, c.1650, inlaid with ivory and mother-of-pearl. Further family portraits hang both in the oak-

Arthur Devis' portrait of William Hasell, 1760; Dalemain.

panelled Drawing Room with its two elegant Adam Brothers mirrors, and in the Dining Room with its fine lacquer coromandel screen.

The first floor Fretwork Room, so called from its ribbed plasterwork ceiling, contains a good early-17th-century portrait of the famous heiress Lady Anne Clifford by Bracken, an artist from Kirkby Lonsdale, and two 18th-century globes, one terrestrial, the other celestial.

Doddington Hall Lincolnshire

Mr and Mrs A. G. Jarvis

5 miles W of Lincoln

This magnificent late Elizabethan mansion has been successively the home of the Tailors, Husseys, Delavals of Seaton Delaval and since 1829 of the Jarvises. Built between 1593 and 1600 by Robert Smythson, the architect of Hardwick, its exterior remains basically unchanged. The interior, however, was largely altered in the 1760s by Thomas Lumby, a Lincoln carpenter, whose fine craftsmanship is evident on the front staircase and in the splendid Long Gallery.

Among important family portraits are two by Dahl, two by Reynolds, especially that of Lord and Lady Pollington, marvellously framed, which dominates the Long Gallery, and Lawrence's of Mrs Sarah Gunman in the Parlour. Other notable paintings include Lely's *Cymon at the Fountain*, also in the Parlour, and, on the Upper Stairs, an interesting group of late-17th- and early-18th-century nautical views. Brussels 17th-century tapestries adorn the first-floor landing and the adjoining Holly Room. On the right, in the Tiger Room, stands an impressive George I four-poster bed, slept in by the Duke of Cumberland at Seaton Delaval in 1745.

In the White Hall (or Dining Room) is a good set of Cromwellian bobbin-turned oak chairs, a 16th-century oak refectory table, restored in the 19th century, with stretcher ends carved as dogs' heads, and two mid-16th-century Venetian chests made of cypress wood.

Medieval scold's bridle at Doddington Hall.

A less pleasant reminder of the past are the gibbeting irons and the medieval scold's bridle for malicious gossips.

On the Front Stairs are two late-17th-century English black and gold chinoiserie cabinets, close to which hangs Doddington's other portrait by Reynolds, a full-length of Sir Francis Delaval, an extravagant gambler and man of fashion. Two Neapolitan mid-17th-century ebony cabinets with panels of painted glass and two 18th-century English chests of drawers with Dutch marquetry panels stand in the Drawing Room with its fine 1720 glass chandeliers, a satinwood Broadwood piano, 1805, and papier mâché gilt wall decorations and mirror frames, *c*.1775. French Napoleonic prisoners of war made the chess set of turned bone while at Dover Castle.

English air-twist glass is displayed on the

Upper Staircase, late-18th-century Meissen and Nymphenburg porcelain in the White Hall, Jesuit ware and 18th- and 19th-century Oriental ceramics in the Parlour; and in the Long Gallery a good collection of 17th- and 18th-century Chinese ceramics together with Bow, Caughley, Leeds, Liverpool, Lowestoft and Meissen porcelain.

Dodington House Avon

Major Sir Simon Codrington, Bt

200 yards N of exit 18 at Tormarton on M4 where it is crossed by A46 10 miles N of Bath

This noble stone mansion with its massive portico, supported on six Corinthian columns, stands amid mature timber overlooking the park landscaped by 'Capability' Brown in 1764. The house is of Elizabethan origin and its rebuilding by James Wyatt, started in 1796 for Christopher Bethell Codrington, was probably his finest achievement in the neo-classical manner and certainly his last, for he was killed in a coaching accident before the house was finished, a task which Wyatville completed.

The Entrance Hall's character is one of dignified Roman splendour. The pattern of the compartmented ceiling is reflected in the floor, paved with red and white Painswick stone, with brass inlay and black marble. A screen of scagliola columns, with their Composite capitals richly gilded, stands on steps at each end of the Hall; beyond each is an alcove sheltering a black marble bust, one of Nelson, the other of Wellington, and a splendid marble and amber topped table. Above Wyatt's stove hangs Archer Shee's fine portrait of Dodington's builder, Christopher Bethell Codrington.

Elegant mahogany, brass and ebony bookcases in numbered order line the Library; a writing table built into one of them conceals an architect's table. Here also are two card tables and a drum table by Sheraton, Chippendale chairs, a Regency mahogany sarcophagus wine cooler and a set of Wedgwood pottery carpet bowls. The octagonal Garden Vestibule contains a black and gold lacquer cabinet, c.1710, and a fine Queen Anne walnut bureau.

The graceful Regency Drawing Room has magnificent mahogany double doors, inlaid with ebony and satinwood; above them is repeated the elegant winged-griffin pattern of the frieze. Other noteworthy objects include the Irish glass chandelier, one of a pair, the 16th-century Venetian table with marble top inlaid with semi-precious stones, a Sheraton mahogany worktable, a Louis XV sofa and chairs and an unusual marble chimneypiece with a great Chippendale mirror above. On each side are Chippendale wall brackets, each supporting a chestnut holder made of Pontypool ware. The restrained Dining Room (formerly the Breakfast Room) with scagliola pilasters preserves most of its original furniture, including the two sideboards, the splendid crescent-shaped hunting table, the Sheraton chamber organ and the wall brackets with carved eagle supports. The great central staircase, dividing into two on the half-landing, is enriched with rococo ironwork taken from Fonthill Splendens, the home of William Beckford's father, demolished in 1808.

A fascinating exhibition, created in the Vaults, displays Wyatt's original plans for the house together with documents and posters about slavery, West Indian pictures and maps, and various Elizabethan charters.

Dorfold Hall Cheshire

Mr R. C. Roundell

1 mile W of Nantwich on A51 to Tarporley

This handsome Jacobean mansion of diapered brick with stone quoins was built in 1616 for Ralph Wilbraham, a member of a respected Cheshire family with strong legal connections. Acquired in 1754 by James Tomkinson, a Nantwich lawyer, the property was handed down by inheritance via the Tollemache family to the present owner.

The Entrance Porch leads into a small Hall and then into the Dining Room, previously a much larger one, which has a fine plasterwork

ceiling; Johnson's portrait of Ralph Wilbraham hangs close to the Georgian chimneypiece
in the Adam style, said to come from a City of
London inn; a pickled pine chimneypiece with
a similar provenance is in the Library. The
attractive plasterwork ceiling here, said to be
by Samuel Wyatt, shows a pair of billing doves
at its centre and symbols of the four seasons at
the corners. This room contains some 18th-
century furniture and Oriental porcelain.

The best room is the Great Chamber,
reached by a staircase with Jacobean balustrad-
ing; it has a barrel-vaulted ceiling with highly
intricate strapwork and pendant enrichments,
made in 1621, with panelling and a carved
frieze of the period. The tympana above the
end walls are also stuccoed. There is a large
stone chimneypiece with Roman Doric columns; the panelling is decorated with tapering
pilasters.

King James' Room at the top of the Staircase
has a fine plaster overmantel on which the royal
arms are emblazoned. The visit from James I
never materialized.

Down House Kent

The Royal College of Surgeons of England

In Downe, 5½ miles s of Bromley, off A233

Down House is maintained as a memorial to
Charles Darwin (1809–82), the famous scientist
who lived here 1842–82. His wife was a
Wedgwood. The Old Study, where he worked
for thirty-seven years, and the Drawing Room
are furnished much as they were when he lived;
the latter contains family portraits, Wedgwood
plaques, miniatures, two fans with paintings of
plants mentioned in Darwin's works, letters
and many other mementos.

The other rooms also contain paintings,
including Russian portraits of Darwin and his
associates, presented by the Darwin Museum in
Moscow on the centenary of the publication of
The Origin of Species, and four by Joseph
Wright of Derby, together with photographs,
showcases with fine examples of the great
scientist's letters, publications, notebooks and

his instruments. The walls of the New Study,
used by Darwin during his last three years, now
display the various stages of the evolution of
living things.

Drumlanrig Castle
Dumfries and Galloway

The Duke of Buccleuch and Queensberry

3 miles N of Thornhill off A76

William Douglas, later 1st Duke of Queensberry, took more than a decade between 1679
and 1691 to build the present Castle. It nearly
ruined him but the result more than justified
the effort. Drumlanrig is the most complete
and splendid example of the mixture of Gothic
and Renaissance styles with Palladian elements
to be found north of the Border, and possibly
in Britain. The entrance show-front dem-
onstrates High Baroque at its most impressive. The Castle stands four square above
double curving staircases sweeping upwards
from the forecourt; the cupola-crowned
towers at each corner of the Castle adding to
the effect of dignity and grandeur. It is thought
that Sir William Bruce may have been
consulted about the plan but more likely
architects were Robert Mylne, the King's
master mason, or James Smith, his son-in-law.

The interior is on an equally princely scale.
The Drawing Room Ante-room, for example,
is panelled and decorated with limewood
carvings in Grinling Gibbons style and of a
comparable quality. The Staircase Hall boasts
one of the earliest wooden balustraded stairs in
Scotland.

As at Bowhill the richness of the Montagu-
Douglas-Scott heritage is everywhere apparent
in furnishings and works of art. The Buccleuch
descent brought such treasures as two extraordinary Louis XIV cabinets – a gift from
Charles II to his son the Duke of Monmouth
– a Flemish ebony cabinet and a set of
chairs and settees, whose covers were reputedly worked by his Duchess. The French
furniture includes pieces by such masters as

Cressent, Migeon, Lebas, C. C. Saunier and Roussel. The English furniture is scarcely less outstanding; late Carolean chairs, a Queen Anne day-bed and chairs with their original cut velvet covering, a magnificent pair of *verre églomisé* mirrors, silver sconces bearing the cypher of Queen Mary by Arthur Mainwaring, a gigantic Charles II silver candelabrum, Chippendale giltwood sconces, Matthias Lock mirrors; a Boulle timepiece by Cressent, a beautiful little grandmother clock, examples by Knibb and other English makers, family silver including a huge wine cistern, Sèvres and Chelsea porcelain. At Drumlanrig it is hard to avoid an almost endless catalogue.

Lastly and most importantly are the paintings; above all Rembrandt's *Old Woman Reading* which has been in the Buccleuch collection since 1750. It is shown in the Hall close to the splendid Holbein portrait of Sir Nicholas Carew, portraits by Clouet and Van Cleef, works by Murillo and of the school of Correggio. The Boudoir contains Dutch cabinet pictures by Cuyp, Ostade and Teniers.

Rembrandt Old Woman Reading, *1655; Drumlanrig Castle.*

There are innumerable family portraits, including the Duke of Monmouth, a particularly appealing early Reynolds of Lady Elizabeth Montagu whose marriage to the 3rd Duke brought the Montagu inheritance to the Buccleuch family, and a Gainsborough of her mother, the Duchess of Montagu. Kneller, Hudson, Richardson, Ramsay represent the major portraitists of their day, just as the painting of the 8th Duchess of Buccleuch by de Laszlo exemplifies the art of the present century.

English watercolour painting seems peculiarly appropriate to the setting of Drumlanrig – the long valley of the Nith which gently descends from the high hills of the central and western Border range. The paintings include topographical subjects by Paul Sandby and Philip Shepherd, and views of Drumlanrig and its surroundings by Queen Victoria's drawing master, William Leitch.

Dunrobin Castle Highlands

The Countess of Sutherland

½ mile NE of Golspie on A9

The most northerly of Scotland's great houses and the largest in the northern Highlands, Dunrobin is delectably set against a backdrop of heather-covered hillside just above the pale sandy shore of the North Sea, looking straight across to Norway. Although it is the seat of the Countess of Sutherland, 24th holder of the title, whose family can trace its ancestry straight back to the 12th century, Dunrobin is demonstrably a mid-19th-century English building. Designed by Barry for the 2nd Duke of Sutherland, the style is 'Franco-Scots' with pointed turrets, a dominant tower roofed like a Swiss-French château, set close beside a clock tower topped by a typically Scottish bell-shaped slate roof. This curious but impressive structure was built in the 1860s and encloses a much older castle, of which only a portion is still visible at the back and from windows overlooking an enclosed courtyard. Nevertheless it was a fitting home for the Dukes of Sutherland, at one time the largest landowners

Michael Wright The Irish Chieftain, *said to be of the 2nd Earl of Tyrone; Dunrobin Castle.*

in Western Europe, possessing almost the whole of the county of Sutherland besides extensive estates in Staffordshire and the Midlands of England.

The 18th Earl of Sutherland died in 1766, leaving an only daughter Elizabeth, who married the 2nd Marquess of Stafford, later created Duke of Sutherland. The Duchess-Countess and her husband made large scale improvements to their estates, communications and townships, which involved the notorious Highland clearances. It was their son who transformed Dunrobin. A serious fire in 1915, when the Castle was used as a naval hospital, destroyed much of Barry's work. In the 1920s Sir Robert Lorimer was commissioned to make good the damage and he simplified and remodelled much of the interior.

The Dining Room, panelled and with an Italianate frieze, is the first example of his work seen by the visitor. It contains some notable family portraits, with which the Castle is well endowed. They include a splendid Ramsay of the 18th Earl wearing the Sutherland tartan kilt and a scarlet jacket, two portraits of the 2nd Duchess by Lawrence and in later life by Winterhalter, and a Romney of the 1st Duke. His wife, Countess of Sutherland in her own right, is depicted several times, the most strikingly in the portrait by Hoppner showing her as a lively and clearly imperious young woman. She was painted both by Reynolds and Lawrence, who was also responsible for a fine portrait of her son, the 2nd Duke. Earlier portraits include anonymous 16th-century likenesses of the 12th Earl (who married Bothwell's divorced wife Jean Gordon) and of Sir Alexander Gordon by Jamesone. There are large impressive portraits of all the dukes and their duchesses, including a striking full length by de Laszlo of Eileen, wife of the 5th Duke. A family group of a different style is Landseer's double portrait of the 3rd Earl and his sister as children with – inevitably – a pet dog. However, the most striking and unusual picture is the full-length by Wright of an Irish chieftain in native dress, said to be of the 2nd Earl of Tyrone, who died in 1616.

The Drawing Room, a long light room overlooking the sea, houses two fine Canalettos and a set of 18th-century Mortlake tapestries in especially good condition, depicting the life of Diogenes. The best furniture in the house is here, including a Louis xv set of *fauteuils* and settees and some restrained and beautiful late-18th-century English pieces. The Library is, unusually, panelled in sycamore wood and the furniture is sturdy Georgian, especially a Chippendale library table and a rent table. There is a large 19th-century globe made in Edinburgh.

There are many relics of Queen Victoria who visited Dunrobin in 1872, including tapestries commissioned for the occasion and an unusual and delightful gilt bed whose four posts are surmounted by figures of doves. Dunrobin is full of fine porcelain, *objets d'art* and of family associations which make this possibly intimidating mansion into a family home.

Dunster Castle Somerset

The National Trust

In Dunster, 2 miles SE of Minehead on A396

The site of Dunster Castle has been occupied for more than a millennium. In 1376 it was acquired by the Luttrell family with whom it remained until 1976 when Lt-Colonel Walter Luttrell, MC, gave it to the National Trust. In 1617 a Jacobean mansion was raised within the medieval castle walls which were demolished during the Commonwealth. Dunster was put in order after the Restoration, the ceilings decorated with fine plasterwork reminiscent of Goudge's distinctive work at Belton and the handsome staircase installed. Its balustrade of

pierced panels is carved from thick elm planks with animals and *putti*, half concealed by waves of acanthus, and with boisterous hunting scenes.

Salvin in 1868–72 demolished the 18th-century augmentations, added the castellation together with two battlemented towers and remodelled the entrance façade. His Outer Hall contains a portrait of Cromwell after Walker and three 'turned' or 'thrown' chairs, the largest of ash, the other two with pear-wood frames and oak seats. In the 16th-century Inner Hall with its 'baronial' chimneypiece by Salvin is a version made in 1591 of Eworth's renowned allegorical portrait of Sir John Luttrell, dated 1550; he is shown rising naked and god-like from a stormy sea, his right arm being grasped

Early-17th-century leather wall hanging showing the story of Antony and Cleopatra; Dunster Castle.

by the figure of Peace. A curious panel painting of the Devise of Sir Thomas Copley is on the east wall.

Portraits by Seeman, Dahl and Vanderbank hang in the late-17th-century Dining Room which contains an elegant 18th-century sideboard and two mahogany urn-shaped wine containers together with a handsome leather screen depicting exotic birds. An unknown cavalier portrayed by Bower is in the Stair Hall. The Morning Room is embellished with late-18th-century giltwood girandoles; the set of mahogany seat furniture is mid-18th century.

In the Gallery beyond is a rare set of brilliantly coloured wall hangings consisting of scenes from the story of Antony and Cleopatra, painted on leather covered with silver foil, which may have been made in the Netherlands some time in the first half of the 17th century. The King Charles' Room contains a plaster overmantel, dated 1620, illustrating the Judgement of Paris, brought from elsewhere in the Castle.

Dunvegan Castle Isle of Skye

John MacLeod of MacLeod

23 miles w of Portree

Gloriously sited on Skye's north-west coast, Dunvegan Castle, the traditional stronghold and home of the Chiefs of MacLeod, has seen some sort of building alteration each century since the erection of the curtain-wall round its rock in 1200. The last tower to need extensive remodelling was the 17th-century south wing, badly damaged by fire in 1938. Interesting collections remain of items from the Stone Age; of 16th- and 17th-century artefacts; of Jacobite relics; the Indian trophies of General MacLeod, 23rd Chief; letters from famous men; relics of St Kilda; medals and decorations. Zoffany's portrait of the General in India and that of the General's second wife, painted with an Indian background, are in the Drawing Room, originally the Great Hall. Later portraits of the same couple by Raeburn

The Dunvegan Cup, a 10th-century Irish bog-oak vessel set in silver in 1493; Dunvegan Castle.

hang in the Dining Room with those by Ramsay of the 22nd Chief, one of his outstanding achievements, and of his second wife.

Many of this romantic castle's treasures are steeped in family history and legend, fascinating as much for their associations as their artistic importance. The Dunvegan Cup, an Irish bog-oak vessel of the 10th century, set in silver in 1493, was given by the O'Neills of Ulster to Rory Mor, the 15th Chief, who had supported them in an uprising against Queen Elizabeth in the late-16th century. Rory Mor's silver-embellished Horn, the horn itself being that of a Kyloe bull, holds nearly two bottles of claret and each new chief is expected to down the contents in one. A rare Jacobite glass, dated 1747, is inscribed to 'The Faithful Palinurus', namely Donald MacLeod of Galtrigall, who faithfully piloted Prince Charles Edward across the waters, 'Over the Sea to Skye'. But it is the Fairy Flag, perhaps woven in the 7th century and from the Island of Rhodes, which is the most famed and venerated object in the Castle. Its powers to save the Clan and act as the protector of family and castle are said to be undoubted.

Dyrham Park Avon

The National Trust

7 miles N of Bath on A46, 2 miles S of M4 (exit 18)

William Blathwayt (?1649–1717) was astute and hardworking not only as a civil servant and diplomat, spending several years at The Hague where he developed a taste for Dutch paintings, but in business as well. In 1686 he married an heiress, Mary Wynter, two years before she inherited the Dyrham estate – Dyrham originally meant a deer park. After her death in 1691, he started rebuilding the dilapidated Tudor manor, employing Samuel Hauduroy, a French architect, to erect the elegant west front (1692–4). By 1698, then at the peak of his career, he was able to commission Talman to erect the impressive east front.

Of the original Tudor house only the Great Hall survives. Its ceiling is enlivened with three scenes by Casali, placed there in 1845; they were originally painted for Alderman Beckford's Fonthill Splendens, which was pulled down by the Alderman's son William, author of *Vathek*, as he needed the stones for Fonthill Abbey. Two further scenes by Casali are on the ceilings of the Cedar and the Walnut Staircases.

Dyrham contains some fine 17th-century Dutch paintings, including works by the younger Teniers, Snyders, Storck, Minderhout, Hondecoeter and Hoogstraeten, whose remarkable *trompe l'oeil View Down a Corridor* is in the gilt leather closet and can

be seen at the end of a long *enfilade* in the east wing. In the Drawing Room is Murillo's *Peasant Woman and Boy*.

The house also has a rich collection of Dutch Delftware (tin glazed earthenware) painted blue, often with exquisite delicacy, including pyramid flower vases, tulip holders and urns of various shapes, some from the designs of Daniel Marot. Delft tile pictures of exotic scenes in contemporary English frames can be seen on either side of the fireplace in the stone-flagged West Hall, where a central lantern hangs from the eagle fixed to the plaster ceiling. In the East Hall the walls are covered with embossed Dutch leather as are the

Hoogstraeten's View Down a Corridor, *1662; Dyrham Park.*

Cromwellian chairs in the West Hall and a screen on the Cedar Staircase. Some of the furniture is also Dutch; the walnut dining chairs in the Great Hall are in Marot's style as is the glorious Dyrham state bed in the Queen Anne Room with its original crimson and yellow velvet hangings, generously on loan from the Lady Lever Art Gallery.

There are James II walnut armchairs and oval pier-glasses, *c*.1745–50, in the East Hall; a fine seaweed marquetry writing table, two *torchères* and a mid-18th-century oval mirror in the Diogenes Room with its two late Mortlake tapestries from the well-known Diogenes series; two elegant rococo looking-glasses, *c*.1760, in the Drawing Room, made of pine and papier-mâché, almost certainly by John Linnell, who probably designed the gilded side-table, *c*.1767, in the same room. The Walnut Staircase Hall contains English painted chairs, *c*.1770, in the 'French taste' and a George III breakfront bookcase of mahogany and beech, in which Caughley and Worcester tea-sets are displayed; the pair of tall oak bookcases or 'presses' in two tiers, which came to William Blathwayt from his uncle, Thomas Povey, are similar to those designed for Pepys and now at Magdalene College, Cambridge.

East Riddlesden Hall
West Yorkshire

The National Trust

1 mile NE of Keighley on s side of A650

The porch, the main part of the Hall and the so-called Banqueting Hall were built by the fiery unpopular Murgatroyds some two years after they acquired the property in 1638; only the façade remains of a later addition, classical in feeling, erected in 1692. The Murgatroyds were also responsible in about 1640 for the isolated building, close to the Hall, whose battlements bear the motto 'Vive le Roy', thus proclaiming their loyalty to Charles I.

Several rooms are embellished with oak panelling and plasterwork on ceiling and frieze, placed there by the family. The contents are not original to the house but have been installed by the National Trust. They include 17th- and early-18th-century portraits, oak and walnut furniture of the same period together with Delftware and 18th- and 19th-century pewter. Outside is a magnificent barn with a finely timbered roof.

Eastnor Castle
Hereford and Worcester

The Hon. Mrs Hervey-Bathurst

2 miles E of Ledbury on Hereford–Tewkesbury road (A438)

Records of the Cocks family go back to the days of Edward I, when they were landowners in Kent. The family first acquired land at Eastnor near Ledbury in about 1600, including the manor house, Castleditch, to which the 1st Baron Somers, a title created in 1784, added a Georgian stone front. However, the 2nd Baron (1760–1841), whose forceful character is revealed by the portrait of him in the Little Library, was determined on a building more in keeping with his rank; in 1812 he laid the foundation stone of this dramatic Gothic castle designed by Smirke, whose feeling for the Classical manner is revealed in the balance and regularity of this more than life-size structure. The building of the Castle was completed in 1820; its cost was over £85,000, a sum which was only found with difficulty. An earldom was conferred on Lord Somers in the following year.

The need to build was inherited by the 1st Earl's son and grandson. The Entrance Hall and the Great Staircase were not subsequently greatly changed, but the 2nd Earl (1788–1852) employed Pugin in 1849 to embellish the Drawing Room in the full flowering of mid-Victorian Gothic; Francis Bernasconi executed the plasterwork, Pugin designed the gilded ornamentation which, together with the furnishings, were carried out by Crace and Co. Gobelins tapestries of 'Alexander' and 'The Seasons' and the Aubusson carpet look surprisingly well under the fan-vaulting, but

Bassano (1515–92) The Last Supper; *Eastnor Castle.*

the main decorations are armorial. Pugin designed the brass chandelier after one in a Nuremberg church and most of the furniture as well.

The 3rd and last Earl (1819–83) was a great admirer of the Italian Renaissance and in the 1860s employed G. E. Fox, who also worked at Longleat, to redecorate the lavish sixty-three-foot long Library with doors and bookcases of Italian walnut inlaid with boxwood, made by Italian craftsmen and erected by the estate carpenters. One of the two stone chimneypieces, carved in Italy, includes a tiny portrait of Garibaldi, then at the height of his fame, depicted as a river god. The tapestries are Flemish but were bought in Mantua. The woodwork in the Little Library is from Siena; the four-poster bed in the State Bedroom is also Italian of the early-17th century. The enormous Great Hall, furnished with armour, including the thirty-three three-quarter suits from Italy, and weapons from as far afield as Scotland and India, has an austere air, somewhat relieved by a stencilled peacock wall decoration taken from a Saracenic cloth. More armour is in the Inner Hall, including two important Bavarian suits, *c.*1520, and a fine

Italian five-fingered *cinquedea* sword with etched blade of the late-15th or early-16th century. The Dining Room was redecorated by the late Lord Somers in 1937, when the Gothic arches were removed.

The family portraits include works ranging from Romney via G. F. Watts to Birley and de Laszlo. G. F. Watts was a great friend of the 3rd Earl and a portrait of his wife and his five early *Allegories* now hang in the Staircase Hall together with his fine *Time and Oblivion.* A splendid *Last Supper* by Bassano is in the State Bedroom and agreeable oil paintings by Hackert in the Dressing Room.

Edgcote Northamptonshire

Mr E. R. Courage

7 miles NE of Banbury on A361 to Chipping Warden

After the destruction by fire of the old manor house soon after 1742, Richard Chauncey, whose family had owned Edgcote since the reign of Henry VIII, commissioned William Jones to build the present house, 1747–52. It

is possible that the plans were made by William Smith of Warwick who was responsible for the stables. John Whitehead carried out the splendid rococo plasterwork ceiling in the Saloon and on the walls and cupola of the Staircase. Newman designed the chimneypieces, the finest of which is in the Saloon, while the woodwork, including that of the handsome overmantels, especially those in the Morning Room and Dining Room, was carved by Abraham Swan.

There is excellent furniture, mainly of the late-17th and 18th centuries, including examples by Cobb, Vile's partner. There are notable pieces in the Drawing Room and Saloon, especially the console tables in the latter. Paintings include two by Bonington in the Saloon and others by or after Cosway, Miereveldt, Metsu and Wissing.

Erddig Clwyd

The National Trust

1 mile s of Wrexham off A483

This late-17th-century mansion is not remarkable for its architecture nor for its site, except that coal-mining directly underneath nearly brought it down in ruin, but for two types of treasure. First there is its marvellous collection of early Georgian furniture, some of it of legendary quality; almost every item noted in the inventory of 1726 is still there. Second there is what might be described as a human treasure established by the Yorke family, who lived here for nearly 250 years; this is an affectionate and unique record first portrayed in paint and later in photography, always accompanied by doggerel verse, of the more important servants, beginning with the negro coachboy of the early-18th century and ending with a group photograph taken just before World War I; their portraits by journeyman painters hang in the Servants' Hall and the photographs along the basement corridor.

The building of Erddig in 1684–7 hastened the ruin of Joshua Edisbury, heavily in debt to Elihu Yale, among others, so that John Meller

ABOVE *The state bed at Erddig, bought in 1720, with embroidered Chinese silk hangings.*

RIGHT *Late-17th-century blue and white Delft vase painted with the arms of William and Mary; Erddig.*

acquired it in 1716 at a bargain price and filled it with the finest contemporary furniture available. He died a bachelor in 1733, so the property passed to his nephew, Simon Yorke I (1696–1767), whose first cousin was created Earl of Hardwicke. Later Yorkes of Erddig lived the life of quiet country gentry on their estate remote from the winds of fashion. However Philip Yorke I (all sons were either Simon or Philip), who re-dressed the eroded brick exterior of the west front and carried out some internal reorganization in 1772–3, consulting James Wyatt but using a local architect, was an MP. Hopper was responsible for the neo-classical Dining Room in 1826. During the present century the house fell deeply into decay with the owners unable to cope. In 1973, Philip Yorke III, the last of the family, very generously presented Erddig together with 1,942 acres to the National Trust, which has since completely restored it, together with the joiners' store, the sawpit, the blacksmith's shop and the other buildings in the Estate Yard, all of them now in working order for the benefit of visitors.

The family portraits, including Gainsborough's *Philip Yorke I* and that of his wife by Cotes, are in the Dining Room, whose table and chairs were supplied by Gillow in 1827. More portraits are in the Entrance Hall, three of them by Kneller and the fourth by John Verelst; others, including paintings of the royal family of Bohemia, are in the upstairs Gallery.

The Saloon, made from two rooms in 1770, contains magnificent gilt pier-glasses and gilt gesso girandoles supplied by John Belchier; the walnut chairs are described in the 1726 inventory as '8 caffoy walnut tree chairs' and the Boulle dressing table of about 1700 is described surprisingly as 'Henry VIII's writing desk' in John Loveday's diary of a tour in 1732. Equally fine furniture is in the Tapestry Room, the Library and in the State Bedroom where stands the celebrated state bed, bought by John Meller in 1720; its glorious embroidered Chinese silk hangings may originally have come from Elihu Yale, Governor of Fort St George, India, 1682–90, as well as the splendid lacquer screen close by. The green japanned chairs here have also retained their original decoration and coverings. Throughout, the condition of the furniture is remarkably unspoilt.

Other delights include the Soho tapestries in the Tapestry Room, in which is a late-17th-century blue and white Delft vase bearing the arms of William and Mary; the unique pair of Chelsea 'Red Anchor' sauce tureens in the shape of plaice in the Saloon, together with Chelsea 'Gold Anchor' chocolate cups, maiolica from Urbino, Meissen and Worcester porcelain and fine Ch'ien Lung ceramics; the mother-of-pearl models of the Chinese pagoda and ruins of Palmyra made between 1765 and 1780 by Elizabeth Radcliffe, Mrs Yorke's companion and a lady's maid; the mahogany furniture by the Royal cabinet maker, John Cobb, introduced into the house in 1770 by Philip Yorke I; the excellent silver in the Butler's Pantry; and the Family Museum, with human skulls and a hornets' nest.

Euston Hall Suffolk

The Duke of Grafton

3 miles SE of Thetford, off A1008 to Ixworth

There was a medieval dwelling here originally belonging to the abbey of Bury St Edmunds, but the present house was built 1666–70 for the Earl of Arlington, Charles II's Secretary of State and a loyal supporter of the Stuarts. His only daughter was married to Henry FitzRoy, son of Charles II and Barbara Villiers, Duchess of Cleveland. He was created Duke of Grafton and inherited Euston, where his descendants still live. The restrained rose-brick façade seen today was part of the house remodelled by Matthew Brettingham in the 1740s, most of which was burnt down in 1902, including the ceilings painted by Verrio. The Hall was then rebuilt but this part was demolished in 1952 because it was no longer manageable. Euston Hall contains good furniture but its principal glory is the outstanding collection of Stuart portraits.

Daniel Mytens George Villiers, Duke of Buckingham, 1626; *Euston Hall.*

Van Dyck Henrietta Maria, 1636; *Euston Hall.*

The Outer Hall is dominated by the large portrait of Charles I by or after Van Dyck: the original is in the Louvre. Van Dyck also painted the fine group of Charles I's five eldest children. The furniture consists of 19th-century copies of 18th-century styles. In the Inner Hall is Reynolds' likeness of the first wife of the 3rd Duke and Lely's magnificent state portrait of Charles II, tired and melancholy, towards the end of his life. Close by is the painting of the Duchess of Cleveland by Lely with that of her father, Viscount Grandison, by Van Dyck. Chinese 18th-century armorial plates are in the showcase.

The Small Dining Room contains Dance's portrait of the 3rd Duke, a view of Euston in the 18th century with a deer hunt in progress and Stubbs' magnificent *Mares and Foals by the River at Euston*; under it is a George II side-table by James Moore. The most interesting furniture in the Dining Room is the pair of late-17th-century mirrors and the mid-18th-century dining chairs. Here are more portraits by Van Dyck of Henrietta Maria and a delightful likeness of Charles II in exile before the Restoration by Philippe de Champaigne, Lely's Lord Arlington, his fine James Duke of York and Mignard's Duchess of Orleans. Lely and Reynolds are represented on the Staircase, where also hangs Birley's portrait of the present

Duke and one of Kent's designs for landscaping the park. A cheerful painting of the great ball at The Hague the night before Charles II's return to England is also here.

A further splendid collection of Stuart portraits is in the Square, off the first floor landing, including works by Wissing (the Duke of Monmouth), Daniel Mytens (the Duke of Buckingham) and others by Van Dyck, Lely (Prince Rupert) and Van Loo.

Eye Manor Hereford and Worcester

Mr and Mrs Christopher Sandford

$3\frac{1}{2}$ miles N of Leominster, $1\frac{1}{4}$ miles W of A49

This unassuming rose-pink Carolean manor house stands next to a 12th-century church, with a knot-garden on the other side. It was built by a West Indian sugar planter, Ferdinando Gorges, for his retirement. Little change has been made since. Its principal glory is the unusually high quality of the ceiling plasterwork, perhaps made by stuccoists from Holyrood Palace, who are thought to have also worked in the neighbourhood.

The ceiling in the wainscoted Dining Hall is divided into nine rectangular coved panels and decorated with swags, drapery and at the intersections with roses. The Turkish carpet was a gift from the late Turkish Sultan, Abdul Hamid II, to Mrs Sandford's grandfather, who was Chairman of the Imperial Ottoman Bank. The oak and elm refectory table, *c*.1700, was acquired from a local inn.

The ceiling of the Great Parlour is even more impressive with its decorations of flowers, fruit and leaves together with four side panels, each with a lively scene portraying, for example,

Page from the Book of Songs *illustrated by Lettice Sandford; one of the books printed by the Golden Cockerel Press, 1933–59; Eye Manor.*

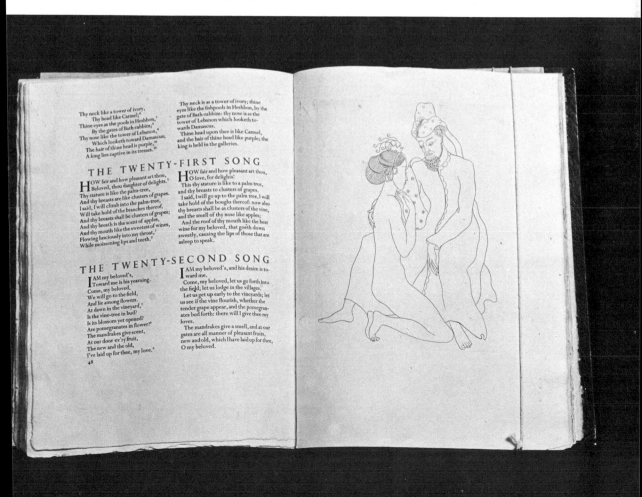

Hercules and the Hydra and a spaniel flushing a wild duck. The walls are lined with bolection-moulded panelling. A hunting scene by Jan Wyck hangs over the fireplace with its moulded stone surround. The walnut marquetry cabinet and the two mahogany and walnut chairs are Dutch of the mid-18th century, while the mahogany wine coolers and the fire-stool on cabriole legs with claw and ball toes are mid-18th-century Irish 'Chippendale', of which a number of fine pieces were inherited from Mr Sandford's father and his mother, Mary, Lady Carbery, to whom the Rowlandson colour prints, La Cave water-colours, and needlework pictures also belonged.

The portrait over the Study chimneypiece is a version of William of Orange dressed for war, painted *c.*1685 at The Hague by Wissing, while the miniatures are attributed to Mary Hadfield, Cosway's wife. On the Carolean Staircase with twisted walnut balusters is a portrait of Lord Stafford attributed to Lely.

Of the other ceilings, perhaps that in the Small Parlour is the most impressive with its oval central wreath of fruit and foliage with cherubs in the spandrels.

There are several collections: one is of Victorian and Edwardian christening robes, bonnets and lesson books; another of fifty-six costume dolls; a great collection of corn dollies, mostly made by Mrs Sandford, but also from all corners of the globe, made from palm fronds, maize husks, bamboo and other materials; in addition examples of straw-marquetry and marquetry-collage are displayed.

In the South-West Bedroom are splendid examples of books designed by Mr Sandford when from 1933 to 1959 he directed the Golden Cockerel Press.

Falkland Palace Fife

The National Trust for Scotland

In Falkland, 11 miles N of Kirkcaldy on A912

Except for Holyroodhouse and parts of Edinburgh and Stirling Castles, Falkland alone survives of the dwellings of the monarchs of Scotland. But the building today is only a small portion of the 16th-century palace erected close to a much older castle which had been the property of the Macduffs, Earls of Fife, before becoming a royal possession about 1440. Falkland in its heyday was more a royal home than a place of state, where, in the brief bright dawn of the Renaissance before the storms of the Reformation, the cultured James IV and James V with their French and English queens held court, hunted, danced and sang.

The south range and the massive fortified gatehouse are the only parts to have survived more or less intact. Begun by James IV who was married for a few months only to Madeleine, daughter of François I, and later to Margaret Tudor, Henry VIII's sister, it was extended and embellished by James V. The result has been called 'a display of early Renaissance architecture without parallel in the British Isles'. French influence was paramount; French masons and Scottish craftsmen trained in France were employed and some of their names are known; Moyce Martyne, Thomas French, Hector Beato, Nicholas Roy. The architect was the King's bastard cousin, Sir James Hamilton of Finnart. This fiery nobleman had spent some years at the French court and had a wild and adventurous career, being ultimately beheaded. He was also responsible for reconstructing the palace at Stirling Castle which has great similarities with Falkland. The early death of James V put a stop to the building although his widow, the Queen Regent, completed the roofing. Here Mary Queen of Scots spent part of her childhood and James VI, her unlikely son, spent his wedding night, giving the palace next day to his queen as a 'Morrowing Gift'. Charles I visited Falkland, but after Cromwellian troops burnt down the north range in 1654 the palace was left to decay. It has always remained the property of the sovereign, in the care of hereditary keepers. In 1881, the 3rd Marquess of Bute became Hereditary Constable, Captain and Keeper. He completely rebuilt the south range and gatehouse (now the keeper's quarters) and on the east range, the Cross House, all that

RIGHT *Robert Adam's two-storeyed oval staircase, c.1777, at Culzean Castle.*

ABOVE *View of the restored King's Bedchamber, Falkland Palace, with its early-17th-century 'Golden Bed of Brahan'.*
LEFT *The Cabinet Room, Felbrigg Hall, containing paintings collected by William Windham II on his Grand Tour.*

remained of the royal apartments. In 1952, Major Michael Crichton Stuart, his grandson, appointed the National Trust for Scotland as Deputy Keeper in perpetuity.

The visitor is able to see the Chapel Royal in the south range which retains a little of its original fixed furnishings, possibly fragments of the royal pew and most of the painted ceiling decorated with the arms and cyphers of Charles I and his queen, who came to Falkland in 1633, and the frieze, which has painted windows exactly reflecting the real ones opposite. A 17th-century Flemish tapestry hangs behind the altar and there is a fine Italian Baroque madonna and an icon made by Polish airmen stationed at Falkland during the World War II. The Chapel is approached from the long Tapestry Gallery where stained glass windows, ceiling, wall panelling and oak floor all testify to the quality of the Marquess of Bute's 19th-century craftsmen.

The only other furnished room is also a remarkable example of reconstruction, the King's Bedchamber, part of the Cross House, which had a privy and narrow stair to the courtyard below. The redecoration was not finished until 1955 and it now appears as it was originally, brilliantly coloured with painted tempera ceiling, frieze and window shutters, and a huge coat of arms above the fireplace. It contains the Baroque 'Golden Bed of Brahan' dating from the early-17th century which has been given to the Trust.

architect, on his return from a protracted Grand Tour in which he acquired views of Rome and Venice by Pannini and Canaletto and much classical marble statuary.

The lively rococo plasterwork ceilings in the cool Entrance Hall and in the elegant Dining Room are by William Perritt. The overmantels in both rooms are of carved wood with broken pediments, each containing a classical bust. The Entrance Hall has a patterned stone floor, shallow oval niches containing marble busts of Roman emperors and goddesses, and fine mahogany doors.

In the Dining Room, the Pannini and Canaletto views are spaced on the walls in gloriously elaborate rococo plasterwork frames. The original canvases, sold early in this century, have since been replaced with facsimiles which might have won approval in the 18th century, a period when good copies of fine paintings were preferred to inferior originals. In addition there are panels enclosing beautifully wrought plasterwork festoons illustrating Holbech's sporting and musical interests. The notable furniture includes two pairs of marble-topped tables in the Chippendale manner and a mahogany wine cooler.

The Staircase Hall is lit by an oval skylight, installed in the mid-18th century, surrounded by 17th-century plasterwork. The staircase itself was partly destroyed by fire in 1920, though it has since been reconstructed to the same 18th-century design, with fluted oak balusters and curving handrail.

Farnborough Hall Warwickshire

The National Trust

6 miles N of Banbury, ½ mile W of A423

Originally a late medieval manor house, built by the de Rale or Raleigh family, this stately dark honey-coloured stone house was partly rebuilt at the end of the 17th century by William Holbech, whose father had acquired the property some ten years earlier. His son, William Holbech the younger, was responsible for remodelling the house on a much larger scale, probably using Sanderson Miller as his

Felbrigg Hall Norfolk

The National Trust

3 miles S of Cromer, W of B1436

Felbrigg with its outstanding furniture, paintings and porcelain lies three miles from the coast, protected from the North Sea winds by its ancient spreading woods. The Jacobean wing, built above the cellars of the medieval Hall, was erected by Sir John Wyndham in the 1620s for his son, Thomas Windham, who left Somerset to settle at Felbrigg. A new brick

LEFT *The Dining Room, Farnborough Hall, with its rococo plasterwork picture frames and panels.*

The Chinese Bedroom, Felbrigg Hall; its hand-painted wallpaper was added by James Paine in the 1750s.

wing was added by William Windham I in the 1680s, to be considerably altered for William Windham II by Paine in the 1750s. William Windham III was Secretary at War for seven years under the younger Pitt. In 1863 the estate was sold to John Ketton, a prosperous merchant, whose daughter married Thomas Wyndham Cremer; their son Robert Wyndham Ketton-Cremer, a distinguished biographer and historian, left the estate to the National Trust in 1970.

There are family portraits by Lely, Kneller, Reynolds, and one of R. W. Ketton-Cremer by Allan Gwynne-Jones, two excellent views of London by Samuel Scott, a set of four seascapes attributed to the younger Van de Velde, but the most interesting are the paintings collected by William Windham II during his Grand Tour and which are now on the walls of the Cabinet, a room designed specially by Paine to accommodate them. They include the largest collection outside the British Museum and the Fitzwilliam Museum, Cambridge, of views of Roman antiquities and the Campagna by Busiri, the Roman *vedutista*: twenty-six are painted in gouache, the rest in oil. In addition there are views by de Vlieger, Van Poelenburgh, Bakhuyzen, Storck and Van der Poel. The Cabinet also contains an excellent Boulle-style Louis XIV writing table (*bureau plat*).

The plasterwork ceilings of the Dining Room and the Cabinet were designed by Paine and made under the supervision of Joseph Rose Sr. That in the Drawing Room with rich panels of fruit, foliage and game birds is dated 1687. The carpets both here and in the Great Hall are mid-19th-century English Savonnerie. Upstairs is Paine's Gothic Library of 1754–5, the books mainly collected by William Windham II who personally bound many of them. Paine also added the remarkable hand-painted Chinese wallpaper to the Chinese Bedroom which contains a pair of Chinese Chippendale chairs and a Chinese lacquered writing desk, 1730.

There is a fascinating miscellany of ceramics; it includes an 18th-century Dutch Delft cistern, a Lowestoft mug and bowl, *c.*1760, and two 18th-century English Delft bowls in the Great Hall; 18th-century Meissen porcelain, and an early-19th-century Staffordshire teapot given to Mr Ketton-Cremer by the late Queen Mary in the Drawing Room; and in the Cabinet a pair of 18th-century Fukien ware libation cups, a pair of white Plymouth shell-shaped salts, *c.*1770, and a small white Bow porcelain figure of Harlequin after Kändler. Busts by Nollekens and Chantrey are in the Great Hall and R. W. Ketton-Cremer's collected works.

Fenton House London

The National Trust

On w side of Hampstead off Holly Hill, 300 yards N of Hampstead underground station

Visitors entering Fenton House, an enchanting small country house, brick-built in 1693, seven years before the discovery of the nearby springs which transformed Hampstead into a popular spa, may be welcomed by the tinkling sound of a spinet or clavichord. Most of the keyboard instruments were collected by the late Major Benton Fletcher and bequeathed to the National Trust in 1937, the earliest being the five-sided Italian spinet made by Marcus Siculus in 1540. This important collection includes virginals, harpsichords and pianos mainly from the 17th to the early-19th century and among the distinguished makers are

Robert Hatley, Burkat Shudi, Jacob and Abraham Kirkman and John Broadwood; most of them may be played.

The fragile delicacy of these sounds makes an ideal background to enjoy the outstanding collections of English, Continental and Oriental porcelain and the fine furniture given to the National Trust by the late Lady Binning with the house. The English porcelain includes early hard paste Bristol (including 'The Classical Seasons') and Plymouth, many Chelsea 'Gold Anchor' groups and works from 'The Girl on a Swing' factory, excellent pieces from Bow, Longton Hall, Derby and especially from Worcester. There are marvellous examples of Meissen, many figures modelled by Kändler and by his successors, Reinecke, Eberlein and Meyer, and of Nymphenburg, Frankenthal, Höchst and Ludwigsburg.

The Chinese wares range from the white-

Grand pianoforte, c.1775, by Dutchman Americus Backers; Fenton House.

'Lady in a hooped Skirt' modelled by Kändler, Meissen, c.1750; Fenton House.

glazed dishes of the Sung Dynasty (960–1279) to the blue-and-white and later polychrome wares of the Ch'ing Dynasty (1644–1912) including a wide collection of the K'ang Hsi period (1662–1722). In addition there are collections of Staffordshire pottery, Chelsea snuff bottles and English enamel ware.

The Dining Room contains good quality Regency furniture, including the lyre-back chairs and the yew-wood wine cooler; even more interesting are the splendid English red lacquer pier-glass, *c.*1700, and the mahogany dining chairs with Gothic decoration. Among other excellent pieces are the Queen Anne 'pie-crust' table, and the small mahogany work table in the rococo style of Cobb in the Blue Porcelain Room and the enchanting painted satinwood furniture in the Drawing Room, especially the chairs with partly caned backs. There are two delightful alabaster and blue-john urns flanking a larger alabaster urn above the Porcelain Room fireplace. The paintings include two watercolour river scenes by Marlow, a drawing of a river landscape by Jan Breughel I, 17th-century stumpwork and needlework pictures and a series of birds and flowers by Samuel Dixon.

Finchcocks Kent

Mr and Mrs Richard Burnett

1 mile w of Goudhurst off A262

This handsome, notably Baroque, red-brick mansion, built in 1725, contains a splendid collection of keyboard instruments, the rooms echoing with music when they are played. The ceiling of the present Entrance Hall is embellished with an intriguing decoration, a fanciful half-human, half-fish, sea-borne Neptune, by Loudon Sainthill. The craftsmanship of door cases, floors, the balusters of the gracious staircase, is everywhere excellent.

Every room, including the spacious Staircase Hall, contains one or more 18th- or 19th-century instruments, often in magnificent cases of various woods, sometimes enriched with ivory or ormolu. They include a two-manual harpsichord by Jacob Kirkman, London, 1756; a Broadwood grand piano, London, 1801; and a house organ by John Byfield, London, 1766. Among other makers are Johann Fritz (Vienna), Conrad Graf (Vienna), Clementi, Collard and Collard, and Jones, Round and Co. There are also examples of early keyboard instruments made on the premises by Derek Adlam.

Firle Place East Sussex

The Viscount Gage KCVO

4 miles SE of Lewes on A27 to Eastbourne

This stately grey stone mansion stands close to the steep wooded northern slope of Firle Beacon, the highest point of the Downs east of Lewes; to the north and east stretches well wooded parkland. Sir John Gage, whose family was established in Gloucestershire, acquired this property in 1446 through marriage to an heiress; their descendants have included distinguished courtiers, soldiers and statesmen.

Much of Firle Place, which is of Tudor origin, was built by Sir John's grandson, another Sir John (1479–1556), who loyally served Henry VIII and was given important offices, including the Chancellorship of the Duchy of Lancaster. Staunchly Catholic, the family was subject to the persecution suffered by recusants, although Sir John (d. 1633) was created a Baronet in 1622.

The 7th Baronet (1695–1744) joined the Church of England, as did his cousin, Thomas (d. 1754); both engaged in politics and the latter, who inherited Firle Place in 1744, was created a Viscount. They were responsible for the 18th-century alterations which give the house its present appearance. Its Tudor origin is not, however, completely effaced; there is a Tudor doorway in the Staircase Hall and the plasterwork ceiling of the Great Hall conceals but does not replace the hammerbeam roof from which it is suspended.

Firle contains notable collections of furniture, porcelain and especially of paintings which, in addition to the Gage portraits, have come from the great Cowper collection at Panshanger, near Hertford, from Fawsley, Northamptonshire, and from Taplow Court, Buckinghamshire. Van Dyck's magnificent group *John, Count of Nassau and Family* dominates the Great Hall, where also hangs a splendid 17th-century Beauvais tapestry, one of a pair; the other is being repaired.

In the white and gold enriched Drawing Room with balancing Ionic screens are full-length portraits by Gainsborough, Reynolds and David Martin. There are two pairs of gilt side-tables, one with a garlanded fox as supporter, and an engaging set of lattice-backed Chippendale-type chairs. On the first floor landing is Johnson's portrait of the 1st Baronet. The Italian paintings are in the adjoining Drawing Room. Over the fireplace is Fra Bartolomeo's superb *Holy Family and the Infant St John*; there are also two portraits by Domenico Puligo, a head by Moroni, a portrait of Piero de Medici by an unknown hand, and two small Venetian views by Francesco Guardi. There is also a head by Rubens. The furniture is mainly French of the Louis XV and XVI periods, including pieces stamped by Riesener and Leleu. Two English display cabinets veneered in satinwood with marquetry, almost certainly by Chippendale,

contain mainly Sèvres porcelain, 1765–78.

The Ante-room contains excellent examples of 'Red Anchor' Chelsea and cups and saucers from the St Cloud factory in Kakiemon style. Reynolds' portrait of Lord Huntly and works by the younger Teniers and Van Goyen embellish the walls.

In the magnificent Long Gallery hang superb portraits by Reynolds and Lawrence, Hoppner and Beach; there are also fine works by Copley, two Zoffanys, and an enchanting small full-length portrait of the 2nd Viscount as a young man by Arthur Devis. Pride of place is given to the younger Teniers' glorious large painting *The Wine Harvest*. The furniture includes a mid-18th-century Italian suite of sofas and armchairs with richly carved rococo-style gilt frames, two fine pairs of French commodes, one *c.*1725 and the other a little later, a splendid roll-top *escritoire*, *c.*1770, in the manner of Riesener and an attractive pair of English oval wall mirrors, *c.*1750. Here also is Firle's finest Sèvres porcelain, magnificent soft-paste pieces painted in the factory's principal

Roll-top escritoire, c.1770, in the manner of Riesener; Firle Place.

colours – *bleu céleste*, *gros bleu*, the even darker *bleu-du-roi*, green, rose – and a remarkable turquoise dinner service decorated with the distinctive *œil de perdrix* pattern of *c.*1770. Elsewhere are good examples of 18th-century Chinese and Japanese wares.

John Piper's view of Firle and a fine Turner watercolour are in the Cowper Bedroom. A small Rembrandt, *Head of a Jew*, and a splendid *Landscape with Windmill* by Koninck are in the Dining Room which is not always on public view.

Floors Castle Borders

The Duke of Roxburghe

A view of the Castle painted in 1809 shows the house to have been a plain rectangular block with forceful projections at each corner set against a background of trees; in the foreground, parkland slopes gently down to the River Tweed. The woods, park and river remain unaltered but the house was transformed about 1849 by William Playfair; he added extensive low wings, heightened the towers and crowned every available roof space with turrets and cupolas, over sixty in all. The effect is immensely impressive, a 'stately home' *par excellence*.

The architect and builder of the Georgian house was William Adam who worked at Floors from 1721 onwards for the 5th Earl and 1st Duke of Roxburghe. Little of Adam's interior survives save for the entrance hall. The decoration and much of the furniture, tapestries and ceramics with which Floors is richly endowed are due to the taste and a skill of the 8th Duchess, an American heiress, whose husband succeeded as 8th Duke in 1892.

The furniture is predominantly 18th-century French, many pieces stamped by the *maîtres ébénistes* of Louis XV and XVI. The reign of Louis XIV is represented by a most striking large bracket clock in a tortoise-shell ormolu-mounted case by Gribelin of Paris. There is a great deal of 18th-century seat furniture, including a set of carved and gilt armchairs in the Ballroom. An unusual tulipwood Louis XV dressing table is stamped JME and a tall cabinet of the period is also made of tulipwood with marquetry and restrained ormulo mounts.

A fine commode signed by Joubert of 1773 is from the bedroom of the Comtesse d'Artois at Versailles. Another notable piece is a Louis XVI ebony and Boulle *bureau plat* by Durand. The Ballroom contains the most important of the English furniture, notably a rare set of Charles II gilt armchairs and four Queen Anne walnut chairs with cane backs and embroidered seat covers. There are Kentian gilt console tables and cabinets, 17th-century black and gold lacquer cabinets, and a William and Mary suite of chairs and high-backed settee covered with blue velvet.

Family interest in the Far East, above all the 8th Duchess's, was not confined to English and Dutch chinoiserie. There is a great deal of first quality Chinese porcelain ranging from T'ang and Ming figures, and a fine pair of Yung Cheng vases, to K'ang Hsi and Ch'ien Lung *famille rose* and *famille verte* pieces. The Meissen china is particularly fine among the European porcelain collection and the smaller objects include a collection of Battersea enamel boxes which is outstanding.

Floors is no less liberally furnished with tapestries, again mostly acquired by the American Duchess May. Perhaps the rarest is a late-15th-century Brussels panel of the Pentecost, probably intended as a single piece for a chapel. The Drawing Room is hung with a Brussels set in very different style and subject, *The Triumph of the Gods*, dating from the 1720s. The panelled Ballroom has a set of Gobelins tapestries, *Les Portières des Dieux*, from designs of Claude Autran Le Jeune.

The paintings are predominantly family portraits although there is a collection of *vedute* of the school of Canaletto, a Ruysdael landscape and some fascinating topographical pictures by Tillemans, Nelson and others. The earliest portraits are of the 1st Earl of Roxburghe and his wife by Jamesone; the most dominating the large Raeburn portrait painted between 1807 and 1812 of James, 5th Duke. After a protracted lawsuit he succeeded in his claim to the dukedom and, re-marrying a week after his first wife's death, was able to celebrate the birth of a son at the age of 81. Small wonder that in his portrait he looks pleased with life. In a very different vein is the conversation piece of the 3rd Duke and a group of friends (which includes the painter Zoffany) painted in Florence by Thomas Patch in the 1770s. This duke, who remained a bachelor after un-successfully courting Queen Charlotte's sister, became a celebrated bibliophile and collected the famous Roxburghe library, sadly dispersed after his death.

The works of established portraitists are well represented, from Kneller and Lely to Rey-nolds and Beechey and, more unusually in Scotland, Hoppner who painted the 3rd Duke. Three ravishing 18th-century female portraits

were hung with great effect by Duchess May in her Needle Room: Peg Woffington by Hogarth and two unnamed ladies, one by Ramsay and the other by Alexis Grimoux.

Florence Court Co. Fermanagh

The National Trust

7 miles sw of Enniskillen on A32

Florence Court, standing on Fermanagh's mountainous border with County Cavan, was built by the Cole family, later Earls of Enniskillen, in about 1760 but in an earlier Georgian style, echoing that of James Gibbs. Elegant but not large, the interior is embel-lished with Georgian craftsmanship at its finest – door furniture, staircase with fluted balusters and a yew wood handrail, pedimented door-

Late-15th-century Brussels tapestry showing the Day of the Pentecost; Floors Castle.

The 15th-century Monks' Refectory, Forde Abbey, its 19th-century screen made from Breton bedsteads.

ways, pine bookshelves and a fine marble-paved floor in the Hall. A serious fire in 1955 caused considerable damage to the house; happily very complete records made possible its successful restoration.

Of outstanding charm is the rococo plasterwork, to be seen in the panels on the stairway walls and especially on the Dining Room ceiling, which displays an eagle with four cherubs blowing the winds to the four corners of the globe, the work perhaps of Robert West of Dublin. The delightful ceiling of the Venetian Room is a post-fire reproduction. In the Drawing Room is an agreeable series of military portraits by Brocas.

Forde Abbey Dorset

The Trustees of Mr G. D. Roper

4 miles SE of Chard, 7 miles W of Crewkerne

Built in the 12th century as a Cistercian monastery, Forde Abbey underwent many changes before its final metamorphosis into a Commonwealth country house in the mid-17th century, largely through alterations initiated by Sir Edmund Prideaux, Attorney General to Cromwell in 1649, the year in which he acquired the property. The estate passed by marriage to the Gwyn family who sold it in 1846 to an ancestor of the present occupant. Here is much fine craftsmanship, such as the painted and gilded roof of the Great Hall and the elegant mid-17th-century panelling on its east wall, the rich but soberly decorated Chapel screen and the exuberant pierced acanthus foliage of the Great Staircase's balustrade, repeated on the inside wall by *trompe l'œil* painting, and the newels topped by carved baskets of fruit.

There are bold plasterwork ceilings above the Great Staircase, in the Oak Room with its white and gold doorcase, and in the Saloon, whose ceiling oval centre contains carved and painted armorials, flanked by panels which naïvely represent 'The Murder of Abel' and 'The Sacrifice of Isaac'. The line of the pilasters dividing the panelled walls matches the pattern of the frieze and ceiling; the sobriety of the brown paint on the panels is enhanced by the gold enrichment, especially on the elaborate overmantel frame above the fireplace. The Saloon's outstanding feature is the five early-18th-century tapestries, woven, to fit the walls, at Mortlake from the Raphael cartoons now in the Victoria and Albert Museum and probably a gift from Queen Anne to Sir Francis Gwyn, her Secretary at War. The tapestry on the thirteen long-back Stuart chairs and two stools is also from Mortlake. The Saloon also contains two splendid Italian *cassoni* gilded and painted with topographical scenes.

The carved and pierced screen in the Refectory, a room restored late in the 19th century, is made unusually from Breton bedsteads; portraits by Mary Beale hang on the west wall of the Great Hall, an attractive Flemish painting of three peasant women is in the Oak Room and elsewhere are sketches by Reynolds and works by Henry Bright, Lord Methuen and Keble Martin.

Forty Hall Middlesex

The London Borough of Enfield

Forty Hill, Enfield

This fine three-storeyed Jacobean house, later considerably altered, was built between 1629 and 1636 for Sir Nicolas Raynton, whose portrait of 1643, attributed to Dobson, is in the Raynton Room. Bold strapwork plaster ceilings are Jacobean as are the Dining Room fireplace and screen with Italianate shell motifs, but the elegant plaster swags of musical instruments which embellish the Entrance Hall together with medallions containing heads representing the four seasons are late-18th century.

There are family portraits of the Meyer family who lived here in the 19th century but the most interesting is by Jan Mytens of Henrietta Anne, Duchess of Orleans, fifth daughter of Charles I, in its original marquetry frame. Recently restored by the Enfield Borough, Forty Hall is now a museum with the beginnings of interesting collections of furniture, especially a cream lacquer cabinet on a gilt stand and two long-back Charles II chairs, and of glass, ceramics, pewter and silver together with much of local interest, including watercolours.

Gaulden Manor Somerset

Mr and Mrs James Le Gendre Starkie

9 miles NW of Taunton, 1 mile E of Tolland church

Gaulden Manor, once owned by Taunton Priory, was surrendered to Henry VIII on the Dissolution of the Monasteries. It is remarkable for the magnificent plasterwork ceiling in the Great Hall, with its enormous pendant and great roundels, displaying religious themes, which was installed by a member of the Turberville family. The frieze is believed to represent happenings in the life of James Turberville, Bishop of Exeter under Queen Mary Tudor, who refused to give the Oath of Supremacy to Queen Elizabeth I; after imprisonment in the Tower, he may have lived here in retirement.

The bold overmantel with its various Turberville coats of arms was placed there by John Turberville who acquired the property in 1639 after the Wolcott family had departed for America in 1630, where they prospered; a descendant, Oliver Wolcott, signed the Declaration of Independence.

Gaulden Manor, always used as a farm, was in a poor state when purchased in 1966 by the present owners, who have undertaken a thorough programme of redecoration, cleaning the important plasterwork features in the Great Hall and the room called the Chapel.

Gawsworth Hall Cheshire

The Roper-Richards family

3 miles s of Macclesfield on road to Congleton (A536)

This delightful half-timbered manor house was originally quadrangular, built round a courtyard during the 16th century, when it was the home of the Fitton family. Here lived Mary Fitton, who may have been the 'Dark Lady' of Shakespeare's sonnets, a romantic association that has added further to the charm of the house. Towards the end of the 17th century, Gawsworth Hall was considerably reduced in size by the demolition of the west wing and part of the south wing.

Inside is a wealth of exposed timbers, a fine plaster frieze in the Antechamber, some good period oak furniture and a large, wide-ranging collection of mostly Victorian paintings and of 19th-century sculpture. There is also a carriage museum.

Gawthorpe Hall Lancashire

The National Trust

On E outskirts of Padiham, N of A6711

This handsome late Elizabethan mansion, built in 1600–5 but extensively remodelled by Barry 1850–2, was given to the National Trust in 1970 by Lord Shuttleworth, whose family had lived hereabouts for nearly 700 years. Now leased to the Lancashire County Council and administered by Nelson and Colne College of Further Education, it houses the splendid collections of textiles, embroideries, toys, lace, basketry, metalwork, costumes, ceramics and glass created by the late Miss Rachel Kay-Shuttleworth. These collections, the largest of their type outside London, are available for study to students from all over Britain, and will form the core of a Craft House. The outbuildings, some of them dating from the 17th century, are being renovated for this purpose.

The outstanding Drawing Room, 1604, regarded by many as the finest of its period in Lancashire, retains its original Renaissance panelling, whose two upper ranges are inlaid with marquetry; the lower of the two, which has curved arches, is especially impressive. Its overmantel with two carved figures in Elizabethan costume, its frieze with men, beasts and mythical figures, and its splendidly elaborate plasterwork ceiling with pendants are almost certainly the work of local craftsmen, as is the impressive Long Gallery ceiling on which oak leaves, filberts, grapes, shells and squirrels are intricately entwined. Many of the bedrooms also retain original ceilings and friezes.

The house contains good early furniture, mainly oak, including an early-17th-century bed in the Grey Room, its hangings made by Miss Kay-Shuttleworth; an extremely rare turned chair; another of fruitwood, *c*.1580, on three legs; two fine carved armchairs with marquetry back panels; and a mid-17th-century Italian harpsichord in a walnut case.

Glamis Castle Tayside

The Earl of Strathmore and Kinghorne

10 miles N of Dundee off A928

Glamis holds a special place today in the nation's affections as the childhood home of Queen Elizabeth the Queen Mother, but its royal connections began long ago. It was one of the hunting lodges of the kings of Scotland from the 11th to the 14th century when Sir John Lyon of Forteviot, a great personage at the court of Robert II, was granted the Thanage of Glamis in 1372. The present Lord Strathmore is a direct descendant of Sir John.

The Chapel at Glamis
Castle, consecrated in
1688 and decorated by
the Dutch artist de Wett
with scenes from the life
of Christ. One of
the panels (below)
shows Christ wearing
a large black hat of
17th-century fashion.

The lords of Glamis continued to serve their sovereigns and the 9th Lord Glamis, Keeper of the Guard and one of James VI's Privy Councillors, was created Earl of Kinghorne in 1606. His son was a friend and supporter of Montrose, but parted company from him and aided the Covenanters against the king. He died impoverished, but Patrick, the 3rd Earl, restored the family fortunes and was responsible for much of the building and decoration of the Castle as it is today. In the 18th century the 9th Earl married Eleanor Bowes, heiress to her father's extensive property in Durham and Yorkshire, and the family name thereafter has been Bowes Lyon. In the 19th century the 13th and 14th Earls were granted United Kingdom peerages; the latter was the father of Queen Elizabeth the Queen Mother.

The Castle is approached from a long avenue across flat wooded lands of the Vale of Strathmore. The tall central tower block is flanked by lower wings and surrounded by wide lawns. In a formal garden below the east wing is a celebrated sundial placed there by the 3rd Earl between 1671 and 1680. His bust, possibly by the Dutch sculptor Sandvoort, is inset in a niche above the front door in the round staircase tower. It is also possible that Sandvoort was responsible for work within the tower and the vast stone fireplace in the Great Hall. Family tradition maintains that this may have been built to Inigo Jones' designs, but there is no documentary evidence to support this contention. A more certain provenance is that Wyatt was the architect of the Dining Room rebuilt after the north wing was burnt down in 1800. This is the first room seen by the visitor and uncharacteristic of Glamis in its early-19th-century decoration and furnishing. More typical is the Crypt with its Jacobean and Carolean 17th-century furniture, and the magnificent Great Hall above with a splendid barrel-vaulted plaster ceiling dated 1621 and containing a series of family portraits, many in ornate 17th-century gilt frames. The large group of the 3rd Earl by Medina dominates one wall. The Earl and his eldest son are dressed in flesh-coloured armour, a convention of the time, somewhat startling to the beholder. Other portraits include a French one of the 9th Lord Glamis as a sensitive, steady-eyed youth, with his secretary George Bothwell depicted on the reverse side.

From the Drawing Room the visitor enters the Chapel, which has ceiling and walls decorated with scenes of the life of Christ by de Wett, for which the contract remains in the house. One panel, *Christ as a Gardener*, depicts Him wearing a large, black, unmistakably 17th-century hat, one of only two such paintings known.

Glamis is also notable for the fine set of Mortlake tapestries of the Life of Nebuchadnez-zar, the only other set being at Knole. King Malcolm's Room contains bed hangings worked by the 2nd Countess at the end of the 17th century in the same style as the Traquair embroideries. The Royal Apartments arranged by the 14th Countess for her youngest daughter when Duchess of York have two fine four-poster beds, one with headboard and hangings worked by her.

There is some good 17th-century furniture at Glamis and a notable collection of porcelain, in particular a fine service of Ch'ien Lung armorial export china.

Perhaps Glamis' most unusual treasure is the set of jester's motley, the Strathmores being the last family in Britain to have their own jester.

Glemham Hall Suffolk

Lady Blanche Cobbold

At Little Glemham on A12, between Wickham Market and Saxmundham

This impressive red-brick Elizabethan mansion became the home in 1923 of Colonel John Murray Cobbold, killed when the Guards Chapel was hit by a bomb in 1944, and his wife Lady Blanche Cobbold, a daughter of the 9th Duke of Devonshire, who lives here.

Glemham was originally built for the Glemham family but underwent considerable alteration in the early-18th century when it was acquired by Dudley North, married to Catherine, daughter of Elihu Yale who founded his famous university at New Haven, Connecticut. The result impaired its exterior charm but embellished the interior, especially the Hall with its screen of fluted Corinthian columns and bolection pine panelling, now stripped of the original white paint. The ground and first-floor rooms are also panelled, the wood exposed and mellow in the Library but overpainted elsewhere. There is fine furniture in the Hall, dating from William and Mary to George I, including a notable veneered walnut cabinet (inlaid with holly and sycamore floral marquetry) and three chests also in walnut veneer, one with seaweed marquetry and the others with elaborate inlaid patterns of figured woods. Beyond is the handsome and spacious Staircase of oak inlaid with walnut. Chairs include tall Carolean uprights and Queen Anne spoon backs. Throughout are good pieces of furniture representative mainly of the 18th century, including both the Chippendale table on tripod pedestals and the wide sideboard in the Dining Room, and several Oriental lacquered pieces.. The furniture and furnishings are primarily for use rather than display and an air of traditional, unpretentious good taste prevails.

Cavendish and Cobbold family portraits adorn the Dining Room and Library. There are a few 17th-century Dutch paintings, a landscape each by Constable and Gainsborough and watercolours of Old Ipswich by local artists. The Staircase from the Smoking Room, originally the Chapel, to the top of the house is hung with amusing mezzotints of 18th-century life. There are collections of Oriental ceramics – *famille verte, famille rose* and Imari – while English porcelain is represented by Chelsea, Davenport, Derby and Worcester.

Glynde Place East Sussex

The Viscount Hampden

4 miles SE of Lewes on A27 to Eastbourne or on A265

This splendid early Elizabethan courtyard mansion with its fine views eastwards over parkland towards the more distant Downs stands a little to the north of the South Downs in the picturesque village of Glynde. Built of brick and flint, *c.*1569, it was erected for William Morley, whose ancestors had settled on this estate by the 12th century. In 1679, the property passed by marriage to the Trevor family and in 1824 in the same way to the Brand family with whom it remains today.

The exterior has been little changed during the last 400 years but the interior underwent modifications in the 17th and 18th centuries. The alterations to the long, low Entrance Hall were made about 1758 by Richard Trevor, Bishop of Durham, son of the 1st Lord Trevor who had been Lord Chief Justice in Queen Anne's reign. A portrait of the Bishop by an unknown hand reveals handsome features with an incipient double chin and a pious expression which may have prompted George II's reference to him as the 'Beauty of Holiness'. He

Rubens' original sketch 'The Apotheosis of James I' for the ceiling design of the Banqueting Hall, Whitehall; Glynde Place.

introduced two screens of columns, one at each end, made of wood and painted to imitate marble; he also installed the two stone fireplaces over which are bronze reliefs by Francesco Bertos, a sculptor who had worked in Rome earlier in the century. Flanking the entrance doorway is a pair of full-length portraits of George III and Queen Charlotte, painted on their coronation by Ramsay, who produced some 200 sets for the occasion.

The Long Gallery above, created *c.*1679–86, retains its late-17th-century character, with Corinthian pilasters and broken pedimented doorcases. The walls are wainscoted with large bolection moulded panels and there is a finely carved overmantel with flowers, fruit and vegetables in the manner of Gibbons. Its stone fireplace and the bronze relief of Christ entering Jerusalem, also by Bertos, were placed here by the Bishop when altering the Hall.

Glynde contains good 18th-century English furniture, but of most importance are the 17th- and 18th-century family portraits, mainly of the Trevors, of which there are three by Johnson in splendidly carved frames, two each by Lely and Kneller and others by Gainsborough, Greuze, Hoppner and Zoffany. In the Drawing Room is Rubens' cartoon for the ceiling of the Whitehall Banqueting Hall.

Godinton Park Kent

Mr Alan Wyndham Green

1½ miles w of Ashford, off Maidstone road at Potters Corner (A20)

This pleasing quadrangular house of mellow red brick with stone dressings of late-16th- and early-17th-century origin encloses a late-15th-century hall house. The east front is probably early-17th-century; its curved gables are reminiscent of similar features at Knole and Blickling. '1628' was placed on the rainwater heads by Captain Nicholas Toke, a colourful personality who married five times. His family had acquired Godinton between 1485 and 1513 and his descendants lived here until 1896 when most of the contents were sold; these have been replaced with carefully chosen examples of the same periods.

Godinton's most fascinating feature is its rich carving, some of which, like the linenfold panelling in the Great Hall, was brought from elsewhere early in the 19th century. The Great Hall is basically 15th century with a well-preserved 14th-century chestnut tie beam still in position. The ceiling was installed by Captain Nicholas Toke to hide the medieval roof with its aperture through which smoke from the central fireplace could escape. The chimneypiece, like those in the 18th-century Palladian Dining Room and in the Great Chamber, is of beautifully carved marble from

Carved chestnut staircase, dated 1628, but probably with additions made in the 1800s; Godinton Park.

nearby Bethersden. The rich wood carving round it, perhaps Flemish and bearing the date of 1584, was installed in the 1800s. The furniture is mainly late-17th century, together with examples of Queen Anne walnut.

The Priest's Room, its panelling installed in the 1920s and which contains a notable French confessional box, may with the Gallery immediately above have formed the pre-Reformation chapel. The Gallery, redesigned by Sir Reginald Blomfield in the 1900s, contains a good Aubusson carpet, Louis XV chairs covered with Beauvais tapestry, Sheraton and Hepplewhite satinwood furniture and a French walnut commode displaying Sèvres porcelain. There are also examples of Dr Wall Worcester, Chelsea and 18th-century Chinese porcelain.

A lavishly carved chestnut Staircase, basically 17th century as indicated by the date 1628 on the central newel post but to which further intricate carving was probably added in the 1800s, leads to the Great Chamber, magnificent not only for the carved overmantel but also for the frieze which on the north and west sides shows pikemen at drill; the rest of it depicts field sports. There is also a splendidly carved overmantel in the First Library, dated 1631.

Godolphin House Cornwall

Mr S. E. Schofield

5 miles NW of Helston between Townshend and Godolphin Cross

The approach to this evocatively named granite manor house through woods from a country lane leaves the visitor completely unprepared for the sudden magnificent view of this Jacobean colonnaded house. Two wings at each end form three sides of a quadrangle; on the fourth side is what remains of the Great Hall of a much larger mansion which was destroyed in 1805. The property came to the Godolphin family – through marriage, late in the 14th century – who became immensely rich from mining tin. Its most distinguished member was the 1st Earl of Godolphin who

served four successive monarchs from Charles I to Queen Anne, until his death in 1712. The house went by marriage to the Dukes of Leeds in 1785 and was afterwards almost completely neglected. Its very successful and quite unpretentious restoration was started by the present owner who acquired the estate in 1937.

The interior is uncluttered and much of the panelling original. The Entrance Hall contains an impressive carved oak chimneypiece and two very early paintings by the late Peter Lanyon, a widely admired post-war Cornish artist. In the Dining Room Wootton's painting of the famous Arab horse, 'Godolphin Arabian', hangs close to that of the 2nd Earl of Godolphin, its owner. There are good furniture pieces, some original to the house and retrieved by Mr Schofield.

The first-floor Library contains a fine William and Mary marquetry cabinet; in the adjoining Elizabethan Room, with its original frieze, is an intricately carved Elizabethan oak bed, c.1590, with a wooden canopy. Beyond is the gracious King's Room, which was enlarged in the 16th century; its plasterwork ceiling is Georgian but retains the original Elizabethan pendants. Here is a splendid carved Renaissance entablature of 1604, with coats of arms above and its columns carved criss-cross in pineapple style, made to commemorate a wedding.

Goodwood House West Sussex

The Goodwood Estate Company Ltd

3½ miles NE of Chichester, approach roads A285 and A286

The 1st Duke of Richmond, born in 1672, was the natural son of Charles II and the beautiful Louise de Quérouaille, Duchess of Portsmouth. He bought Goodwood in 1697 as a hunting box – the Charlton, the first fox-hunt to be formed in England, was established nearby. The 3rd Duke first employed Chambers, c.1760, to develop the original building here. Chambers created the Long Hall, part of which had been the entrance hall to the older house, but it was James Wyatt towards the end of the century who set about building an enormous octagon-shaped mansion with a tower at each corner; only the three wings now standing were completed when the scheme was halted because of the expense. The interior has recently been redecorated to show off its splendid collections of paintings, furniture and porcelain.

Foremost are the royal portraits, including two by Van Dyck, one of Charles I, his Queen and two eldest children and the other of Charles I's five oldest children; Lely's candid state portrait of Charles II; Kneller's early masterpiece, the Duke of Monmouth, and Vanderbank's Queen Caroline, one of his finest works. Among other portraits are works by Dahl, Wissing, Van Loo, Hudson, Reynolds (notably the 3rd Duke of Richmond), Hoppner, Lawrence (the 5th Duchess) and Grant. Four of Canaletto's best known paintings, especially the view of St Paul's and the River Thames from Richmond House, are here. In addition there are two seascapes by Samuel

Scott, one of Rodney's bombardment of Le Havre and, in the elegant Long Hall, three notable sporting scenes by Stubbs and five horse paintings by Wootton.

In the Yellow Drawing Room is some of Goodwood's finest furniture, including four magnificent inlaid marquetry commodes, three of them stamped with the names of Courturier, Dubois and Latz respectively, together with fine examples of Meissen porcelain; more excellent French furniture is in the Card Room. A remarkable Charles II marquetry cabinet on matching stand, inlaid with ivory and fruit woods, stands in the Green Hall together with Chinese and Japanese lacquerwork, the latter incorporated in a Louis XV *secrétaire à abattant*, stamped BVRB (Bernard Van Risen Burgh). The State Dining Room chairs, their backs once adorned with crocodiles, are in the Egyptian manner of Thomas Hope and there are sarcophagus-shaped wine coolers. The Tsar of Russia was entertained here in 1814.

George Stubbs (1724–1806) The Duke of Richmond's Racehorses at Exercise; *Goodwood House.*

Louis XV Gobelins tapestry illustrating Don Quixote *in the Tapestry Drawing Room, Goodwood House.*

In the circular Card Room are three cabinets of Sèvres porcelain, gloriously painted by the most distinguished artists associated with the royal porcelain factory. There is more Sèvres in the alcove at the end of the Yellow Drawing Room, flanked by Chelsea mazarin-blue handled cups and two finely decorated Chelsea beakers. Four Louis XV Gobelins tapestries, illustrating episodes from *Don Quixote*, hang in the Tapestry Drawing Room, whose unusual marble fireplace is the work of John Bacon: the ceiling is decorated in the style of Adam and contains further excellent examples of English and French 18th-century furniture, especially the set of Louis XV chairs and settees, upholstered in the original Lyons velvet and

stamped with the name of Delanois. The early Axminster carpet in the Card Room was especially made for this room.

Gorhambury House Hertfordshire

The Earl of Verulam

2¾ miles N of St Albans near A5

The present dignified Palladian mansion, built 1777–84 to designs by Robert Taylor for the 3rd Lord Grimston, replaced the Tudor home, now a preserved ruin nearby, built about 1570 by Sir Nicholas Bacon, the father of the great essayist Sir Francis Bacon, Lord Chancellor

Panel from the Tudor enamelled glass window at Gorhambury House.

family portraits, four paintings by Sir Nathaniel Bacon, an amateur of great distinction who painted only for his family. Here is his remarkable full-length self-portrait, one of his wife and two of the cook maid.

In the elegant Yellow Drawing Room with attractive Chippendale-style chairs and a period organ hang two fine paintings by Reynolds; one is of the four children of the 2nd Viscount Grimston and the other of the Hon. Mrs Walter. Other portraitists represented here include Batoni, Ramsay and Beale. The delightful carved white marble fireplace, with antique red marble insets, is by Piranesi, as is that in the Library, which contains some of Bacon's books and above the shelves more family portraits by, among others, Lely, Wissing, Dahl, Kneller and Riley.

Grey's Court Oxfordshire

The National Trust

At Rotherfield Greys NW of Henley-on-Thames on road to Peppard

The oldest of this romantic group of buildings, standing on a hill amid beech woods, are the crenellated Great Tower, built in the mid-14th century, and the three smaller medieval towers. The house itself, built of flint and brick with stone dressings, is mainly 16th century with later additions in the 17th and 18th centuries, although the Kitchen retains some earlier features. In about 1760 the Drawing Room and the so-called Schoolroom were embellished with elegant plasterwork, perhaps by Roberts of Oxford.

The furniture is mainly English of the late-17th and early-18th centuries; there are also two fine large Swiss dower chests. The Drawing Room boasts a lovely 18th-century marble chimneypiece; that of carved stone in the Schoolroom is also 18th century. In the pleasant unpretentious Hall are cabinets of fine English porcelain, especially of Chelsea. The Dining Room has six watercolours by Brangwyn and in the Schoolroom are several mementos of Sir Henry Irving.

under James I, whose portrait is in the Dining Room.

The Great Hall, designed as a cube, contains features from the Tudor house, including the carved Purbeck marble fireplace and the rare enamelled 16th-century glass windows. The portraits in the Hall Gallery are of recent generations of the Grimston family, Earls of Verulam, who succeeded to Gorhambury. Below the Gallery are royal Stuart portraits by De Critz, Lely and Huysmans (Catherine of Braganza). Kneller painted the equestrian portrait of George I and Daniel Mytens that of the 1st Lord Baltimore to whom Charles I granted land in Maryland. The white marble bust of Pope Clement XIV is by Hewetson, one of four versions in England. Here is one of the earliest known English hand-made pile carpets, dated 1570.

The Ball Room contains, among other

Haddo House Grampian

The National Trust for Scotland

2 miles N of Tarves, 20 miles N of Aberdeen

The House of Kellie, where Haddo House now stands, had been the home of the Gordons of Methlick for centuries when it was burnt down in 1644 by Covenanting forces led by the Marquess of Argyll, who broke his promise of safe conduct to Sir John Gordon and sent him to Edinburgh for trial and execution. In 1731 the 2nd Earl of Aberdeen commissioned William Adam to build him a grand new house and the imposing central block dates from that time. Adam's entrance was on the first floor, reached from a broad balustraded terrace. The entrance was remodelled in 1880 by the 7th Earl and 1st Marquess of Aberdeen to whom the house as it is today is almost entirely due. He rearranged and redecorated the interior in the Adam Revival style then in vogue and called in Edinburgh and London firms to do

the work, which was carried out to a very high standard of craftsmanship. It is a style that speaks to us today less of the refined and sometimes emasculated elegance of Robert Adam's designs than of the decade of Queen Victoria's Diamond Jubilee and the grandeur of the official residences of her representatives in every quarter of the globe. It was a world in which Lord Aberdeen played a distinguished role. Son of a Prime Minister, he became twice Viceroy of Ireland and Governor-General of Canada.

The Georgian sequence of the reception rooms was retained but only the one-time Entrance Hall retains its 18th-century panelling and carved overdoors. The marble bust of Queen Victoria which dominates the chimney-piece was given to her Prime Minister after she stayed at Haddo in 1851. Two of the most important paintings hang in this room — a portrait of Lord Aberdeen as a young man by Lawrence and one of Guizot, the French statesman, by Paul de la Roche, painted in

Reception room, Haddo House, decorated in Adam Revival style in 1880 for Lord Aberdeen.

1838. Eighteenth-century portraiture is best represented by a full-length by Batoni of Lord Haddo, who died before his father, the 3rd Earl. The latter was painted by Mossman in 1741. A collection of 19th-century watercolours by members of the family reveals the high quality of amateur talent so often found in the living rooms and corridors of country houses. The work of Countess Ishbel, wife of the 1st Marquess, is notable. A watercolour by James Giles, landscape gardener as well as topographical artist, depicts Balmoral Castle before Prince Albert rebuilt it. Four marble busts of contemporary statesmen by Chantrey embellish an ante-room simply known as The Square. It contains a pair of fine early George II giltwood mirrors. Most of the furniture is 18th-century reproduction and was installed in the 1880s together with carpets, curtains and wallhangings. There are a few good Georgian pieces, notably an Irish satinwood bureau-bookcase, with painted decorations, that was given to the 1st Marquess and his wife and restored to the house, after some wanderings, by the late Queen Mary.

A set of fine porcelain plates and dishes hand-painted by Canadian women artists was presented to Lady Aberdeen in 1898. It depicts Canadian views, birds and animals and is displayed in a corridor leading to the Library, contrived in 1880 out of the old stable block. Beyond, steps lead down and back to the Chapel, a building of considerable architectural interest. It was the last work of G. E. Street, who also designed the fittings. The east window is by Burne-Jones.

Haddon Hall Derbyshire

The Duke of Rutland

2 miles SE of Bakewell on A6

Recorded in Domesday Book, Haddon Hall in the Peak District was added to and altered by the Vernon family from the beginning of the 13th century. Since 1567 when Dorothy Vernon, married to John Manners, inherited it from her father, it has belonged to the Manners family. Their descendants succeeded in 1641 to the Earldom of Rutland, elevated in 1703 to a Dukedom, and the family concentrated their resources on Belvoir Castle. Thus, since early in the 17th century, Haddon Hall slumbered undisturbed until the 9th Duke (1886–1940) lovingly and expertly restored it at the beginning of this century.

In addition to its ancient dignity, its fine gardens and beautiful site above the River Wye, Haddon is remarkable for its wood carving, its panelling and its fine tapestries, although sixty pieces were destroyed by fire in 1925. One of the oldest pieces hangs in the Banqueting Hall above the dais; dating from *c*.1460, it displays the Royal Arms of England in which the lions of England are quartered with the lilies of France on a *mille fleurs* background. Here also is one of a set of five early-17th-century Mortlake tapestries depicting the Senses; three more are on the Staircase landing and the fifth is in the Ante-room to the State Bedroom (now used as a shop), in which there are 16th-century Brussels tapestries of hunting scenes.

The Banqueting Hall and Minstrels' Gallery were restored with oak from the family estates. The Dining Room is remarkable for its ceiling with its original painted decorations (restored in 1926) interspersed with panels bearing heraldic emblems; the panelled frieze also contains heraldic emblems, with more carvings in the panelling in the alcove and over the fireplace. The Great Chamber, in addition to the 17th-century Flemish tapestries of woodland scenes, contains 16th- and 17th-century furniture: more pieces are in the Long Gallery with its glorious Renaissance carved panelling.

The Chapel, whose font and arches are Norman, contains several 15th-century frescoes, including one of St Christopher and two of St Nicholas. The splendid 15th-century Nottingham alabaster reredos was brought here by the 9th Duke. Paintings include a good example of Hondecoeter's work in the Banqueting Hall. Particularly enjoyable is Rex Whistler's view of Haddon from a neighbouring height, 1933. The ancient Kitchens contain their contemporary fittings, including bread or 'dole' cupboards.

Pier-glasses and tables, c.1758, in the Tapestry Room, Hagley Hall.

Hagley Hall West Midlands

The Viscount and Viscountess Cobham

12 miles from Birmingham just off A456 to Kidderminster

Hagley Hall, facing west towards the Malvern Hills, is a handsome sandstone mansion built in Palladian style by Sanderson Miller. It was commissioned by the 1st Lord Lyttelton in 1756 to replace a previous Elizabethan manor house. The Lytteltons, an ancient Worcestershire family, were then already allied by marriage to the Temples and in 1889 inherited the Cobham title, when the Temple main line became extinct.

A highly distinguished feature of Hagley is the glorious rococo plasterwork by Vassalli, shown to advantage in the White Hall by the pale yellow of the walls. Not only was he responsible for the delicately contrived Hall ceiling, but also for the medallions, the statues in the niches and for the two panels; that over the carved stone chimneypiece, supported at each end by doughty figures, shows Pan spiritedly winning the love of Diana and bears his signature. Also in the Hall are busts of Roman emperors; those of Rubens and Van Dyck are by Rysbrack. The mahogany tables at the north end are attributed to Goodison, although later somewhat altered. Vassalli also worked with splendid effect on the ceilings in the Dining Room, whose walls are hung with graceful swags; in the Drawing Room, where his plasterwork surrounds paintings by 'Athenian' Stuart; in the Van Dyck Room, whose ceiling and frieze he embellished with vines and cornucopias, and in the Gallery where he introduced a chinoiserie theme, complete with ho-ho birds.

The portraits range from mid-17th century down to the present. Those of the 10th Viscount, who was Governor-General of New Zealand, 1957–62, and of his wife by the Australian William Dargie and Edward Halliday respectively are in the Boudoir, which also contains an engaging drawing by Queen Victoria, given to Sarah Lyttelton, a governess of the royal children. Elsewhere on the *piano nobile* are works by Lely (the 3rd Viscount Brouncker, 1620–84), Batoni, Riley, Van Loo, Jervas, Wootton, Reynolds, Ramsay and West. The 17th-century paintings in the Gallery, their stained-pine frames mainly carved by Thomas Johnson, were bequeathed by Lord Brouncker to Sir Charles Lyttelton, Bt. One of the most interesting portraits is that of Admiral Sir Thomas Smith by Richard Wilson, painted in 1740, ten years before the artist's departure for Italy to concentrate on landscapes. Other paintings include an Arcadian scene by Cipriani, *Supper at Emmaus* attributed to Lafosse and a view of Chepstow Castle, 1847, by Barker of Bath, together with many others on the two staircases. A delightful pair of small landscapes by Zuccarelli flanks the Library chimneypiece. The Van Dycks in the Van Dyck Room include a portrait of the 2nd Earl of Carlisle and *Descent from the Cross*; also here is Van Reymerswaele's genre scene *The Misers*.

The superbly preserved tapestries woven at the Soho factory in the 1720s, perhaps to designs by Clermont, were acquired before the room was built, so it was probably designed for them. The giltwood settees and chairs are also covered with tapestry. The elaborate oak overmantel and some of the panelling in the Barrel Room, which was made in 1926 after the fire, came from the earlier Elizabethan manor. An unusual mahogany writing table in the Library has paired console legs at the four corners. There are fine pier-glasses and console tables in the Tapestry Room and the Gallery.

Ham House Richmond, Surrey

The National Trust leased to the Department of the Environment and managed by the Victoria and Albert Museum

Close to the Thames, w of A307 at Petersham

This red-brick mansion, built in 1610 and later enlarged, gloriously reflects the Baroque splendours of the Restoration. It then belonged to the lovely, rapacious Elizabeth, Lady Dysart, and her second husband, the ruthless Duke of Lauderdale, a favourite of Charles II. Lely painted her revealingly in the loveliness of youth and later with the Duke, coarsened by age: these portraits hang in the Gallery above the Great Hall. The property belonged to the descendants of Sir Lyonel Tollemache, 3rd Baronet, her first husband, until given in 1948 to the National Trust.

Most of the late Stuart furniture listed in an inventory drawn up in 1679 can be identified in the house today. The 4th Earl of Dysart, the Duchess of Lauderdale's grandson by her first marriage, added the gilded X-frame chairs and sofas, gilded pier-glasses and the green and red velvet suite of seat furniture on his accession in 1727, but since then time seems magically to have stood still.

There are masterly 17th- and 18th-century portraits, mainly in the Great Hall and the Long Gallery, by Lely, Kneller, Ashfield, Johnson, Wright (Col. John Russell), Vanderbank and Reynolds. Other paintings, many of them inset above doors and fireplaces, include four 'Sea Pieces' by the younger Van de Velde, two views of Naples and a sea port by Wyck in the Queen's Closet, and some fine early miniatures, including works by Hilliard and Oliver. There are ceilings painted by Francis Cleyn and by Verrio or his school. Some walls are hung with tapestries, probably Soho, others with damask (mainly modern copies), while the Marble Dining Room most unusually retains its original gilt-leather wall-hangings. Elsewhere deal was painted in imitation of marble and of the then fashionable walnut.

RIGHT *(below) Dressing commode of inlaid satinwood, 1773, by Thomas Chippendale at Harewood House; (above) Carriera's portrait of Horace Walpole, Houghton Hall.*

ABOVE *Armchair, c.1665, carved with dolphins and with the original silk tissue covering; Ham House.*
RIGHT *Writing cabinet venerred with burr-walnut and ebony, embellished with silver mounts, c.1670; Ham House.*

The furnishings and paintings which were listed in the 1679 and 1683 inventories include a superb writing cabinet or scriptor, veneered with burr-walnut and ebony and embellished with silver mounts, in the Duke's Closet; the furniture in the Green Closet, including 'one ebony table garnished with silver'; and the ornate cabinets, especially that of Japanese lacquer on a fanciful Dutch gilt table, in the Long Gallery. An example from each of the splendid sets of upholstered chairs still covered with the original textiles, including that carved with dolphins, is in the Museum Room together with a display of period costumes and other fabrics. The Lauderdales' wealth is everywhere lavishly revealed in the fine ceiling plasterwork, rich lacquer furniture (especially that in the Ante-Chamber to the Queen's Bedchamber with its silver fire tongs, particularly admired by Horace Walpole, and an outstandingly fine kingwood writing cabinet mounted with silver), the carved and pierced panels of the Great Staircase's balustrade and the K'ang Hsi ceramics.

Hampton Court Palace
Middlesex

The Department of the Environment

On N bank of Thames at Hampton Court

Except for Windsor Castle, Hampton Court is the most spectacular of all royal palaces. The scale and grandeur of the building, set in beautiful gardens, and the richness of its historical associations are matched by its glorious paintings. Its State Rooms contain a large proportion of the royal collection of paintings which, together with those at Windsor and Kensington Palace, form the richest known of all private collections.

This vast Tudor edifice, then larger than any royal dwelling, was started in 1515 by Cardinal Wolsey as his country house, within easy reach of Westminster by barge down the Thames. Wolsey, having overstepped himself, gave it to Henry VIII, who then disgraced him and extended the buildings. The second great building era came with William III who

LEFT *The Spangle Bedroom, Knole; the silk appliqué embroidery dates from c.1610.*

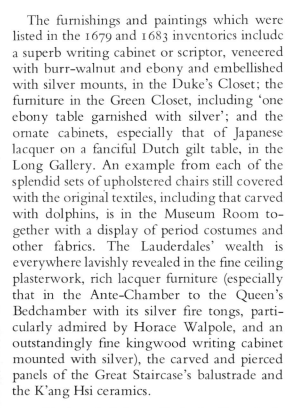

Joos van Cleve's portrait of Henry VIII;
Hampton Court

commissioned Wren to extend the palace; his work is most evident in the State Rooms round Fountains Court, which replaced the earlier structure. Wren was assisted by Talman and Hawksmoor. William III lost interest after the death of his wife, Queen Mary, and the interior decoration was not completed until after the Hanoverian succession. George II was the last monarch to live here.

The State Rooms, which were first opened to the public by Queen Victoria, are reached up the King's Staircase, embellished by the vast allegorical composition painted in its upper walls and ceiling by Verrio, who also decorated the King's State Bedroom and Dressing Room and the Queen's Drawing Room; it is probable that he was assisted by Thornhill who later painted the ceiling of the Queen's Bedroom. The paintings include the lovely little 13th-century Duccio triptych and other early primitives collected by the Prince Consort. Then there are the Venetian masterpieces, some of them acquired by Charles I from the Mantua sale, including Tintoretto's *Nine Muses*, Giorgione's *Shepherd with a Pipe* and

Titian's *Lucretia*. Other Italian painters represented are Lotto, Bassano, Correggio, Andrea del Sarto, Gentile da Fabriano, Feti, and Sebastiano Ricci (especially *Christ in the House of Simon*).

Among the English portraits are Lely's sumptuous 'Windsor Beauties' and Kneller's staider 'Hampton Court Beauties'. Earlier portraitists include Van Dyck, Honthorst and Daniel Mytens, Holbein (*Christ at the Tomb*), Mabuse, Gheeraerts, the younger Lucas Cranach and Pieter Breughel the Elder (*Massacre of the Innocents*). The Wolsey Rooms, off the King's Guard Room with its vast trophies of weapons, contain an unusual anti-Papal allegory by Girolamo Treviso, and Hapsburg portraits by Alonso Sanchez Coello. Philippe de Champaigne's renowned *Cardinal Richelieu* is in the Haunted Gallery.

Hampton Court also possesses fine tapestries. In the Watching Chamber are Flemish tapestries, four of them representing the conflict of the Virtues and Vices, *c*.1500. Brussels 17th-century tapestries woven in 1662 to Gobelins designs by Charles Le Brun hang in the Queen's Gallery. William III's Orangery contains the magnificent cartoons of *The Triumph of Caesar*. Grinling Gibbons carved the oak reredos, designed by Wren, in the lavishly decorated Tudor Chapel. Jean Tijou moulded the beautiful wrought-iron balustrade of the Queen's State Staircase.

The Great Palace is surrounded on three sides by gardens which echo in their purpose and design the changes of taste as clearly as do the different periods of the Palace.

Hanbury Hall
Hereford and Worcester

The National Trust

2½ miles E of Droitwich on B4090

This dignified red-brick country gentleman's residence was built by Thomas Vernon (1654–1721), who amassed over £100,000 as a barrister. His marble bust, probably by Francis Bird, blandly surveys the scene from a niche

RIGHT *The Hall Staircase, decorated with murals in full Baroque style by James Thornhill; Hanbury Hall.*

over the Hall fireplace – with good reason since he was able to commission Thornhill at the height of his fame to decorate the walls and ceiling of the open-well Staircase rising from the Hall. A swirling, Baroque assembly of classical deities crowds the Staircase ceiling, from which Mercury flies down waving a print of the notorious Dr Sacheverell, found guilty of seditious preaching in 1710. The other scenes are taken from the story of Achilles. Two more paintings by Thornhill are on the ceiling of the Long Room. The monochrome *trompe l'œil* on the Hall ceiling is probably by an assistant.

The fine furniture in the Drawing Room includes two long settees and elbow chairs of carved giltwood *c.*1780, and the handsome small Sheraton oval urn table of satinwood and giltwood. The mahogany pie-crust table *c.*1765 and the set of Hepplewhite 'interlaced heart' chairs are part of the Watney collection. The Worcester porcelain includes some fine transfer-printed pieces. Other excellent pieces come from the Merrill Trust.

The Long Room has been furnished to display splendid 18th- and early-19th-century Derby, Chelsea and Bow porcelain figures, Dutch, Flemish and French flower paintings, and fine examples of 18th-century seat furniture, including some by Chippendale, which all form part of the collection generously given by Mr R. S. Watney. Also notable is the delicately carved rococo chimneypiece and overmantel. The remarkable walnut Queen Anne chairs in the Blue Bedroom are on loan from the Lady Lever Art Gallery.

Hardwick Hall Derbyshire

The National Trust

2 miles s of Chesterfield–Mansfield road (A617)

Designed by Robert Smythson for that inveterate builder, the rich and powerful Bess of Hardwick, this great mansion in the Derbyshire hills, perhaps the finest late

Detail of 'Playing Boys' set of tapestries, Hatton Garden workshop, 1679–85; Hardwick Hall.

Elizabethan house in existence, was created in 1591-7. Derogatorily described as 'more glass than wall', it is remarkable for its perpendicular design, its windows which are progressively taller from ground to second floor where the State Rooms are sited, and for its wealth of 16th- and 17th-century tapestries, Elizabethan embroidery and plasterwork. Hardwick was gradually deserted in favour of Chatsworth, the second family home, by Bess's descendants, the Earls, later Dukes, of Devonshire, which meant that the tides of changing fashion rarely reached Hardwick. Bess herself would today recognize many of the items she had so imaginatively acquired and listed in the 1601 inventory.

In the Hall are eight Brussels mid-17th-century tapestries to designs by Jacob Jordaens, but most remarkable of all are the large needlework hangings in early 20th-century frames forming a screen, depicting 'Heroines accompanied by Virtues' on one side with 'The Virtues and their Contraries' on the other, once attributed to Mary Queen of Scots. There are bold plaster strapwork panels at the north end and around Bess's coat of arms over the fireplace; also noteworthy are her great jewel-chest and the Cromwellian armour.

More fine tapestries from Flanders, Brussels, Mortlake and Hatton Garden line the walls of the staircases, landings, the superb High Great Chamber, the stupendous Long Gallery, and most of the other rooms. Needlework, much of it fashioned by Bess and her attendants, is to be seen in the Drawing Room (three framed embroideries, originally cushions), in the High Great Chamber, in the corridor outside the Mary Queen of Scots Room (including pieces from late medieval church vestments), on the North Stairs and especially in the Paved Room, where some of the embroidery is almost certainly the work of Mary Queen of Scots herself, although she had died four years before Hardwick was started. Outstanding is the tester and backcloth of Lapiere's state bed, made for Chatsworth in 1697, but since the last century used to form the central canopy in the Long Gallery. Other embroideries hang from beds and embellish seat furniture, and rare early

Elizabethan embroidered bedcovering on one of the state beds at Hardwick Hall.

carpets are seen covering tables, as was the custom in Bess's day; a magnificent Ushak carpet is on the long table on the half-landing and another Ushak and a Shah Abbas (silk) carpet are on long tables in the two bays of the Long Gallery.

Fine plasterwork is everywhere in evidence: over the door into Bess's private Withdrawing Room, and over the chimneypiece in the Drawing Room; the magnificent plasterwork frieze in the High Great Chamber is very probably the work of Abraham Smith, and still retains some of its original colour. The overmantel in the Paved Room shows Ceres with a cornucopia, and there is a remarkable plasterwork overdoor on the landing of each staircase. Also impressive are the great chimneypieces made of marble with ebony-coloured cartouches, and the alabaster over-mantels of Thomas Accres, especially the bas-relief of Apollo and the Muses in the

The Music Room, Harewood House, designed by Robert Adam, with furniture by Chippendale, plasterwork by Joseph Rose Jr and ceiling paintings by Angelica Kauffmann.

Withdrawing Room and the Marriage of Tobias in the Blue Room. The great array of family portraits from the reign of Queen Elizabeth onwards is concentrated mainly in the Dining Room and in the Long Gallery where they traditionally hang over the tapestries. They include works by and after Mytens, Kneller, Amigoni, Dahl and Wissing together with attributions to Larkin, the elder Bettes and Hoare.

The furniture, except that in the Drawing Room, is mainly of the 16th and 17th centuries. A great set of Jacobean 'farthingale' chairs and stools, en suite with two state chairs, is in the High Great Chamber, which also contains a remarkable large Elizabethan walnut table inlaid with cards, musical instruments and other marquetry designs. The 'sea dog' table, so described in the 1601 inventory, and the elaborate cupboard opposite the chimneypiece c.1570, regarded by many as probably the two finest pieces of Elizabethan furniture to survive in England, are in the State Withdrawing Room together with the excellent Elizabethan square oak table inlaid with playing cards. The Long Gallery contains a late-17th-century set of walnut stools with carved stretchers and red velvet cushions.

Pedestal and urn with ormolu mounts veneered with rosewood and inlaid with satinwood, c.1770, by Thomas Chippendale; Harewood House.

Harewood House West Yorkshire

The Earl of Harewood

8 miles N of Leeds on the Leeds–Harrogate road (A61)

Edwin Lascelles, 1st Baron Harewood, commissioned John Carr of York to design his new house, on which building started in 1759. Soon afterwards he met Robert Adam, recently back from his Grand Tour, and brought him in to co-operate with Carr on the exterior. Adam later became responsible for all the interior decorations. The brilliantly successful results of the Adam-Carr alliance can be seen from the fine collection of topographical watercolours of Harewood House by Girtin, Malton, Turner and Varley in the Princess Royal's Sitting Room. Barry added a third storey in 1843 whereby much of the neo-classical appearance was lost, but except for the Dining Room, which was redesigned by Barry, Adam's interior decorations have remained very largely unchanged.

Harewood was Adam's first great country-house achievement. In carrying out his exquisite interior decoration, he employed the younger Joseph Rose for most of the plasterwork, Biagio Rebecca for the decorative paintings in the Old Library and on the ceiling of the magnificent Gallery and Angelica Kauffmann for the oval paintings incorporated above the pier-glasses in the Gallery as well as the roundels in the ceiling of the Music Room, on whose walls are classical scenes by Zucchi. William Collins, another noted stuccoist, worked with Rose in the Entrance Hall. Adam was responsible for such details as the pattern of the Music Room carpet echoing that of its ceiling. Much of the furniture was made by Chippendale in a character completely sympathetic to Adam's conception; the superb inlaid furniture in the Princess Royal's Sitting Room, the elaborately intricate pelmets in wood, carved to simulate taffeta hangings, in the Gallery together with the mirrors and console tables, the seat furniture and the *torchères*, the Music Room gilt chairs and sofas are all his.

Two members of the Lascelles family at Harewood have been keen collectors. The 1st Viscount Lascelles, son of the 1st Earl, acquired the fine Sèvres porcelain in the China Room, the 17th- and 18th-century Chinese porcelain in the Gallery and the topographical water-colours mentioned above. The 6th Earl (1882–1947), who married HRH The Princess Royal, daughter of King George V, and inherited the property of his great-uncle, the last Marquess of Clanricarde, collected the splendid old master paintings in the Rose Drawing Room and the Green Drawing Room; among them are portraits by Titian, Tintoretto and Veronese, two Madonnas by Giovanni Bellini and a haunting El Greco.

There is a fine representative collection of family portraits from the 18th century onwards, including the work of such masters as Reynolds (especially his Lady Worsley), Gainsborough, Romney, Hoppner, Lawrence, Grant (Henry, the 3rd Earl) down to Munnings and William Nicholson. Winterhalter's Charlotte, Lady Canning, which hangs in the Gallery, was painted for Queen Victoria and given by King George V to the 6th Earl.

Harrington Hall Lincolnshire

Lady Maitland

5 miles E of Horncastle off A158

This delightful pink-brick Carolean manor house, built on a medieval stone base, stands amid gardens associated with Tennyson – they were probably the original of Maud's garden. The medieval house was rebuilt about 1535 and, except for the Elizabethan porch tower, remodelled in 1673 by Vincent Amcotts. The property was acquired in 1950 by Sir John Maitland, then MP for Horncastle.

The Hall with fine panelling of about 1710 contains a court cupboard of 1687 and a fireback of the Three Crowns in an oak tree, commemorating Charles II's escape after the Battle of Worcester. Over the fireplace is an early-19th-century portrait of John Maitland, MP for Chippenham, riding a horse later given by him to the Prince Regent. Here also is a typical scene by Morland.

The Dining Room also boasts 18th-century panelling; its chairs and sideboard, inlaid with the Greek key pattern in ebony, are Regency, as is the corner cupboard with mourning bands. Over the fireplace is a landscape by Vollerdt, dated 1755. Among the family portraits is one of a Jacobite member swearing allegiance to the Young Pretender by David Martin, a disciple of Ramsay.

The panelling in the Drawing Room is late-17th century. Here are several pleasing pieces of furniture, including a William and Mary walnut cabinet, a Dutch marquetry bureau and a Dutch china cabinet, both 18th century, and a Hepplewhite satinwood bookcase, c.1810. David Teniers' *Kitchen Interior* hangs above the fireplace. A landscape by Adriaen Van de Velde is in the Morning Room which contains mid-18th-century mahogany furniture.

There is a good Staircase with a delightful baluster, dating from c.1720, a Carolean fireplace in the Morning Room, discovered behind later additions by Sir John Maitland, and good examples of Dresden and Chinese *famille rose* porcelain. Here also is a good quality mahogany breakfront bookcase and an unusually small Queen Anne gesso table.

Hatfield House Hertfordshire

The Marquess of Salisbury

2 miles E of M1, close to Hatfield railway station

The north front of this glorious red-brick Jacobean mansion shows the power and pride of the great Cecil family, chief ministers to Henry VIII, Elizabeth I and James I, while the south front adds subtlety and grace to its virtues. These qualities are to be found

The 'Ermine' portrait of Queen Elizabeth I, 1585, by Nicholas Hilliard; Hatfield House.

throughout the splendid interior.

In the superb Marble Hall, the Jacobean successor to the medieval Great Hall, the elaborately carved wood screen, the Minstrels' Gallery and much of the panelling are original, as are the refectory tables. The Brussels tapestries are 17th century. The woodwork and plasterwork of the ceiling are also Jacobean and its 1878 paintings and slightly over-elaborate surrounds in no way detract from the Hall's period splendour.

Here and on the fine Italian Renaissance carved oak Staircase are royal and family portraits. Among the former are the famous 'Rainbow' and 'Ermine' portraits of Elizabeth I, the latter by Hilliard; both are a reminder that the Queen spent much of her childhood here and heard the news of her accession in the nearby park. The 'Rainbow' portrait is so called because she carries in her hand a rainbow, symbol of peace; on her sleeve is a serpent, emblem of wisdom. The 'Ermine' portrait shows a live ermine, symbolizing purity and virginity. The family portraitists range from the elder de Critz (1st Earl of Salisbury) to

Derek Hill. There are notable portraits by Dahl, Wissing, Reynolds (the 1st Marchioness), Romney, Lawrence, Richmond and Augustus John, some of them in King James I's Drawing Room, so named because of the life-size statue of that monarch worked by the French sculptor Maximilian Colt in Caen stone over the fireplace; the furniture here, including several fine French pieces, is mainly late-18th century.

The impressive Long Gallery contains a hat, gloves and stockings of the Virgin Queen, a magnificently ornate crystal posset set given to Philip of Spain and Queen Mary on their betrothal, two fine sets of James II chairs covered with Italian silk and several late-17th- and early-18th-century ornate cabinets, including some in lacquer. In the North Gallery is Charles I's cradle and a chair of state with its stool which once belonged to Queen Anne.

In the panelled Winter Dining Room with its impressive chimneypiece is a portrait of Charles I by Mytens and a modish one of George III by Beechey. The Library's neo-classical chimneypiece encloses a portrait of the 1st Earl of Salisbury in mosaic made in Venice and taken from a painting by the elder de Critz: there is also a family group, including the 5th Marquess and Lord David Cecil, by Edward Halliday.

The Chapel, which survived the 1835 fire and whose ground floor was entirely re-modelled between 1869 and 1880, retains its original Flemish stained glass and its original decorations in the Gallery, with portraits of the early saints in the panels under each arch. The fine 'Four Seasons' tapestries in the Armoury were made in 1611 by Ralph Sheldon.

Haughley Park Suffolk

Mr and Mrs A. J. Williams

Off A45, 10 miles E of Bury St Edmunds, 3 miles NW of Stowmarket

This pleasant E-shaped red-brick Jacobean house, standing amid well-kept gardens, was built *c.*1620 by Sir John Sulyard, member of an old Suffolk family. The present owners

The neo-classical Hall by James Wyatt; Heveningham Hall.

acquired the house in 1957, four years before much of it was gutted by fire. The restoration has been well done, especially the Staircase with solid oak treads which is a replica of the original one of 1620. There are several paintings of the 17th-century Dutch school and some interesting furniture.

Heveningham Hall Suffolk

Department of the Environment

4½ miles s w of Halesworth, entrance on Peasenhall–Walpole road

Sir Joshua Vanneck, a member of a prominent Dutch mercantile family in the City of London, purchased the Heveningham estate in 1752, a year after having been made a Baronet. It included a small Queen Anne house which Sir Robert Taylor was commissioned in 1777 by Sir Gerard, the 2nd Baronet, to enlarge into what became, after Ickworth, the grandest mansion in Suffolk. The 3rd Baronet was ennobled in 1796 as Lord Huntingfield and his descendants lived here until 1970 when the estate was sold to the Ministry of Housing and Local Government because of taxation and soaring maintenance costs.

The exterior and the Morning Room interior were completed by 1780 when Taylor was replaced by young James Wyatt, then rising rapidly in reputation, who became responsible for the rest of the interior, including the design of some of the furniture. The Hall is undoubtedly one of the finest neo-classical rooms to survive; the semi-circular vaulted ceiling with its Gothic echoes, the marble floor which reflects the pattern of the ceiling, the specially designed doors and furniture and the use of colour create a completely satisfying harmony. The same masterly and controlled inventiveness applies to the Dining Room, Library, Saloon and the Etruscan Room, which still contain Wyatt's original furniture; the painting of the medallions, roundels and friezes was executed by Biagio Rebecca. The colour in these rooms, as in the Hall, emphasizes the elegant charm of this most civilized period. The Drawing Room alone was not completed by Wyatt.

There are several good portraits on loan from the Vanneck family and other sources, including works by Reynolds, Mercier, Cotes and William Nicholson; these are in the Morning Room, Drawing Room and Passage Room, the only rooms in which pictures were meant to be hung. There are others on the Staircase Hall and in the Smoking Room. Upstairs the Yellow Dressing Room contains various plans by 'Capability' Brown for the park seen from its window, together with a modern restoration plan now in hand.

(Because of possible future changes here, intending visitors should first check that the Hall is open.)

ABOVE *Lucas Cranach's portrait of the Greek scholar Philip Melancthon; Hever Castle.* BELOW *Suit of armour, German, c.1520; Hever Castle.*

Hever Castle Kent

The Lord Astor of Hever

3 miles SE of Edenbridge off B2026

An enchanting small castellated and moated manor house, originating in the 13th century and later the home of Anne Boleyn whom Henry VIII courted here, Hever Castle was acquired in 1903 in dilapidated condition by William Waldorf Astor, who imaginatively restored and redecorated it in Tudor style with 20th-century comfort and convenience. All fragments of the original structure were preserved, and all additions made to the highest standard. Thus the oak panelling in the Drawing Room is inlaid with black bog-oak and holly, copied from the renowned 16th-century room once at Sizergh Castle.

Its vast range of treasures is similar in concept to those of Anglesey Abbey and consists of objects of the finest quality, chosen for their rarity or association. There are Tudor portraits, including Henry VIII, Anne Boleyn and Anne of Cleves, and of French royalty, the latter by François Clouet. Here also are Martin Luther and Philip Melancthon by the elder Cranach.

Other paintings include splendid works by Guardi, Canaletto, Hogarth and Turner.

In the Dining Hall, the owners of the superb suits of armour include Francis I and Henry II of France. In the Long Gallery is more 16th-century armour, both Italian and German, together with the gilt and enamel inlaid helmet of the last Moorish King of Granada. The large 16th-century casket of rock crystal is Venetian, given by Pope Clement VIII to Marie de Medici on the birth of Louis XIII in 1601. Other treasures include a fine collection of crystals, some engraved, ranging from the 15th to the 19th century.

The Council Chamber contains a 16th-century biretta belonging to a Venetian Doge, Italian 16th- and 17th-century ecclesiastical vestments and a 16th-century Flemish alabaster figure of the Madonna. There are collections of ivories in the Morning Room and on the stairs and landing. Anne Boleyn's Prayer Book and a Bible signed by Martin Luther are in Anne Boleyn's Oratory.

Hinchingbrooke House
Cambridgeshire

Hinchingbrooke School

½ mile W of Huntingdon on A604

Once a nunnery, of which much fascinating evidence remains, Hinchingbrooke became the country home successively of the Cromwell family and, until recently, of the Montagu family, Earls of Sandwich. Added to, altered, considerably damaged by fire in 1830, it was partly restored by Edward Blore; his drawings are in the Chapter House Room. A gracious Staircase with fine carved panels incorporated into the balustrade, the newel posts crowned with bowls of fruit, c.1660, was installed in the 1950s from a now demolished house in Essex. Excellent mid-18th-century stained glass by William Peckitt of York is in the Library together with rich oak carving, including a 16th-century fireplace and a 19th-century copy, their overmantels framing portraits of the 1st Earl and his wife. Other Montagu

Carved Staircase, c.1660, at Hinchingbrooke House.

portraits include works by Jonathan Richardson and Robert Buhler, RA. The Dining Room contains a fine oak refectory table (with three modern copies) and a notable carved oak court cupboard, both 17th century.

Since 1962, Hinchingbrooke has been the sixth form centre of Hinchingbrooke School.

Hoghton Tower Lancashire

Sir Bernard de Hoghton, Bt

5 miles E of Preston on A675

The de Hoghton family has lived at Hoghton since the 11th century and goes back even further but the present picturesque mansion, with its two courtyards crowning the hill top, was rebuilt between 1563 and 1565. James I was entertained here with a large retinue in 1617 and knighted 'the Sir Loin of Beef' in the

Banqueting Hall, which contains a good Jacobean table. Neglected from the mid-18th century onwards, the house started to be restored in the 1860s for Sir Henry de Hoghton, 9th Baronet, by Paley and Austin.

There is some good 16th-century panelling, furniture by Gillow, Worcester (Barr, Flight and Barr) porcelain, and a collection of dolls' houses, but sadly most of the family collections have been lost by fire.

Holker Hall Cumbria

Mr Hugh Cavendish

½ mile N of Cark off the Haverthwaite road, 4 miles sw of Grange-over-Sands

The original building of 1604 was later extended, only to suffer a disastrous fire in 1871. The rebuilding of the west wing was carried out handsomely by Paley and Austin for the 7th Duke of Devonshire in Victorian Tudor style. In addition to its paintings and furniture, visitors will be impressed by the spaciousness of the interior and the fine craftsmanship everywhere, especially in the Long Gallery, Staircase and Hall.

The Library with its Derbyshire alabaster fireplaces contains a portrait of James II by Riley, family portraits by Richmond and a fine drawing by Sargent. In the Drawing Room are elegant French 18th-century furniture, a fine Dutch 17th-century inlaid table, a Chinese Chippendale table, Hepplewhite sofas and chairs, a screen with embroidery attributed to Mary Queen of Scots, and a Carrara marble fireplace. Paintings include a tumultuous battle-scene by Salvator Rosa, *Storm at Sea* by Vernet and others by Jacob van Ruisdael, Gaspard Poussin and W. J. Müller.

Wyck's *Old Whitehaven Docks* dominates the Billiards Room, which also contains Reynolds' caricature of four English visitors to Rome, including Sir William Lowther, who then owned Holker.

Family portraits in the Dining Room, with its fine set of Chippendale dining chairs, include works by Hoppner, Reynolds and Jonathan Richardson and a fine self-portrait by Van Dyck. The Wedgwood Dressing Room has a fireplace with blue and white Wedgwood jasper ware, the plaques and frames by Thorvaldsen and a fascinating screen showing scenes of Russia and Russians cut out from newspapers and magazines during the Crimean War by the 7th Duke's children. Two 18th-century Italian *bombé* commodes and two rural landscapes made from Dutch tiles are in the adjoining bedroom, which also contains an attractive 18th-century French *armoire de Dieppe* (cupboard).

Holkham Hall Norfolk

The Viscount Coke

2 miles w of Wells s of A149 from Wells to Hunstanton

Thomas Coke (1697–1759), created 1st Earl of Leicester in 1744, was left an orphan when aged only ten. Inheriting a vast fortune from his Norfolk estates, he set out at fifteen on the Grand Tour, which lasted for six years, accompanied for a time by Kent, and during which he started to amass the libraries, antiquities and paintings which his yet unbuilt mansion was eventually to house. Reclaimed from heathland on which oak and beech trees were planted as early as 1712, the park at Holkham was started in 1720 but the foundations for the Hall were only dug in 1734 and the mansion's completion some thirty years later came after its creator's death. Since then it has suffered no basic change.

Holkham's Palladian design was conceived by Lord Leicester in conjunction with Lord Burlington and Kent, who sketched the plans, adapted from Palladio's Villa Mocenigo, and was built by the elder Matthew Brettingham. The achievement is lavish without ostentation and enormously impressive. Sir Nikolaus Pevsner has written that Holkham 'has the most consistently palatial interior of any mansion in England'.

The first floor is reached by a broad Staircase from the ground-floor level through the

Rubens Return of the Holy Family *(below) in the Saloon, Holkham Hall. This room (left), with its gilded ceiling and walls hung with crimson Genoese velvet, contains furniture designed by William Kent.*

pillared marble Hall whose cold austerity contrasts with the warm magnificence of the State Rooms, especially the Saloon. Their walls, when not hung with subdued velvets or tapestries, are plain ivory and gold as in the North Dining Room and in the Statue Gallery and Tribunes, which contain antique sculptures collected in Italy by Coke and later by the younger Brettingham; the only additional colour is provided by the fine English Axminster carpet in the former room and in the latter by the red furnishings of the armchairs and settees designed, like much of the other furniture, by Kent, who was also responsible for the marble fireplaces and the decorative wall features in the North Dining Room. In addition there is the splendour of the ceilings, elaborate but unfussy, the two pier-glasses by Whittle, the Brussels and Mortlake tapestries, the Genoa velvet wall coverings, the pair of side-tables into which Michael Rys-brack incorporated mosaics from Hadrian's

182

Villa near Tivoli and, above all, the paintings.

The portraits include works by Gerard (Sir Edward Coke, 1552–1634, Lord Chief Justice and founder of the family's fortune), Gainsborough (Coke of Norfolk, who became the 1st Earl of Leicester of the second creation), several by Van Dyck (especially his Duc d'Arenberg) and others by Johnson, Lely, Kneller, Trevisani and Batoni. The Landscape Room contains seven by Claude, three by Nicolas and four by Gaspard Poussin; perhaps Claude's finest painting at Holkham is his *Apollo flaying Marsias* in the Drawing Room. In the North Dressing Room is Bastiano di Sangallo's contemporary copy of Michelangelo's cartoon for one side of the Great Council's Hall, Florence, which was maliciously destroyed, leaving this as the only version in existence. The Saloon is dominated by Rubens' *Return of the Holy Family*. The Italian 17th century is well represented by the works of Reni, Maratta, Giordano and Annibale Carracci.

Honington Hall Warwickshire

Sir John Wiggin, Bt

In Shipston-on-Stour, 10 miles s of Stratford-on-Avon, $\frac{1}{2}$ mile E of A34

This gracious small Caroline mansion of brick with stone dressing stands close to the River Stour in placid rural surroundings. It was acquired by the present owner's family in 1923. Originally Honington Hall was erected c.1680 for Sir Henry Parker, Bt, but the building of the remarkable octagonal Saloon, designed in Burlingtonian character by John Freeman, the re-siting of the Staircase and the addition of the glorious plasterwork, which adds such distinction to the interior, were undertaken by Joseph Townsend who bought the property in the 1730s. The work was carried out c.1750–2 under the supervision of William Jones, although some of the plasterwork may have been of a slightly earlier date. There is probably no other house of this size where the Georgian decoration is so finely wrought.

The Hall, with its white stone flagging and black marble squares, is embellished by elaborately framed plasterwork panels depicting the Arts and Trojan scenes; the Baroque overmantel with the head of Flora in its richly devised frame is verging on the rococo. The ceiling is decorated with arabesques and representations of the Seasons. The Hall Staircase, made of oak with a stylish wrought-iron balustrade, can be seen through one of the highly ornate frames.

The Oak Room is distinguished for the fine bolection moulding of its panelling, for its white-veined, highly carved marble chimney-piece, and for the doorcase leading to the Boudoir, with winged sphinxes in the frieze and *amoretti* disporting themselves on the pediment. The plasterwork on the Boudoir ceiling is perhaps by Thomas Roberts of Oxford or by Charles Stanley; it is at its most exuberant in the octagonal Saloon with its coffered ceiling; each of the eight corners is adorned with a riotous rococo swag enclosing a medallioned portrait. The Saloon doorcases are equally elaborate. In comparison, the Dining Room with panelling and plasterwork of a rather later date is simplicity itself.

Hopetoun House Lothian

The Marquess of Linlithgow

2 miles from the Forth Road Bridge at South Queensferry off A904

Sir William Bruce, the foremost architect of his age north of the Border, was asked in 1696 to draw up plans for a fine new house and magnificent park for the newly married laird, Charles Hope, later 1st Earl of Hopetoun. Work began about 1700 and was completed in four years. Twenty years later William Adam was asked to transform the house into a grand mansion and the result was a building Adam felt to be his masterpiece.

Approached from a long drive close to the glittering waters of the Firth of Forth, Adam's show front is a tall central block surmounted by a balustrade linked to low pavilions by curving colonnades embracing a broad gravelled forecourt. However, the garden front is Bruce's work, and, in contrast, has a graceful dignified Palladian façade. Bruce's beautifully proportioned rooms include the former gilded panelled Entrance Hall, the Earl's Bedroom – later decorated in rococo style – and above all, the central Staircase, also panelled and decorated with carved frieze and borders, which now surround modern landscape murals. This leads up to a suite of wainscoted bedchambers and ante-rooms, containing fine Dutch and English 17th-century furniture and a set of Soho tapestries made for Hopetoun at the Vanderbank factory *c.*1700. The scrolled ironwork balustrade of a secondary staircase of the same date, by a local craftsman, is worthy of particular attention.

The suite of grand state apartments on the ground floor was decorated for the 2nd Earl after 1748 by William Adam's more famous sons, Robert and John, and represents a complete change of taste and style. As an example of their early work, Hopetoun is outstanding. Approached from a cool classical Entrance Hall with stone floor and inset with marble reliefs (part of the great art collection inherited by the 1st Countess from her brother, the Marquess of Annandale), the first room, the Yellow Drawing Room, is in dramatic contrast. Hung with rich yellow damask it has a fine coved ceiling with rococo details picked out in gilt above a deep gilded frieze. The style is robust, almost Kentian. The best of the furniture, including ornate pier-glasses and console tables, is by James Cullen, a little known rival of Chippendale. He was also responsible for the elaborate mirrors and large suite of chairs and settees in the Red Drawing Room, the largest and most impressive of the suite. The wonderful ceiling is one of Adam's most original works in rococo style and includes elements of the fashionable chinoiserie. The large marble fireplace was sculptured by Rysbrack from designs sent from Rome. The 2nd Earl sent Robert Adam to Italy with Lord Hope and his younger brother, later the 3rd Earl, in 1754, a visit which was to have great consequences for English architecture and design. This is commemorated in a portrait

Mid-18th-century pier-glass and console table by James Cullen; Hopetoun House.

painted in Rome by Dance of the two young Hopes and their tutor.

The third room was originally a state bedroom with an elaborate gilt bed designed by Lock and supplied by Cullen in 1768. This was transferred to another room and the bedchamber converted into a dining room about 1820. It is now a fine example of late restrained Regency decoration.

The Hopes were of French origin and thought to have laid the foundations of their fortune as Edinburgh merchants early in the 16th century. They gave loyal service to the crown during the 17th and 18th centuries, and the tradition of public service continued during the 19th and the present century. The 7th Earl and 1st Marquess of Linlithgow was Governor of Victoria and first Governor-General of Australia in 1900 and the 2nd Marquess was

Viceroy of India 1936 to 1943.

There are many family portraits covering 300 years of family occupancy. They range from works by David Allan, who painted the 1st Earl with his grand new house in the background, to the 4th Earl in the uniform of the Royal Company of Archers, the King's bodyguard in Scotland, by Watson Gordon, and ceremonial portraits of the Governor-General and the Viceroy. There is a Ramsay of the 2nd Earl and a large flamboyant portrait of Lord Annandale by Procaccini, a pupil of Maratta. The Annandale collection was mostly sold in the 19th century but was replaced, largely by pictures of the Venetian, Flemish and Dutch schools. These include a group of musician brothers by Passarotti and a contemporary copy of Rembrandt's *Old Woman*, the original of which is in the National Gallery in London. The allegorical scenes painted over doors and fireplaces in the Bruce rooms were painted by Tideman, who was commissioned to produce thirty-seven works in 1703.

Houghton Hall Norfolk

The Marquess of Cholmondeley

13 miles E of King's Lynn, 10 miles w of Fakenham (A148)

This outstanding example of Palladian architecture with its glorious State Rooms, the house encased in pale golden stone, was erected for Sir Robert Walpole, Prime Minister 1721–42, later 1st Earl of Orford. The Hall was designed by Colen Campbell in 1721 and built 1722–35 under Ripley's supervision. The direct line became extinct on the death in 1797 of the writer Horace Walpole, the 4th Earl and the great Prime Minister's youngest son, when the estate passed through the female line to the 4th Earl and 1st Marquess of Cholmondeley, Lord Great Chamberlain of England, an office held by the family in alternate reigns.

Sir Robert Walpole instructed William Kent to decorate the State Rooms and Kent's hand is to be seen everywhere: in the *chiaroscuro* murals on the Great Staircase; in the painted ceilings; in the design of the furniture, especially in the Stone Hall where there are two sets, covered in green velvet, one in walnut and the other in gesso; in the mahogany and gilt chairs and sofas in the Saloon, covered with crimson Utrecht wool velvet, except for one sofa which is in the same Genoa silk velvet as the chairs in the Marble Parlour and the glorious bed in the Green Velvet Bedchamber; and in the various Baroque pier-glasses and marble-topped side-tables, usually of giltwood, and in the painted table in the White Drawing Room. Kent used Artari as stuccador for the Stone Hall ceiling, its central coat of arms on a pale blue background, and Rysbrack for the magnificent

Mortlake tapestries, 1670, woven in gold thread with Stuart portraits in the Tapestry Room, Houghton Hall.

fireplaces and overmantels in the Stone Hall and the Marble Parlour: Sir Robert's bust in the former chamber is also his.

Sir Robert made a magnificent collection of paintings, unhappily sold to the Empress Catherine of Russia by the eccentric 3rd Lord Orford in order to pay off his debts. The paintings in the Cabinet Room were replaced by the magnificent Chinese hand-painted wallpaper. The present paintings are nearly all portraits, including Wootton's sturdy Sir Robert with hounds on the easel in the Stone Hall and others by Kneller, Batoni, Beale, Van Loo, Carriera (pastels of Sir Robert's three sons), Zoffany, Hoppner, Reynolds, Seeman, Jervas (Gulfridus, Sir Robert's brother, surrounded by gilded carving by Gibbons in the Common Parlour) and Sargent (the Dowager Lady Cholmondeley).

Some of the finest furniture was once Sir Philip Sassoon's, brother-in-law of the 5th Marquess, including the magnificent red lacquer bureau and its companion green lacquer Louis xv bureau, signed by Macret and Boudin respectively, the three small Louis xv tables, two with Sèvres tops, in the White Drawing Room, and the Queen Anne lacquer tables in the Cabinet Room. There is a magnificent pair of rococo chinoiserie mirrors in the Cabinet Room and two Louis xiv Boulle marriage chests with bronze mounts in the Saloon where stands a large musical clock originally made for the Turkish market; it plays a different tune for each day of the week. The two thrones from designs by Pugin in the Tapestry Dressing Room came from the Palace of Westminster.

Among other notable treasures are the great bronze copy of Le Sueur's Greek Gladiator on the Great Staircase; the bronze 18th-century copy by Girardon of the Laocoön group belonging to the Vatican, in the Stone Hall, which also contains a bust of a Greek prince whose head is antique but the body 18th century; the Chinese armorial plates in the Marble Parlour, and in the Saloon the Sèvres vases, decorated with seascapes after Morin, which stand on a small Sèvres tray which was once owned by Horace Walpole.

The House of the Binns Lothian

The National Trust for Scotland

3½ miles E of Linlithgow on A904 Queensferry road

There is written evidence dating from 1335 of the 'land of the Bynnes' and of a house there before 1478. In 1599 James, Lord Lindsey of the Byres, sold the property to Sir William Livingstone, who in turn sold it to Thomas Dalzell, a cadet of the ancient family of Dalzell of Dalzell, later Earls of Carnwath. These high-sounding names are somewhat at odds with the existing modest 17th-century house with 19th-century Gothic castellations that sits protected from the bitter east winds by the slopes of twin hills named the Binns. But the Dalzells were never far away from national events from the 16th century to the present day and one member of the family, General Tam, who served three monarchs during a remarkable career in the 17th century, has stamped the house with the mark of his personality. (The family name is pronounced Dee-yell.)

The first Thomas Dalzell was one of the 'hungerie Scots' to accompany James VI to London on the king's accession to the English throne. He made his fortune in the south and returned to Scotland to enlarge and redecorate his newly acquired property. Thomas's splendidly ornate plasterwork, possibly the work of Italian craftsmen or of Scottish workmen trained by the Italians, remains in the four principal rooms. The King's Room, prepared as a state bedroom, has a deeply moulded frieze of fruit, a medallion of heroes' heads, a heavy central pendant and the Royal Coat of Arms. The High Hall ceiling has geometrical patterns, heraldic devices and the royal arms over the fireplace dated 1630.

General Tam was the second Thomas of the Binns. Always a staunch king's man, he signed the petition of the nobles opposing Charles I's attempts to introduce the Prayer Book to Scotland, but refused to act against the Crown. He saw service in Ireland and when Charles was executed in 1649 he swore never to cut his hair or beard until a king be restored. A half-length portrait at the Binns attests the truth of the story. He fought at Worcester and joined Charles II in exile after escaping from the Tower of London. He then went to Russia and became a general and Russian nobleman. He returned at the Restoration and was made commander-in-chief of the King's forces in Scotland. Charged with suppressing the Covenanters, his enemies called him 'the Bloodie Muscouvite' but he could also be merciful.

His relics are to be found throughout the house from the tall riding boots hanging over the Dining Room fireplace, his spurs, trunk, silver camp spoon and huge comb, his great two-handed 14th-century ceremonial longsword bearing the Passau mark, to his Bible, one of the earliest printed in Scotland, the New Testament in 1611 and the Old Testament in 1613. There is some good Regency furniture and early-19th-century family portraits.

Hughenden Manor
Buckinghamshire

The National Trust

1½ miles N of High Wycombe on the w side of A4128

Benjamin Disraeli acquired the Hughenden estate in the wooded Chilterns in 1848, shortly before becoming leader of the Conservative Party. His beloved wife refashioned the unpretentious late-18th-century mansion in the Victorian Tudor Gothic style. The charm of this heavy red-brick house stems from the almost tangible atmosphere left by the great statesman.

In the Hall and Staircase hang portraits of Victorian statesmen and others in what he called his 'Gallery of Friendship'. Family portraits have pride of place in the Gothic Drawing Room, with others in the Disraeli Room and the heavy, sombre Dining Room.

Tam Dalzell's Bible, printed in 1613, at the House of the Binns.

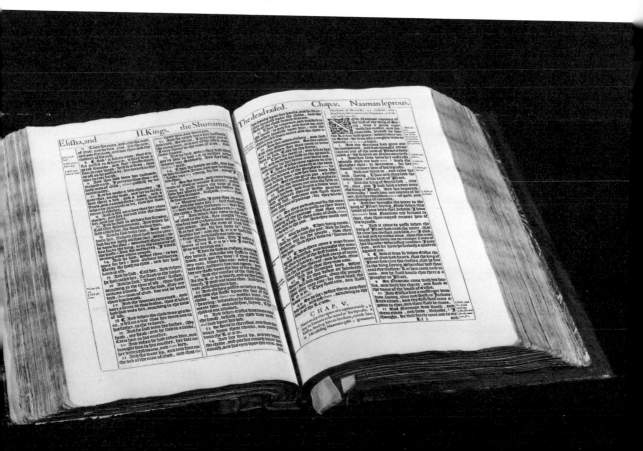

Francis Grant's portrait of Benjamin Disraeli, 1852, at Hughenden Manor.

The other rooms, including the Politicians' Room, the Berlin Congress Room, the Royal Room, his Library and Study, bear witness to his personal and political associations and achievements during his brilliant career.

Hutton-in-the-Forest Cumbria

The Lord and Lady Inglewood

6 miles NW of Penrith on B5305 Wigton road

This mansion consists of a startling number of building styles, reflecting its long history which stretches back to the late-13th century. The oldest part is the 14th-century pele tower, raised by the de Hutton family when homes near the Scottish Border were inevitably also fortresses. This tower is linked by a late-17th-century Baroque centrepiece by Edward Addison, a local architect, to a second, sandstone tower designed by Anthony Salvin early in his career in the 1820s. He was recalled half a century later to modernize the house,

when further additions were made. The Long Gallery, the upper storey of the 1640s wing thrusting out from the pele tower, was much restored at this time.

A progress through the house is equally a journey through the centuries. After the Entrance Hall in the 14th-century tower with its armoury and mantrap comes the late-17th-century Cupid Staircase. Installed by the energetic Sir George Fletcher (d. 1700) whose daughter and heiress brought Hutton to the Vane family of County Durham, its carved wooden panels depict boisterous cupids tumbling amid acanthus foliage. Appropriately, the large Mortlake tapestry at the head of the stairs has more cupids at play, one of the 'Playing Boys' series. The Long Gallery contains family portraits, late Stuart furniture, and blue and white Chinese porcelain and Delftware.

Salvin's influence is strong in the Library and in the 1871 Drawing Room, kept just as it was in Victorian times with a clutter of *objets d'art*, china cabinets, artificial flowers under glass domes and furniture of various styles. Some of the Dining Room furniture is by Gillow and the portraits are mainly of the Vane family. The wallpapers in this room and in 'Lady Darlington's' 18th-century bedroom are by William Morris.

Ickworth Suffolk

The National Trust

3 miles SW of Bury St Edmunds on W side of A143

This grandiose, most unusual house, although Palladian in principle, consists of a central oval building surmounted by a dome joined to two large rectangular pavilions by curving wings. It was started in 1795 to plans probably commissioned in Rome by Frederick Augustus Hervey, 4th Earl of Bristol and Bishop of Derry (1730–1803) who succeeded in 1779 to the title and an annual income totalling about £40,000, half of which came from his bishopric.

The mitred Earl planned to use the two wing corridors and pavilions for displaying the

William Hogarth The Holland House Group, *c.1637; Ickworth.*

magnificent Hervey collections of paintings, furniture, silver and sculpture to which he intended to add the treasures which he had amassed mainly in Italy during his peregrinations through Europe; unhappily the last were seized in Rome by the invading French in 1798. When the Earl died five years later, his son, the 5th Earl and later 1st Marquess, considered demolishing this highly impractical building, but he eventually completed it in 1829, making the east pavilion the family residence. The Rotunda was used for guests and entertaining and the corridors and central Hall for exhibition purposes; the west pavilion was never completed internally.

In the Hall and Staircase well, dominated by Flaxman's large group, the *Fury of Athamas*, are family portraits, including Van Loo's *John,*

Lord Hervey, 1741, whose bust by Bouchardon stands close by, Kauffmann's likeness of the Earl-Bishop over the chimneypiece and full-length portraits by Seeman of the 1st Earl and his second wife.

The Dining Room, decorated and furnished by the 1st Marquess between 1824 and 1829 with good quality mainly contemporary furniture, is hung with more family portraits, including works by Hoppner, Lawrence and Grant; the pair of mid-18th-century gilt rococo pier-glasses and tables are Italian, perhaps purchased by the 2nd Earl in Turin where he went as Ambassador in 1755. The dining table holds part of the outstanding collection of Hervey silver. The rococo candelabra bearing George II's arms are by Simon le Sage and two of the soup tureens with the 2nd Earl's arms by Kandler. Robert Cooper fashioned the great Baroque wine cistern in 1680.

The Library and Drawing Room contain a remarkable collection of paintings. There are more family portraits, including Hogarth's famous *Holland House Group*, and a conversation piece portraying the 3rd Earl with some of his family by Gravelot to which Hayman probably contributed additional figures, but the outstanding canvas is Velazquez's portrait of the Infante Balthasar Carlos, son of Philip IV of Spain. Gainsborough painted both the naval 3rd Earl, known as 'Casanova' Hervey because of amorous exploits revealed in his outspoken diaries, and the eldest son of the 4th Earl, while the 4th Earl-Bishop is portrayed in Naples by Madame Vigée Lebrun.

There are important pieces of French furniture, including a marquetry *bureau de dame* stamped by Pierre Roussel and a small marquetry upright *secrétaire* stamped by Pierre Migeon. Both rooms have a magnificent pair of Portuguese rococo 'trumos' or combined pier-tables and glasses. In addition there are busts by Nollekens, glorious Sèvres and Meissen porcelain and fine chandeliers.

Much of the Ickworth silver, mainly collected by the 1st and 2nd Earls and displayed in the West Corridor, is outstanding with

Marquetry bureau de dame, c.1760, by Pierre Roussel; Ickworth.

Rococo silver soup tureen by Fredericke Kandler, 1752; Ickworth.

many early-18th-century pieces by refugee Huguenot makers such as Paul Crespin, Paul de Lamerie, Pierre Harache, Simon Pantin, Pierre Platel and Philip Rollos, and further rococo examples by Frederick Kandler and Simon le Sage. Other treasures include the 18th-century Chinese export service, the State Room chimneypieces, lacquered furniture, J. D. Crace's Pompeian Room (completed in 1879), fine Doccia porcelain, dress swords and outstanding miniatures and fans.

Ightham Mote Kent

Mr C. H. Robinson

Ivy Hatch, 6 miles E of Sevenoaks, off A25 and A227

Waters run down into the north-west of the hollow in which this romantic mainly medieval mansion lies, to fill the moat and finally drain into a tributary of the Medway. Extensively remodelled early in the 16th

One of the grotesque figure corbels which support the 14th-century roof in the Great Hall, Ightham Mote.

century, this splendid house, built round a courtyard, has been lived in for 600 years.

The fascinating Great Hall was built in the Decorated style in the 14th century, but the oak panelling was designed by Norman Shaw in about 1872. The stained glass in the five-light Perpendicular window in the west wall contains fine early-16th-century stained glass. The open timbered roof is carried by carved corbels which represent grotesque figures whose expressions testify to the weight of their burden.

There are fine examples of carved wood on the double doors of the Crypt, on the Jacobean Staircase with its newel post representing a Saracen's head and in the splendid Renaissance overmantel and frieze, also carved with Saracens' heads, in the Drawing Room, whose walls are hung with 18th-century hand-painted Chinese wallpaper.

The Tudor Chapel is notable for its ceiling. The ribs of the wooden barrel-vault are painted with chevrons in the Tudor livery colours of green and white with intervening panels, some with royal badges and others with lozenges of green and white. Although the colouring is somewhat faded, the ceiling as a whole still resembles the rich decorations of the temporary galleries and pavilions set up for court festivities in the 16th century.

Ingatestone Hall Essex

The Lord Petre and Essex County Council

½ mile SE of Ingatestone off B1002

After the surrender of Barking Abbey in 1539, the manor of Ingatestone became the property of the Petre family of Devon origin. William Petre, who built the Hall, served three Tudor monarchs as Secretary of State; his son was ennobled in 1603.

After a long absence the family returned here after World War I and restored the Hall. Its north wing is now occupied by the Essex Record Office for exhibition purposes while the Tudor Long Gallery, also open to the public, contains some excellent furniture, including two marquetry commodes, a 16th-century virginal, 18th-century Chinese armorial wares and family portraits by Romney, Raeburn and Casali.

Inveraray Castle Strathclyde

The Duke of Argyll

On Loch Fyne ½ mile NE of Inveraray

MacCailein Mor, Chief of the Clan Campbell, is the oldest and proudest of all the honours, titles and hereditary offices held by the family, Earls, Marquesses and Dukes of Argyll. The long history of the clan, one of the largest and most powerful in Scottish history, is traditionally traced back to the 11th century. Inveraray Castle has been the seat of the family since 1474 when the 1st Earl moved from the ancient stronghold at Loch Awe. In the 17th century the 1st Marquess, Montrose's adversary and a staunch Covenanter, was executed after the Restoration of Charles II. His son

The Armoury Hall, Inveraray Castle.

suffered a similar fate but his grandson was a vigorous supporter of William of Orange and was created Duke of Argyll in 1701. The 3rd Duke inherited in 1743 and at once set about building a new castle in Inveraray. His idea was based on a Vanbrugh design drawn as early as 1720; Roger Morris, who had already worked for the Duke in Kent, was called in to realize his concept. His remarkable building, the marriage of a late Elizabethan layout with Gothic details, is one of the earliest 18th-century buildings in this style. Work began in 1744 only to be interrupted by the '45 Jacobite rising. It was renewed in 1746 and the house was finished in 1768. The plan included demolishing an earlier 15th-century castle, removing the middle of the old town of Inveraray and re-siting it in its present position round the harbour and finally transforming the surrounding land into a landscaped park. The Augustan orderliness of the trim little town presided over by the Castle set on the banks of a remote sea loch must have seemed as exotic in the mid-18th century as the townships of New England or Virginia across the Atlantic.

By 1773, when the 'grandeur and elegance of this princely seat' impressed Dr Johnson, the Castle was occupied, but the 5th Duke who succeeded in 1750 altered and redecorated much of the interior of the Castle during the next twenty years, and completed the rebuilding of Inveraray town. His architect was Robert Mylne, member of a dynasty of master masons particularly associated with Holyrood, who altered the internal arrangements and redecorated the principal rooms. Despite a serious fire in 1877 (after which Salvin made some further alterations to turrets and roof line) and a second conflagration in 1975, Inveraray Castle is substantially unchanged today.

Mylne's designs are in brilliant contrast to the Gothic exterior. Delicately classical in the current French style, they include a new Dining Room contrived out of part of the original Long Gallery. The ceiling was cast in London by John Papworth, the cornice and frieze are by John Clayton. The wall painting was done by two Frenchmen, Girard and Guingard, whose work only survives at Inveraray Castle. They had been employed at Carlton House and the work is of the highest quality. Some seat furniture, in French style, was made in the Castle by Edinburgh cabinet-makers and the gilding was also done *in situ* by Dupasquier who was also responsible for work in the Tapestry Drawing Room. This room is hung with Beauvais tapestries of the *Pastorales* set after Huet designs, ordered by the Duke in Paris and completed in 1787. It is thought to be the only set still in the room for which it was commissioned. The overdoors were appropriately painted by Girard, his colleague having died at Inveraray. *Confidantes* and *fauteuils* were supplied by Linnell about 1775. Inveraray is remarkable for the quantity of French and French-style 18th-century gilded chairs, covered with contemporary tapestry.

It is notable too for the many family portraits ranging in date from the rare portrait of three young Campbell brothers, by Adam de Colone, signed and dated 1624, to a delightful equestrian portrait of George Campbell, afterwards 8th Duke of Argyll, as a small boy painted by J. F. Herring in 1827. There is the 1st Duke and his sons by Medina, the 2nd and the 3rd Duke by Allan Ramsay, the 5th Duke and his brother-in-law, Field-Marshal Seymour Conway, by Gainsborough. The children of the 5th Duke are depicted in four sensitive portraits by Opie. Their mother, the celebrated Irish beauty Elizabeth Gunning, was the widow of the Duke of Hamilton before her marriage to the 5th Duke, and was not only twice a duchess but the mother of four dukes. Her eldest son who became Duke of Hamilton is seen in a full-length portrait by Batoni, and the Duchess herself is depicted in a gentle pastel by the Scottish pastel-painter and miniaturist Catherine Read. Captain Lord William Campbell RN, Governor successively of Nova Scotia and South Carolina, was painted by Cotes.

The Castle has royal associations. Queen Victoria's fourth daughter, Princess Louise, married the Marquess of Lorne, later 9th Duke of Argyll, in 1871. The Victorian Room contains many reminders of her time, notably her portrait after Winterhalter and a maple-wood writing desk given as a wedding present by the Queen. The Princess was an accomplished sculptor.

A feature not to be overlooked is the magnificent display of arms arranged in decorative patterns in the Armoury Hall, which soars to nearly 100 feet.

Kedleston Hall Derbyshire

The Viscount Scarsdale

4½ miles NW of Derby on Derby–Hulland road via Derby ring road to Queensway

The approach through the park to the formal Palladian north façade of Derbyshire's finest Georgian mansion little prepares the visitor for Robert Adam's superb interior and the glorious south front created *c*.1759–65. Sir Nathaniel Curzon, 1st Baron Scarsdale, a

learned patron of the arts, was not content with Smith of Warwick's Queen Anne residence which he inherited. The elder Brettingham provided the overall plan *c*.1758, was succeeded briefly by Paine, and then in turn replaced by Robert Adam, who had recently returned from Italy imbued with the principles and details of Roman architecture seen both in Rome and at Spalato, the site of the Emperor Diocletian's palace.

The impact of the stupendous Marble Hall is overwhelming. Adam designed it, supported by twenty great fluted Corinthian columns and pilasters of Nottingham alabaster, as a Roman *atrium* and the adjoining circular Saloon as the *vestibulum*. George Richardson, formerly one of Adam's draughtsmen, designed the plasterwork on the ceiling, which was executed by Joseph Rose Jr; Richardson may also have been responsible for the overmantels, one of which contains a painting after Gravelot and the other one after

The Marble Hall designed by Robert Adam as a Roman atrium; Kedleston Hall.

Domenichino. The plasterwork in the other rooms on the *piano nobile* is also by Rose. Adam himself designed the sarcophagus benches and perhaps the superb griffin grates and fire-irons. The panels in *chiaroscuro*, possibly by William Hamilton, depict scenes from the ancient world.

The magnificence of the Hall is echoed in the Saloon rotunda, whose framed paintings of ruins are also by Hamilton, the *chiaroscuro* panels depicting English historical scenes by Rebecca and the plasterwork by Rose. There are highly unusual cast-iron stoves in the shape of classical altars in the alcoves while the furniture reflects the influence of Adam.

Kedleston contains splendid paintings. In the Music Room is a version of Bassano's *Moses Striking the Rock*, works by Giordano (*The Triumph of Bacchus*), a Guercino, three seascapes by Van Diest and a view of Naples by Occhiali. Here also is an impressive and exceptionally rare set of 18th-century rosewood armchairs, their backs with a pierced radial design. The organ case is by Adam. Ivory chairs, supposedly owned by Tipoo Sahib of Mysore, and two early-17th-century Flemish tapestries are in the Tapestry Corridor.

Fine Dutch and Italian paintings, including works by Cuyp (*Landscape in the Rhine Valley*), de Momper (*Naaman's Journey*), Veronese and Reni, embellish the State Drawing Room. Spang made the classical styled marble chimneypiece. Linnell was responsible for the card tables and the splendid merfolk ornate settees, made partly to Adam's design. The great silver cistern was made from caskets presented to Lord Curzon of Kedleston when Viceroy of India, 1898–1905.

The Library, its bookcases by Adam, contains Van Dyck's *Sir Peter Rycaut* and more Dutch and Italian paintings by Lotto, Koninck and Salvator Rosa. Royal and family portraits by Van Dyck, Miereveldt, Lely, Johnson, Kneller, Hone and Reinagle dominate the State Boudoir; particularly impressive is the splendid looking-glass decorated with a palm motif, as are the State Bed and other furniture in the adjoining State Bedroom which, together with the Dressing Room, is enriched by further

Merfolk supporting the arm of one of the 18th-century settees at Kedleston Hall.

distinguished family portraits by the elder Jonathan Richardson, Lely, Honthorst, Reynolds, Soldi, Hoppner and Kauffmann.

The gracious State Dining Room, its ceiling enriched with paintings by Zucchi, displays paintings set into the walls by Claude, Romanelli, Schiavone, Snyders and Zuccarelli. 'Athenian' Stuart's classical ormolu tripod stands here. In the semi-domed apse at one end are fine curved tables and an impressive wine cooler of Sicilian jasper. In the Portrait Corridor are portraits of Lord Curzon and his first wife in vice-regal robes, early Derby porcelain and a model of Nelson's flagship, *Victory*. An unusual feature of Kedleston is the imaginative use of Derbyshire blue-john in some of the chimneypieces.

Kellie Castle Fife

The National Trust for Scotland

3 miles NNW of Pittenweem off A921

The original baronial keep of Kellie was probably a simple tower dating from about the 14th century. Its history is traceable as far back as the 11th century when it was the principal seat of the great Saxon family of Siward, Earl of Northumbria, who served King Malcolm I. In 1360 the Siward heiress Helen resigned the lands to a cousin, Sir Walter Oliphant, whose descendant sold the estate in 1613 to Thomas Erskine, afterwards 1st Earl of Kellie. In 1834 the title and the property passed to the 9th Earl of Mar. Forty years later the house stood empty and decaying, the contents sold at 'a muckle roup'. It was rescued by an Edinburgh professor, the father of Robert Lorimer the architect. In 1948 his son Hew bought the Castle and continued, with his wife, the work of restoring and refurbishing Kellie Castle. The house and its enchanting walled garden bear

17th-century plasterwork showing the Erskine and Dalzell coat of arms; Kellie Castle.

witness to the Lorimers' success. In 1950 it was acquired by the National Trust for Scotland.

Although the history of the demesne of Kellie is so long, no trace of the Siwards has survived, and little of the Oliphants and Erskines, save for the arms and initials of members of these families who contributed to the building of the Castle and the magnificent 17th-century interior plasterwork. It is the decoration of the four principal chambers that gives distinction to Kellie. The Great Hall is fifty feet long with long sash windows on the south side illuminating the room with the pale bright light associated with the North Sea coast. There are two pilastered fireplaces and a decorated plaster ceiling 'of noble simplicity' with heraldic panels bearing fruit and laurel wreaths which dates from 1660. The walls have discreet late-17th- or early-18th-century panelling. The smaller Withdrawing Room next door, now the Dining Room, is decorated with striking and unusual panelling of the Restoration period, all painted with romantic idyllic landscape scenes. A fine 16th-century Flemish tapestry *Europa and the Bull* covers one wall of the room that also contains a good French provincial pearwood *armoire, c.*1680, a fine gate-leg table and a carved wood figure of St Christopher of the same period. On the floor above, the Principal Bedroom has a deeply coved plaster ceiling of an elaborate ornate design of vine boughs, leaves and grapes. The central ceiling painting of Mount Olympus is by De Wett who was employed at the same time by Sir William Bruce at Holyroodhouse on both portrait and decorative ceiling paintings. The adjacent Earl's Room has another deep-coved decorated plaster ceiling with a central heraldic panel displaying the arms of the 4th Earl of Kellie and his wife.

Kensington Palace London

The Department of the Environment

Kensington Gardens, London

William III and Mary II, his Queen, acquired Nottingham House, an early Jacobean mansion, as a country retreat in 1689, changed its name to Kensington House and instructed Wren, assisted by Hawksmoor, to improve it. Queen Anne, George I, who commissioned Kent to decorate much of the interior, and George II all used this magnificent palace but George III preferred to live at Buckingham House. The Duke of Kent was allocated apartments here, and it was here that his daughter, Princess Victoria, was awakened in 1837 with the news of her accession to the throne. For long unused, except intermittently as a museum, the State Apartments were refurnished in 1956 with important paintings and furniture from the royal collection and opened to the public.

Entry is up the Queen's Staircase and into Queen Mary's Gallery which shows Wren's sober restraint; the plainness of the oak panelling and white ceiling of the Gallery is relieved only by the rich cornice and the carved and gilded mirrors over the door heads. The superb surrounds of the mirrors over the fireplaces were carved by Grinling Gibbons in 1691. The distinguished portraits include Kneller's *Peter the Great*, Hannemann's *William, Prince of Orange*, and those of William III and Queen Mary II by Wissing.

In Queen Mary's Closet, the most important picture is the flower-piece by Daniel Seghers. It also contains Kneller's portrait of Queen Anne and her son, the Duke of Gloucester, and her husband, Prince George of Denmark, by Dahl. In Queen Mary's Dining Room is the fine Allori of Judith with the head of Holofernes, small Dutch and Flemish pictures and 17th- and 18th-century Chinese porcelain. Her Drawing Room has a more elaborately carved cornice, a pastoral landscape by the younger Teniers, a flower-piece by Bogdani and an important portrait of Robert Boyle by J. Kerseboom. The hangings of the state bed in Queen Mary's Bedroom are original.

The Privy Chamber contains fine Mortlake tapestries, *c.*1623 and a series of busts of scientists and philosophers, while in the Presence Chamber are Rysbrack's notable terracotta busts of George II and Queen Caroline as well as a gloriously elaborate

Wind-dial, 1694, by Robert Morden above the mantelpiece in the King's Gallery, Kensington Palace.

Kentwell Hall

overmantel probably carved by Gibbons. The ceilings of both rooms, commissioned by George I, are by Kent; the latter ceiling shows the earliest known use of arabesque patterns in the Pompeian manner and is a forerunner of Robert Adam's style. Beyond them is the King's Staircase; Kent painted the lower walls with trophies and masks and the upper walls with spectators looking out from under arches, a vigorous if not an entirely successful achievement. The Staircase is embellished with an excellent wrought-iron balustrade by Tijou.

The King's Gallery, its ceiling depicting scenes from the *Odyssey* by Kent, contains 17th-century Flemish, Spanish and Italian pictures, the most important being Rubens' glorious *Jupiter and Antiope*, Van Dyck's outstanding *Cupid and Psyche* and a large *Boar Hunt* by Snyders at his best. A wind-dial, 1694, by Robert Morden serves as overmantel.

John Martin's splendid *Eve of the Deluge* dominates the Duchess of Kent's Dressing Room. Some of Queen Victoria's toys are in the Ante-room, while her adjoining bedroom contains typical mid-Victorian genre paintings. Kent's most successful ceiling is probably that in the King's Drawing Room; its splendid chimneypiece was carved by James Richards in 1724 and an elaborate clock, with paintings by Amigoni, silver bas-reliefs by Rysbrack and surmounted by the bronze figure of Atlas by Roubiliac, occupies its centre. The Council Chamber is hung with pictures of the Great Exhibition of 1851 and dominated by an Indian ivory throne. The Roman style Cupola Room, the work of Kent, has a ceiling reminiscent of Chiswick House and a fine bas-relief by Rysbrack above the fireplace.

Kentwell Hall Suffolk

Mr J. Patrick Phillips

On A134 at N end of Long Melford

This red-brick Tudor mansion, probably built in the 1550s, belonged to the Clopton family, who settled here towards the end of the 14th century. The main Staircase is late-17th

century and the Great Hall chimneypiece *c.*1720. Thomas Hopper, who also worked at nearby Melford Hall, was responsible for rebuilding the central block after a serious fire in 1827, which he did in Elizabethan style. The design and decoration of the Great Hall, complete with Minstrels' Gallery, and the main Dining Room, both of which rise through one and a half floors, thus encroaching on the original Long Gallery, are entirely his. Their dark brown panelling is in fact plaster; its sombre effect in the Dining Room will be alleviated when the paint on the walls above the wainscoting has been completely stripped to reveal Hopper's patterned wall design. There are several pieces of fine oak furniture, both period and 19th-century imitation.

The present owner acquired Kentwell in 1971 when the mansion was in very poor condition. Since then he has valiantly put in hand a steady programme of restoration.

Kenwood London

The Greater London Council

Between Hampstead Heath and Highgate

Kenwood was acquired from the 3rd Earl of Bute by the 1st Earl of Mansfield in 1754. Ten years later he called in Robert Adam whose neo-classical Library is one of his finest achievements; 'for sheer simplicity of construction and refinement of decoration,' James Lees-Milne has written, 'Robert Adam never surpassed his efforts in this room.' Especially noteworthy are the painted panels by Antonio Zucchi amid the arabesques by Joseph Rose Jr.

Kenwood's present glory is the Iveagh Bequest, the renowned collection of paintings, mainly English, Dutch and Flemish, made by the 1st Earl of Iveagh. Perhaps the three outstanding masterpieces are Rembrandt's *Self-Portrait*, Vermeer's *The Guitar Player* and Frans Hals' *Pieter van den Broecke*. The English paintings include fine examples by Gainsborough, including *Mary, Countess Howe* and his pastoral *Going to Market*; by Reynolds, especially *Lady Mary Leslie, Mrs Musters as*

The neo-classical Library by Robert Adam at Kenwood.

Hebe, Lady Chambers, and the paintings of children such as *The Infant Academy* and the portraits of the Brummell children. Van Dyck is worthily represented by *Henrietta of Lorraine*; Raeburn by *Sir George Sinclair as a Boy* and Romney by, among several, *Anne, Countess of Albemarle and Her Son*. There is a splendid view of Dordrecht by Cuyp, good examples of Guardi and Boucher, a fine portrait by Lawrence of Miss Murray, works by Angelica Kauffmann, an early Turner, *Fishermen on a Lee Shore*, and works by Morland and Hoppner.

There is excellent 18th-century English furniture at Kenwood, including two neo-classical side-tables, *c.1795*, in the Dining Room; fine matching carved and gilded chairs, in which motifs derived from Stuart and Revett's *Antiquities of Athens*, 1762, have been incorporated, in the Library; a carved mahogany pedestal, *c.1795–9*, in the Vestibule; two commodes in the Old Tea Room with harewood veneer, inlaid with vases, flowers, etc., *c.1775*; a fine overmantel mirror with carved giltwood frame, *c.1775*, in the Music Room; and John Sandforth's remarkable late-18th-century mahogany long-case clock in the Lobby.

On view on the first floor during the winter months are Lady Maufe's collection of 18th-century shoe buckles and part of Mrs John Hull Grundy's collection of 18th- and 19th-century jewellery; in the summer exhibitions are held of the work of 18th-century English painters.

Jan Vermeer The Guitar Player, *c.1671 (above), and Thomas Gainsborough* Mary Countess of Howe, *c.1765 (below); Kenwood.*

Kew Palace London

The Department of the Environment

Close to s bank of the Thames, Kew

Kew Palace, or the Dutch House, by far the smallest of the royal palaces, was built in 1631 for a Flemish merchant. It became the favourite home of George III and Queen Charlotte when their family was young. The King remained at Windsor after 1804 but the Queen continued to use Kew on occasion and died here in 1818. The Palace contains portraits of the royal pair

The Breakfast Room, Kew Palace; Bogdani's painting of a flight of ducks is early-18th century.

by Zoffany and of their Continental kinsfolk, including that of Christian VII of Denmark by Nathaniel Dance. There are entertaining paintings of a dinner and a tea-party by Marcellus Laroon, an early-18th-century flight of ducks by Jakob Bogdani and an agreeable rustic view of cattle at a fountain by Berchem. The period furniture is sparse but good. Noteworthy is the Queen's bamboo four-poster bed, topped by palm fronds. The Pages' Waiting Room contains an intriguing regal miscellany with miniature and needlework portraits, scent bottles, buttons and alphabetical ivory counters. There is a fine model of a Palladian country palace by Kent.

Killerton House Devonshire

The National Trust

7 miles NE of Exeter on w side of
Exeter–Cullompton road (B3181; formerly A38)

Sir Richard Acland, 15th Baronet, whose portrait by Bernard Dunstan hangs in the Library, gave Killerton House, renowned for its glorious gardens, to the National Trust in 1944 together with over 6,000 acres. Built *c*.1775, the house was much altered in 1900.

Besides the family portraits there are two notable collections. In the Corridor between the Music Room and the Drawing Room is a splendid assembly of drawings of the members of Grillion's Club, a London dining-club of which the 10th Baronet was a founder member in 1812 and to which many distinguished personalities have belonged. The earlier drawings were by Joseph Slater (d. 1847) and the rest by George Richmond.

The second is the remarkable Paulise de Bush Collection of Costume, formed between 1940 and 1970 and exhibited on the first floor. The garments displayed are for the period from 1750 onwards.

The chamber organ in the Music Room was built in 1807 by William Gray. Above the chimneypiece hangs a portrait of Hannah More by H. W. Pickersgill commissioned by the 10th Baronet, a great admirer of her work. There is also an impressive mahogany china cabinet in this room, containing examples of Flight and Barr Worcester porcelain, Chamberlain Worcester, Derby, Spode and Sèvres porcelain. In the Drawing Room is W. H. Funk's formidable portrait of Gertrude, wife of the 12th Baronet, facing that of her husband by Herkomer. A larger than life portrait of the 10th Baronet by Owen hangs on the Staircase.

Knebworth House Hertfordshire

The Hon. David Lytton Cobbold

1 mile s of Stevenage; road access from A1 (M) at Stevenage

Knebworth was acquired in 1490 by Sir Robert Lytton, a favourite of Henry VII; wealthy and powerful, he converted the medieval structure into a quadrangular Tudor brick mansion, which stood until 1811, when Mrs Bulwer demolished all but one wing. She encased this side, containing the Banqueting Hall, in stucco; her son, Edward Bulwer-Lytton, who became renowned as a novelist and was created 1st Baron Lytton, further embellished the house in High Victorian Gothic. His son Robert became Viceroy of India and 1st Earl of Lytton.

Sir Edwin Lutyens, a son-in-law of the 1st Earl, redesigned much of the interior and gardens in the early-20th century. The present Entrance Hall is his work; here there is a set of high-backed early-18th-century chairs. The romantic Banqueting Hall contains an early Jacobean screen with Gallery above at one end, while the pedimented pine panelling and overmantel, c.1660, reflect Inigo Jones' influence; the early-19th-century dining chairs are of applewood. Here and in the White Drawing Room, which was also designed by Lutyens, are family portraits by Gheeraerts, Lely and Riley; particularly noteworthy are the portraits of Sir Philip Sidney by John de Critz and of Sir Rowland Lytton by an unknown hand. In the White Drawing Room are two early-18th-century Italian tortoiseshell and ivory cabinets and a third, veneered in tortoiseshell and inset with ivory and ormolu, from Flanders. The Lutyens Library contains, in addition to the literary collection of Bulwer-Lytton, a sketch by G. F. Watts of the 1st Earl, a Chinese *ting* (a tripod bronze ritual vessel), c.500 BC, and several cabinets of memorabilia.

Crace, collaborating closely with Bulwer-Lytton, designed the elaborate Staircase and the glorious Victorian Gothic State Drawing Room, with Gothic furniture, some also by Crace, in which hangs Maclise's genre painting of Edward IV visiting Caxton's printing press; his portrait of the novelist is in the Ante-room. Nearby, in Bulwer-Lytton's Study, is a portrait of him by E. M. Ward.

The Falkland Room is hung with excellent 18th-century Chinese hand-painted wallpaper. The Queen Elizabeth room, very much Tudor in character, contains 16th- and 17th-century paintings, including an amusing example of 17th-century propaganda showing nun, monk and baby.

Knightshayes Court Devon

The National Trust

2 miles N of Tiverton

Knightshayes Court, best known for its remarkable garden which was created as recently as 1950, was built, 1869–79, for John Heathcoat-Amory, MP, later created a baronet;

he was the grandson of John Heathcoat of Derbyshire, a progressive lace-maker who successfully moved his thriving business from the Midlands, where his mill had been destroyed by Luddites in 1815, to Tiverton. In 1973 on the death of the 3rd Baronet, the property together with most of its contents was generously made over to the Trust.

Burges was the original architect. He completed the building and started on the interior decoration, 1869–74, but was then sacked for his dilatoriness and replaced by J. G. Crace, who had largely completed the task by 1882. Much of his work was later painted over by the 1st Baronet's wife, although some has since been uncovered and restored by the Trust.

The spacious, well-balanced Hall, which faces north, contains full-length portraits of the 1st and 2nd Baronets. A set of early-18th-century Dutch marquetry chairs stands against the walls. Here and in the stairwell are corbel figures of men and beasts designed by Burges; on the end wall is a notable design for a panel of ceramic tiles by William de Morgan. A cast of Epstein's *Deirdre* stands on the table. The newel posts on the Staircase are carved in the shape of talbots, the hound of the Amory family crest.

The spacious ground-floor reception rooms, facing south, contain some good furniture together with a small collection of paintings. The walnut dining chairs, made in Wales before 1850, are a Gothic adaptation of their 18th-century predecessors. On the ceiling,. Crace's painted design has been restored. There is a collection of 17th-century Italian maiolica and a handsome brass chandelier in the Morning Room. The Library mahogany chairs with pierced splats are George II; there is a delightful *Madonna and Child with St James and St Sebastian* by Matteo di Giovanni above the chimneypiece and close by a version of Sebastiano Ricci's *Christ Healing the Lame Man at the Pool at Bethesda*.

The Drawing Room paintings include Rubens' fine *Stormy Landscape*, c.1630, two rare flower-pieces by Constable, a version of Claude's *Apollo and the Cumaean Sibyl* and a sketch attributed to Turner, *The 'Sun of Venice'*

The 'Sun of Venice' going to Sea, *attributed to Turner; Knightshayes Court.*

going to Sea. There are good examples of English and French mid-18th-century furniture and of green Dr Wall Worcester porcelain.

At the foot of the Back Stairs is a small portrait of Lady Amory, the widow of the 3rd Baronet, who still lives here, and under it a case of medals she won as Miss Joyce Wethered, holder of the Ladies' Open Golf Championship title four times between 1920 and 1928.

Knole Kent

The National Trust

At Tonbridge end of Sevenoaks, off A21

This vast grey mansion of Kentish ragstone in its spreading park is one of the most important and probably the largest country house in Britain. Reminiscent of a very grand Oxford college with its seven paved or grassed

Parcel-gilt toilet set, c.1673; Knole.

quadrangles and supposedly countless rooms, Knole grew from the 13th to the 18th century; there is little of a later date. Owned successively by Archbishops of Canterbury and Tudor monarchs, Knole was given by Elizabeth I to her cousin Thomas Sackville, 1st Earl of Dorset, poet and statesman, whose descendants still live here.

Knole's 17th-century furniture with its original covers, much of it of royal provenance from Whitehall and Hampton Court, is unique. It was acquired by the 6th Earl of Dorset who, as Lord Chamberlain to William III, was entitled to remove for his own use outmoded royal furniture. King James II's huge carved and gilded bed with its rich green velvet hangings and his gilt furniture, attributed to Thomas Roberts, in the Venetian Ambassador's Room, is superb. Another magnificent bed, also made for James II when Duke of York, its hangings woven with thread of silver and gold with faded coral silk lining, probably made in France, is in the King's Bedroom, which also contains Knole's renowned silver furniture. There are two remarkable suites of Jacobean furniture, covered in the original, now much faded, crimson velvet in the Leicester Gallery, their frames gessoed and decorated with red and gold arabesque patterns; here also is the 'Knole settee', *c.*1610, once probably a chair of state set up beneath a canopy. The seat furniture in the Brown Gallery, including the X-framed armchairs, is also 17th century.

The black and silver high-backed chairs in Lady Betty Germain's Rooms date from the reign of William III; Louis XIV probably presented to the 6th Earl the important set of French 17th-century furniture which stands at the end of the Cartoon Gallery. This consists of a richly carved gilt table, its ebony top inlaid with brass and pewter, and two candle-stands *en suite*, their stems carved in the shape of *putti*. The set is attributed to the royal designer and *ébéniste* Pierre Golle.

There are fine examples of tapestry and needlework, notably the late-16th- and early-17th-century Flemish tapestries in the Venetian Ambassador's Bedroom, showing scenes from

Orlando Furioso by Franz Spierincx. The silk *appliqué* embroidery in a strapwork pattern which covers the bed and the seat furniture in the Spangle Bedroom is also exceptionally rare, dating from about 1610.

The Reynolds Room, hung with 18th-century crimson woollen velvet, contains splendid portraits, including ten by or attributed to Reynolds, mainly of contemporary personalities such as Dr Johnson, Oliver Goldsmith and David Garrick. Other distinguished portraits at Knole include works by Gainsborough, Hoppner and Romney; perhaps the most impressive are the full-length portraits of the 3rd Earl of Dorset and his wife, now attributed to Larkin. Van Dyck, Dobson, Kneller and Jervas are also well represented.

Other notable features include the fireplace probably by Cornelius Cuer and the plaster-work ceiling and frieze by Richard Dungan, 1605–7, in the vast Ballroom, which is hung with Sackville portraits and contains Sèvres porcelain given by Napoleon to the 3rd Duchess of Dorset; the late-16th-century Persian carpet in the Reynolds Room; the Charles I billiard table, a great rarity, in the Old Billiard Room; and the nude plaster figure of the 3rd Duke's mistress at the foot of the Great Staircase.

Marble-topped octagonal stone table, c.1550, at Lacock Abbey.

Lacock Abbey Wiltshire

The National Trust

In Lacock village, 3 miles N of Melksham, 3 miles s of Chippenham E of A350

Originally a nunnery, erected close to the gentle Avon, Lacock Abbey was acquired on its dissolution in 1539 by William Sharington, a profiteer whose crest significantly was the scorpion. He cleverly adapted the buildings into a private house without destroying its character; the cloisters and surrounding rooms are still intact. His niece married into the Talbot family with whom Lacock remained until it passed to the National Trust in 1944 together with the village.

The most impressive room, the Hall, was built in the graceful rococo Gothic manner, 1754–5, for John Ivory Talbot by Sanderson Miller. The dramatic terracotta figures, standing in niches under Gothic canopies, were executed by the Austrian, V. A. Sederbach, c.1756, whose 'performances' were said to be 'easy and not expensive'. The shallow tunnel-vaulted ceiling is emblazoned with the arms of Talbot's friends; on its completion, Talbot gave them 'a grand sacrifice to Bacchus'. Here are four Gothic tables of yew, twelve mahogany hall chairs, and in the fireplace, handsome brass andirons, c.1680.

Two grotesque medieval carvings, one of stone and the other of wood, are in the Brown Gallery. Family portraits in the Stone Gallery include two by Dahl; here also is a fine Gothic marble-topped table and a set of early-17th-century English chairs with carved scalloped backs, later repainted. The delicately carved stone chimneypiece was probably the work, *c.*1550, of John Chapman, the stonemason, who it is thought also made the remarkable stone table, now standing in Sharington's Tower, its marble top supported by four satyrs holding buckets of fruit.

In the Blue Parlour are more family portraits, two by Kneller and one by Gainsborough, another by Seeman, and 18th-century English and Oriental lacquer furniture; there is also a cabinet, probably Italian, on a Charles II stand, carved and originally gilded. More family portraits are in the South Gallery. The Dining Room with classical frieze and pedimented doorcases possesses a fine rococo table and mirror and Cornelis van Haarlem's allegorical painting *Peace and the Arts.*

Lacock was the home of W. H. Fox Talbot, a prominent pioneer of photography whose achievements are recorded in the fascinating recently created museum in Lacock village.

Lamb House, Rye, East Sussex

The National Trust

In West Street

Lamb House stands in cobbled West Street and has changed little since it was built in 1722. Its unpretentious good taste and the indication of a quiet garden behind its adjoining wall are characteristics widely found in buildings of this period. Its associations, however, are exceptional. George I was snowed up here for three days, after being blown ashore nearby in 1726. From 1898 until he was compelled by ill-health to return to London in 1914, it was the home of the novelist, Henry James. A. C. Benson, Master of Magdalene College, Cambridge, and his brother, E. F. Benson the novelist, were subsequently tenants, as was more recently H. Montgomery Hyde, the biographer. Only the Hall with its elegant staircase and two ground-floor rooms are shown: a portrait of George I hangs in one but it is the personality of Henry James, mementos of whom are displayed, which pervades the house.

Lamport Hall Northamptonshire

Lamport Hall Preservation Trust Ltd

8 miles N of Northampton on A508

John Isham, a successful London merchant, and his brother, members of an ancient Northamptonshire family probably of Saxon origin, acquired the Lamport estate in 1560 and proceeded to re-build the manor house there. John's shrewd personality, caught by an unknown painter, dominates the Entrance Hall, where he is seen hand on skull, remembering one of the family mottoes that 'In Things Transitory Resteth no Glory'; other portraitists here and in the Vestibule include Van Miereveldt and Lely.

Sir Justinian Isham commissioned John Webb in 1654 to build what is now the central block of the south-west front, over which the family motto is repeated, but the wings on either side and the attractive Library were added by Francis Smith of Warwick in 1732, later well furnished in the Regency manner. Francis' son, William Smith, later added the south wing.

The splendid Library collection includes the 1638 Bible which once belonged to Charles I. The busts over the 1819 bookcases represent English men of letters. Over the fireplace hangs the portrait of the 6th Isham Baronet as a boy; the other likeness is of Sir Thomas, the 3rd Baronet, painted in Rome while on the Grand Tour in 1677 by Maratta; he commissioned the large scale *Venus and the Death of Adonis* by Ludovico Gimignani now in the Summer Drawing Room. The latter chamber contains family portraits by Lely, Gaspars and Bokshoorn, both of whom worked in Lely's *atelier,* and Kneller; there is a fine Kentian console table and an early Worcester dessert service.

The magnificent Music Room, originally designed as an entrance hall by John Webb, rises the full height of the house; the delightful plasterwork ceiling and frieze of 1740 were made to designs by William Smith and echo the Isham swan motif on Webb's impressive chimneypiece carved by Cibber. The yellow marble *tazza* was acquired in 1678. There are

Chinese early-17th-century hardwood (hua-li) cupboard; Langton Hall.

more family portraits by Hudson and Archer Shee, together with a bust of the 5th Baronet by Scheemakers, but the most impressive works are Van Dyck's equestrian painting of Charles I, one of several versions, and of Anne of Denmark, James I's queen, by Paul Van Somer, a version of which is also in the royal collection. Other noteworthy paintings include Van Dyck's *Christ and St John as Infants* and an *Adoration of the Shepherds* by Reni. A fine Chinese 18th-century armorial service is displayed in the China Passage, while in the Cabinet Room are two impressive Venetian cabinets and a Florentine altar table with a *pietre dure* design.

Langton Hall Leicestershire

Mr G. R. Spencer

In West Langton, 4½ miles N of Market Harborough

Langton Hall is built on a long-inhabited site: it is mentioned in Domesday Book and Roman remains have been found nearby. The house, a harmonious jumble of styles mainly of the 16th to 18th centuries, stands in gardens amid

ancient timber and is surrounded by glorious country.

The lower half of the large stone-flagged Entrance Hall is panelled with home-grown cedar. The paintings include a version of *Judith Holding the Head of Holofernes*, after Allori. There is a good 17th-century Flemish tapestry and some chairs of the French Louis Philippe period, but the pieces of outstanding interest are the Chinese early-17th-century hardwood (*hua-li* or *huang-hua-li*) cupboards and altar tables. Other Oriental items include a Japanese bow with arrows and two Chinese pictures, carved from cork. The Drawing Room walls are remarkable for being covered with Venetian lace.

Lanhydrock House Cornwall

The National Trust

2½ miles SE of Bodmin

The Lanhydrock estate, acquired in 1620 by Sir Richard Robartes, a Truro merchant and banker, created 1st Baron Robartes in 1624, remained in the Robartes family until the 7th Viscount Clifden gave it to the National Trust

Detail, showing Adam and Eve, of the plasterwork ceiling in the Gallery, Lanhydrock House.

Chinese porcelain. On its walls are portraits by Arthur Devis and Romney.

The Gallery in the north wing which was spared from fire is Lanhydrock's most remarkable feature, especially the original plasterwork of the barrel-vaulted ceiling, whose twenty-four panels illustrate Old Testament incidents from the Creation to the Burial of Isaac. The bookshelves, which replaced much of the 17th-century panelling in the Victorian era, contain an unusually good collection of 17th-century books.

A fine portrait of the 1st Baron, resplendent in his Stuart court costume, hangs on the Oak Staircase. George Richmond's portraits of the 1st Lord and Lady Robartes, 1844, are in the Inner Hall.

in 1953. The house, built 1630–40, underwent various changes but a disastrous fire in 1881 destroyed all but the north wing. It was rebuilt by Richard Coad, and the pleasure of visiting Lanhydrock is to see this late Victorian restoration of a largely Jacobean house in which solid comfort was the architect's first priority. William Morris wallpapers embellish many of the rooms.

The Steward's Room is hung with plans and views of the house at various stages and the Corner Room contains souvenirs of this century's four coronations. The Morning Room possesses 17th-century tapestries; one is Flemish and the other, of a merrymaking party, possibly from Mortlake. Here also is a beechwood writing table, *c.*1710, overlaid with brass and tortoiseshell in the Boulle manner. The spacious well-proportioned Drawing Room, furnished with pieces from Wimpole Hall, which once belonged to the Robartes family, contains a long, low, elegant English suite of two pairs of settees, *c.*1720, on carved walnut legs with lion's paw feet, two mid-18th-century Dutch marquetry serpentine fronted chests, English carved giltwood side-tables, *c.*1730, and an intriguing 17th-century Italian cabinet of ebonized wood, veneered in tortoiseshell and decorated with gilt brass, urns and candelabra of blue-john Derbyshire spar. There is also good 17th- and 18th-century

Lauriston Castle Edinburgh

The City of Edinburgh Council

$4\frac{1}{2}$ miles NW of the city, off the A90 Cramond and Queensferry road

Three periods of Scottish architectural styles separated by 400 years are represented at Lauriston. A late-16th-century tower house (built by Sir Archibald Napier, father of the inventor of logarithms) was enlarged by William Burn, the Edinburgh architect, in 1827. He added a rectangular structure in what was then described as English Jacobean style, but which is now immediately recognizable as 19th-century Scottish. This was extended in 1872. Burn's agreeable and incoherent addition looks out over the Firth of Forth to the Fife coast. Lauriston's distinction lies in the interior, decorated and furnished between 1903 and 1919 by the last owner of the house, William Robert Reid, whose widow left the house and contents to the City of Edinburgh in 1926. He was the owner of a successful firm of Edinburgh cabinet-makers which specialized in fitting out railway Pullman cars. Mrs Reid was the daughter of the founder of an equally successful firm of sanitary engineers, who installed the magnificent plumbing, heating and lighting.

Good craftsmanship was the quality most admired and sought after by the Reids – artistic criteria came second – and the results of their adherence to these standards can be seen throughout the home. There is an immense amount of furniture, mostly of the 18th century, both English and Continental, often standing in juxtaposition to reproductions of these styles made by Morison and Co., the firm owned and managed by William Reid. Commodes abound – English, French and Italian, *bombé*, veneered, inlaid – in every room from the Library to the Bathrooms. There are Chippendale chairs, a late-18th-century architect's desk, an Adam-style side-table, a Spanish inlaid cabinet *c.*1800, gilt and marble

Spanish inlaid cabinet, c.1800;
Lauriston Castle.

topped tables, Régence and Regency pieces, George II gilt mirrors, Louis XVI *secrétaires* and *bureaux à plat* and two Matthias Lock design giltwood mirrors. A fine breakfront bookcase houses the greater part of the Reids' comprehensive collection of blue-john Derbyshire fluorspar. There are a great number of clocks, including one by Ellicot.

Although furniture was the Reids' major passion, their collecting interests were wide-ranging. Lauriston contains a small but notable collection of casts from intaglios by James Tassie (1735–99) of Glasgow and a number of curious wool mosaics manufactured for about twenty years by a single Yorkshire firm *c.*1850. The Dining Room contains 17th-century tapestries, one signed by Reydams dating from *c.*1650. The visual arts evidently held less appeal for William Reid but he had a liking for prints and engravings, mainly of the 18th century, the skill of the engraver being of more consideration than that of the artist.

Leeds Castle Kent

Leeds Castle Foundation

6 miles SE of Maidstone on B2163 Leeds–Sutton Valence road

The origins of this romantically sited Castle, built on two islands surrounded by the still waters of a mere, stretch back to the 12th century; it has been much altered over the years. The impressive stone interior of one building is from the early-19th century; the gloriette, or inner castle, was built at various times from the 13th to the 16th centuries. The walls are embellished with 16th- and 17th-century Brussels and Flemish tapestries, although a very rare late-15th-century Flemish tapestry hangs in Henry VIII's Banqueting Hall, together with a magnificent carpet made in India, probably by Persian craftsmen. The fine quality furniture, mainly 16th- and 17th-century, is of oak. In the Queen's Bedroom is a splendid early-16th-century triptych of the Virgin and Child from St Catherine's Church, Cologne, by the Master of the St Ursula

Egyptian bronze cat, c.600 BC (left) and Eugene Boudin Beach Scene (right); Leeds Castle.

Legend, and another by Niccolo di Pietro Gerini is in the King's Private Chapel together with four bas-relief panels of the Annunciation and Birth of the Holy Child.

By contrast, scenes from Parisian life by Constantin Guys line the landing approach to the comfortable modern Conference Room, embellished with a fine collection of works by 19th-century French artists including Boudin, Lepine, Fantin-Latour, Degas (pastel of a dancer), Toulouse-Lautrec, C. Pissarro and Rousseau, gravely surveyed by an Egyptian bronze cat (a mummy-case), c.600 BC. The Yellow Drawing Room with finely carved pedimented doorcase contains two flower paintings by Monnoyer and an 18th-century French mirror in a bronze frame. The pine panelling of the Thorpe Hall Room was designed by Webb c.1660; here hangs a painting by Jean-François Millet.

Leighton Hall Lancashire

Mrs and Mrs R. J. G. Reynolds

2 miles w of A6 through Yealand Conyers village

The white limestone house, rebuilt in 1760–3 in mid-Georgian style after a fire in 1715 had destroyed the medieval house, was given a graceful 'Gothic' façade between 1800 and 1810. Richard Gillow, the distinguished

Lancaster furniture maker, whose descendants live here, acquired the property in 1826 from a cousin. It stands at the foot of a great winding drive with the distant Lakeland mountains forming an enchanting background. The Entrance Hall, embellished with a Gothic Revival screen beyond which rises an elegant curved stone staircase, contains an unusual eight-winged table by Gillow and a fine Louis xv bracket clock by Blakey of Paris.

18th-century games table by Gillow at Leighton Hall.

The Dining Room is furnished with early examples of furniture made by Richard Gillow, whose portrait hangs here, together with that of Mrs J. R. Reynolds, the owner's mother, by Edward Seago; a further Seago study is in the Music Room. Gillow is again represented in the pleasant Victorian Drawing Room by a fine 18th-century games table. The paintings include two Venetian views by Guardi, two scenes by Morland, a landscape by J. B. Pyne and a Jordaens of a flautist with companions.

There is interesting Victorian furniture in the agreeably proportioned bedrooms.

Leith Hall Grampian

The National Trust for Scotland

1 mile w of Kennethmont on B9002

The scenery of the upper reaches of the wide Garioch strath 'is not entitled to be called striking, but is generally pleasing', wrote a correspondent in 1854. It has changed little since then and the description applies equally well to the modest unpretentious house. It was begun in 1649 by James Leith of Aberdeen, whose family had moved there some 200 years before. The simple rectangular 17th-century house was enlarged at intervals until by the late 19th century it had reached its present proportions, enclosing a rectangular courtyard. There are a few concessions to passing fashions; Venetian and sash windows relieve the simple façades, topped by corbelled corner turrets.

Family fortunes waxed and waned: Jacobite sympathies, successive minorities, an unexpected legacy. The lairds followed well-established practice after the depressed and unsettled condition of the first half of the 18th century by becoming notable soldiers or sailors and it is their mark that gives the house its flavour. Military paintings predominate; they include a large battle scene of the Siege of San Sebastian in 1813 when General James Leith-Hay and his nephew Andrew, laird 1838–62, distinguished themselves, and a copy of the *Thin Red Line*, the most famous picture of the battle of Balaclava in 1857, in which Sir Andrew's son, Alexander Sebastian, took part. There are delightful contemporary watercolours depicting army life with the 93rd Regiment, later the Argyll and Sutherland Highlanders. Pictures by Orlando Norie vividly depict the siege and relief of Lucknow by the 93rd the following year. The era of the Indian Mutiny is also recalled by some of the personal jewellery of the last King of Oudh, including the walking stick of his queen, which contains a tiny phial of poison in the ferrule. North America is strikingly represented by the costume of a Red Indian chief presented to Alexander Sebastian before he left Canada in 1848 after ten years' service. Perhaps the most interesting of the military relics is a large powder horn, dated 1759 and bearing the name of Lt John Leith of the Royal Highland Regiment, which is engraved with maps of the Hudson and Mohawk valleys showing the forts between New York and Lake Ontario, and recalls the English and French struggles for the control of North America.

Among the otherwise undistinguished family portraits, three stand out: a study of Sir Andrew by Hayter for a composite picture of the House of Commons, painted in 1833, and two paintings of him and his wife by Northcote. The furniture at Leith Hall fits its setting, restrained and simple, and includes an unusual set of elm dining-room chairs, an early-19th-century Scottish sideboard and a pair of elegant late-18th-century cutlery urns.

Levens Hall Cumbria

Mr O. R. Bagot

5 miles s of Kendal on Milnthorpe road (A6)

Grey-stone Levens Hall is largely Elizabethan, enclosing a much older structure, with late-17th-century additions. The Great Hall and the two Drawing Rooms are panelled, the latter also embellished with splendid oak-carved chimneypieces, one dated 1595. The overmantel of the Dining Room, in which is a fine

Limoges enamel crucifix, 13th century;
Levens Hall.

Marquess of Wellesley and the Emperor Alexander of Russia, a 13th-century Limoges enamel cross, a fine French clock with ormolu embellishments, some good Dutch marquetry furniture, two mirrors, a delightful *Woman Sewing* by Sickert and several scenes by Diaz, a member of the Barbizon School.

On the Staircase is a painting by Hondecoeter and a cabinet containing 17th- and 18th-century glasses. The Library pictures include a child portrait by Cuyp, a portrait by Owen of Sir Charles Bagot and an enjoyable flower painting by Bosschaert. The bedrooms contain early patchwork made of Indian chintz, Gillow furniture and some small watercolour scenes by de Wint.

There is also a wide-ranging collection of steam engines, illustrating the development of industrial steam power from 1820 to 1920.

Lindisfarne Castle
Northumberland

The National Trust

On Holy Island or Lindisfarne, 5 miles E of Beal across the sands

set of Charles II cane-backed chairs, is also carved and its walls embossed with Spanish leather. All four rooms have ribbed plaster-work ceilings, interspersed with decorative devices and pendants, and filled with an agreeable miscellany of *objets d'art*.

The Great Hall contains a charming Mother and Child by the Florentine Bicci di Lorenzo, *c.*1430, Cromwellian armour, model ships, and a William and Mary long-case clock. In the Drawing Room is a copy by Rubens of a painting of Anne of Hungary, family portraits by or attributed to Lely and Hudson, together with scenes by Constable and J. S. Cotman. Here is an enchanting little Charles II side-table with double spiral turned legs, a water-gilt mirror of the same period, four excellent William and Mary *torchères* and a harpsichord by Shudi, 1773.

In the Small Dining Room's show-case are displayed miniatures of, among others, the

Lindisfarne, a tiny island on the wind-swept Northumbrian coast which is connected to the mainland by a causeway only at low tide, was a great centre of Christianity. St Aidan and St Cuthbert lived here in the 7th century and the ruins of an 11th-century Benedictine abbey can still be seen. The Castle, originally a fort and subsequently a coast-guard station, is perched dramatically on an outcrop of rock and was converted with great skill and imagination into a country house by the architect Sir Edwin Lutyens in 1902–7. His personality is everywhere – in the herringbone pattern of the brickwork floors; in the model of the Dutch three-masted ship which hangs from the ceiling in the Ship Room, now the comfortable Sitting Room; in the specially designed door-catches throughout the Castle; and in the placing of the map of Holy Island above the Entrance Hall fireplace which is connected to a weather vane on the roof and used as a wind indicator.

Some of the furniture is to Lutyens' design, including the dresser and refectory table in the Kitchen and the oval oak Dining Room table. Other notable pieces are the Charles II walnut chairs, the painted Dutch china cabinet and the Flemish walnut writing table, both 17th-century, in the Ship Room; the Flemish four-poster beds in the Long and East Bedrooms; the Queen Anne walnut tallboy in the Long Gallery and the fine oak chest-of-drawers, *c.*1660, inlaid with mother-of-pearl and ivory, in the Upper Gallery.

Littlecote Wiltshire

Mr D. S. Wills

3 miles w of Hungerford, just off A4 at Froxfield

This large and impressive early red-brick Tudor manor house, *c.*1490–1520, close to the sedate River Kennet, contains two particularly unusual features. The first is the restrained Cromwellian chapel, thought to be the only complete example in existence, in which the altar is replaced by a high oak pulpit; it contains a notable set of early-17th-century needlework panels. The second is the Dutch Parlour, whose walls are covered with paintings, many of merry-making scenes, traditionally attributed to Dutch prisoners-of-war held here during the wars of Charles II. The early-18th-century painted ceiling depicts Justice and Fame attended by cupids, supporting the Popham arms and commemorating Sir John Popham, Lord Chief Justice, who acquired Littlecote in 1589; his portrait is in the Great Hall. The Popham family held Littlecote until 1922, when the property was acquired by the late Sir Ernest Salter Wills, Bt, whose descendants live here.

In the spacious Great Hall stands a thirty-foot long shovel-board table, believed to be the longest in existence, 'turn' chairs, one made for a child, and an oak finger stock for prisoners. Above the panelling is a view of Littlecote by Wyck and an equestrian portrait by an unknown hand of Colonel Alexander Popham – his buff coat, breast plate and sword, together

with the buff coats worn by his Cromwellian garrison and trophies of their weapons, including cavalry pistols, are also on display.

The Drawing Room, formed in the mid-18th century and altered again in 1810, contains good Chippendale furniture in the Chinese style, complemented by hand-painted Chinese wallpaper and richly carved mahogany doors. There are fine gilt mirrors and *torchères* and an excellent Aubusson carpet with the coat of arms of Louis XV. Another Aubusson carpet which once belonged to Queen Charlotte, wife of George III, is in the Library, also formed in 1810; the oak shelves are curved to the room's design. The satinwood furniture is Sheraton. The furniture in the Brick Hall is oak of the 16th and 17th centuries; the portrait of Charles,

Finger stocks supposedly used on prisoners by Judge Popham, who acquired Littlecote in 1589.

Duc de Bourbon is by Sebastiano Piombo.

A large late-17th-century Brussels tapestry with William III's coat of arms as King of England hangs in the William of Orange Bedroom with a late-16th-century oak four-poster bed; the portrait of Lord Cobham, Lord Chamberlain to Elizabeth I, is attributed to Moro.

There are superb needlework hangings in the Haunted Bedroom and a fascinating needlework panel of the Roman pavement found in Littlecote Park in 1728, which has recently been rediscovered. There is a fine display of Dr Wall Worcester porcelain in the adjoining corridor.

The handsome oak-panelled Long Gallery contains Popham family portraits, including one by Dahl, two fine Antwerp cabinets inlaid with tortoiseshell, collections of paperweights and cow cream jugs, fine crystal chandeliers, a Queen Anne needlework carpet before the fireplace and Chippendale armchairs covered with needlework of similar design.

18th-century needlework panel of the Roman mosaic pavement found in Littlecote Park.

Little Moreton Hall Cheshire

The National Trust

4 miles sw of Congleton off A34

Little Moreton Hall was described by the late Robin Fedden as 'the most picturesque half-timbered house in the country'. As the interior is largely empty, it is possible to admire to the full the ingenuity of Tudor and Elizabethan craftsmanship in the excellent carpentry, plasterwork, glazing and painting. Started about 1480 as an H-shaped house consisting of two wings on either side of a Great Hall, which still stands, it was added to in 1559 and again after John Moreton succeeded in 1563, so that by 1580 Little Moreton Hall looked much as it does today. The Moreton family were first established here in the 13th century; the last member of the family died in 1912 when the property passed to a cousin, Charles Thomas Abraham, later Bishop of Derby, who, together with his son, offered this remarkable black and white house to the Trust in 1937.

A handsome oak refectory table, an octagonal table and a low 'Cubborde of boxes', the last two items mentioned in the 1601 inventory, stand in the Great Hall. The pewter in the show-case includes an early-17th-century salver bearing the wolf's-head crest of the Moretons on its rim.

The Moreton crest is also to be seen on the 16th-century glass in the Withdrawing Room, whose ceiling is panelled with moulded beams and on whose plaster chimneypiece are the royal arms and supporters of Queen Elizabeth I; another bearing the Moreton arms and flanked by the figures of Justice and Mercy is in the Upper Porch Room. There are painted scenes from the Apocrypha and blackletter texts on the upper part of the Parlour wall and similar texts with decorative borders on the north and west walls of the chancel in the Chapel, for which there was a vogue between 1570 and 1610 when any sort of figure subject was taboo in churches. Plasterwork designs embellish the gables at either end of the Long Gallery, one of which incorporates the figure of Destiny and the other that of Fortune.

Tudor and Elizabethan craftsmanship shown (above) in the Upper Porch Room, Little Moreton Hall, with its plaster chimneypiece bearing the Moreton arms, and (below) in the Great Hall whose oak refectory table is listed in the 1601 inventory.

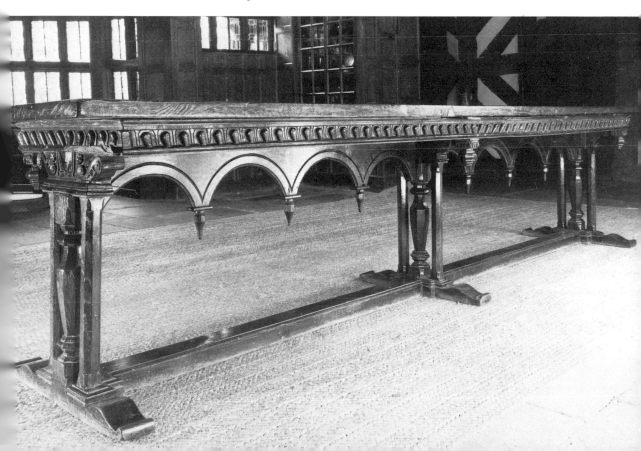

Longleat Wiltshire

The Marquess of Bath

4 miles sw of Warminster on A362

The exterior of this magnificent Elizabethan 'prodigy house' was designed by Smythson for Sir John Thynne, who prospered greatly under Henry VIII, while the great park in which it stands is one of 'Capability' Brown's finest achievements: both have undergone little change. The interior structure was, however, much altered by Wyatville, c.1800–10; only the Elizabethan Great Hall with its magnificent stone chimneypiece, its hammerbeam roof and its Minstrels' Gallery above the finely carved screen remains unaltered. Here hang eight splendid hunting and equestrian scenes by Wootton.

The way to the State Rooms leads through the Lower East Corridor which contains portraits by Miereveldt and Johnson, late-16th-century Brussels tapestries and fine examples of Oriental ceramics; fascinating mementos of Winston Churchill are displayed in cabinets.

The Ante-Library is the first of seven rooms, four on the ground and three on the first floor, which were sumptuously, almost overwhelmingly, decorated in Italian High Renaissance style to the order of the 4th Marquess: the work was carried out by Italian craftsmen under the direction of John Crace in the 1860s. These rooms contain distinguished family portraits by or attributed to Larkin (*Lady Thynne* c.1610), Gower (*Countess of Leicester* c.1585), Robert Peake the Elder, Gheeraerts, Van Dyck, Johnson, Lely, Wissing, Riley, Closterman, Kneller, Dahl, Beale, Vanderbank, Lawrence and Hoppner. The 19th and 20th centuries are represented by Watts, George Richmond, Orpen, Sargent and Graham Sutherland (the 6th and present Marquess).

The Saloon is hung with early-16th-century French and Flemish tapestries. The State Drawing Room walls are richly covered with Genoese velvet, c.1650, on which are hung mainly 16th-century Flemish, Italian and Dutch religious paintings, among them *Rest on the Flight into Egypt* attributed to Titian. In the Lower Dining Room and the State Dining Room are fine examples of silver and silver-gilt, ranging from the cup made 1626–7 for Thomas Coventry, Lord Keeper, to 19th-century works by Garrard, including the 1837 silver centrepiece on the State Dining Room table, representing the death in the Civil War of Sir Bevill Grenville.

The furniture includes 18th-century English

Jan Siberechts' painting of Longleat, 1675 (left), and Graham Sutherland's portrait of Longleat's present owner, the 6th Marquess of Bath (right).

Chippendale style chairs in the Breakfast Room, 17th-century Portuguese-Indian ebony chairs in the Lower Dining Room, French Boulle writing tables in the Saloon, together with a glorious inlaid Louis XV gaming table by Guillaume Kemp. Other magnificent pieces are in the State Drawing Room, including the *bonheur-du-jour* by Severin, c.1760, and Talleyrand's writing table with ormolu mounts in the form of laurel sprays and made by Pierre Garnier.

Meissen animals by Kändler are displayed in the Minstrels' Gallery, and in the Dress Corridor there are cases containing Sèvres, Worcester, Chelsea and Crown Derby porcelain. The family's coronation robes are displayed in the same corridor. The Dressing Room is hung with fine 18th-century Chinese wallpaper.

The walls flanking Wyatville's Grand Staircase are hung with royal and other portraits, and at the foot of the staircase is the family state coach, built c.1750.

Loseley House Surrey

Mr J. R. More-Molyneux

2½ miles SW of Guildford, 1½ miles N of Godalming

Loseley House, built in the 1560s by Sir William More, one of Queen Elizabeth's advisers, is still inhabited by his descendants. Although later somewhat altered, it remains essentially an Elizabethan mansion, one of the finest in south-east England.

The panels on either side of the elaborate chimneypiece in the Great Hall and those opposite, painted with decorative designs and heraldic devices, are said to come from long vanished Nonsuch Palace, built for Catherine Parr by Henry VIII at Ewell, Surrey. The distinctive panelling under the great family portrait of Sir More Molyneux and his family, dated 1739, and the series of grotesque panels, perhaps Italian, in the Gallery probably have the same origin. The full-length portraits of James I and his queen commemorate their visit

Two of the series of painted panels, c.1538, said to be from Henry VIII's Nonsuch Palace; Loseley House.

to Loseley. Particularly attractive is the portrait of Edward VI painted in the manner of Holbein. Much of the heraldic glass in the windows is original.

The Library contains finely carved woodwork, especially the overmantel with the arms and initials of Queen Elizabeth above it, dated 1570. The outstanding chimneypiece is in the Drawing Room, carved from a single piece of chalk and probably copied from one at Nonsuch. Among the portraits is that, perhaps Flemish, of Sir William More with a skull; below it stands a splendid South German inlaid chest on which is depicted a decaying city. The excellent furniture includes a fine Queen Anne walnut cabinet. Also noteworthy is the Drawing Room plasterwork ceiling and its frieze, enlivened with moorhens and cockatrices; the pier between the windows is in the shape of a lion's paw. The storm scene is by the younger Van de Velde.

On the Staircase hangs a remarkable Elizabethan allegorical painting. The first-floor panelled bedrooms contain 17th-century Mortlake, Antwerp and Oudenarde tapestries and, in Queen Elizabeth's Room, an unusual oak pelmet depicting a boar hunt.

Lotherton Hall West Yorkshire

The Leeds Metropolitan District Council

1 mile E of A1 at Aberford on the Towton road (B1217)

Originally a small 18th-century house, Lotherton Hall assumed its present larger proportions very early this century. It was given to Leeds in 1968 by Sir Alvary and Lady Gascoigne together with the family art collection and a generous endowment fund.

The Gascoigne collection comprises mainly 18th-century furniture and paintings to which 19th-century pieces have been added, together with 19th-century porcelain and a fine collection of works by English sculptors working in Rome between 1750 and 1850. In the Oriental Gallery the magnificent collection of early Chinese ceramics bequeathed by Frank Savery to Leeds has been added to the Far Eastern works owned by the Gascoignes. Elsewhere are fine examples of contemporary ceramic works by the late Bernard Leach and his pupils, including Michael Cardew, and a collection of historical costumes to which examples of costume by distinguished contemporary designers starting with Bill Gibb are being added annually. An enlightened use of the Gascoigne endowment fund is to commission an increasing amount of contemporary work in various fields.

Outstanding among the Gascoigne paintings are Batoni's portrait of the 8th Gascoigne Baronet, and one of his grandfather, the 6th

Baronet, probably by Trevisani, both commissioned on the Grand Tour, Wheatley's remarkable Irish House of Commons, 1780, and an agreeable late-18th-century painting of a mounted hunting group. The 19th-century porcelain includes fine quality painted vases from, among others, the Derby, Worcester, Swansea and Coalbrookdale factories. To the gold and silver Gascoigne racing trophies have been added fine precious metal works from the mid-19th century onwards. The furniture includes pieces by Burges, A. W. Pugin and by Ernest Gimson and Peter Waals. Hewetson, Banks and Gott are among the sculptors.

The glorious Chinese ceramics date from the Neolithic period to the early Ming dynasty, with special emphasis on the 11th- and 12th-century T'ang dynasty, represented by a horse, funerary sculpture and the glazed earthenware camel from the Gascoigne Collection.

'The Gascoigne camel'; Lotherton Hall.

Lullingstone Castle Kent

Mr Guy Hart Dyke

2 miles s of Farningham on A225

Lullingstone Castle, a manor mentioned in Domesday Book, was acquired in 1361 by the Peche family, ancestors of the present owner. There are notable memorials to them and to their Hart and Dyke descendants in the Norman church of St Botolph across the lawn from the house, which was built by Sir John Peche in the reign of Henry VII and later remodelled under Queen Anne. Sir John's jousting helmet, won when challenging Henry VII at a tournament in 1494, is in the Drawing Room. A massive Tudor gatehouse stands on the third side of the lawn. There was once a second gatehouse, as shown in the large picture of this group of rose-red brick buildings, probably by a journeyman painter *c.*1725, which hangs above the Great Hall fireplace: it was demolished *c.*1760. To the south stretches the lake with gloriously wooded banks. The estate passed by marriage from the Peche family during the Tudor period to the Harts who lived here until it went again by marriage to the Dykes in 1738.

Both the Great Hall and the Drawing Room are impressive, especially the latter with its Elizabethan plaster barrel-vaulted ceiling, decorated with strapwork, pendants and roundels of Roman emperors. These rooms and others have fine early-18th-century oak panelling; that in the Drawing Room is embellished with fluted Corinthian columns. Among other family mementos here are a large Elizabethan alms dish and a collection of fans.

Of the family portraits the most interesting is the triptych in the Great Hall, dated 1575, showing seventy-nine-year-old Sir Percyval Hart, between his two sons, wearing the silver ceremonial knife as the King's Chief Server. The same knife is worn by his grandson, Sir Percyval Hart II, in his likeness in the Drawing Room. Other portraits include two of the Dykes, father and son, who remodelled the garden, by Domenico van Schmissen in the Great Hall; more portraits are in the

Drawing Room, in the State Bedroom, with its finely wrought needlework hangings made early this century, the Library and at the foot of the splendid early-18th-century Staircase, built with shallow treads to aid the ailing Queen Anne who more than once visited Lullingstone; her portrait is in the Drawing Room.

Luton Hoo Bedfordshire

The Wernher family

2 miles s of Luton on A6129

Soon after the 3rd Earl of Bute had acquired the Luton Hoo estate, he commissioned Robert Adam in 1767 to expand and modernize the house already there. Further extensive alterations were started by Smirke in the 1820s and were barely completed by the time of the disastrous fire of 1843, after which the Bute family left. The present mansion is basically the work of Mewes, the architect of the Ritz and Waldorf Hotels in London, who was employed by Sir Julius Wernher, 1st Baronet, after he had acquired Luton Hoo in 1903. The skill with which Sir Julius developed a great mining interest in South Africa is reflected in the discernment with which he assembled his remarkably fine art collections, displayed in a rich Edwardian setting.

The Dutch Room contains good 17th-century Dutch paintings by Dou, Frans Hals, Hobbema, Metsu, van Ostade and the younger Van de Velde and there are works by Hoppner, Cosway, Ibbetson and Patrick Naysmith in the English Room. The most important paintings hang in the Main Gallery, including works by Filippino Lippi, Bermejo, Memlinc, Titian, Altdorfer and Rubens' oil sketch *Diana and her Hounds*. Here also are Flemish tapestries, Renaissance jewellery and Italian maiolica. An outstanding collection of Byzantine and French ivories, extending from the 10th to the 14th centuries, is displayed in the Ivory Room.

In the Blue Hall are excellent 18th-century French tapestries woven at Gobelins while Beauvais tapestry work, depicting scenes from La Fontaine, covers the suite of Louis XVI

Hans Memlinc (c.1435–94) Virgin and Child *(above)
and Bartolomé Bermejo* St Michael, *c.1480 (left);
Luton Hoo.*

belonged to the Duke of Cumberland, the son
of George III, who became King of Hanover in
1837.

Sir Harold Wernher, 2nd Baronet, married
Lady Zia, daughter of the Grand Duke Michael
of Russia from whom was inherited the
important collection of Fabergé gold, jewelled
and enamelled objects, made with the greatest
ingenuity. Two basement rooms are devoted
to Imperial family portraits and other Russian
mementos.

A superb collection of English 18th-century
porcelain, made by Lady Ludlow whose first
husband was Sir Julius, can be seen off the
Upper Corridor. Here and in the Lower
Corridor are further impressive displays of
German stoneware, 16th- and 17th-century
German silver-gilt and Limoges enamels of the
same period, 16th-century Turkish pottery and
a small collection of English furniture over
which presides Sir Joshua Reynolds' portrait of
Lady Caroline Price. The Brown Jack Room,
named after Sir Harold's horse which won
twenty-five races for him, contains horse
paintings by Munnings and others.

armchairs and sofa. Here also are fine examples
of Sèvres porcelain, including part of a service
ordered by Catherine the Great of Russia.
There is another remarkable set of Beauvais
tapestries, *The Story of the King of China*,
framed by Italian marble in the opulent Dining
Room, glittering with candelabra, candlesticks, knives, forks and spoons which once

Lydiard Park Wiltshire

The Borough of Thamesdown

3 miles w of Swindon, just N of A420, signposted Lydiard Tregoze

Lydiard Park was reconstructed in the Palladian style from an older house between 1745 and 1749 for the 2nd Viscount St John, whose family remained here until nearly two centuries later. Acquired by the Swindon Corporation in 1943, it has since been splendidly restored.

The impressive Entrance Hall has a fine coved ceiling and chimneypiece, its panelling crowned with garlands and heads. The ground-floor State Rooms have well-wrought plasterwork ceilings, each of which reflects the character of the room it adorns; that of the Library has thick stuccoed bands enriched with gold.

The woodwork is also elaborate and finely carved and the chimneypieces throughout are of a high standard. the Library's white-painted bookcases, topped by open pediments enclosing busts, are original. The furniture is not original to the house, but appropriate period pieces have been brought in, mainly 18th century and Regency, while the interesting folding writing desk in the Library is of the Empire period.

Nearly all the paintings are portraits, many of them of the St John family, thirty-two of which were acquired from Lord Bolingbroke. Others include twenty-three family pictures given to the National Trust by the late Colonel R. ff. Willis (1875–1958) and, by his wish, lent to the former Corporation of Swindon to hang at Lydiard Park. The painters commissioned to record the likenesses of this well-established family whose sons served in the forces or traded overseas include West and Downman, with attributions to Beechey, Pickering and Tilly Kettle. The excellent three-quarter-length portraits of Richard Willis (1724–80), who died at the siege of Grenada in the West Indies, and of his wife may be by Pine or Hoare, although previously attributed first to Ramsay and then to Cotes.

Lyme Park Cheshire

The National Trust–Stockport Corporation

½ mile w of Disley on Stockport–Burton road

Sir Thomas Danyers was given Lyme, high up on the edge of the Peak District, by Edward III in 1346 in gratitude for his feat of capturing the Constable of France at Crécy. His daughter married the 1st Sir Piers Legh and their descendants continued to live at Lyme until 1946 when the Trust was given the property; it is maintained by Stockport Corporation. The Leghs were a family of soldiers and huntsmen and reared a prized breed of mastiff, now extinct, at Lyme. One accompanied Sir Piers Legh II at Agincourt, another Prince Rupert in the Civil War, and it is this unusual type of dog that is supposedly portrayed in Velazquez's *Las Meninas*, a copy of which hangs at Lyme Park.

A Tudor mansion was raised in 1550 to replace the medieval house but it is a massive and imposing Palladian edifice that we see today, partly the work of Leoni in the 1720s, although Elizabethan characteristics remain. The entrance Hall with its Ionic columns is hung with three fine Mortlake tapestries illustrating the story of Hero and Leander from a set of six designed by Cleyn, c.1623–36. The Baroque ceiling above the Grand Staircase is by Conseiglio and Polfreman, and a local carver, James Moore, worked on the Staircase. The impressive Saloon has carved Corinthian pilasters and wainscot, which may also be Moore's work, and remarkable limewood carving that could be by Gibbons. The delicate rococo ceiling retains its original gilding. This room contains sound early Georgian furniture, especially the set of six walnut chairs covered in yellow damask, a George II giltwood chandelier and a 17th-century Kouba carpet.

The Long Gallery and especially the Drawing Room retain something of their original Elizabethan character. The latter is embellished with vigorous strapwork, a deep frieze with grotesque masks above oak panelling, and Queen Elizabeth I's arms in the overmantel. The early Chippendale chairs in the Stag Parlour are covered with pieces of the

The Stag Parlour, Lyme Park, where the early Chippendale chairs are covered with the cloak worn by Charles I to the scaffold.

cloak worn by Charles I on the scaffold and it was in this room that the local Jacobite gentry met to plot against William III in the 1690s.

Lytes Cary Somerset

The National Trust

On w side of Fosse Way (A37), 2½ miles NE of Ilchester

This peaceful stone medieval manor house was the home of the gifted Lyte family from the 13th to the 18th century. Henry Lyte, who took over the property after 1588, was a keen botanist whose *Niewe Herball* of 1578 he dedicated to Elizabeth I. His son Thomas was also able to flatter his monarch by tracing King James I's genealogy back to Brutus.

The grey-stone buildings range from the 14th-century Chapel, the 15th-century Hall and the 16th-century additions on the south front to the 18th-century building on the north and the west front, erected in 1907 by Sir Walter Jenner, 2nd Baronet, who restored the property and left it to the Trust. The interior contains much good English 16th- to 18th-century furniture, much of it collected by Sir Walter Jenner.

In the Great Hall is a fine example of the traditional oak refectory table, supported by four turned legs joined by stretchers, a James I and a Cromwellian carved oak armchair, two dwarf female 'companions' in somewhat singed leather by the original fireplace, a 17th-century Aubusson tapestry, Delft blue and white tulip vases and an enchanting 17th-century 'cottage' birdcage.

The great Parlour retains its early-17th-century panelling with Ionic pilasters, uncovered intact early this century. The furniture here is mainly late Stuart and includes an elegant William and Mary laburnum-wood table on six S-shaped legs, its rectangular top inlaid with oyster veneer, a lacquer bureau of the same period, surmounted by a shaped and broken pediment with three parcel gilt urns, and a Queen Anne walnut tallboy on a stand with cabriole legs.

A collection of drinking glasses and, unexpectedly, two ceramic busts of the Emperor Alexander I of Russia are in the Little Parlour, together with a semi-circular mahogany drinking table, a James II armchair and a late Stuart walnut bureau. The Great Chamber with an inner porch of linenfold panelling is remarkable for its coved and ribbed plaster ceiling, *c.*1533; it contains a winged armchair upholstered in green damask and fine examples of William III and Queen Anne walnut cabinets. A delightful William III burr walnut chest stands in the Little Chamber.

Manderston Borders

Mr and Mrs Adrian Palmer

2 miles E of Duns on A6105

The highest possible standards of design, craftsmanship and materials, regardless of expense, were demanded by the millionaire Sir James Miller when Manderston was re-modelled and redecorated for him between 1900 and 1905. They make Manderston one of the most outstanding Edwardian country houses in Britain.

Sir James married the daughter of the Earl of Scarsdale in 1893, who was the sister of Lord Curzon the great Viceroy, and the influence of Kedleston, their family home, had considerable bearing on his plans for Manderston. Sir James had already become a highly successful racehorse breeder and he began his transformation of the property by building the stable block, which cost him £20,000. The most magnificent of their type at that or possibly any other time, they are built of dressed stone; stalls and arched roof are of teak with polished brass posts and the names of the horses – all starting with M – are engraved on marble plaques. The harness room is of polished mahogany with a marble floor. Never can horses have been so royally housed. The marble dairy with vaulted roof and marble boss, the gardener's Scots baronial house and the domestic offices are all of the same fabulous standard of workmanship and material that is the hallmark of the house.

View from the Hall into the Dining Room at Manderston.

Louis XVI reproduction furniture and the huge central crystal chandelier, the effect is dazzlingly opulent as it must have been at the first and, sadly, only ball given at Manderston in 1905, for Sir James died the next year.

Manderston is not a house to visit for great paintings or furniture acquired through the accidents of inheritance. Rather it is a superb period piece, furnished and decorated exactly to the taste of its owner, who expected and obtained the best of everything that the Edwardian age could provide in luxury, comfort and convenience. There are competent 19th-century family portraits, fine porcelain of the turn of the present century, a collection of blue-john fluor spar said to be the largest in Scotland, and statuary, mostly of the 19th century, provided by Duveen. There is some Louis XV furniture, including a fine pair of kingwood commodes, and a set of three Louis XVI chairs with covers worked by Mrs Bailie, eldest daughter of the first Miller owner of Manderston, as well as four chairs covered in silk *petit point* needlework by her daughter, whose grandson now carries on the family tradition.

Mapledurham Oxfordshire

Mr J. J. Eyston

4 miles NW of Reading of Caversham–Woodcote road (A4074)

The architect employed was John Kinross who worked for the Marquess of Bute at Falkland. The quality of his work – particularly in the plaster ceilings executed by Italian craftsmen – is such that without written evidence it is impossible to distinguish original 18th-century work from his reconstructions.

The simple ceiling in the Library/Billiard Room is the nearest to Adam style and the Dining Room, Drawing Room and Ballroom are outstanding examples of the taste and workmanship of the time. This last room, decorated in primrose and white – Sir James' racing colours – is hung with embossed velvet, the curtains woven in gold and silver thread. The materials look as good as new and with the

This large red-brick Elizabethan house lies close to the Thames at its most glorious. Building began *c.*1585 for Sir Richard Blount whose descendants still live here, and the house contains several original features, although many changes were made in the 18th and 19th centuries, when the Elizabethan Great Hall was remodelled into the present small Entrance Hall flanked by the Dining Room and Library. The Hall, its panelling installed in 1831, is dominated by Dobson's portrait of Sir Charles Blount (*c.*1598–1644) and by grotesque English 17th- and 18th-century carved animal heads which probably symbolize such vices as gluttony and deceit. Two startled deer flanking the fireplace were each carved from a single tree.

The Library contains notable portraits of Michael Blount (1743–1821) and his second wife by Romney and one by Soldi of the German composer Hasse, but Mapledurham's finest portrait is in the Dining Room – Larkin's *Lady St John of Bletso* (*c.*1615). The background of this admirable full-length figure constitutes one of the earliest painted English landscapes. Other good portraits include Gilbert Jackson's *Boy with Staff* on the Staircase, that of Mannock Strickland by Riley in the Dining Room, Johnson's *Young Girl with a Rattle* and Kneller's *Alexander Pope* in the Boudoir. Pope was a frequent visitor to Mapledurham and corresponded with the sisters Martha and Teresa Blount, whose portrait by Jervas is in the Saloon.

Other enjoyable paintings include a vast canvas depicting a rural scene of game being carried home, attributed to Jan Fyt and, in the Dining Room, a good example of

Hondecoeter's work and a flower-piece by the elder Verbruggen in which roses and peonies are used as symbols of mortality. The central dark panel of this painting may once have shown Christ's body being taken down from the Cross but it was painted out when the Catholic faith, to which the Blounts have adhered for over 350 years, was virtually proscribed in England.

Several fine early Jacobean plaster ceilings survive, including that in the Saloon. This room contains two massive giltwood marble-topped tables in the style of Kent (one of them supporting a fine Boulle clock case) a sofa with lion masks, Chippendale chairs and a Chinese lacquer cabinet (*c.*1690) on an English stand. Good furniture is to be found throughout.

The huge Great Staircase, Tudor in origin, is particularly impressive and in considerable contrast with the charming little Catholic Gothic Chapel, built *c.*1789.

The Gothic Chapel, c.1789, at Mapledurham.

Marble Hill House

Twickenham, Middlesex

The Greater London Council

On the Richmond road

This elegant Palladian villa, recently restored by the GLC, was built for Henrietta Howard, later Countess of Suffolk, the mistress of George II, who contributed £12,000 towards

The chimneypiece in the Great Room, Marble Hill House.

the costs. The house is suitably furnished with pieces from the George II period. The white and gold cube-shaped Great Room, reached by a shapely mahogany staircase from the ground floor, has considerable charm and contains a splendid chimneypiece. Admirable paintings in the house include a view of the nearby Thames by Richard Wilson, and portraits by Hogarth, Reynolds, Hayman, Thomas Hudson, Vanderbank and Cotes, besides genre paintings by Gravelot and Mercier.

Melbourne Hall Derbyshire

The Marquess of Lothian

In Melbourne 8 miles s of Derby on A514 to Ashby-de-la-Zouch

This muted grey-stone Jacobean mansion, nestling close to the fine Norman church of St Michael at the southern end of the little town of Melbourne, has retained its original modest character in spite of enlargements in c.1725. It was acquired from the church early in the 17th century by Sir John Coke, Principal Private Secretary to Charles I in the eleven years preceding the Civil War, and has come by marriage to the Kerrs, Marquesses of Lothian, via the Lamb, Temple and Cowper families. Two Prime Ministers have lived here; William Lamb, 2nd Viscount Melbourne, and Henry Temple, 3rd Viscount Palmerston. The 11th Marquess of Lothian initiated in the late 1930s the 'Country House Scheme' whereby historic country houses and their contents could, subject to public access, pass without taxation to the National Trust.

Portraits of distinction adorn the ground-floor rooms. Johnson's likeness of Sir John Coke, emphasizing his benign yet immensely shrewd character, is in the panelled Dining Room with Lely's fine portrait of the 2nd Earl of Chesterfield and his wife, and others by Kneller, Dahl, Jervas and Hudson. Hoppner's *Lady Melbourne*, mother of Queen Victoria's first Prime Minister, is in the Library, with a superb version by Bassano of *Moses Striking the Rock*, an architectural *capriccio* by Pannini, and

View of the Front Hall and oak Staircase at Melbourne Hall.

works by Susstrice and Snyders. Kneller's large canvases of Queen Anne, her husband Prince George of Denmark and George I dominate the Drawing Room, which also contains Dahl's likeness of the elegant Thomas Coke, Queen Anne's Vice-Chamberlain. In the Front Hall are early-17th-century Leventhorpe family portraits and an enchanting one of Lady Amabel Cowper in the centre of a mirror, while there are 20th-century studies in the Study by Eric Kennington and Simon Elwes. Particularly interesting is the extravaganza *Four Children of John Coke of Melbourne* by Huysmans, who was patronized by the Catholic supporters of Charles II's wife, Catherine of Braganza: it hangs on the oak Staircase and is his most important work in England. Other paintings here include a flower study by Monnoyer, and works by Bogdani and Hondecoeter. A portrait of Kaiser Wilhelm II hangs in the Entrance Hall; he presented the glass standing on the giltwood table

beneath *Queen Anne* in the Drawing Room to Admiral of the Fleet Lord Walter Kerr.

In the Dining Room is a full set of Charles II long-back chairs, six with and six without arms. There are two Chinese travelling chests in the Entrance Hall together with an impressive mahogany serpentine blanket chest and a little horseshoe emblem taken from Napoleon after Waterloo and presented to Lord Lothian by the Duke of Wellington. Early Bristol and Bohemian glass is displayed in the Drawing Room where there is also a lace fan once belonging to the Empress Eugénie. Also on view are examples of American Sandwich glass, various autographed letters, Lord Melbourne's Bible box, Sir John Coke's fine iron-bound dispatch box and Chinese export wares.

The House Chapel should be visited because of the altarpiece, a crucifixion by Guercino, and the Lippo Memmi, 1360, which is the oldest painting in the house.

227

Melford Hall Suffolk

The National Trust

In Long Melford, 3 miles N of Sudbury

In 1578 Queen Elizabeth journeyed through Suffolk, when according to a contemporary account, 'there was suche sumptuous feastings and bankets as seldom in anie parte of the worlde there hath been seene afore. The Maister of the Rolles, Sir William Cordell, was the first that begawne this greate feasting at his house of Melforde.' Cordell had first rented the manor on the Dissolution of the Monasteries and in 1554 he acquired outright possession. He built the red-brick mansion soon afterwards, not in Elizabethan but in the more restrained Tudor manner.

Sir Harry Parker, 6th Baronet and related to the Parkers of Saltram, acquired much of the contents as well as Melford Hall in 1786, and portraits of the Cordell family are displayed with those of Parkers on the panelled walls of the two-storeyed Banqueting Hall. Among several panels of armorial glass in the Hall windows is the shield of John Winthrop, first Governor of Massachusetts. Here also are two marquetry Nonsuch chests, a suite of high-back Charles II chairs and several ivory figures from Goa which, with the magnificent collection of Oriental ceramics meant for the King of Spain, were taken from the *Santissima*

Chinese vase and plate, Ch'ien Lung period, 1745–55, part of the treasure captured by Admiral Sir Hyde Parker from the Spanish; Melford Hall.

Trinidad, captured at Manila in 1762 by Admiral Sir Hyde Parker, 5th Baronet. Romney's portrait of this hard-hitting sailor, who accompanied Anson round the world, dominates the magnificent Regency Library designed by Thomas Hopper.

The Library consists of a small octagonal room, its shelves of rosewood lined and mounted with brass anthemions, and a larger room, separated from the smaller by two scagliola columns, whose fine oak bookshelves are beautifully veneered with burr walnut and bands of ebony. The larger also contains paintings by Dominic Serres of naval actions fought by the 5th Baronet and his second son, Sir Hyde Parker, who was in command with Nelson at Copenhagen in 1801, when the Danish fleet was destroyed. The latter's magnificent portrait, also by Romney, is on the grand early-19th-century Staircase, embellished at upper storey level by an Ionic colonnade; here hang works by Cuyp, Siberechts and Wouvermans. The Hyde Parker Room in the north wing, which was gutted by fire in 1942 and since restored by Sir William Hyde Parker, 11th Baronet, contains further family portraits, including works by Northcote and Beerstraten, some fine furniture, including a pair of rococo console tables, and 18th-century silver. In the adjoining Blue Drawing Room are, among other noteworthy pieces, a Queen Anne burr walnut card table, a Louis XV writing desk inlaid with Sèvres plaques and a rare 'seaweed' marquetry clock, which only needs winding once a year, together with 17th- and 18th-century Dutch paintings, much fine quality Chinese *famille rose* and *famille verte* porcelain, and a splendid rococo fireplace.

Mellerstain Borders

The Lord Binning

Between Kelso and Gordon off A6089

In a setting as harmonious as its name, Mellerstain looks out above a formal terraced garden over a gentle southern slope to the

Robert Adam's Library, Mellerstain.

distant Cheviot Hills beyond the Tweed. It was built between 1725 and 1776 by two generations of architects for two successive owners. William Adam built the wings for George Baillie; Robert, his more famous son, designed the linking central block and decorated the interior for the Hon. George Baillie-Hamilton, who inherited the estate from his great-uncle. Although Adam's castellated three-storeyed building with its bold projection on the north and a contrasting flat façade on the southern garden front may not be his most successful, the interior and especially the suite of reception rooms is a triumph. The Library, an outstanding creation, is one of the loveliest of all his rooms. The ceiling, repainted in its original colour scheme of delicate greens and grey-blue, has a central roundel, probably by Zucchi. A frieze of low-relief figures in the

classical style runs round the room above inset bookcases. The marble chimneypiece is not Adam's design, but those in the adjoining Music Room are his. This room is painted in pale blues and lilacs, with doors, frieze, cornice and plasterwork ceiling picked out in white, deeper blue and dark green. The pier-glasses and side-tables are again Adam's design. The more ornate Drawing Room is decorated in grey, lilac and soft yellow with gold damask wall hangings. A smaller Sitting Room has an unusual Gothic-style ceiling, once again Adam's work, which is seen too in the Gallery on the top of the house. Its barrel-vaulted ceiling antedates later neo-classical rooms, as for instance the Library at Stourhead, by a quarter of a century. The decoration was left unfinished but the ceiling design is on display. Adam also designed a marble-lined bathroom.

Mellerstain contains an unusually diverse collection of paintings. Family portraits include that of the famous Lady Grisell Baillie, heroine of the late-17th century, painted in maturity by Maria Verelst, as were her two daughters, one of whom was also the subject of a Ramsay portrait. He also painted the delicate and perceptive study of two Hamilton children. Gainsborough is represented by a portrait of the Hon. Mrs George Baillie, wife of Adam's patron who is depicted by David Martin. Two portraits by Aikman stand out: the 1st Earl of Marchmount, Lady Grisell's father, and another double child portrait. There are also a number of 16th-century Dutch paintings, notably *Girl with Fruit* by Nicolas Maes, landscapes and seascapes. A portrait of the Prince d'Angri is by Van Dyck. The Italian school is mainly represented by 17th-century religious works by Bassano and Correggio. Apart from the Adam-designed furniture, there are some good English pieces: a pair of Queen Anne gilt gesso side-tables, a Sheraton satinwood commode and mirror *en suite*, 17th-century marquetry side-tables and stout comfortable Georgian library chairs. More unexpected in this urbane 18th-century house is a large early-16th-century Flemish hunting tapestry.

Milton Abbey Dorset

The Governors of Milton Abbey School

9 miles s w of Blandford just N of A354 at Milton Abbas

Apart from the magnificent church, the only one of Milton Abbey's monastic buildings still standing is the Great Hall, completed in 1498. It has a fine hammerbeam roof and elaborately carved free-standing screens. The other monastic buildings were replaced in the late-18th century by Chambers' restrained Gothic mansion, built as a country house in lovely rural surroundings for Joseph Damer, Earl of Dorchester. It is now a public school.

Much of the west wing's interior was designed in neo-classical style by James Wyatt.

The Music Room displays eighteen full-length 18th-century portraits, nearly all copies, inset in white carved frames with decorative swags beneath. On the main Staircase, which has lyre-shaped balusters, are two portraits by Angelica Kauffmann. The first-floor Ballroom possesses a fine Wyatt barrel-vaulted ceiling with a frieze of winged griffins; similar decorations embellish the adjoining rooms.

Milton Manor House Berkshire

Surgeon-Captain and Mrs E.J. Mockler

In Milton village, 4 miles s of Abingdon, 1 mile w of Sutton Courtenay on B4016

The manor's three-storey-high Dutch style central block with its steep hipped roof was erected by the Calton family *c.*1663. About a century later two wings were added, one of which contains Milton's outstanding feature, the remarkable Gothic Library, still maintained in its original aubergine colour. Its bookcases, windows, fireplace and seat furniture are all in the Gothic style particularly associated with Horace Walpole's mansion at Strawberry Hill, Twickenham, started in 1748. The Barrett family who undertook these additions are featured in the delightful overmantel conversation piece by Highmore. The Library also

Worcester teapot, Dr Wall period, c.1750–80; Milton Manor House.

contains a good collection of porcelain, including fine examples of Bristol, Worcester, Liverpool, Spode, Crown Derby and Rockingham as well as Chantilly and Chinese 18th-century wares.

The Hall contains an unusual 17th-century red-pine fireplace and overmantel carved with two rustic maids bearing cornucopias. A family group by Thomas de Keyser hangs in the Drawing Room, whose marble fireplace and bold plaster ceiling reflect the influence of Webb. On the first floor are family portraits, including Kneller's *Churchill Sisters*, excellent hand-painted Chinese wallpaper in the Chinese Bedroom and, above the Library, the Chapel, also in Strawberry Hill Gothic, and containing Murillo's *Assumption*, *Four Gospellers* by Bloemart and a Flemish triptych, *The Adoration of the Magi*.

Moccas Court
Hereford and Worcester

Mr Richard Chester-Master

13 miles w of Hereford by River Wye, 1 mile off B4352

Judging by the little Norman church nearby, Moccas has long been occupied but the elegant red-brick mansion is late-18th-century. In 1771 Catherine, heiress to the Moccas estate of the ancient Cornewall family which is descended from Henry II (the senior branch of which owned Berrington), married Sir George Amyand Bt, a successful London banker of Huguenot descent who took Cornewall as his surname. Their descendants owned Moccas until 1962, when the estate was inherited by the present owner's father. Mr Richard Chester-

The Library in Strawberry Hill Gothic style at Milton Manor House.

The late-18th-century circular Drawing Room with wall panels of paper printed at the Reveillon factory, Paris; Moccas Court.

Master is now restoring and refurnishing the house, its original contents having been sold in 1946.

In 1775 Sir George consulted Robert Adam about the design of a new house, and later consulted Lancelot Brown and Humphry Repton about its picturesque surroundings, but he in fact employed Anthony Keck to carry out the construction. A dramatic effect is achieved by the approach up steps into the impressive Hall from which a magnificent cantilevered staircase curves up to the semi-circular first-floor landing, lit from the domed and decorated ceiling above. The Hall contains a Georgian breakfront bookcase, above which is a portrait of Catherine Cornewall as a girl.

The Music or South Drawing Room is embellished with a fine gilded frieze of musical instruments, a theme repeated on the marble chimneypiece. It contains good furniture but the outstanding piece is the recently acquired Chippendale commode, which was originally made for Moccas. Ariana Egerton, a gifted amateur artist, painted the early-19th-century portrait of her two sisters, one playing on a harp. In the Library, its chimneypiece of red scagliola, is more good 18th-century furniture, both English and French.

The Circular Drawing Room is a delightful if unexpected climax to a tour of the house. The recently restored delicate ceiling, frieze, doorcases and chimneypiece are to designs by Adam, dated 1781, but the elaborate wall panels are not painted but of paper from the Reveillon wallpaper factory of Paris. No fires were allowed to be lit in this room in order to prevent the paper being discoloured by smoke.

Plasterwork relief in the Elizabethan Great Hall, Montacute.

Montacute Somerset

The National Trust

In Montacute village, 4 miles w of Yeovil

Few of the original contents remain at Montacute from 1601 when this poetic Elizabethan golden stone house, built to emphasize the importance of Edward Phelips, Master of the Rolls, was completed. Happily the interior has gradually been refurnished through generous bequests, especially that of Sir Malcolm Stewart, and through loans from museums and from the Phelips family. Phelips portraits hang in, among other places, the Great Hall with its Elizabethan screen, its bucolic plasterwork relief of a hen-pecked husband, its superb 16th-century heraldic glass (also in the first-floor Library) and its fine set of high-backed walnut chairs, c.1690.

Other noteworthy features are the interior porch in the Library and the rich tapestries. These include a late-15th-century Flemish tapestry showing scenes from the Labours of Hercules, and a fine Gobelins tapestry, dated 1788, entitled 'The Hunter' from the *Nouvelles Indes* series. Particularly fine is the 15th-century *millefleurs* tapestry in wool and silk, probably from Tournai, showing an armoured knight carrying a banner and mounted on a richly caparisoned horse.

Today Montacute's greatest treasure is the magnificent collection of Elizabethan and Jacobean portraits in the spacious Long Gallery, on permanent loan from the National Portrait Gallery in co-operation with the National Trust to whom Montacute came in 1931. Many of the greatest personalities and some of the finest portrait painters of this period are represented, including Steven van der Meulen, the younger Gheeraerts, Mytens and Johnson.

233

Moor Park Mansion

Hertfordshire

The Three Rivers District Council

1 mile SE of Rickmansworth

The Club House of the Moor Park Golf Club must be the most elegant in existence. The estate, whose origins are Norman, was owned by, among others, the 3rd Earl of Bedford and the ill-fated Duke of Monmouth. The present mansion was designed by Leoni on an older foundation for Benjamin Hoskyn Styles, 'the richest adventurer in the South Sea Scheme', who sold his holdings in the company before its 'bubble' burst, and restored the house in the grandest manner, including its encasement in Portland stone.

The decoration of the cube-shaped main Hall was entrusted to Thornhill who organized a neo-Palladian scheme of pictures let into feigned plaster frames. However, Thornhill quarrelled with Styles and was replaced by the Venetian Amigoni, whose four *style galant* paintings from the story of Io and Argos, taken from Ovid's *Metamorphoses*, now dominate the Hall beneath the gallery. The magnificent

The King's Room, Moseley Old Hall, the house where Charles II hid after the Battle of Worcester, 1651.

plasterwork of the two trophies, one on each side of the entrance, the double fish-tailed *putti* supporting the frames of the paintings and the splendid figures over the door pediments are perhaps by Bagutti, as is the ceiling and surrounds in the White Drawing Room. The ceiling painting, including the *trompe-l'œil* cupola, is by Brunetti, another North Italian compatriot of Leoni, who also painted the architectural and sculptural decoration around Sleter's figure paintings on the Staircase to the Gallery and in the Saloon. Sleter was also responsible for the *chiaroscuro* pictures in the Hall Gallery.

The ceiling of the long Ball Room, now the Dining Room, was designed c.1765 by Robert Adam and decorated by Cipriani for Sir Lawrence Dundas, 1st Baronet, who then owned Moor Park. During World War II, the mansion was the headquarters of the 2nd Airborne Corps.

Moseley Old Hall West Midlands

The National Trust

4 miles N of Wolverhampton, E of A449 Stafford road

It was in the priest hole of this house that Charles II hid from Commonwealth forces after the Battle of Worcester in 1651. His handwritten letter thanking Jane Lane for her help is in the show-case in the Entrance Hall.

Moseley Old Hall was originally built c.1600 but was much altered in 1870 when the whole building was encased in brick. It was empty when it came to the National Trust in 1962 and has since been furnished largely with 17th-century oak furniture. The interesting contents include a Lambeth Delft 'Blue Dash' charger of 1670, a brass bed warmer of 1649, four pieces of 17th-century stumpwork in a case in the King's Room, and in the Catholic Chapel on the second floor the Spanish crucifix that belonged to the Whitgreave family who lived here from early in the 17th century until 1925. There are portraits of Thomas Whitgreave, Jane Lane and King Charles by unknown hands.

234

Mount Edgcumbe Cornwall

The City of Plymouth and County of Cornwall

Across the Tamar by the Cremyll ferry from Plymouth or B3247 from Antony

Mount Edgcumbe, which stands in picturesque parkland and enjoys splendid views of Plymouth across the River Tamar, is the seat of the Earls of Mount Edgcumbe, who still occupy the house. First built in the mid-16th century and altered and extended two centuries later, it was gutted by German incendiary bombs in 1941; the house has since been rebuilt.

The Hall, modernized with a Staircase leading direct to the first floor, is still top-lit by clerestory windows. It contains family portraits including the only Reynolds, that of the 2nd Earl, to survive the bombing. Here also are a fine Aubusson tapestry and several family relics.

The books in the Library came mainly from the family's London house and the long-case clock of 1610 from Cotehele, the original home of the Edgcumbe family. The furniture here is mostly Hepplewhite. In the octagonal Morning Room are Cromwellian chairs of 1650. The contents of the main Drawing Room are partly George II and partly 17th-century

from Cotehele; here also are three fine seascapes by Van de Velde. The Dining Room contains two 16th-century Flemish hunting scenes from Cotehele, more Hepplewhite furniture and two Bronze Age Celtic horns.

Mount Stewart Co. Down

The National Trust

On E shore of Strangford Lough, 5 miles SE of Newtownards

Mount Stewart was started in 1804 by the 1st Marquess of Londonderry to designs by Dance, who built the west wing, and was completed for the 3rd Marquess in the late 1840s probably to designs left by William Vitruvius Morrison, an eminent Irish Greek Revival architect. Its somewhat prosaic exterior is in contrast with its fascinating interior and contents, which include mementos of Lord Castlereagh, son of the 1st Marquess, who represented Britain at the Congress of Vienna. The interior decoration today owes much to the 7th Marchioness, a leading political hostess in the 1930s whose husband was a minister under MacDonald and Baldwin. The superb

George Stubbs' painting of Hambletonian, the famous racehorse, 1799; Mount Stewart.

gardens were given to the National Trust in 1955 by Lady Londonderry and her daughter, Lady Mairi Bury donated the house to the Trust in 1976. Many of the contents are generously on loan from her.

Morrison's impressive Hall, a classical octagon with two pairs of Ionic pillars screening two side halls, is lit centrally by a large dome. Its cabinets contain a splendid 18th-century Chinese export armorial service. Here also is an impressive Greek Pentelic marble tombstone, *c.*350 B C. Morrison's black and white Hall with its mid-18th-century English mahogany ladder-back chairs, Venetian chairs covered in red velvet and a Dutch apothecary's cabinet, leads to Dance's West Staircase, its delicate cast-iron balustrade and mahogany handrail inlaid with ebony by John Ferguson. The Staircase is dominated by Stubbs' outstanding painting of the celebrated thoroughbred racehorse, Hambletonian, whose owner, Sir Henry Vane-Tempest, was the father-in-law of the 3rd Marquess of Londonderry. Other equestrian pictures are in the Entrance Hall, the gallery of the Hall and in the Dining Room, in which hang Mengs' fine portrait of Robert Stewart, later 1st Marquess, painted when he was in Rome, and two by Kneller. The 7th Marquess and Marchioness are portrayed by de Laszlo in Lady Londonderry's Sitting Room while Batoni's likeness of the 1st Marquess's brother when in Rome is in the Drawing Room.

The Dining Room contains the twenty-two Empire chairs used by the delegates at the Congress of Vienna: the backs and seats were embroidered with the arms of those present and the states they represented in *petit point* on a gold ground, worked by nuns in Nantes for the 7th Marchioness. Here also is a splendid pair of Adam-style oval urn-shaped mahogany wine coolers. In the Castlereagh Room is a fine set of Regency mahogany bookcases, a display case containing mementos of the great statesman's career and an entertaining set of caricature statuettes in plaster by Jean Pierre Danton, *c.*1833. The Music Room is Dance's most elegant achievement, the pattern of the plasterwork ceiling reflected by the oak

and mahogany floor with a central pattern.

A large early Biedermeyer walnut writing desk is in the Drawing Room with three fine Aubusson carpets, two 18th-century Italian pier-glasses and a notable collection of objects of vertu.

Muncaster Castle Cumbria

Sir William Pennington-Ramsden, Bt

1 mile SE of Ravenglass village on A595

Muncaster Castle stands high on a magnificent site, perhaps Roman, among the Cumbrian coastal hills, guarding the western approaches to Eskdale and the Lake District beyond. The glorious views round three-quarters of the compass caused Edward VII when Prince of Wales to declare them the most perfect in Europe. The oldest part of the present castle is the 14th-century pele tower, but the Pennington family were already here in the previous century. Later additions include the impressive octagonal Library, 1780, on the site of the 14th-century kitchens, remodelled by Salvin in the 1860s when he was employed to do extensive restoration work.

The spacious flag-stoned Entrance Hall contains elaborate panelling, two horse studies by Ferneley, two fine Flemish wood carvings, a medieval Burgundian soldier carved in lime wood, several family portraits by or after Gainsborough and Kneller, and a rare likeness above the Library entrance of King Henry VI, who was sheltered here after his defeat at Towton in 1464. According to tradition, the grateful Henry gave the Pennington family the delicate enamelled 15th-century glass bowl, known as 'the luck' of Muncaster; as long as it remains intact, the Pennington succession at Muncaster is assured.

The Dining Room, its walls above the panelling covered with gilded and embossed leather, contains a set of Charles II walnut chairs, silver by Paul Storr, Velazquez's *Boy with a Falcon* and portraits by, among others, Van Dyck and Hoppner. More portraits, some

The black and white octagonal Hall by William Morrison; Mount Stewart.

attributed to Lely, hang on the walls of the brass-railed gallery of the Library, enriched by William and Mary furniture, unusual Dutch circular six-legged chairs, a fine collection of miniature furniture made by apprentices late in the 17th century, several Italian bronzes, including Cellini's *Satyr on a Sea Horse*, and two Munnings portraits.

In the bedrooms are splendid fireplaces, elaborate carved beds, chests and Flemish tapestries, all of the 16th century. A despondent portrait of Shelton, the last Muncaster jester, hangs in the nearby passageway.

The barrel-vaulted Drawing Room, its ceiling enlivened by Italian stuccoists, was built in 1861 and contains further excellent family portraits by, among others, Hudson, Reynolds, Lawrence, Watts and de Laszlo and an attractive Flemish alabaster figurine.

Nether Winchenden

Buckinghamshire

Mrs John Spencer Bernard

In Lower Winchenden village, 7 miles w of Aylesbury on A418

This fascinating stone mansion close to the River Thame, medieval in origin, was monastic property until the Dissolution and retains many features of the Tudor period, including the splendid chimneys. In the 18th century it was inherited by the Bernard family, to whom it still belongs. Sir Francis Bernard was Governor of Massachusetts and New Jersey and his youngest son, Scrope, became Under Secretary of State to Lord Grenville. Some of the large collection of letters and documents from this period are usually on display and are particularly interesting to American visitors. Sir Scrope made extensive alterations to the house from 1798 in Georgian Gothic style, with charming results.

The Parlour is notable for its delightful early Renaissance carved frieze and beams, *c.*1530, decorated with foliage, heads in profile and grotesques, including a mermaid, and for its Tudor carved woodwork and linenfold panel-

ling. The fireplace with its carved festoons is Georgian. By contrast, the Renaissance stone fireplace in the Great Hall carved with harpies, birds, fruit and a goblet at its centre is probably of the late-16th century. Here also is a rare 16th-century Flemish tapestry depicting Henry VIII surrounded by his courtiers and clergy. The ribbed plaster ceiling at its east end dates from about 1805. There is good oak furniture in the Entrance Hall, including a refectory table, and the house contains a number of 'country house' portraits.

Newburgh Priory North Yorkshire

Sir George Wombwell, Bt

In Coxwold, 5 miles from Easingwold, off A19

Newburgh Priory, gloriously situated on the edge of the pleasant village of Coxwold, was acquired from Henry VIII after the Dissolution of the Monasteries by Anthony Bellasis, cleric and lawyer who together with his brother Richard made a fortune from the suppression of monasteries. Richard's son, Sir William Bellasis (d. 1604), converted the priory into a home. His grandson was ennobled by Charles I, taking the title of Fauconberg. The 17th-century history of the family with its strong Roman Catholic associations reflects the hazards of the times. The circumspect 2nd Viscount, raised to an Earldom in 1689, was basically royalist although he married Oliver Cromwell's third daughter. The Protector's body is supposedly at rest in the bricked-up tomb in the upper part of the house, where there is a display of Roman coins found on the estate, a shield dating back to Roman times, and the saddle and pistols of Lord Bellasis of Worlaby, the 2nd Viscount's brother, who was an outstanding royalist commander in the Civil War. The 4th Viscount (1699–1774, 1st Earl of the second creation) was largely responsible for remodelling much of Newburgh. In 1825, the Fauconberg title became extinct and the property passed by the female line to the Wombwell family.

The impressive stone mansion has undergone many changes, including part destruction of the central block. After considerable deterioration, a valiant and successful restoration programme in the 1960s has saved everything possible, but the Gallery range is still open to the sky.

The dark panelled Black Gallery, thought to be part of the original 1145 structure, contains a set of Charles II carved walnut armchairs and early family portraits. Margaret Fairfax, wife of Sir William Bellasis, is seen here in an attractive portrait of 1558; other portraits include the two sisters of the 3rd Viscount, who both became nuns in their teens, and a portrait of Oliver Cromwell after Hudson. In the adjoining Justice Room is Soldi's fine conversation piece of the 4th Viscount Fauconberg and his family.

The Dining Room, previously the Library, may have been remodelled by the 4th Viscount; here are full-length portraits of the 2nd Viscount and Mary Cromwell, his wife, which hang here with other family likenesses. The room's outstanding feature is the remarkable Renaissance stone chimneypiece dated 1615 and almost certainly carved by Nicholas Stone, later the master mason of the Whitehall Banqueting House; the superb oval relief of Venus is flanked by *putti*, one on each side, with

George Romney's portrait of Lady Anne Wombwell (1768–1808) at Newburgh Priory.

The Renaissance stone chimneypiece, 1615, by Nicholas Stone in the Dining Room, Newburgh Priory.

the figures of Mars and Diana at either end.

The Small and the Large Drawing Rooms both have glorious plasterwork ceilings by Cortese, of Italian-Swiss origin who settled in York. They contain family portraits, among them an enchanting painting of two girls, one of them with a squirrel, by Mercier and others by Beale, Huysmans, Romney (Lady Anne Wombwell) and Hoppner. Two large paintings of a stag hunt by Snyders are in the Small Drawing Room together with a self-portrait by Soldi. The Large Drawing Room contains a fine mid-18th-century marble chimneypiece and a set of chairs of the same period covered in their original needlework.

There are good examples of English New Hall and Crown Derby porcelain on the China Staircase and of royal blue Worcester in the Small Drawing Room.

OPPOSITE *Fabergé gold and enamel cigarette box (above) and Chelsea porcelain, c.1760 (below); Luton Hoo.*

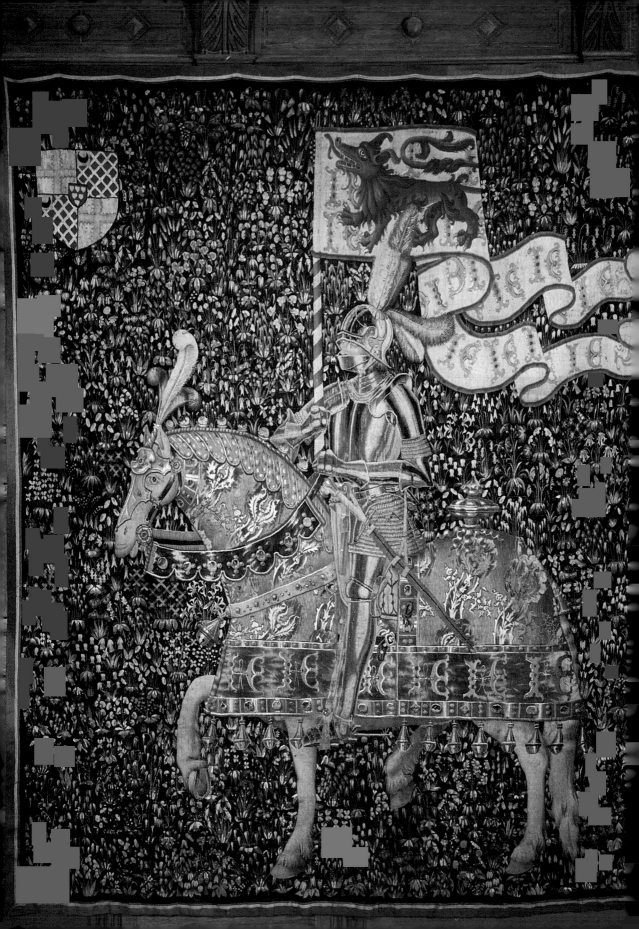

ABOVE *Adam's Tapestry Room, Newby Hall, designed to house the Gobelins tapestry set 'Les Amours des Dieux', 1769.*

Newby Hall North Yorkshire

Mr R. E. J. Compton

4 miles SE of Ripon on Boroughbridge road (B6265)

The original rectangular red-brick house, standing close to the lovely River Ure, was built *c*.1690 in the Wren style, if not by Wren himself, for Sir Edward Blackett, member of a respected Northumberland family. In 1748 the estate was acquired from the Blacketts by Richard Weddell for his son William, who became renowned as a collector of the arts and who returned in 1765 from Rome with a splendid assembly of antique sculpture. William commissioned Robert Adam in 1766 to alter Newby Hall to house this collection and Adam changed the southern of the two wings

for this purpose. In 1785 Lady Bute wrote to Mrs Delany: 'You must have heard of the elegance and magnificence of Mr Weddell's house, all ornamented by Mr Adam in his highest (and indeed, I think his best) taste.'

On Weddell's death in 1792, the estate passed to his cousin Thomas Robinson, 3rd Lord Grantham, later Earl de Grey, who in 1802 added the Regency Dining Room. In 1874, a Billiard Room was built above the Dining Room, together with a staircase leading to it, by his grandson Robert Vyner, whose daughter Mary married Lord Alwyne Compton, son of the 4th Marquess of Northampton, the grandparents of the present owner, Mr Robin Compton.

Above the Regency Dining Room fireplace is a delightful contemporary painting of the children of the 1st Lord Grantham, who was

LEFT *Millefleurs tapestry from Tournai, c.1481, of a knight in armour on horseback; Montacute.* 243

The 'Hare picture', a satire of the Charles I period by an unknown artist; Newhouse.

British Ambassador at Vienna, 1730–47, and who received from the Empress Maria-Theresa the two portraits of her and one of her husband, painted by Van Loo, which hang on the north wall. The room contains fine examples of Chippendale furniture designed by Robert Adam – a rectangular pair of satinwood and mahogany tables, two satinwood and mahogany plinths with urns, and three pedestals supporting splendid alabaster vases. The dining-room chairs and mahogany dining table with gadrooned borders on carved cabriole legs and claw and ball feet are also thought to be Chippendale.

The Billiard Room contains Vyner family mementos; Sir Robert Vyner (1633–88) was a leading goldsmith and banker to Charles II. Nearby is a prodigious international collection of chamberpots. In the Drawing Room is an impressive collection of 18th- and early-19th-

century English and Continental porcelain, a very fine Lawrence of Lady Theodosia Vyner, a satinwood commode and French furniture.

The magnificent Entrance Hall was designed by Robert Adam; its plasterwork ceiling and military trophy panels are dated 1771, by Joseph Rose Jr. It contains a large pastoral painting by Rosa de Tivoli, a mahogany cased organ thought to be by James Stuart and a superb black, grey and white Sicilian marble floor. The elegant main Staircase has fine Cippolino marble columns at the base brought from Italy by William Weddell, and contains portraits by Kneller and Batoni, a large painted George III pier-table by Adam and a Boulle-designed Louis XIV commode with clock.

Adam made the Tapestry Room to fit the beautiful set of Gobelins tapestries, *Les Amours des Dieux*, ordered by William Weddell in 1766. The giltwood chairs and sofas covered with matching needlework were made by Chippendale. The ceiling paintings are by Zucchi. The Library, with Corinthian columns at each end, is also to Adam's design; the plasterwork ceiling by Joseph Rose is decorated with paintings by Angelica Kauffmann. The room contains French and English furniture.

The renowned Sculpture Gallery in three compartments remains exactly as Adam and Weddell arranged it, its rotunda and terminating apse 'the meticulous reconstruction of a Roman interior'. Among this superb collection of busts and statues, the finest is the 'Venus' from the Barbarini Palace in Rome.

Newhouse Wiltshire

Mr and Mrs George Jeffreys

9 miles s of Salisbury, 3 miles from Downton off B3080

This remarkable brick house, begun *c*.1619, has three wings in the shape of the letter Y with a hexagonal centre, possibly meant to represent the Trinity. It contains interesting mementos of Nelson, a family relation, including glass, tableware and linen from HMS *Victory*, and

there are attributions to Knapton and Riley among the family pictures. However, the most extraordinary of the paintings is the large 'Hare picture', a fascinating satire of the Charles I period showing hares hunting, killing and eating men.

The furniture includes Cromwellian, late Stuart and Louis XVI chairs and a handsome Breton dresser. A carved wooden Breton saint stands on the Staircase and there is a fine Queen Anne quilt, probably made by travelling male embroiderers, in the East Bedroom.

Newstead Abbey Nottinghamshire

Nottingham City Council

11 miles N of Nottingham on Mansfield road (A60)

Newstead Abbey was purchased in 1540 after the Dissolution of the Monasteries by Sir John Byron of Colwick. By the time his great-great-grandson was created a baron by Charles I in 1643, the estate was much depleted and by 1798, when the property was inherited by the ten-year-old 6th Baron, the future poet George Gordon Byron, it was decayed and mortgaged. Lord Byron stayed here intermittently and

Detail of Thomas Phillips' portrait of the poet Byron, 1813 (above), and Peter Tillemans' painting of the west front of Newstead Abbey, c.1730 (left).

parts of the house were repaired, inadequately, in 1808–9. His last visit was in 1814, the year before he left for Europe under a cloud of scandal, and in 1817 Byron sold the whole estate to Colonel Wildman who restored the Abbey to designs by John Shaw. It was presented to the City of Nottingham by Sir Julien Cahn in 1931.

Today the Abbey is a memorial to Lord Byron and contains numerous mementos of the great poet's tempestuous life. His bedroom still contains his bed, with ponderous coronets at each corner of the tester, and there are portraits in the North Gallery of Byron at Cambridge, of Claire Clairmont, one of his mistresses, of his uncongenial wife, Annabella Milbanke, and of his beloved Newfoundland dog, Boatswain. Here also are busts of Byron and of Lady Caroline Lamb, the wife of Prime Minister Lord Melbourne; their notorious affair became the scandal of London society. More touching are the shoe lasts made to correct Byron's deformed right foot and the black leather helmet designed by Byron himself before setting out in 1823 to fight for

Mahogany breakfront bookcase by Gillow of Lancaster; Normanby Hall.

Greece's independence. He died of fever in malaria-ridden Missolonghi in April 1824.

Part of the important Roe Collection of the poet's manuscripts, letters and first editions are in the East Gallery, and more letters are kept in the Charles II Room. Phillips' familiar portrait of Byron, one of three originals, hangs over the fireplace in the heavily restored Salon, which has an unusual plasterwork ceiling dated 1631–3, perhaps of Dutch design, and a view of the Abbey's west front, painted c.1730 by Tillemans for the 4th Baron.

Normanby Hall Humberside

The Scunthorpe Corporation

4 miles N of Scunthorpe on B1430

The finest house to have stood at Normanby may have been that commissioned by the 3rd Lord Sheffield from Robert Smythson, who also built Hardwick and Doddington Hall, Lincolnshire, but no traces of it remain in the present mansion, which was erected in Regency style by Sir Robert Smirke between 1820 and 1830 for Sir Robert Sheffield, 4th Baronet. It was later considerably enlarged, 1905–7, for Sir Berkeley Sheffield by Brierley of York, who replaced the wall between the Entrance Hall and Inner Hall with the present Ionic colonnade, its capitals picked out in gilt, green and red.

The Scunthorpe Corporation, which acquired Normanby from the Sheffield family in 1963, has imaginatively set about restoring and furnishing the rooms in early-19th-century character, helped by contemporary inventories dated 1829 and 1840. The East and West Silk Drawing Rooms, with silk hangings which may be original, contain several Sheffield portraits, including one of John Sheffield, 3rd Earl of Mulgrave, later Duke of Buckingham and Normanby, who died without an heir. There are good examples of furniture by Gillow of Lancaster, especially the handsome mahogany breakfront bookcase in the Library. A growing costume collection of the mid-19th century onwards is displayed upstairs.

Norton Conyers North Yorkshire

Sir Richard Graham, Bt

3½ miles N of Ripon near Wath, 1½ miles from A1

This attractive country house of rendered brick with Dutch gables and a fine walled garden, thought to be the original of Thornfield Hall in Charlotte Brontë's *Jane Eyre*, dates from the end of the 15th century. It was built by the Norton family and forfeited to the Crown as a result of Richard Norton's part in the ill-fated Catholic Rebellion of 1569. It was acquired in 1624 by Richard Graham, who was made a Baronet by Charles I in 1629, and whose descendants still live here. He probably added the main staircase and the gables in about 1630. Further additions such as the plasterwork ceilings in the Parlour and Dining Room were made late in the 18th century. The structure has altered little since 1774, the date of the view of the house in the Hall.

Family portraits in the Hall include one attributed to Priwitzer of Richard, younger son of the 1st Baronet, who was himself raised to a baronetcy by Charles II, and one of the 7th Baronet by Beechey. Here also is a large painting by Ferneley of the Quorn Hunt and a late-18th-century Chinese screen with pictures on one side and text on the other, mounted on a modern base. A fine portrait by Batoni of Sir Humphrey Morice with his hounds hangs in the Dining Room, together with two by Romney. An air of gentle charm pervades throughout.

Nostell Priory West Yorkshire

The National Trust

6 miles SE of Wakefield on N side of A638

Originally a 12th-century priory, Nostell was suppressed in 1536 by Henry VIII. The property was acquired in 1654 by Rowland Winn whose brother was created a baronet at the Restoration and a descendant, Sir Rowland (1820–93), held high political office under Queen Victoria and was created Lord St

Chippendale giltwood marble-topped table to Adam's design, 1777; Nostell Priory.

Oswald in 1885. His great-grandson, who lives here and owns the contents, conveyed the Priory to the National Trust in 1953.

Sir Rowland Winn, 4th Baronet, commissioned James Paine in 1733 to build a new house at Nostell, perhaps based on a plan by Colen Campbell. Paine was responsible for the overall design and for the delightful rococo decoration of much of the interior, including the two Staircases (one for the family, the other for visitors), the Dining, Amber and Breakfast Rooms, the State Bedchamber and State Dressing Room. He employed Perritt and Joseph Rose Sr to execute his exuberantly attractive plasterwork designs and recorded that their achievement was 'inferior to none of the Performances of the best *Italians* that ever worked in this Kingdom'.

The 5th Baronet, on succeeding in 1765, replaced Paine with Robert Adam to complete the decoration of the house in his by then fashionable manner and to curb some of Paine's extravagancies. Adam accordingly decorated the Top Hall, Saloon, Library, Tapestry and Billiard Rooms; he designed the wall panels painted with grotesques in the Dining Room and the chimneypieces in the State Dressing Room, the Amber and the Breakfast Rooms.

Joseph Rose Jr was used to carry out Adam's typically inventive and beautiful ceilings. Zucchi was commissioned to paint the medallions over the doors in Paine's Dining Room and the classical landscapes in the Saloon and the Tapestry Room; the latter room contains three Brussels tapestries from a set of the 'Four Continents', *c.*1750. Since the 5th Baronet's death in 1785, the house has changed little and most of its superb furnishings are original.

Nostell is renowned for an outstanding collection of furniture by the elder Chippendale both in his earlier Director style and in the neo-classical manner to designs by Adam; many of the original bills survive. The Adam-Chippendale association is particularly happy in the Library, which contains the latter's outstanding Library table. Equally impressive is the green and gold japanned furniture in the State Bedroom and Dressing Room for which Chippendale also provided the Chinese hand-painted wallpaper. A pair of side tables by Paine in the Dining Room show Kent's influence. There are fine paintings, among them the portraits of the 4th Baronet and of his brother,

The Oak Room with its 16th-century four-poster bed; Oakes Park.

Colonel Edmund Winn, by Henry Pickering. Other treasures include a magnificent ebony cabinet, its drawers faced in *pietre dure*, on a stand supported by ebony negroes; the magical Dolls' House of *c.*1730 at the far end of the Lower Hall, complete with its original miniature fittings, traditionally attributed to the young Chippendale who was born at nearby Otley; and the largest known Chinese armorial dinner service of over 600 pieces.

Oakes Park South Yorkshire

Major and Mrs T. Bagshawe

4 miles s of Sheffield on B6054

This sturdy well-proportioned house looking south into Derbyshire is much younger than the Bagshawe family which is known to have been established in the neighbourhood of the Peak District since at least 1318. The existence of a house here was first noted in a deed of 1468 but the present building took shape soon after the Restoration, with subsequent alterations and improvements in 1811, when the central porch was added, and again in 1827.

The Oakes came by marriage to the Bagshawes early in the 18th century and has been passed down to the present owners by inheritance, sometimes through the female line. Its contents reflect the changing yet conservative tastes of well-established and respected gentry more interested in comfort and tradition than ostentation. In the Drawing and Dining Rooms and on the excellent oak Main Staircase are good 'country house' portraits of the family ranging over the past three centuries, several of which are attributed to Kneller, Dahl and Hudson, but the majority of which are by unknown hands.

The handsome oak panelling with Ionic pilasters in the Drawing Room is of good quality. There are many interesting examples of 16th- and 17th-century oak furniture, including the heavily carved 'Chancel Chair' in the Front Hall and the four-poster bed in the Oak Room. The Dining Room contains Chippendale and Hepplewhite style chairs and a

The Dining Room at Oakes Park; George Pike's organ, 1792, is flanked by marble statues by Francis Chantrey.

1792 organ, built by George Pike and enclosed in a handsome Sheraton breakfront mahogany case which matches the large sideboard; it is flanked by marble statues by Chantrey, the distinguished 19th-century sculptor who was a friend of the family. Other examples of his work are to be seen in the house. G. F. Watts is also represented by two family conversation pieces. There is good Sheffield plate, several fine tapestries on show and displays of late-19th- to early-20th-century costumes in the Small Bedroom and of Victorian baby clothes and toys in the Nursery.

Oakwell Hall West Yorkshire

The Kirklees Metropolitan Council

In Birstall

Standing near the old village centre of Birstall, Oakwell Hall has undergone little change since the 17th century. Originally a timber house erected in the 15th century, it was remodelled and cased in local sandstone in 1583 by one John Batt (1535–1607); he and his father could well be described as early property developers. Further improvements were undertaken in the

Oak 17th-century open-work gates at Oakwell Park, designed to keep dogs out of the upper floor.

principal bedroom's overmantel repeats the Tuscan pillar scheme; around its grate are curious carved wood panels which may have recently been placed here.

Ormesby Hall Cleveland

The National Trust

3 miles SE of Middlesbrough, S of A174

James Pennyman, whose grandson was made a Baronet after the Restoration, acquired the Ormesby estate in 1600 but the present house was built in about 1750 and the Adamesque decorations added by the prodigal 6th Baronet in the 1770s. The late Colonel J. B. W. Pennyman bequeathed Ormesby to the Trust in 1962.

Although built in the mid-18th century, the house has an earlier character and is of special interest for its rich decoration, carried out by craftsmen from York, then a centre for decorative artists. The central part of the ceiling of the Entrance Hall, screened by Ionic columns at both ends, is emphasized by the circle within a square; the oak leaves on the frieze and doorcases and the Vitruvian scrolls on the dado are typically Palladian. The Library is of the same period. Sir James, 6th Baronet, whose small full-length portrait in the Dining Room was painted by Reynolds for £20, was responsible for the elegant plaster-work ceilings in the Dining and Drawing Rooms; their Adamesque designs were probably by Carr of York. But the most impressive feature of the house is the elegant Gallery with its mid-18th-century panelling and its pedimented doorways. The principal bedrooms are equally richly decorated.

first half of the 17th century by local masons using local materials. John Batt's descendants owned the Hall well into the 18th century, although a number emigrated to Virginia early in the 17th century. Between 1841 and 1851, the Hall was run as a girls' boarding school by friends of Charlotte Brontë, who described it in her novel *Shirley*.

Oakwell is a good example of the sort of home inhabited by wealthy Yorkshire land-owners, and of the skills of Yorkshire craftsmen. An oak screen, framed by three pairs of Tuscan columns, stands at one end of the Great Hall. Oak is to be seen on every side, in the 17th-century panelling and the open-well Staircase, built out at the side of the huge fireplace; at its foot are open-work gates of oak to keep the dogs out of the upper floor. The

Osborne House Isle of Wight

The Department of the Environment

1 mile SE of East Cowes

Queen Victoria and Prince Albert, with their ever growing family, felt the need for a quiet retreat away from state functions and in 1845 they acquired at their own expense an ideal site on the Isle of Wight. The present Italianate villa with its two campaniles and its Grand Corridor running round the courtyard was designed by the Prince Consort with practical advice from Thomas Cubitt, who built it. The Pavilion, the first part to be built, was occupied by the Royal Family in 1846 and soon afterwards the Household Wing and the Wing for the Queen's guests were added. In 1890 another wing, which contains the Durbar Room, was constructed. Osborne, standing in magnificent gardens, was increasingly used by Queen Victoria in her widowhood and it was here that she died in 1901.

The influence of Prince Albert is widespread throughout this great country house, which retains its contemporary decorations and furnishings. The elaborate Minton tile design of the floor of the corridor between the Pavilion vestibule and exit was to his design, as was the elaborately decorated billiards table, made by Magnus, in the Billiards Room, which also contains an enormous porcelain vase given by Tsar Nicholas to the Queen in 1844 and painted with views of his palace at St Petersburg. The widowed queen insisted that every possible feature in the house and grounds remained as it was during her husband's lifetime and so it largely remains today.

The rooms opening out of the Grand Corridor, including the Billiards Room, contain painted ceilings. The five rooms of the Private Suite upstairs are carpeted with Brussels carpets. In the Drawing Room is a grand piano by Erard, decorated with ormolu mounts and plaques of coloured porcelain bearing representations of famous Italian paintings, a theme repeated on the six cabinets. Mary Thorneycroft sculpted the life-size marble statues of the royal children who are also featured on porcelain plaques in a nearby rosewood cabinet. In the Dining Room hang royal portraits after Winterhalter. Throughout the apartments are displayed gifts presented to the Queen over the years, including fine Continental porcelain, especially from the Berlin factory.

The remarkable Durbar Room was added in honour of the Queen's possessions in India in which she took particular interest, especially after she was proclaimed Empress of India in 1876. It was designed by John Lockwood Kipling, Rudyard Kipling's father, who had been Curator of the Lahore Museum. The ceiling and walls above the Burmese teak dado are deeply and intricately decorated in plasterwork. Many Indian pieces in finely wrought gold and silver are on display; the embroidered ceremonial addresses and commemorative items of the 1887 and 1897 jubilees are particularly impressive. The adjoining corridor is devoted almost entirely to Indian subjects, including paintings of the Queen's Indian soldiers, many by the Czech painter, Rudolph Swoboda.

Osterley Park Middlesex

The National Trust, administered by the Victoria and Albert Museum

Just N of A4 near Osterley station

Very few great houses of the 18th century have almost completely retained their character but Osterley is one. Its contemporary decoration remains largely intact, while its rooms contain their original furniture, uncluttered with later additions. This red-brick mansion was built in the 1570s but underwent a neo-classical transformation by Robert Adam for the Child banking family between 1761 and 1780. Chambers may have been involved shortly before Adam took charge and much of the furniture in the Gallery (as well as the fireplace and ceiling in the Breakfast Room) may be his. However, the girandoles and pier-glasses in the Gallery are to Adam's design and probably also the great sofas, one at each end under a Hoppner portrait.

The cold pale blue-grey and white Entrance Hall is entirely to Adam's design with its marble floor reflecting the bold, elegant design of the ceiling plasterwork, as well as the apses at each end, the sculptured classical figures in their niches, the chimneypieces and fire-grates, and

Furniture designed by Robert Adam for Osterley Park:
(left) tripod candlestand, 1776, in the Tapestry Room
and (above) satinwood commode veneered with harewood, c.1773, in the Drawing Room.

the four trophy panels flanking the entrance into the Long Gallery. The other rooms were also designed by Adam, each aiming at achieving a unity of its own.

The Eating Room is notable for its vine and ivy plasterwork ceiling; the pier-glasses above the marble-topped tables, the graceful sideboard with urns by Linnell and the lyre-back chairs both here and in the Library were designed by Adam. In the Library, where the white bookcases are supported by Ionic pillars, the gloriously inventive ceiling, picked out in colour, with inset paintings by Zucchi and Cipriani, marks a stage in Adam's trend in his later years to more intricate, delicate patterns, seen at its extreme on the walls of the Etruscan Dressing Room which Horace Walpole particularly disliked.

The Drawing Room shows Adam at his grandest; his highly imaginative plaster ceiling is echoed by the Moorfields carpet. Here also is a pair of outstanding commodes veneered with harewood and inlaid with classical motifs, which are seen again on the architraves above the door and on the chimneypiece. The pier-glasses are notable for their enormous glass plates brought with much difficulty from France. Walpole described this room as 'worthy of Eve before the Fall'. The magnificent tapestries in the Tapestry Room were woven after Boucher and signed by Jacques Neilson, a fellow Scot and aquaintance of Adam's, who was in charge of the Gobelins works in Paris, 1749–88. Adam designed the elaborate bed in the State Bedroom.

Osterley passed in 1804 by marriage to the 5th Earl of Jersey and was given by the 9th Earl to the National Trust in 1949.

Oxburgh Hall Norfolk

The National Trust

7 miles sw of Swaffham on s side of Stoke Ferry road

The Bedingfeld family, traditionally of Norman origin, settled in Suffolk between 1087 and 1102. Oxburgh came to them by marriage and in 1482 Edmund Bedingfeld received Edward IV's permission to fortify Oxburgh, surrounded by its moat, with battlements. Loyal to the Stuarts and to the Old Faith, the family was granted a baronetcy in 1661 by Charles II. The 6th Baronet assumed the additional name of Paston in 1830. Oxburgh was faced with demolition after World War II but the Dowager Lady Paston-Bedingfeld, mother of the 9th and present Baronet, repurchased the Hall and presented it to the National Trust in 1952.

Oxburgh's greatest glory is its remarkable 15th-century brickwork Gatehouse, which has escaped both restoration and modernization. Not so the rest of the house; the Great Hall was demolished in 1775 and partly replaced by the large Saloon block, and the 6th Baronet employed the younger Pugin to give the rest of the house an air of Victorian Tudor. Its contents reflect its continuing ownership by one family for nearly 500 years.

The King's Room in the Gatehouse contains a votive picture of the 1st Baronet and family under the protection of the Virgin Mary, to

The King's Room, with its Elizabethan wall hangings, in the 15th-century Gatehouse, Oxburgh Hall.

celebrate the family's survival during the Civil War, 13th-century charters, royal letters of the Tudor period written to the family and two delicate wood carvings by Gibbons. The painted glass is Continental of the 16th and 17th centuries. Some of the furniture as well as the armour here and elsewhere in the house is on loan. Also on loan is the elaborate 1647 tapestry map of part of the home counties in the Queen's Room. Nearby in a small room are the celebrated needlework hangings of Mary Queen of Scots and Bess of Hardwick, Countess of Shrewsbury, displayed under controlled conditions.

There are family portraits on the walls of the stairs and in various rooms. In the Small Dining Room with its elaborately Victorian and earlier carved panels and furniture, relieved by the plain Lambeth armorial dinner service, c.1725, is a portrait of the 3rd Earl of Burlington, one of whose sisters was married to the 3rd Baronet. In the Saloon is an attractive one by an unknown artist of the 3rd Baronet as a boy, c.1690, wearing a grey smock over a white petticoat, his shoes tied with red ribbon. Opie's portrait of Charlotte Jerningham, wife of the 5th Baronet, is in the Old Drawing Room. The walls of the corridor and stairs are decorated with late-17th-century embossed and painted Spanish leather.

Packwood House Warwickshire

The National Trust

1 mile E of Hockley Heath, off A34 Birmingham–Stratford road

Packwood is famous for its remarkable yew topiary garden, partly planted c.1650–70, which represents the Sermon on the Mount. The interior of the Tudor farmhouse to which additions had been made in the mid-17th century was much altered both before and after World War I by Mr Alfred Ash and his son, Mr Baron Ash, who in 1941 gave the property to the National Trust.

Packwood has a fine collection of tapestries, both English (Mortlake and Soho) and Continental (Dutch, Flemish and French), which embellish the Long Gallery, the Hall, the Inner Hall and the Great Hall with its Soho tapestries of Africa and America, c.1733. There are also panels of mid-17th-century 'Turkey' work in the Inner Hall and other examples covering an oak chair and footstool in the Ireton Room. The stained glass in the Dining Room and the Study is Flemish of the early 17th century; the heraldic panels in the Great Hall were made in 1921 except for that bearing Queen Mary's coat-of-arms which commemorates her visit to Packwood in 1927.

Good furniture includes a 14th-century oak refectory table top from Baddesley Clinton on early-17th-century supports in the Great Hall together with a notable suite of six George I walnut chairs and four late-17th-century Italian walnut chairs covered in Utrecht velvet, a rare Charles II oak cupboard inlaid with mother-of-pearl in the Dining Room and a Queen Anne chest of drawers on a stand, inlaid with seaweed marquetry, in the Drawing Room, where a walnut spinet is the earliest known example of the work of Thomas Hitchcock the younger, active 1690–1715. A fine Dr Wall Worcester china tea service is in the Study and there is much good panelling and other woodwork, which is not indigenous to the house.

Charles II oak cupboard inlaid with mother-of-pearl; Packwood House.

The Elizabethan Great Hall, Parham Park, with its original stone fireplace and carved oak screen, and array of 16th- and 17th-century portraits.

Parham Park West Sussex

Mr and Mrs P. A. Tritton and the Hon. Clive and Mrs Gibson

4 miles SE of Pulborough on A283

This restrained grey-stone Elizabethan manor house stands in its large deer park with the South Downs looming in the distance and Chanctonbury Ring close by. Parham was expanded in 1577, shortly before Queen Elizabeth I dined here, and was acquired in 1601 by the Bysshopp family, who remained here until 1922 when the 17th Baroness Zouche of Haryngworth sold the property to Clive Pearson, the younger son of the 1st Viscount Cowdray. His eldest daughter and her husband, Mr and Mrs P. A. Tritton, now live here together with their nephew and his wife, the Hon. Clive and Mrs Gibson. Alterations, mainly internal, were made at different times and much careful work has been done during

the past fifty years to emphasize Parham's original Elizabethan character.

The house contains highly distinguished collections of paintings, furniture, carpets and needlework, made all the more pleasurable by their careful arrangement. The paintings, many of them of great historical interest, are probably the best known of all the treasures. In the Entrance Hall are equestrian and sporting paintings by Barlow, Seymour and Wootton, and Reynolds' magisterial likeness of Alderman Beckford (whose son built Fonthill Abbey) with St Paul's Cathedral as background. An enchanting marble relief of a marine Venus by John Deare and a fine view of Venice by Bellotto embellish the Upper Hall, which leads into the double-cube Great Hall with its original stone fireplace and a gloriously carved Elizabethan oak screen.

Here hangs an impressive array of 16th- and 17th-century portraits. They include a sumptuously robed Queen Elizabeth I by an

255

unknown hand, her sleeves painted with a symbolic design of silkworms and mulberry leaves; Edward VI and a version of Henry Howard, Earl of Surrey, who was executed by Henry VIII, both by Scrots (Stretes); Elizabeth's favourite, the Earl of Essex, by Gheeraerts; Sir Thomas Gresham by Steven van der Meulen, 1563; Isaac Oliver's Henry Prince of Wales, James I's eldest son, riding a white horse; one of Lord Burghley attributed to Mor; and likenesses of Thomas Bysshopp, created a baronet in 1620, and his family.

Other fine portraits in the house include Daniel Mytens' *Charles I when Prince of Wales*; Larkin's *Countess of Denbigh*, *c.*1616; Bartolomé Gonzalez's comely *Infanta Maria Anna of Spain* to whom Charles was briefly betrothed; and works by Van Dyck (his magnificent *Ann Kirke*, dresser to Queen Henrietta Maria), the younger Pourbus, Wright, Johnson, Lely, Kneller (*Mrs Dunch*), Riley, Closterman, Arthur Devis and Soldi.

Those of Prince Charles, his family and associates are in the Great Parlour.

The Green Room is devoted to Sir Joseph Banks, Bt, President of the Royal Society 1778–1820. Reynolds' portrait of him was made soon after his return from accompanying Captain Cook as botanist on his first circumnavigation of the world in the *Endeavour*, 1768–71. A fascinating reminder of the stage of exploration at that period is the omission of the south coast of Australia on one of Banks' globes. Here also are Stubbs' paintings of a kangaroo and dingo dog, done from skins Banks brought back from Australia, and Reynolds' fine full-length painting of Omai, a native of Tahiti brought to England by Cook after his second expedition and lionized by London Society. William Parry's painting shows him being introduced by Banks to Dr Solander, his Swedish secretary. This room also contains portraits by Gainsborough, Romney and Hoppner.

Among the notable early English furniture

Yew four-poster bed designed by John Makepeace; Parnham House.

are a fine Elizabethan bulbous-legged table and small Tudor oak chest, in the Great Hall; two oak chests of drawers, one *c.*1603 and the other *c.*1666, in the Great Chamber; a Spanish *vargueño* or travelling chest and a 17th-century Awabi shell-covered chest from Nagasaki in the Great Parlour; a George II walnut and gilt looking-glass in the First Floor Lobby; painted Sheraton beechwood chairs in the elegant 18th-century Saloon and, in the West Room, a long-case clock by Edward Stanton and a triangular ombre card table. There are splendid carpets and rugs from Turkey, Persia and India.

The magnificent needlework includes that attributed to Mary Queen of Scots on the four-poster bed in the Great Chamber; worked on the back is a figure said to resemble Marie de Medici. Also in the Great Chamber is a remarkably delicate rendering on a cushion of the story of Moses found in the bulrushes. Fine 17th-century needlework embellishes six French upright chairs and an English armchair in the Great Parlour; there are curtains and wall coverings of Hungarian stitch in the Great Chamber, the West Room and the Ante-room. The Long Gallery, its ceiling pleasingly decorated in tempera by the late Oliver Messel, contains John Rising's painting of the 12th Lord Zouche with the Parham Troop of Yeomanry, said occasionally to have drilled here on foot, and a variety of fascinating displays; in a bedroom off it is a remarkable collection of Stuart needlework pictures.

Parnham House Dorset

Mr John Makepeace

½ mile s of Beaminster

This fine Tudor house, built in 1585 of golden Ham Hill stone, was enlarged and embellished by John Nash in 1810. The character of the interior was somewhat spoiled during the 19th century but has recently been imaginatively restored and is now the setting for the unique furniture designed by John Makepeace, Parnham's owner, and made by his skilled young craftsmen in the adjoining workshops.

His School for Craftsmen in Wood is also housed at Parnham. The Drawing Room is used as a gallery for exhibitions of the work of living artists and craftsmen, while the Library has the Museum of Woodcraft which includes a comprehensive collection of woodworking tools, both ancient and modern.

Pencarrow Cornwall

The Molesworth-St Aubyn family

4 miles NW of Bodmin off A389 and B3266 at Washaway

The Pencarrow estate was inherited by John Molesworth, Auditor for the Duchy of Cornwall to Queen Elizabeth I, whose grandson became Governor of Jamaica and was created a baronet by William III. The present restrained Palladian house, surrounded by gardens and fine timber, was built in the 1760s. Sir William Molesworth, 8th Baronet, who became Secretary of State for the Colonies, extended the Music Room *c.*1830 to create a shrine for a marble Venus from Rome; the room still retains its mid-18th-century rococo ceiling of the four seasons. At the same time he installed pinewood panelling, bookcases and a display cabinet for his English, European and Oriental porcelain, especially of the K'ang Hsi Chinese period, in the Entrance Hall, which he converted into a Library. Above the cases hang the inherited Arscott family portraits; Beechey's likeness of the 6th Baronet who completed the house is above the chimney-piece.

Among other family portraits are the group of eleven by Reynolds in the Dining Room; the splendid conversation piece of the four Misses St Aubyn with St Michael's Mount in the background by Arthur Devis in the Ante-room, its walls covered with Chinese linen; and, in the Drawing Room, Northcote's likeness of the last Arscott squire and Wissing's 8th Earl of Pembroke. In the Inner Hall is a version of Edward Bower's tragic portrait of Charles I at his trial, together with two most enjoyable London views by Samuel Scott.

The Drawing Room contains a fine Chinese

ABOVE *The Music Room extension, c.1830, to house the marble Venus at Pencarrow.*

BELOW *Oak screen in the Great Hall, Penhow Castle, which dates back to the 14th century.*

lacquer cabinet, an 18th-century Chinese bowl, embellished with views of Pencarrow, a small group of miniatures by the fireplace, and flowered damask curtains and chair covers from a Spanish ship captured in the Philippines in 1762. There is good furniture throughout but especially noteworthy are the two carved Kentian tables in the Inner Hall.

Penhow Castle Gwent

Mr Stephen Weeks

On A48 midway between Chepstow and Newport

Standing above the traditional old road from England into South Wales, Penhow was one of six strongholds built in the 12th century to guard Chepstow Castle from Welsh attack. In the 14th century a Hall was added which was divided into a Lower and a Great Hall above in c.1485. A Tudor wing was also erected on the opposite side of the courtyard and given a Restoration façade c.1670.

The fortress was the home of a French family from St Maur in Touraine who followed the Normans to England. Their name became corrupted to Seymour and it was from this family that Lady Jane Seymour and the Dukes of Somerset descended. In the 18th century Penhow Castle became a farm house and fell into decay until it was acquired in 1973 by the present owner, who set about restoring the complex of buildings with imagination tempered by scholarship.

The Norman Keep Room, with its massive thirteen-foot-long elm tabletop and walls which incorporate the occasional Roman brick, and the Seymour Chamber above, containing a fine metal-bound Indian chest and a stone from the abbey of St Maur-sur-Loire kept here in a gilded wooden tabernacle of 14th-century design, are now as solid as they were 800 years ago. The Lower Hall, with its tiled floor and a diversity of finds from the moat, and the Great Hall are happily revived. The fine quality oak for the latter's screen comes from the Hutton-in-the-Forest estate in Cumbria and against it on a pedestal stands a

19th-century wooden angel from Oberammergau. The Great Hall's firedogs are from St Maur.

The late-17th-century Dining Room with little swags over the fireplace, and the Old Parlour with a painted architectural fantasy in its overmantel, are both decorated with good bolection panelling and later plasterwork ceilings. Engravings of the Castle hang on the walls.

Penrhyn Castle Gwynedd

The National Trust

1 mile E of Bangor off A5

The vast echoing interior of this enormous castle, built between about 1827 and 1837 in the short-lived neo-Norman style by the versatile Thomas Hopper, is almost everywhere exuberantly decorated – ceiling, arches, balustrades – with designs of many origins in addition to Norman; the stained-glass windows in the Great Hall, with its floor of Mona marble, are by Willement and the plasterwork attributed to Bernasconi. Nevertheless, it is a homogeneous achievement, the work of one man who had a free hand in the design and choice not only of the architecture but of the decoration and furniture as well, with superb and sometimes startling results. Slate is widely used, as seen in the billiard table and in the enormous slate bed in one of the principal bedrooms. However, when Queen Victoria came here in 1859, she slept in the massive carved oak bed designed by Hopper in the State Bedroom.

Slate appropriately is the main source of the wealth which built Penrhyn. The slate quarries

The Library, Penrhyn Castle, designed and furnished in neo-Norman style in the 1830s.

Sir Philip Sidney's funeral helmet (above) and (left) Gheeraerts' painting of Lady Sidney and her children, c.1595; Penshurst Place.

in the nearby Nant Ffrancon valley were developed by Richard Pennant (?1737–1808), who already had a considerable fortune from his Jamaican estate. Pennant, who in 1783 became Baron Penrhyn of Penrhyn, Co. Louth, was annually exporting some 12,000 tons of slate by 1792. As he had no children, his estates passed to a grandson of his sister, George Hay Dawkins (1763–1840), who assumed the name of Pennant and rebuilt the Castle. He was succeeded by his elder daughter's husband, Edward Gordon Douglas, who added the name of Pennant to his surname and was created 1st Baron Penrhyn of Llandegai. In 1951 the Castle was conveyed to the National Trust with part of the vast Penrhyn estates.

The furniture is everywhere larger than life as, for example, the two chairs in the Entrance Hall whose arms are formed of winged cherubim, and the elaborate side-table in the Great Hall with its entwined dolphin supports made of slate. In the Dining Room, whose walls, ceiling and sideboards have neo-Norman decoration, are the paintings collected by the 1st Lord Penrhyn of Llandegai. Portraits by Romney and Herkomer are in the Breakfast Room. The fascinating Doll Museum contains dolls from all over the world, including Japan, the Arctic and Java.

Penshurst Place Kent

The Rt. Hon. Viscount De L'Isle vc, kg

In Penshurst Village, 3½ miles w of Tonbridge

Originally built in the 14th century, Penshurst Place was extended in the 16th and 17th centuries and underwent some 19th-century Gothic restoration and rebuilding. It came to the Sidney family in 1552 and it was here that Philip Sidney, soldier and poet, was born. The glorious Barons Hall, built about 1340, with its central hearth, is the finest example of its kind still standing; the magnificent chestnut roof is supported by life-sized figures. The trestle tables are mid-15th-century and the three-tiered screen, the weapons and armour, including Sir Philip Sidney's funeral helmet, are 16th-century. Here are two state swords: one belonged to Elizabeth I's favourite, Lord Leicester; the other was given to Field-Marshal Lord Gort vc, Lord De L'Isle's father-in-law, by the people of Malta in gratitude for his leadership during the siege of the island in World War II.

The Crypt is now the Armoury. Above it is the State Dining Room which contains family portraits of the 16th century, including a fine Gheeraerts of Lady Sidney and her children, *c.*1595. The furniture is mainly 18th-century. In Queen Elizabeth's Room, the glorious green and rose damask material with an appliqué design, *c.*1695, which covers the late Stuart shell-headed day-bed and matching chairs, has the same delightful design and colouring as the wall hangings. Here also is a card table with original *petit point* needlework, attributed to William Kent, and handsome late-17th-century crystal chandeliers which are among the earliest known. Next is the Tapestry Room with two fine late-17th-century Brussels tapestries and a French Gothic tapestry *c.*1520; a Dutch cabinet, each drawer framing a Dutch 17th-century painting; a Kentian gilt table with inlaid marble top and a Florentine 17th-century cabinet inlaid with *pietre dure*.

In the Long Gallery a portrait of Elizabeth I hangs above an effigy cast in lead from her death mask. The portraits include that of Sir Henry Sidney, attributed to Eworth, Lely's of Lord Romney as a boy, Johnson's *The 2nd Earl of Leicester* and others by Kneller, Wissing and Highmore. Elaborate gilt and marble-topped tables are ranged along the panelled walls and there is Indo-Portuguese ebony and ivory furniture. A William III four-poster bed hung with contemporary green velvet is in the Panelled Room below, with red lacquer furniture of the late-17th and early-18th centuries. The Nether Gallery reached through an archway contains sculptures, furniture and tapestries mainly from France and Italy. The Toy Museum in the 19th-century wing will intrigue the young of all ages.

Petworth House West Sussex

The National Trust

In Petworth, $5\frac{1}{4}$ miles E of Midhurst (A272/A283)

It is impossible to pass through Petworth without being conscious of the great house which occupies the west side of this pleasant town. Only its great wall and backyards are visible from the road but on entering the park the visitor will see the magnificent west front of the house, remodelled between 1688 and 1693 by the 6th Duke of Somerset, and the exquisitely romantic landscape designed by 'Capability' Brown in 1752 and so marvellously depicted in Turner's two sublime paintings of the park at sunset, which hang in the Turner Room with eleven other of the master's canvases.

The Northumberland Percys' connection with Petworth began in 1150 but it was after the Reformation, when the Percys were suspect because of their Catholicism (the 7th Earl was executed), that the 9th Earl was forced to live at Petworth away from his northern stronghold.

One of the two views of Petworth park at sunset by Turner, painted in the early 1830s; Petworth House.

The 11th Earl left an only daughter as heiress, who was married three times before her sixteenth birthday, on the third occasion in 1682 to the 'Proud' 6th Duke of Somerset. The 7th Duke died childless and the Percy titles and estates were therefore divided: Petworth, the vast Cumbrian estate and the Egremont Earldom went to the son of his daughter, married to Sir William Wyndham. Petworth has since descended through the male line to the present Lord Egremont and Leconfield who still lives here.

The outstanding collection of paintings at Petworth was started by the 10th Earl of Northumberland (1602–88), who acquired the splendid Van Dycks, notably those of Strafford and of Sir Robert and Lady Shirley, Titian's superb *Man in a Black Plumed Hat*, the eight small religious pictures by Elsheimer and several of the Lelys. The Proud' Duke commissioned the 'Petworth Beauties', representing ladies at Queen Anne's Court, from Dahl and Kneller, who portrayed the Queen herself. He also added the magnificent Claude and employed Laguerre to paint the walls and ceiling of the Grand Staircase after a fire in 1714.

The majority of the 17th- and 18th-century Dutch, Italian and French paintings were acquired by the 2nd Earl of Egremont (1710–63), who is said to have died from a surfeit of turtle dinners. Among these paintings are works by Hobbema, Cuyp, Van Goyen, the younger Teniers, van Ruysdael, Gaspard Poussin, Le Nain and Bellotto. The 2nd Earl also acquired the important collection of ancient marble sculpture, dating from the 4th century BC, through the Hellenistic period to Imperial Rome; the outstanding piece is the head of Aphrodite long attributed to Praxiteles.

The 3rd Earl's (1751–1837) greatest interest was the patronage of contemporary British artists and the acquisition of their works, both painting and sculpture. He enormously admired Turner, twenty of whose oils are at Petworth; he also bought works by Gainsborough, Zoffany, Richard Wilson, Blake, Fuseli and de Loutherbourg, as well as contemporary portraits by Reynolds, North-

Titian (c.1487/90–1576) Man in a Black Plumed Hat; *Petworth House.*

cote, Opie, Romney, and especially by Thomas Phillips. Among sculptors he favoured Flaxman, Nollekens, Chantrey, Rossi and Carew, and extended the North Gallery about 1826 probably as a setting for Flaxman's last great work, *St Michael and Satan*.

The furniture and wood-carving are also magnificent. The early-17th century contributed the black and gilt walnut chairs, nine with shell-shaped backs and nine painted with a coronet. In the Carved Room is the superlative pair of double picture frames by Grinling Gibbons on either side of the chimneypiece, together with magnificent work by John Selden and his early-19th-century successor at Petworth, Jonathan Ritson; there is further fine work by Selden in the Marble Hall. The outstanding pier-glasses and some of the French pieces of furniture were acquired by the 2nd Earl of Egremont.

There are also fine examples on display of Oriental, English and French porcelain, most of them 18th century.

Philipps House Dinton, Wiltshire

The National Trust

9 miles W of Salisbury on B3089, just N of Dinton village

Philipps House, Dinton, was completed in 1817 for the Wyndham family, which had long owned the estate, to the neo-classical designs of Jeffrey Wyatt, later to assume the name of Wyatville to distinguish himself from his uncle, James Wyatt. The house took its present name when the estate was acquired from the Wyndhams by Bertram Philipps in 1917: it came to the National Trust in 1943.

The airy, well-proportioned state rooms with their finely moulded ceilings are mainly furnished with Regency furniture, especially the Dining Room. The most impressive interior feature is undoubtedly the great central Staircase, its treads of Portland stone, which divides into two on the half-landing; it is lit from a circular lantern in the roof above. The mahogany doors and other fittings are of fine quality throughout. A pair of classical landscapes by Orizonte hang with other Italian scenes in the Drawing Room.

Plas Newydd Isle of Anglesey

The National Trust

2 miles from Menai Bridge on A4080

Plas Newydd on Anglesey, looking across the Menai Straits to Snowdonia from one of the loveliest sites in Wales, was occupied by the Griffith family of Penrhyn from about 1470 and a new house was built here soon afterwards. The property descended to Sir Nicholas Bayly, 2nd Baronet, whose marriage in 1737 to Caroline Paget brought the title of 9th Baron Paget of Beaudesert (in Staffordshire) to their son, who was the father of Field-Marshal Henry William (Bayly) Paget, 2nd Earl of Uxbridge (of the 2nd creation), made 1st Marquess of Anglesey for commanding the cavalry at Waterloo. The 9th Baron Paget, 1st Earl of Uxbridge, converted the original manor house into a noble 18th-century mansion. The Gothic and classical interiors, created 1793–9 by James Wyatt, assisted by Joseph Potter of Lichfield, remained unchanged until the 1930s when the 6th Marquess (1885–1947) entirely remodelled the north wing and made the long Dining Room, brilliantly decorated by the late Rex Whistler.

The Entrance Hall and Music Room are in the Gothic taste. The former rises through two storeys with a graceful plasterwork fan-vault ceiling and contains a shrewd, severe contemporary portrait of the 1st Lord Paget of Beaudesert (1505–63), one of Henry VIII's chief advisers, two vast paintings by Snyders and banners commemorating the Peninsular and Waterloo campaigns. In the Music Room, originally the Great Hall, are an elaborately carved chimneypiece, vaulted plasterwork ceiling and good family portraits, especially Lawrence's likeness of the 1st Marquess (of Waterloo fame) and that of Lady Caroline Villiers, his first wife, by Hoppner. The Staircase Hall with its elegant cast-iron balustrade contains late-18th-century neo-classical console tables with curving gilt supports and rams' heads, a fine neo-classical pier-glass in Wyatt's style, an impressive portrait of Catherine Knevitt, wife of the 2nd Lord Paget, by Gheeraerts, one of Caroline Paget, Lady Bayly, by Hudson and eight scenes of Marlborough's campaigns by Laguerre. In Lady Anglesey's Bedroom, decorated with advice from the late Sybil Colefax in the 1930s, is a pair of superbly carved gilt rococo girandoles after Chippendale designs and in her husband's Bedroom a splendid late-17th- or early-18th-century state bed.

The reception rooms facing Snowdonia, excluding the two Rex Whistler rooms, are neo-classical in style with elegant friezes by Wyatt. The fine gilt gesso pier-glasses in the Ante-room with their original Vauxhall plates and the large gilt console tables, their tops painted to resemble black marble, are late-17th- or early-18th-century and came from Beaudesert. A pair of Napoleonic Sèvres vases decorated with scenes from the Emperor's campaigns are an indirect reminder of the 1st Marquess's military achievements. Louis XV period painted chairs, upholstered in *toile de Jouy*, stand here and in the Octagon Room, which contains a Regency writing table with a brass gallery and an interesting pair of early-19th-century rococo games tables. The white marble chimneypiece is by the elder Westmacott, as is that in the Saloon, which is

Details of Rex Whistler's idealized version of the Menai Straits, a mural which stretches the full length of the Dining Room at Plas Newydd.

dominated by four large pastoral landscapes by Balthasar Paul Ommeganck; in addition there are magnificent gilt pier-glasses and tables, the latter in the manner of Kent, a mahogany architect's table of about 1760, a pair of George I period mirrors, Queen Anne walnut and padouk wood chairs and likenesses of the 1st and 2nd Marquesses. In the Breakfast Room are two fine seascapes by Peter Monamy and two by John Thomas Serres. The mahogany breakfast table is of Chippendale design.

There is a fascinating Rex Whistler exhibition in what was the Billiard Room and in the Dining Room his most celebrated painting, without doubt a masterpiece. On a single canvas stretching the length of the room is depicted a gloriously idealized view of the Menai Straits, in which can be recognized the steeple of St Martin-in-the-Fields, Trajan's column and other architectural landmarks. The Cavalry Museum, where hangs Denis Dighton's vast picture of Waterloo, is devoted to the 1st Marquess's campaign equipment; it also contains a fine portrait of him by Winterhalter. Adjoining is the interesting Ryan collection of militaria, mainly uniforms and headgear.

Polesden Lacey Surrey

The National Trust

1½ miles s of Great Bookham off A246 Leatherhead–Guildford road

The present house, a Regency villa built in the 1820s, replaced an earlier Caroline house once belonging to Richard Brinsley Sheridan, politician and playwright. Surrounded by splendidly laid out gardens and wooded hills, it was acquired in 1906 by Captain the Hon. Ronald Greville (d. 1908) and his wife, a distinguished Edwardian hostess. Between them they remodelled much of the interior, including the embellishment of the Drawing Room with its immensely sumptuous carved and gilt Italian panelling. Mrs Greville's father, William McEwan, left her the nucleus of a fine collection of paintings, furniture and other objects of art to which she subsequently added. Here in 1909 she entertained King Edward VII, and here in 1923 King George VI and Queen Elizabeth, then the Duke and Duchess of York, spent part of their honeymoon.

The Corridor contains Dutch paintings,

LEFT *Louis XV commode, c.1765, with pictorial chinoiserie panels; Polesden Lacey.*

RIGHT *The Tapestry Room, Nostell Priory, with Brussels tapestries, c.1750, and ceiling designed by Robert Adam.*

acquired mostly in the 1890s, among them a small, luminous landscape by Cuyp, two delightful interiors by the younger Teniers, a fine coastal view by Van Goyen and works by Salomon van Ruysdael, Jacob van Ruisdael, de Hoogh, van der Heyden, Adriaen and Isaac van Ostade, the younger Van de Velde and Terborch. Also displayed here are some 14th- to 16th-century Flemish and Italian paintings, including works by the Sienese, Luca di

Famille rose goose tureen, Ch'ien Lung period, c.1760; Polesden Lacey.

Tommé, Perugino and Van Orley. Among fine English portraits in the Dining Room are four by Raeburn, a Reynolds, a brilliant Lawrence (*The Masters Pattison*) and a Richardson.

Polesden contains excellent French furniture, mainly in the Dining Room, Drawing Room and Tea Room, ranging from the Renaissance to the early-19th century. There are superb Louis XV and XVI giltwood chairs, commodes, bureaux and *tables ambulantes*, often veneered in tulipwood and kingswood, inlaid with floral marquetry and mounted with ormolu; some are signed by distinguished *ébénistes*, including Genty, Roussel and Wolff. One of the most important pieces, stamped by both Tuart and Demoulin, who may have repaired it at a later date, is the *secrétaire à abattant*, lacquered and with ormolu mounts, in the Dining Room, where a fine English serpentine commode, c.1770, on which Chinese lacquer was also used, stands under the portrait of William McEwan. There is also good English furniture, the chairs often covered with fine needlework, in the Library, Study and Corridor.

There is a splendid collection of Chinese *famille verte* and *famille rose* porcelain in the Dining Room, the Corridor and Hall, and good examples of Meissen, Nymphenburg,

Fürstenburg, Bristol and Derby porcelain, much of it figurative. There are fine Persian carpets, mainly from Fereghan and Hamadan, although that in the Library is Chinese, *c*.1860. In addition there is a magnificent collection of silver, much of it English late-17th century, some of whose decoration reveals Mrs Greville's enjoyment of chinoiserie.

Fine Flemish tapestries embellish the Hall where the principal feature, placed on the fireplace wall, is the sombre richness of the oak panelling carved by Edward Pierce, taken from Wren's city church of St Matthew, Friday Street, which was demolished in 1881. There is a notable collection of 16th-century Italian maiolica in a show-case on the Hall Staircase including several plates painted by Francesco Xanto Avelli of Urbino.

Pollok House Strathclyde

The City of Glasgow District Council

3½ miles sw of Glasgow city centre, off the Pollokshaws road

Secluded in a wooded park with views over gently sloping fields, it is hard to realize that Pollok House lies within the boundaries of Scotland's largest city. Now administered as an art gallery by Glasgow District Council, to whom it was presented in 1967 by Mrs Anne Maxwell Macdonald and her family, Pollok has been connected with the Maxwells for 700 years. The family is thought to have descended from a Saxon nobleman dispossessed by the Normans in the 11th century, who came north to serve the Scottish kings. About 1269 Sir John Maxwell became the first laird of Pollok, and as lowland lairds they lived, in the main peacefully, for the next 300 years. Strong covenanting views brought the family fortunes low but after the succession of William of

LEFT *(above) The Edwardian Drawing Room, Polesden Lacey; (below, far left) Silver wine cooler, 1812, by Paul Storr, Petworth House; (below, left)* Reflection *by Matthew Smith, part of Rockingham Castle's collection of 20th-century paintings.*

El Greco Lady in a Fur Wrap, *c.1577; Pollok House.*

Orange and Mary they revived and in 1732 the 2nd Baronet commissioned William Adam to build him a new house, 1748–52, which is now the central three-storeyed block with a steeply hipped roof of the present Pollok House. In 1890 the 10th Baronet commissioned the second phase and work continued for some twenty years, during which time Sir John laid out the present garden with formal terraces flanked by garden pavilions. Little of the original decoration remains, with the notable exception of Clayton's plasterwork in the Drawing Room and fireplaces in the main corridor. Some of the furniture has been added since Pollok was given to the City of Glasgow, including a fine rosewood bookcase made by William Trotter of Edinburgh about 1820 and a pair of George II mahogany settees from the collection of the Earl of Moray. The superb long-case clock was made for the Maxwell family in the 1760s by John Craig of Glasgow. There are some very good examples of English and Oriental porcelain set out.

It is, however, for its remarkable collection

of paintings, particularly Spanish, that Pollok is so justly renowned. A unique example of Scottish connoisseurship, the collection was formed by one man, William Stirling of Keir who inherited Pollok from his maternal uncle in 1863 and became Sir William Stirling Maxwell, 9th Baronet. He had a rare knowledge of Spanish art and his *Annals of the Artists of Spain*, published in 1848, was for many years the standard English work. Apart from the Bowes Museum Collection at Barnard Castle in Yorkshire, the Stirling Maxwell collection is the most comprehensive private collection in Britain. It was mainly formed between 1842 and 1859, some of the most outstanding paintings being bought at the 1853 sale of King Louis Philippe's collection, when Sir William acquired two El Grecos: the enchanting *Lady in a Fur Wrap*, *c.* 1577 and *Portrait of a Man*, *c.*1590. The same year he acquired *Adam and Eve* by Cano and two Goyas, *Boys playing at Soldiers* and *Boys playing at Seesaw* which have affinities in style with his cartoons for tapestries dating from the 1770s. There is also a set of the

William Blake Adam Naming the Beasts, *1810; Pollok House.*

Goya (1746–1828) Boys playing at Seesaw; *Pollok House.*

last of Goya's four series of etchings, *Los Disparates*.

The Pollok Collection includes works by nearly all the great Spanish masters: a notable Murillo, *Madonna and Child with St John*, a strangely disturbing portrait of an unnamed royal baby by Claudio Coello, works by Carreño de Miranda, Morales, Caxes, Valdés Leal and Luis Tristán, besides many anonymous paintings from the 16th and 17th centuries. There are few Italian works with the exception of a Zuccaro portrait of Queen Elizabeth and a Venetian scene attributed to Guardi. Seventeenth-century Dutch and Flemish painting is represented by Miereveldt, Jan Steen, Berchem and Jordaens. The British paintings cover widely differing periods, from an Isaac Oliver miniature to a family portrait of the last baronet by Nicholson painted 1910–11, and include portraits by Hogarth, Romney and a Nasmyth landscape, but the glory of the British painting is without doubt the twin half-lengths of *Eve Naming the Birds* and *Adam Naming the Beasts* by William Blake.

Powderham Castle Devonshire

The Earl and Countess of Devon

8 miles s w of Exeter off A379 to Dawlish

A branch of the ancient and distinguished family of de Courtenay came to England in 1151 with Eleanor of Aquitaine, the bride of Henry II, and acquired Powderham by marriage at the end of the 14th century. Many alterations and additions were made to the Castle, especially in the 18th and 19th centuries; the last part to be built was the Victorian Tudor Banqueting Hall, started by the 10th Earl and completed by the 11th. It was the latter who commissioned in his father's memory the massive heraldic fireplace, similar to that installed by Peter Courtenay, Bishop of Exeter, in his palace in 1478. At one end of the Hall, facing the Gallery, is Hudson's portrait, 1756, of Sir William Courtenay, created Viscount Courtenay in 1761, and his family. It was the 1st Viscount who acquired the pair of elaborate rosewood bookcases with broken

Rosewood bookcases with broken pediments and brass inlay, 1740, in the Ante-room, Powderham Castle.

pediments and brass inlay, signed J. Channon, 1740, now in the Ante-room with family and other portraits, including two by Kneller.

The First Library beyond contains portraits by Hudson, Cosway and Downman, and has an elegant chimneypiece and two handsome pier-glasses. The later Music Room was designed *c*.1790 by James Wyatt for the 3rd Viscount Courtenay, who, when a boy, was scandalously involved with William Beckford. He later successfully claimed the title of Earl of Devon, in abeyance since 1556, to become the 9th Earl. This room has a handsome Carrara marble neo-classical chimneypiece by Sir Richard Westmacott, and a bronze grate, 1788, by Thomire. There is a fine domed ceiling, an Axminster carpet by Thomas Whitty, Wedgwood vases on the chimneypiece and gilt furniture, the chair arms shaped as dolphins from the family crest, probably made by the firm of Marsh and Tatham who were responsible for similar pieces in the Second Library; some of the 3rd Viscount's thirteen sisters made the embroidered white satin covers of the sofas.

More family portraits by Hudson, Downman and Cosway hang in the Second Library. The China Room, containing much good porcelain, mainly French, leads to the magnificent blue Staircase Hall, enriched with ivory, with its excellent rococo plasterwork, *c*. 1754–6, crowned by the mask of Apollo in the ceiling lantern. In the adjoining Marble Hall, partly oak panelled with tapestries above, is a huge long-case clock by Stumbels of Totnes and mahogany chairs bearing the family crest. The pleasant White Drawing Room has a view of the Castle by John White Abbott, while there are good portraits by Reynolds, Opie and Johnson in the 18th-century School Room.

Powis Castle Powys

The National Trust

w of A483 Welshpool–Newtown road

To find not only fine portraits and furniture of the Herbert family but also relics of Tipoo Sahib, the formidable Sultan of Mysore, in a dramatic castle guarding the Welsh Marches and the upper reaches of the Severn is an unexpected pleasure. The delicately carved cedarwood day-bed of the Sultan and a large collection of Chinese and Indian bronzes, the earliest being of the 15th century, are to be seen in the Ballroom at Powis; they were inherited and added to by the 2nd Lord Clive, son of Clive of India, who married the daughter of the 1st Earl of Powis of the second creation. In 1804 Lord Clive became the 1st Earl of the third creation, taking the name of Herbert in place of Clive; the 6th Earl now lives in the castle.

The origins of Powis, high on a ridge amid terraced gardens and ancient parkland, date from the reign of Edward I. It was purchased by Sir Edward Herbert, younger son of the Earl of Pembroke, in 1587 when the Long Gallery was built and the Dining Room and Oak Drawing Room decorated with fine plasterwork of which a little survives. The 3rd Baron Powis, Sir Edward's great-grandson, created Earl by Charles II and Marquess by James II (who later raised him to a Dukedom) installed the State Bedroom. A comparison of the balusters of the State Bedroom and the Staircase suggests that Winde may have been connected with both. Further work was done by Pritchard of Shrewsbury late in the 18th century but, apart

Isaac Oliver's miniature of Lord Herbert of Cherbury, c.1610–15; Powis Castle.

The Elizabethan Long Gallery at Powis Castle.

from the Ballroom, this was largely superseded by Bodley who remodelled the Dining Room and Oak Drawing Room in the 1900s.

In the Dining Room are family portraits by Dahl, Reynolds, Romney, Dance (*1st Lord Clive*) and Ellis Roberts. Here also are fine carved Chippendale mahogany dining chairs, not all original, and an early-19th-century mahogany wine table, complete with decanter stand and moveable bottle. The Library ceiling is decorated with Lanscroon's depiction of the five daughters of the 1st Marquess. The Library contains a Charles II settee and two armchairs and a small collection of ancient Greek red figure vases, as well as Isaac Oliver's famous miniature of Lord Herbert of Cherbury, which together with the fine Bellotto of Verona in the Oak Room belongs to Lord Powis' trustees. There are also portraits by Kneller, Peake (*Lord Herbert of Cherbury*), Riley, Gainsborough and Dance and part of Tipoo Sahib's Sèvres coffee service in the Oak Drawing Room. The William and Mary furniture includes an oyster walnut sidetable and one with floral marquetry picked out in blue-green stained ivory. Mortlake tapestries adorn the Gateway Room which houses twenty-four miniatures, including the 1st Lord Clive's daughter, by Cosway, and an English 15th-century Book of Hours.

The State Bedroom is remarkable for the state bed's deep alcove, guarded by a railing, reminiscent of Louis XIV's great bed at Versailles and the only one in Britain to retain this arrangement. The Queen Anne silver gesso furniture here, upholstered in Spitalfields velvet, is similar to the set in the Tapestry Room at Erddig. The Elizabethan Long Gallery contains early-18th-century console tables with eagle supports, a French walnut chest with carved portraits, 1538, and an outstanding 16th-century Italian table inlaid with marble and semi-precious stones on a wooden base with carved lions supporting the four corners. The wall clock with a four-hour dial is by

Tompion. The Staircase has fine acanthus carved balusters and treads inlaid with holly; the walls are embellished with murals by Lanscroon, 1705, and the ceiling is by Verrio. The Blue Drawing Room, whose ceiling is also by Lanscroon, contains two English black lacquer commodes, perhaps by Pierre Langlois, which incorporate Japanese lacquer panels.

Preston Manor East Sussex

The Borough of Brighton

On Brighton road to London at Preston Park

Perhaps the site of a Saxon settlement as suggested by its name of Preste-ton, meaning a priest's holding, the Manor stands partly on 13th-century foundations. Subsequently added to and altered, it took its present shape in about 1738. In 1905 major additions were made to the house which substantially changed its character and Preston Manor today presents the appearance of an opulent Edwardian country house. Charles Thomas-Stanford bequeathed

South German cabinet, c.1570–80; Preston Manor.

the house in 1933 to Brighton Corporation and since then it has been administered as a country-house museum.

It is not known if any of the contents of the house date from the 1738 additions and most of the furniture was purchased by the Stanford family after 1905. Nevertheless, its rooms contain fascinating and wide-ranging collections of both English and European furniture, as well as a notable collection of silver and Sheffield plate. In 1936 the widow of Percy Macquoid, the furniture historian, bequeathed a very important collection of English and European furniture dating from the 16th to the 18th centuries, as well as a small but choice collection of silver and ceramics. There are Stanford family portraits by Shannon and Orpen, a small group of 18th- and 19th-century landscapes by among others Alexander Nasmyth, Robert Anning Bell, and William Shayer, and miniatures, including one of the Duke of Wellington by J. B. Isabey.

Purse Caundle Manor Dorset

Mr R. E. Winckelmann

In Purse Caundle village, 4 miles E of Sherborne

This serene grey manor house, built in the 15th and 16th centuries, compels attention because of the varied texture of its attractive stonework. It stands on a much older site and may once have been a royal hunting lodge since this area was a popular hunting ground of the Plantagenets. Two families built the house. The Lang or Long family, which acquired the property in 1439, was responsible for its older parts, while the Hanhams, who inherited the manor house from the Longs, completed the task.

Both the Great Hall and the Great Chamber are of 15th-century origin. The former is open to the roof and is held together by an elaborate complexity of beams and braces; its frieze consists of panels, most of them quatrefoils with shields or leaves but some with sprays of oak and acorns. The wall panelling is 17th-century as is the balustrade in the Gallery at one end. The Great Chamber has a barrel-shaped roof and a pretty oriel window. The wallpaper was added some fifty years ago.

The house has three late-16th- or early 17th-century oak four-poster beds and other furniture ranging from the Jacobean to the Regency period.

Quebec House Kent

The National Trust

At E end of Westerham on Sevenoaks road, facing B2026 to Chartwell

This modest red-brick house, originally Tudor, is a place of pilgrimage for Canadians and for students of military history. The boyhood home of James Wolfe, its collection of prints and paintings, books, model ships, weapons and personal mementos is a powerful reminder of the career and personality of the hero of Quebec. Two items are particularly remarkable. The pencil profile of Wolfe, drawn by Captain Harvey Smith, an A D C, on a page torn from a field pocket book at the height of battle, is the only living likeness of the adult Wolfe to have survived. Equally evocative is Wolfe's travelling canteen – a rare and handsome example of campaign furniture, equipped to provide a substantial dinner in the comfort and style expected by an 18th-century general officer.

The Queen's House Greenwich

The National Maritime Museum

On s bank of Thames at Greenwich

The Queen's House was Inigo Jones' first architectural achievement, commissioned for James I's Danish wife, Queen Anne, and the first Palladian building in Britain. It spanned what was then the main road to connect the grounds of now long vanished Greenwich Palace with the park beyond. Work started in 1616, halted after Anne's death, was re-started by Charles I and completed by 1636. The house

Detail of the ceiling painted in 16th-century Italian style in the Queen's Bedroom, The Queen's House.

was later enlarged for Charles II and occupied by his widowed mother, Queen Henrietta Maria.

The Great Hall, designed as a cube, has a magnificent black and white marble floor, a painted ceiling in the manner of Thornhill and a first-floor Gallery. There is also a 16th-century Italian style painted ceiling with grotesques in the outer coves in the Queen's Bedroom, perhaps by John de Critz I or by Matthew Gooderick; a splendid spiral 'Tulip Staircase' by Jones with a graceful wrought-iron balustrade decorated with Henrietta Maria's *fleur-de-lis*; and richly decorated ceilings in the Queen's Drawing Room and the West Bridge Room. But the house's principal glory is the superb collection of 17th-century portraits and marine paintings. Lely's portraits include, among others, those of Prince Rupert and of Sir Robert Holmes with Sir Freschville Holles while Daniel Mytens is represented by his portraits of Charles, Earl of Nottingham, who commanded the English fleet against the Armada, and of Robert Rich, Earl of Warwick. The Dutch admirals Cornelis Tromp and De Ruyter, painted by Lely and Hendrick Berckman respectively, are also here, as is a portrait of Inigo Jones himself.

There are fine scenes of the 1673 Battle of Texel by both the elder and younger Van de Velde, painted while they were in England. Other Dutch marine artists include Bakhuyzen, de Vlieger, Storck and van Minderhout. One room is devoted to grisailles, large pen and ink drawings on prepared panels or canvases, a style in which the elder Van de Velde and Cornelis Bouwmeester excelled. There are fine

ship models, some 17th-century furniture and an outstanding collection of engraved glass, a bequest from Claude Jacobs.

Quenby Hall Leicestershire

The Squire de Lisle

7 miles NE of Leicester, near Hungarton

Probably the most important Jacobean house in the county, Quenby Hall, the original home of Stilton cheese, is built of diapered brickwork with stone dressings. Standing high in well-timbered parkland, it faces west with fine views and was erected *c*.1615–20 for George Ashby. It was remodelled in the mid-18th century in contemporary style, which included making the Hall two storeys high, a decision reversed by Bodley in 1905 when he restored the Great

The restored Ballroom at Quenby Hall, its ceiling a copy of one at Knole; the stone chimneypiece is early-17th-century.

Parlour, now the Ballroom, above the Hall. The present owner, of ancient lineage, who acquired the Hall in 1972, has meticulously put the house in excellent condition and moved here belongings from now demolished Garendon Park, formerly the family seat.

The Entrance Hall, with elegant screen, a pedimented chimneypiece and enriched with a Louis xiv Aubusson tapestry and a Felletin Verdure tapestry of the Louis xv period, contains a fine portrait of an unknown lady by a disciple of Hieronimo Custodis. Beyond is the handsome Brown Parlour, its neatly carved panelling consisting of tiers of blank arches and its plaster ceiling decorated with broad bands and pendants. The family portraits in pastels include works by Pond and by Rosalba Carriera, whose likeness of Ambrose Phillipps (1707–37) must have been painted on the Grand Tour – he was a founder member of the Dilettanti Society – as she never visited England.

On the first flight of the oak Staircase is a set of pictures depicting four allegorical figures of women, representing different times of the day. There are also family portraits, including two by Kneller, and a large Italian landscape by Locatelli. In the Library, its Gothic stone fireplace designed by E. W. Pugin, is a fine collection of books, a view of Quenby Hall by Tillemans, 1710, an 18th-century painting of Palm Sunday from Cuzco, Peru, and examples of Korean furniture.

The Ballroom, refurnished with panelling from other rooms, its ceiling a copy of that in the Ballroom at Knole, contains an ornate armorial stone chimneypiece. In addition to family portraits, there is an 18th-century giltwood Spanish table with a painted marble top, and a bronze by Clodion, 1760. Elsewhere there are 18th-century religious paintings from Peru and a splendid collection of pre-Columbian pottery.

In the Pomegranate Room, so-called because of its elaborate plasterwork frieze of pomegranates, is a Jacobean four-poster bed and in the early-17th-century Angel Bedchamber, whose pilasters were mutilated by Roundheads, is a version of de Critz's painting of the 1st Earl of Salisbury.

Raby Castle Durham

The Lord Barnard TD

1 mile N of Staindrop on A688

From Staindrop village the park slopes gently northwards to Raby Castle which, with its nine towers, is the largest medieval stronghold in the county. Cnut traditionally had a fortress in Staindrop and the 11th-century Bulmer's Tower may include part of it. The Nevill family, Earls of Westmorland, owned Raby for three centuries until their downfall in 1569 through participating in the unsuccessful Catholic 'Rising of the Earls' against Elizabeth, which was plotted here in the Barons' Hall. In 1626, the Vane family acquired Raby; they were ennobled as Lords Barnard in 1698 and later became Earls of Darlington and Dukes of Cleveland until the extinction of that particular line in 1891. A cousin then inherited the Barnard title of which the present owner is the eleventh holder.

The Castle has been added to and altered over the centuries. In the 18th century Carr of York made various alterations, including redesigning the Entrance Hall, in the Gothic style, to allow a large coach and horses to pass through it. William Burn, a Scot with a large mid-Victorian practice, altered much of Carr's work and built the heavily ornate Octagon Drawing Room and Dining Room, extended the Barons' Hall and restored the Chapel. The remarkable Kitchen with three huge fireplaces is 14th-century.

Raby contains a fascinating collection of paintings, good English and French furniture and some porcelain. Except for chairs in the Barons' Hall and marquetry pieces in the Library, scarcely anything predates 1714, the year when the 1st Lord Barnard sold the whole of the Castle's contents in anger at his son's marriage. The Small Drawing Room, its ceiling designed by Carr, has an excellent collection of sporting paintings by Marshall, Chalon, J. F. Herring Sr, Francis Sartorius and Wootton. In the Library are a portrait by Batoni, classical ruins by Marco and Sebastiano Ricci, and in the Ante-Library *Embarkation of*

H.B. Chalon The Raby Kennels, *1820; Raby Castle.*

the Queen of Sheba by Claude and Dutch scenes by de Hoogh and the younger Teniers. In Burn's Dining Room are good portraits by Lely, Cornelius de Vos, Hannemann, Amigoni, Reynolds and Hoare. There are further portraits by Lely, Reynolds, Hoppner and Grant in the vast Barons' Hall.

The furniture includes a fine inlaid tortoise-shell cabinet, perhaps 17th-century Italian, in the Ante-Library and French marquetry tables and cabinets, mounted in ormolu, some with Sèvres plaques, in the Octagon Drawing Room. Gillow made the tables in the Dining Room and the red and gold suite in the Barons' Hall which contains a splendid collection of white Meissen birds by Kändler and Kirchner, 1720–35; the pelican is believed to be the largest known Meissen piece in a private collection. There is also Sèvres and Doccia porcelain.

A collection of carriages and fire-engines is also on display.

Ragley Hall Warwickshire

The Marquess of Hertford

2 miles sw of Alcester on A435 to Evesham

James Wyatt's paired staircases and giant portico, added *c.*1783 to the impressive mansion started *c.*1680 by Robert Hooke for the first and last Earl of Conway and his only extant work, only partly prepares the visitor for the stupendous Great Hall, soaring the full height of the building. It was designed by James Gibbs for the 2nd Baron Conway, later created Earl of Hertford and finally Marquess in 1793 for services to the state, and the magnificent rococo plasterwork is by Artari. In the ceiling's central medallion Britannia presides majestically, the spear she holds entirely three-dimensional. Stucco figures of War and Peace in rich rococo frames face each other above the fireplaces. The furniture bearing the family coat-of-arms, encircled by the Garter, was

The Great Hall designed by James Gibbs in the 1750s, with rococo plasterwork by Artari; Ragley Hall.

made for the Hall in 1756 and the marble bust of the Prince of Wales, later George IV, by Nollekens was given by the Prince to commemorate a visit to Ragley.

The original 14th-century castle, now long disappeared, was acquired by Sir John Conway in 1591. It descended after the Earl of Conway's death in 1683 to Francis, created 1st Baron Conway, who was the younger son of Sir Edward Seymour, Speaker in the Long Parliament and grandfather of the 1st Marquess. The house was built gradually. James Gibbs completed the rooms in the 1750s and was responsible for the superb ceilings in the Study, the Green Drawing Room and possibly the Blue Room, although this may have been executed to a French design of the 1740s; the plasterwork was probably done by Artari. Further alterations to the ceilings of several state rooms, notably the Mauve Drawing Room and the Red Saloon, were undertaken by James Wyatt in the 1780s in his most accomplished

neo-classical style. Little has been added or changed since. Ragley became a hospital in World War II and has recently been restored with government grants and with the advice of the late John Fowler.

There are excellent collections of paintings and furniture. Reynolds is prominent with his portrait of Horace Walpole in the comfortable Library, with its carvings over the doors reminiscent of Gibbons. Two of the four portraits in the Blue Room are by Wissing and the other two by Dahl; here are Regency chairs, an English 18th-century chinoiserie cabinet and another made in Italy c.1700. In the Small Dining Room with its elegant chimney-piece are several equestrian paintings by Wootton. The portraits in the Main Dining Room are by Van Loo, Ramsay, Hoppner and von Angeli; the cut-glass and silver cruet set was made in 1804 by Paul Storr. More portraits by Kneller, Hayman, Hoppner and Richmond hang in the Ante-room. The Italian landscape

Detail of Graham Rust's recent mural on the South Staircase Hall at Ragley Hall.

Ranger's House London

The Greater London Council

Chesterfield Walk, Blackheath, London SE10

This late-17th-century villa, the home from 1748 until his death in 1773 of Philip, 4th Earl of Chesterfield, author of the famous 'Letters', has recently been restored and now houses some fifty paintings, nearly all of them highly impressive Jacobean and Stuart portraits from the great 19th-century Suffolk collection, owned by successive Earls of Suffolk and Berkshire, and generously given to the Greater London Council by the Hon. Greville and Mrs Howard.

William Larkin Lady Isabella Rich, c.1610–20, one of the Jacobean portraits at Ranger's House.

in the Mauve Drawing Room is by Vernet, the candlesticks and plates on the mantelshelf are Bow and Spode respectively, and the furniture includes Chippendale and Sheraton pieces.

The Red Saloon contains two outstanding paintings, *The Raising of Lazarus* by Cornelius van Haarlem and *The Holy Family* by Cornelius Schut, as well as works by Lely, Van Loo and Seeman; the furniture is mainly 18th-century French. Chinese Chippendale mirrors, with 18th-century French commodes standing below, embellish the Green Drawing Room, in which good French and English porcelain is displayed together with a pair of ormolu candelabra by Matthew Boulton. There are several excellent Reynolds and a magnificent carpet made in Portugal in 1973 for this room. A noteworthy Morland hangs in the Study, which contains a fine mid-18th-century set of English furniture.

The late Ceri Richards' large and magnificent *Defeat of the Spanish Armada* dominates the North Staircase Hall. The vast mural painting in the South Staircase Hall by Graham Rust entitled *The Temptation* is now nearing completion.

Nine of the full-length Jacobean portraits are by William Larkin, who flourished *c*.1610–20, an artist recently rediscovered through the researches of Dr Roy Strong; these include the richly clad 3rd and 4th Earls of Dorset and seven superb female full-lengths probably commissioned to commemorate the marriage in 1614 of Elizabeth Cecil to Thomas Howard, later the Earl of Berkshire, a title subsequently combined with that of Suffolk. In addition, there are admirable portraits by William Hogarth, Daniel Mytens, Johnson, Lely, Wissing, Kneller, Hudson, and a little known Venetian painter, Antonio David, who worked in Rome for the Old Pretender and is here represented by his splendid portrait of William Howard, Viscount Andover (1714–56).

Rockingham Castle
Northamptonshire

Commander Michael Watson

2 miles N of Corby on A6003

Rockingham Castle, a prominent landmark on its high hill, was built by William the Conqueror and remained a royal residence until the reign of Henry VIII when it was leased by Edward Watson and bought outright by his grandson who established a dynasty from which sprang the Earls and Marquesses of Rockingham and the Earls Sondes. A symbol of the Castle's royal provenance is the iron chest in the Great Hall left there by King John on his last journey in 1216. There is another ancient chest which once belonged to Henry V. Battered by the Roundheads in the Civil War, the Castle has been modified by succeeding generations to serve domestic rather than military purposes. The last building work was in 1850 by Salvin when the Flag Tower was erected.

There are good portraits, mainly of the family, from the Elizabethan period until the 20th century. The Great Hall, completed in 1579, contains a battered portrait of Edward Watson whose descendants still occupy the Castle, together with fine contemporary portraits of Queen Elizabeth I and of Francis I, King of France, by or after Joos van Cleve. Most of the furniture is 17th-century, as is the armour and weapons from the Civil War.

The Long Gallery contains important paintings, including four Ben Marshalls, one depicting the 3rd Lord Sondes and his three brothers with their hounds, an early Reynolds and a later fine portrait of Elizabeth, wife of the 2nd Lord Sondes. There is a charming Zoffany of the children of the 1st Lord Sondes, a conversation piece by Dahl, and portraits by Kauffmann, Lely, Beechey and Beale. The Long Gallery also contains late-17th-century English furniture, a Louis XV writing table and commode, an 18th-century painted sleigh and a pair of semi-circular tables painted by Kauffmann. Opposite the Main Staircase are two portraits of the 1st Lord Rockingham, one painted before and the other (by Dobson) after his imprisonment by Parliament for his loyalty to Charles I; Dobson's portrait of the 1st Lady Rockingham hangs close by. A view by Constable of Hampstead Heath is in the Library.

An unusual and attractive feature is the collection of 20th-century paintings, mainly British, made by the present owner and his uncle, Commander Sir Michael Culme-Seymour RN, 5th Baronet. Among them are

18th-century painted sleigh; Rockingham Castle.

fine representative works by Sir Matthew Smith, Stanley Spencer, Augustus John, Sickert, Robert Colquhoun, Paul Nash and Josef Herman.

Rossdhu Strathclyde

Sir Ivar Colquhoun of Luss, Bt

s of Luss off A82

Dignified and a little sombre, Rossdhu is an eminently civilized house built in 1772 and enlarged in the early 19th century by the addition of a classical portico and low flanking wings. It stands on a small wooded peninsula – *ros dubh* means 'black headland' in Gaelic – on the west shore of Loch Lomond, looking across its island-studded and often treacherous waters to the heights of Ben Lomond. This tranquil setting belies the violent history of the Colquhoun (pronounced Ka-hoon) clan which can be traced back to the misty periods of early Scottish history and is rich in clan warfare, blood feuds, cattle reiving, murder, treachery, and struggles for and against the crown. In the 17th century Sir John Colquhoun, 19th of Luss, was the last person openly to practise black magic. He married Montrose's sister, then eloped with her younger sister and fled abroad to die in exile. This sinister laird was followed by others devoted to more praiseworthy and peaceable pursuits. Sir James, 25th chief and 1st Baronet of a new creation, was a civilized person and the builder of the present house. The chieftains also made notable soldiers, Sir James himself having fought as one of the first Black Watch officers at Dettingen; a descendant became the first Colonel of the Gurkhas in 1800 and one of the large American branch of the clan, Lt Jimmy Calhoun, was killed with General Custer at Little Big Horn. The present laird's father was a legendary soldier in World War I.

Rossdhu reflects little of its turbulent past and is a comfortable family home. The Entrance Hall was repainted by Lorimer early in the 1900s and recently the panelling has been stripped to the original natural wood.

The small Drawing Room has been recently redecorated with modern hand-painted Chinese silk wall hangings made in Hong Kong. It contains part of a set of gilt Adam mirrors originally made for Rossdhu, but sold with much of the contents early this century. Some pieces have been traced and brought back. The large Drawing Room was severely damaged by fire in the early 1900s and was remarkably well restored by Italian craftsmen. It now contains most of the family portraits, which range from anonymous 17th-century paintings to works by Ramsay and Raeburn, notably of Sir James the builder. Two little portraits by Miereveldt are of the Winter Queen, Elizabeth of Bohemia, and her ill-fated husband.

The Library, which was originally the Saloon, contains impressive mahogany breakfront bookcases and has retained the 18th-century rich plasterwork cornice and frieze. A collection of boxing trophies and pictures reflects the achievements and tastes of the late laird, who was a lightweight boxing champion. A whole room is devoted to the remarkable collection of stuffed birds and animals made in the 19th century by his great-grandfather, naturalist and sportsman, the author of a classic work on Scottish Highland sport.

Rousham Park Oxfordshire

Mr C. Cottrell-Dormer

12 miles N of Oxford on Banbury road (A432)

The original house was built *c.*1635 for Sir Robert Dormer, a fervent royalist who, in case of attack during the Civil War, had musket holes made in the oak door into the Entrance Hall, which can still be seen today. They were to no effect as he was imprisoned by Hampden, the Parliamentarian, in 1642.

General James Dormer, on inheriting Rousham in the early 18th century, evidently found the house and grounds too old-fashioned. A friend of Pope and Swift, he was imbued with the Palladian principles of Lord Burlington and with ideas about the

The Great Parlour at Rousham converted from the Library in 1764 when the rococo plasterwork was added; the chimneypiece and overmantel are by Kent.

picturesque in the making of a garden. He commissioned William Kent to redesign the property according to contemporary style and it was Kent who created the renowned gardens, to the delight of Horace Walpole who described the results as 'Kentissimo'. He did not greatly alter the exterior, except to add two wings joined to the house by corridors, nor the general layout of the interior, which retains the original staircases. He did, however, add Georgian cornices, doorcases and chimneypieces to most of the rooms and marvellously redecorated the small Painted Parlour in the grand manner.

The Painted Parlour is one of the most enchanting of 18th-century rooms. Kent painted the ceiling in canvas 'after the grotesk manner ... as the Ancients used', as he once wrote. An oval composition of Bacchus and Venus is at its centre; the white background, painted with arabesques, is overlaid with diagonal red bands, also intricately decorated, and has two landscape vignettes, one at each end. The white marble fireplace with Medusa's head in the entablature is by John Marden; the romantic painting of mountebanks is by Pieter Van Laer in an elaborate carved oak and giltwood overmantel, supported at the sides by crouching eagles (Hussey) or swans (Pevsner). Kent designed the carved brackets to support General Dormer's bronzes, some of the furniture and the carved marble-topped tables.

Kent likewise decorated the room originally used by General Dormer as his library, which in 1764 was converted into the Great Parlour. The bookcases were removed and fine rococo plasterwork added to the doorcases and picture frames by Thomas Roberts of Oxford; this

283

involved lengthening at least one portrait to fit. Kent's unusual vaulted ceiling remains, as well as his white marble chimneypiece, containing both classical and Gothic features, and his giltwood overmantel framing Van Loo's portrait of General Dormer.

Rousham contains memorable portraits. In the Entrance Hall, with its finely patterned wood floor, are works by Johnson (*Sir Robert Dormer*, 1642), Riley, Lely and Kneller, and one attributed to Sanchez Coello. Dobson's portrait of the four kings of France hangs over the chimneypiece in the Dining Room, which also displays Kneller's fine *Sir Charles Cottrell*, *c*.1685, and likenesses by Dahl and West. Dobson is also represented in the Drawing Room along with Hudson and Reynolds. The likeness by Arthur Devis of General Julius Caesar, a member of an Italian family related to the Cottrells, hangs in the Music Room; other members of the family are on the Staircase, together with Kneller's portraits of the poets Pope and Edmund Waller. The Library contains works by Maratta, Berchem and Pannini, a drawing by Rowlandson and three John Piper gouaches of the house and park.

The Dining Room, with mid-17th-century mullioned windows and 17th- and early-18th-century furniture, at Rufford Old Hall; this room is part of the wing added to the central building in 1661.

Rufford Old Hall Lancashire

The National Trust

6 miles N of Ormskirk at N end of Rufford on E side of A59

Rufford is renowned for its late-15th-century Great Hall, for its collection of arms and armour and for the mainly oak furniture of the 17th and early-18th centuries, reflecting local designs and craftsmanship, which Lord Hesketh included with his gift of the property to the National Trust in 1936.

The stone-flagged Great Hall is unique in the exuberant decoration above window level. The elaborate open-timbered roof is supported by five hammerbeam trusses, the hammerbeams terminating in figures of angels with shields, only one of whom now has wings. Also holding up the roof are two free-standing octagonal carved posts cut from two oak trees of slightly different girth. Between these two uprights is an extremely unusual and rare movable screen, panelled on both sides, each of which has a projecting angel: above are three spires carved with late Gothic ornamentation.

Adjoining is the Philip Ashcroft Folk Museum containing fascinating relics from the surrounding countryside of life in the pre-industrial age.

St Fagan's Castle

South Glamorgan

Welsh Folk Museum

$4\frac{1}{2}$ miles w of centre of Cardiff

St Fagan's Castle, now part of the Welsh Folk Museum, was once a residence of the Earls of Plymouth and contains interesting furnishings, such as the elaborate late-16th-century three- and four-legged turned chairs and the oak-carved chimneypiece in the Hall. In the mainly 17th-century Parlour are an elaborately carved oak overmantel, a dresser with pewter, a stumpwork picture in a marquetry frame and a veneered walnut cabinet on twisted legs. A fine carved oak bed with canopy stands in the 17th-

Sampler, 1839, one of the examples of Welsh needlework at St Fagan's Castle.

century bedroom. The Withdrawing Room, with its ribbed ceiling plasterwork of squares, contains a pastoral scene by Bloemen, two Flemish tapestries, late Stuart chairs of various designs and a 1664 virginal with a charming painted scene inside its lid.

Plymouth family portraits hang in the Long Gallery, which possesses an intriguing 18th-century rococo gilt mirror and a Baroque pier-glass. Of special interest is the old Kitchen with its hanging crate to protect the bread from mice, its revolving spit powered by a dog running inside a wheel, its game rack and its Welsh dresser with clock centrepiece.

St Mary's Bramber, West Sussex

Mr and Mrs P. Smart

In Bramber on A283

Standing on a much older site and originally known as the Chapel House, St Mary's is a

The Blue Drawing Room, St Michael's Mount, decorated in Gothic style c.1740

Grade One timber-framed house, one of the finest in Britain. Its interior was altered in Elizabethan and subsequent eras. It contains oak-beamed ceilings and fine panelling, close on 400 years old; the panelling in the Painted Room was specially decorated for the visit of Elizabeth I to simulate views seen through arches. The former owner imaginatively restored what in 1945 was a derelict building and the present owners are continuing the work. Within the house are period furnishings, illustrated books on natural history and the Hendry collection of tropical shells. The later Burgess Hall houses the National Butterfly Museum.

St Michael's Mount Cornwall

The National Trust

½ mile s of Marazion, access by causeway at low tide, at other times by ferry

The cluster of buildings clinging to this romantic, soaring, sea-rimmed rock, first a Benedictine monastery colonized by monks from Mont St Michel, Normandy, then a fortress and since 1660 the home of the St Aubyn family, range from 12th-century to Victorian Gothic. The 3rd Lord St Levan donated it to the National Trust in 1954.

The journey through the castle starts in the compact Armoury. Beyond is the Study of Sir John St Aubyn, 5th Baronet, with family portraits, including excellent miniatures, and a long-case Mounts Bay tidal clock, c.1725. A wooden iron-bound late-15th-century cannon stands in the passage leading to the Breakfast Room, now a white and gold Library, hung with small watercolours of Mont St Michel, Normandy.

The great distinction of the Monks' Refectory, its 15th-century timbers restored 400 years later and known as the Chevy Chase Room, is its bucolic plaster frieze, c.1641, depicting boar, stag and ostrich hunting, bear baiting and the pursuit of a hare. Charles I's royal coat-of-arms stands above it at one end. The armour belonged to the castle's royal garrison in the Civil War. There are good portraits here by Dobson and Walker.

The 12th-century Chapel, restored in the

14th century, possesses a fine Flemish gilt brass chandelier, six Flemish and three larger Nottingham alabaster carvings behind the altar; that of St John the Baptist is outstanding.

The two enchanting Blue Drawing Rooms, converted *c.*1740 from the 1463 Lady Chapel and decorated with Gothic plasterwork, contain excellent Chippendale Gothic furniture, especially in the larger with its barrel-vaulted ceiling and in its Ante-room where a remarkable model of the Mount made out of champagne corks can be admired. These rooms are hung with delightful family portraits by Hudson, Arthur Devis, Gainsborough and the Cornishman Opie, by whom there are further likenesses in the Pink Music Room together with two by Hoare of Bath.

Salisbury Hall Hertfordshire

Mr W. J. Goldsmith

5 miles s of St Albans on A6

Salisbury Hall, a delightful building of russet-coloured bricks surrounded by a moat, is the remaining wing of a much larger mansion. Built mainly in its present shape soon after the Restoration, it was supposedly one of the meeting places of Nell Gwynn and Charles II. In 1905 it became the home of Lady Randolph Churchill on her second marriage to George Cornwallis-West, and it was here that Winston Churchill is said to have first met his future wife, Miss Clementine Hozier.

The site is ancient, possibly Roman, and there is evidence of earlier building in the Hall, where the black and white stone floor stands on three older levels. The remarkable Renaissance frieze of medallions in Totternhoe chalk stone from the Chilterns, each enclosing a Roman head, dates from Henry VII's time when the building then here was remodelled in Tudor style. The medieval tiles in the hearth dating from about 1380 indicate an even earlier structure. The Dining Room chimneypiece of 1640 unusually combines carved stone and wood with painted decoration.

The contents have no connection with the

house lovingly revived by the present owner who acquired it in derelict condition in 1955. They include a late-16th-century Hanseatic chest with decorative inlaid panels, reminiscent in style of a Nonsuch chest, several Charles II chairs and portraits by or after Vanderbank, Mary Beale and Knapton. The attractive Staircase has twist-turned balusters, with carved baskets of fruit on the newel posts.

Salisbury Hall was occupied in World War II by the design department of the De Havilland Aircraft Company, which produced here the first prototype of the Mosquito fighter-bomber. This can be seen in the hangar adjoining the house, together with other examples of early aircraft and a vast and fascinating collection of aircraft models.

Saltram House Devon

The National Trust

2 miles w of Plympton between A38 and A379 main roads

Saltram faces south towards Plymouth Sound on a site long noted for its beauty. Of Tudor origin, the house was converted between 1743 and 1750 into a restrained classical mansion, among the largest in Devon, by John Parker,

Carved giltwood settee, c.1770–1, perhaps made by Chippendale, in the Saloon, Saltram House.

Six-branch candelabra, 1772, by Matthew Boulton, one of four bought for the Saloon, Saltram House.

with pictures. Five are by Reynolds, including another of the 1st Lord Boringdon in his woods with a gun and, over the marble chimneypiece attributed to Sir Henry Cheere, a portrait of his young son, who became the 1st Earl of Morley, with his sister. Works by Vanvitelli and Charles Brooking are also here.

At the north end of the Velvet Drawing Room is a Corinthian pillared screen and a pair of carved giltwood pier-glasses as an overture to Adam's magnificent double-cube Saloon with its elaborate plasterwork ceiling by Joseph Rose, embellished with nine oil-on-paper painted roundels of mythological scenes by Zucchi; its decorative scheme is echoed by the Axminster carpet, which Adam designed. He may also have been responsible for the carved giltwood suite of two settees and eighteen chairs, the picture frames and the four giltwood stands, made perhaps by Chippendale to carry the four blue-john, tortoiseshell and ormolu six-branch candelabra by Boulton. Reynolds' work is again in evidence with his portraits of Theresa Robinson, Lord Boringdon's second wife, and of Paul Ourry.

The Dining Room, originally the Library, is again by Adam, including the exceptionally elegant curved and painted sideboard made to fit into the bay window and flanked by urn-shaped wine coolers on pedestal cupboards. Green enriched with white is the dominant colour here. The pastoral scene, its frame set into the wall above the chimneypiece, is by Zuccarelli; the other paintings are by Zucchi. The green and white dinner service with the Parker family crest is of Marseilles faience. The elegant Staircase Hall, lit by an oval skylight, boasts eight paintings by Angelica Kauffmann, including her sympathetic likeness of Reynolds. Further noteworthy portraits include the nine by Gilbert Stuart in the Library divided into two parts by an Ionic scagliola screen, together with others by Reynolds and Northcote and a self-portrait by Angelica Kauffmann. In the Boudoir are Parker likenesses by John Downman.

There is magnificent furniture everywhere – marble tables from Italy in the Morning Room, pieces in the manner of Boulle and the

spurred on by his wife, Lady Catherine Poulett, whose portrait by Hudson in the George II Entrance Hall supports the comment that she was 'a proud and wilful woman'. In addition to its fine collections of furniture and paintings, Saltram is noted for the Parker family's association with Reynolds, born in nearby Plympton (Lady Catherine is said to have given him his first pencil), and for Robert Adam's decoration of the Saloon and Dining Room. Adam's commission came from John Parker, later the 1st Lord Boringdon, whose portrait, also by Hudson, is in company with that of his mother, Lady Catherine.

The bold ceiling plasterwork in the Entrance Hall, dominated by Mercury, was possibly by Vassalli; that in the Morning Room, also Italian, reveals *putti* with musical instruments floating above Genoa velvet-clad walls, closely hung very rare Louis XVI French *escritoire*, stamped by Evalde, in the Velvet Drawing Room and further excellent French and Italian pieces in the Staircase Hall. The Chinese Dressing Room and the Chinese Chippendale Bedroom show the chinoiserie style to advantage.

Saltram is also rich with English (Bow, Chelsea, Derby, Plymouth, Wedgwood, Worcester) and European (Dutch Delft, Meissen, Sèvres) porcelain and ceramics, with bronzes, mirrors, chandeliers and other objects of art. The 1779 Kitchen is open to inspection.

Sandringham Norfolk

Her Majesty the Queen

8 miles NE of King's Lynn (off A149)

The Sandringham estate was acquired in 1862 for Edward VII when Prince of Wales, as Queen Victoria and the Prince Consort had thought it desirable that the heir to the throne should have his own country establishment on his coming of age. The original house proved

Jean-Edouard Lacretelle's portrait, 1885, of Princess Alexandra riding; Sandringham.

inadequate for the Prince, especially after his marriage in 1863 to Princess Alexandra of Denmark, and the present red-brick mansion with stone dressings, designed in Jacobean style and standing amid magnificent gardens, was completed in 1870. It is furnished and decorated in late Victorian and early Edwardian styles. Sandringham remains the personal property of Her Majesty the Queen and the Royal Family traditionally spend the New Year here.

The Jacobean Entrance Hall and the Saloon together form the principal reception room, separated only by a screen of two wooden Roman Doric columns which supports the Minstrels' Gallery. The Entrance Hall contains von Angeli's excellent portrait of King Edward VII when Prince of Wales, with his family, the first of many royal portraits to be seen throughout the house. In the Saloon are Winterhalter's *Queen Victoria*, 1845, and his *Prince Albert*, 1850, and three fine 17th-century Brussels tapestries. A wide-ranging collection of weapons, especially from India, hangs on the corridor walls. Three painted satinwood armchairs in the Small Drawing Room are covered with tapestry worked by the late Queen Mary in 1935: a wall case contains Continental porcelain from Dresden, Herendt, Copenhagen and Niderviller and portraits of the King and Queen of Denmark, parents-in-law of Edward VII.

Further display cabinets in the Main Drawing Room contain delightful Worcester porcelain, including two plates with exotic birds and part of a service painted with children from the workshop of James Giles; a glorious collection of objects, mainly Chinese, made from quartz, jade, amber, rock crystal and other semi-precious materials; Russian ornaments and drinking vessels in silver and enamel; and a cabinet devoted to fans. There are also late-19th-century royal portraits by Edward Hughes, their white frames enriched with ormolu sprigs, contemporary marble statues by Count Gleichen, a royal cousin, and a French rectangular table on cabriole legs stamped by the 18th-century *ébénistes* Louis Gillet and Léonard Boudin. Both here and in

the Dining Room, whose 19th-century tapestries are inspired by Spanish themes, the
white and gold decor of the elaborate plaster
ceilings and walls achieves a harmonious effect.
The Minton porcelain includes a handsome
dessert service decorated after Landseer. The
Lobby and Ballroom Corridor contain more
portraits of Edward VII when Prince of Wales,
his family and friends on official and less formal
occasions in Britain, Europe and India, and
more late-19th- and early-20th-century bronzes by, among others, Count Gleichen.

A Museum of great interest, containing big
game trophies, vintage cars and archaeological
finds, stands in the grounds nearby.

Scone Palace Perth

The Earl of Mansfield

½ mile W of Old Scone, 1 mile N of Perth on the
A93 Blairgowrie road

For close on a thousand years Scone (pronounced Scoon) was a monastery of the
Culdees, a priory and abbey of Augustinian
Canons. Kings have been inaugurated at Scone
from the legendary times of the 'high kings of
the Picts' to the last coronation in Scotland in
1651 when Charles II was crowned at the
church on nearby Moot Hill. The medieval
Abbey and Bishop's House were burnt by a
mob in 1590 with only the Abbot's house and
royal lodging surviving to form the core of the
present house, which was enlarged and
Gothicized in 1802 by William Atkinson,
Wyatt's pupil. Since 1604, when the 1st Lord
Scone and Viscount Stormont was granted the
property, Scone has remained the possession of
the Murray family, a branch of the Murrays of
Tullibardine (*see* Blair Castle). Its most
renowned member was William Murray,
younger son of the 5th Viscount, later created
Earl of Mansfield, who became Solicitor-
General, Attorney-General and Lord Chief
Justice, Chancellor of the Exchequer of
England, the most famous lawyer of his
century and perhaps of all time. His London
home was Kenwood, but many of his

possessions are at Scone, including several
portraits, notably Reynolds' of himself and one
of his wife. His nephew, the 2nd Earl, had a
brilliant diplomatic career: envoy in Dresden
and Vienna and Ambassador in Paris 1772–8.
The state bed bearing the coat of arms of
George III was presented to him by the king.
He bought much of the great quantity of
French furniture in the house. This includes a
Louis XV *poudreuse*, a *secrétaire* stamped by
Nicolas Petit and a *table-à-mécanisme* by
Topino. The Drawing Room contains a large
and important set of *fauteuils* by Bara, made in
1756. The Boulle commodes and tables *en suite*
are by Levasseur. An exquisite little writing
table by Riesener, stamped with Marie-
Antoinette's cipher, was one of three ordered
and delivered to Marly in 1781.

The wealth of French furniture and some
impressive Italian pieces incline the visitor to
overlook the many fine representative pieces of
18th-century English furniture. Scone contains
some important paintings, mostly family
portraits, including the 1st Earl by Hudson and
by Martin, the 2nd Earl by Batoni and a
delightful Zoffany of his daughter with Dido,
daughter of her uncle's West Indian housekeeper who had been freed from slavery by
Lord Mansfield. There are the conventional
and obligatory royal portraits by Allan
Ramsay and some 17th-century Dutch paintings, by Teniers, Koninck and Seghers.
Sculpture is represented by busts by Bernini,
Rysbrack, Nollekens and others.

The porcelain at Scone is particularly fine,
much of the best being displayed in glazed
bookcases in the Library. Meissen, Sèvres,
Ludwigsburg, together with Chelsea, Derby
and Worcester factories are all well represented. Among the Oriental pieces a pair of
K'ang Hsi *sang de bœuf* vases, mounted in
ormolu and stamped with the French royal
coat of arms, and a set of Ch'ien Lung vases are
outstanding.

The Mansfields have been notable collectors
of smaller works of art and craftsmanship and
Scone is a treasure house in this respect. The
collection of European ivories is one of the
largest in the country and is displayed in the

Writing table by Riesener, c.1781, made for Queen Marie-Antoinette (left) and the unique 1830s Martin ware collection (above) at Scone Palace.

Dining Room. Very different is the unique collection of *objets d'art* made of *papier mâché* by the Martin family who specialized in this craft and patented a process for painting decorative objects with coloured enamels in 1730. The seventy or so objects at Scone comprise one half of the King of France's collection; the other half was sold to the Tsar of Russia and disappeared in the 1917 revolution. An exceptionally large number of interesting and unusual clocks are seen in the house, both French and English, and include examples by such masters as Leduc, Alexandre Beckert and Thomire. The most impressive is perhaps the four-sided clock by Charles Edward Viner.

Little at Scone recalls the ancient house that Atkinson transformed, with the notable exception of the Long Gallery on the ground floor, 168 feet in length. The original floor of Scottish oak is inlaid with a chequered design carried out in dark bog oak. Many kings have walked here: Charles II to his coronation, his grandfather James VI and I perhaps to the adjacent room now called the Duke of Lennox's Room which still contains the monarch's oak table. There are also to be seen here pieces of bed hangings almost certainly embroidered by Mary Queen of Scots and her ladies and two well-preserved pieces of 16th-century needlework.

Shaw's Corner Hertfordshire

The National Trust

Ayot St Lawrence, 3 miles NW of Welwyn

George Bernard Shaw's red-brick house, with its small rooms and commonplace contents, in the remote hamlet of Ayot St Lawrence, contains no material treasure except perhaps for Rodin's bust and Augustus John's vigorous portrait of the playwright and critic. Yet the great man's spirit, boisterous still but gentler than he would sometimes have it, lives on here, evoked by his hats and walking sticks, his meticulous filing cabinet and exercise machine. Even more haunting is his writing cabin hidden among trees with his cane chair and spring bed-frame folded up against the wall.

Augustus John's portrait of George Bernard Shaw at Shaw's Corner.

291

Ceiling painted c.1788 by Charles Catton in the Prince's Room, Sheffield Park.

Sheffield Park East Sussex

Mr and Mrs P. J. Radford

On A275 between Uckfield and Haywards Heath

Sheffield Park was famous at the end of the 19th century because the 3rd Lord Sheffield, a devotee of cricket, initiated the Test Matches between England and Australia, some of which were played on his cricket ground on the west side of Fletching. The Jubilee match of 1896 was attended by the Prince of Wales, later Edward VII, whose room in the house is still called the Prince's Room. In 1954, parts of the gardens and lakes were acquired by the National Trust.

The original 16th-century house was bought in 1769 by John Holroyd, created Baron

OPPOSITE *The double-cube Saloon, Saltram House, with its Adam-designed Axminster carpet.*
BELOW *Pianoforte, c.1790, by Muzio Clementi in the Crystal Drawing Room, Sheffield Park.*

Sheffield in 1780 and later elevated to an earldom. He was a great friend of Edward Gibbon, the author of *The Decline and Fall of the Roman Empire*, who often stayed here and is buried in Fletching church. After the historian's death, his *Memoirs* were put together by Lord Sheffield and published in 1796.

James Wyatt was commissioned in the 1770s to Gothicize the house's appearance. The work included the entire exterior and interior but much of the Tudor house still exists within the present walls. Some unfortunate alterations, mostly to the interior, were made early in this century, which adversely affected the Entrance Hall and the perimeter of the upper landing of the Stair Hall. The present owners, who purchased the house in 1972, are skilfully and steadily restoring it.

The Music Room contains a Broadwood grand piano, *c*.1840, a Regency harp made in Dublin and a William Kent settee. The attractive Dining Room with its gold, yellow and black colour scheme reflects the colours of the marble chimneypiece, but probably the most delightful of all the rooms is the Prince's Room with its remarkable ceiling painted by Charles Catton RA, *c*.1788, the cove alive with tigers and leopards. The comfortable Library, once much used by Edward Gibbon, contains collections made by the present owner of Dickensiana and early printed books. The pleasing Crystal Drawing Room, with its curved end wall and triple window, retains its original Wyatt ceiling and fireplace; here is a pianoforte *c*.1790 by Muzio Clementi, a friend of Mozart.

Sheldon Manor Wiltshire

Major Martin Gibbs DL, JP

2½ miles w of Chippenham

This golden-stone manor house, guarded by ancient trees, its small 15th-century chapel close to the entrance porch, was started in the 13th century on what may have been an even older site. It was acquired by the Gibbs family in 1917. The interior, a home and not a museum, contains furniture in various styles from different places, acquired over many years, pleasantly and unpretentiously displayed, together with some good late-17th- and 18th-century Chinese ceramics.

In the Hall are 17th-century oak tables, 16th-century Spanish travelling chests, a fine cabinet inlaid with ivory and various woods, an 18th-century marquetry long-case clock by James Hubert and a collection of Nailsea glass sticks and flasks. The Dining Room has oak linenfold panelling, an unusual table-settle and a linen press in oak, both mid-17th century, and a high-backed oak settle of the early-18th century. The West Bedroom has an early-17th-century four-poster bed of oak with some of the original valances, a fine late-17th-century walnut chest with seaweed marquetry and a mirror with embroidery in a tortoiseshell frame.

Sherborne Castle Dorset

Mr Simon Wingfield Digby

Off A30, SE of Sherborne

This massive H-shaped mansion was started by Sir Walter Raleigh and enlarged *c*.1625 by the Digby family. In spite of mid-18th-century additions, when 'Capability' Brown created the lake to the north and west, and its spreading parkland to the south, its exterior is proud and forbidding rather than gracious, perhaps a fitting reminder of its five-week siege in 1645 before the Roundheads breached its defences.

The interior design and decoration range from the Elizabethan style, as in the Hall which contains the even earlier Digby tilting helmet, via Jacobean, as seen in the Oak Room with its fine elm table, and Strawberry Hill Gothic, as in the delightful Library, to the Victorian Dining Room or Solarium with its magnificent 1860 heraldic alabaster chimneypiece. There are good family portraits by or attributed to Johnson, Lely, Van Dyck, Daniel Mytens, Kneller, Beale, Kauffmann, Batoni, Reynolds and Hoare of Bath; Grant's portraits in the Solarium of Mrs Murray Stewart and of

LEFT *The mid-18th-century white and gold Saloon, Uppark.*

George Wingfield Digby on horseback were done in collaboration with Landseer who painted the animals.

In the Red Drawing Room is the magnificent *A Procession of Queen Elizabeth* I, *c.*1600, attributed to Robert Peake the Elder, and used by Sir Winston Churchill to illustrate his *History of the English Speaking Peoples*. There is much excellent furniture, mainly English especially of the 18th century, including two remarkable console tables supported by an ostrich with a horseshoe in its beak, the Digby family crest, with accompanying pier-glasses, in the Red Drawing Room; a pair of George III commodes in the manner of Pierre Langlois, the French emigrant *ébéniste*, Oriental lacquer cabinets on Kentian giltwood stands and a Jacobean walnut dispatch box with elaborate brass mounts in the Green Drawing Room.

Especially notable is the George Wingfield Digby Collection of Oriental porcelain, both Chinese and Japanese, professionally displayed and catalogued, from the 16th to the 18th centuries, including late Ming, Wu-Ts'ai style (porcelain in underglaze blue, red and with enamels) and K'ang Hsi. Also impressive are the Japanese Kakiemon and Arita enamelled wares, *c.*1660–1700, and a small group of Hirado porcelain (1751–1843).

Shugborough Staffordshire

The National Trust, administered by Staffordshire County Council

On A513 Rugeley–Stafford road, 5½ miles SE of Stafford

Shugborough was acquired by William Anson in 1624 and the core of this notable house was raised in 1693. William's great-grandson Thomas, a founder member of the Dilettanti Society and MP for Lichfield, extended the house in 1748, adding the wings and building

A Procession of Queen Elizabeth I, *c.1600, attributed to Robert Peake the elder; Sherborne Castle.*

the temples and monuments in the Park. These were partly paid for by his younger brother George, Admiral Anson, created Lord Anson after his spectacular voyage round the world in 1744, which enormously enriched him. James Stuart carried out further work, since swept away, in the 1760s. The Admiral's great nephew, created 1st Viscount Anson in 1806, employed Samuel Wyatt to carry out further extensive remodelling. His son, the 1st Earl, was both a progressive politician and a spendthrift; as a result most of the contents except the family portraits were auctioned off in 1842. Happily, the 2nd Earl acquired fine French furniture and most of the works of art in the house today.

The personality of Admiral Anson permeates the house. Marble busts of him and Lady Anson attributed to Wilton are in the Ante-room to the Dining Room; Hudson's portrait of him is above Scheemakers' marble chimneypiece in the Dining Room, that by Reynolds in the Saloon, while the Sitting Room is hung with prints and engravings of him and kindred naval subjects. Of outstanding interest is the Chinese porcelain he acquired in 1744. The Verandah Room contains the service of 205 circular pieces given him in Canton for the part played by his crew in extinguishing a dangerous fire; each piece includes views of Plymouth Sound and the Eddystone Lighthouse in addition to Chinese scenes. Two earlier *famille verte* dinner services are in the Chinese Chippendale display cabinet in the Blue Drawing Room, standing between Chinese mirrors in elaborate frames, one with its original mirror painting.

Equally important is the French furniture collected by the 2nd Earl. A Louis XVI parquetry *jardinière* is stamped F. Bury and two other fine pieces are in the Blue Drawing Room, while in the Red Drawing Room are pieces bearing the stamp of J. H. Riesener, L. Delaitre, Rübestuck and J. Schmitz. English pieces include white and gilt sideboard tables, *c*.1735, in the Dining Room, bearing the mask of Hercules and lion trophies, attributed to Matthias Lock. The late-18th-century satinwood cabinet off the State Bedroom bears the

Chinese Chippendale display cabinet containing famille verte dinner services; Shugborough.

stamp of Gillow. Also notable is the Wedgwood sauce tureen, 1744, one of 900 pieces supplied to the Empress Catherine of Russia, each painted with a different English scene; this piece depicts Shugborough.

The family portraits include works by Hayter, Reinagle, Grant and Landseer. Landseer also contributed splendid animal sketches to the fine collection, scattered about the house, of 19th-century sporting pictures. There are a number of paintings, by Nicholas Dall and Moses Griffith, of Shugborough and the monuments in the Park.

Finally tribute must be paid to the elegant plasterwork ceilings executed by Vassalli in the Dining Room and Library in 1748 and that in the Red Drawing Room by the younger Joseph Rose to Samuel Wyatt's designs in the 1790s.

There is evidence that both Vassalli and the younger Rose worked at Shugborough for James Stuart in 1763, but no sign of this work remains.

Sissinghurst Castle Kent

The National Trust

2 miles E of Sissinghurst village, off A229
Maidstone—Hawkhurst road

When Sir Harold Nicolson and his wife, Vita Sackville-West, both distinguished writers, acquired Sissinghurst in 1930, they merely rehabilitated what little survived of the 16th-century mansion and concentrated on the creation of the now famous garden. Nevertheless, the Library, with over 4,000 volumes and a few pieces of early Persian pottery, and the first-floor room in the Elizabethan tower,

Early Elizabethan panelling in
the Linenfold Panel Room, Sizergh Castle.

which was Vita Sackville-West's sitting room, retain something of their owner's personalities; the latter contains her own books, Sackville miniatures and mementos of foreign travel.

Sizergh Castle Cumbria

The National Trust

3½ miles S of Kendal, NW of A6/A591 interchange

This ancient rambling building, its pele tower erected *c*.1350 but the rest mainly of the Tudor period, stands amid lovely gardens. Its contents reflect the history of the Strickland family which still lives here after 740 years of occupation. The Stricklands went into temporary exile with James II in 1688 and their loyalty is commemorated by the Stuart portraits by Rigaud in the Dining Room, by the fine K'ang Hsi porcelain tureen mounted with ormolu, a gift from Mary of Modena, James II's Consort, and, in the pele tower museum by the intricately worked Privy Purse of Catherine of Braganza, Charles II's wife, and other intriguing Stuart relics.

The panelling and the early Elizabethan carving are among the finest in existence. There are four gloriously carved chimneypieces dated prior to 1580. The oldest panelling is that in the Linenfold Panel Room, probably dating from Henry VIII's reign. The walls of the Dining Room and the Queen's Room are covered with oak panels; their carved overmantels are superb. The magnificent ornate oak panelling, *c*.1568, of the Inlaid Chamber was sold in 1891 to the Victoria and Albert Museum; its elaborately designed plasterwork ceiling and frieze remain at Sizergh as they were too difficult to move.

Strickland family portraits include works by Lely, Wissing, Kneller (*Sir Thomas Strickland*, 1621–94, who went into exile with the Stuarts), Riley, Romney (*The Rev. William Strickland at his Toilet*), Opie and Owen, two appealing portraits of children probably by Hesketh, an assistant of Dobson and, over the fireplace in the Stone Parlour, an engaging likeness of Thomas Strickland in hunting kit with his horse, by Ferneley, whose painting of a fox with a dead duck is in the pele tower.

There is much good furniture throughout. A Jacobean oak refectory table and Elizabethan oak backless benches with elaborate supports stand on the pele tower's second floor. An unusual French painted slate-topped table, 1708, is in the Upper Hall. The Queen's Room contains a fine Queen Anne walnut cabinet and cushion mirror and three Louis xvi period pieces, including a *bonheur du jour*. Elsewhere are Italian ebony pieces, inlaid with ivory and other woods, an impressive set of walnut Queen Anne chairs on cabriole legs with ball and claw feet, mahogany Chippendale-style chairs and tallboys by Gillow.

Other noteworthy features include Bristol and Nailsea glassware and a collection of English ceramics (Worcester, Lowestoft, Liverpool, Caughley, Whieldon, Leeds and Chelsea).

Sledmere House Humberside

Sir Tatton Sykes, Bt

24 miles E of York on road to Bridlington

Richard Sykes inherited the Sledmere estate in the Yorkshire Wolds from his mother's family, the Kirkbys, in 1748, and set about building a suitable mansion on the site of the original Tudor manor house. In 1761 he was succeeded by his younger brother, the Rev. Mark Sykes, who was created a baronet for services to agriculture. He gave the estate seven years later to his son Christopher, who in due course succeeded to the title. He added to the mansion, commissioned 'Capability' Brown to landscape the park, which involved moving the village to its present site, and employed Joseph Rose Jr to carry out the plasterwork. A disastrous fire in 1911 destroyed much of the interior, which was almost exactly restored by Brierly of York.

The Entrance Hall with the rifles and banners of the Yorkshire Wolds Yeomanry, raised in 1798 during the Napoleonic Wars by Sir Christopher, little prepares the visitor for the triumphant sweep of the Staircase Hall with its Doric screens. It contains Rose's oval medallions of 'The Four Seasons'; the metopes of the frieze bear alternately the Sykes and Kirkby crests. Also here are a superb pair of Italian 18th-century marble vases on white and gilt pedestals and a magnificent set of Chinese Chippendale chairs which line the walls.

The Music Room furnishings include a splendid 18th-century organ case and a fine armorial Ch'ien Lung dinner service. Rose was responsible for its enchanting neo-classical ceiling and also for the wall decorations of the Dining Room, where the original ceiling remains unchanged. Romney's portrait of the aloof Sir Christopher and his wife, Elizabeth Tatton, thought to be the artist's only double portrait, hangs in the Dining Room, with its Hepplewhite chairs and Sheraton sideboard on which stands an excellent pair of Sèvres vases, flanking a marvellous early-18th-century Baroque clock; the vases and clock come from the Orleans collection. Rose also executed the heavier plasterwork of the Drawing Room in which there is a fine Louis xv *bureau de dame* by Dubois and gilt furniture, *c*.1790, made especially for this room by John Robbins, a London cabinet-maker; among the portraits is Romney's *William Tatton Egerton* MP, a family group by Lawrence and Grant's accomplished likeness of Sir Tatton Sykes (1772–1863), the 4th Baronet, renowned as a tyrannical father and a bloodstock breeder.

The paintings in the Study are mainly devoted to the Sledmere Stud by, among others, J. F. Herring Sr and Chalon. The furniture here includes a magnificent early-18th-century South German marquetry bureau cabinet, two Chippendale settees and a card table, as well as part of a set of Chinese Chippendale chairs; the library armchair and stool are by Giles Grendy.

The majestic first-floor Library, running the width of the house, echoes Imperial Roman halls at their grandest. Its book collection would have been even finer if the 4th Baronet had not sold off part of it, rather than his hounds, to pay his inherited debts. Rose designed the barrel- and cross-vaulted ceiling,

picked out in colour and now being restored. The furniture upholstered in red damask is by Giles Grendy. The original carpets were destroyed in the 1911 fire but the pattern was reproduced in mahogany parquetry by Brierly. The two white marble chimneypieces were designed by Sir Christopher.

The ground-floor Turkish Room was built for the 6th Baronet, a distinguished soldier and diplomat who helped draw up the Sykes-Picot Palestine Agreement in 1916. It contains a remarkably pretty and very rare 18th-century Canton enamel table.

Smallhythe Place Kent

The National Trust

2 miles s of Tenterden on E side of Rye road (B2082)

Dame Ellen Terry, the renowned actress, made this timbered house, built c.1480, her home and died here in 1928. Miss Edith Craig converted it into a memorial to her mother and in 1939 presented it to the Trust.

Anyone interested in the theatre will be enthralled by the contents, for Dame Ellen was a great collector of theatrical souvenirs. In the ground-floor Terry Room is furniture from the Lyceum stage; a sketch of her by Sargent; one of her mother, Mrs Benjamin Terry, by Archer Shee; her old make-up basket; a miscellany of snuff boxes, miniatures, costume jewellery and friendship beads from various friends, a letter from Oscar Wilde, theatre programmes and much else. The carved beam over the fireplace once supposedly belonged to Nell Gwynn.

The Dining Room with its oak dresser, pewter mugs and an early-17th-century oak armchair is filled with mementos of other stage personalities, such as David Garrick's knives and forks, Sir Arthur Sullivan's eyeglass, a necklace worn by Fanny Kemble, photographs of Sarah Bernhardt, Rachel and Eleanora Duse, and a plaster cast of Dame Ellen's hand. In the first-floor Costume Room the silk and satin garments still retain their colour and sheen. Among them is the famous beetle dress of

Laura Taylor's painting of Ellen Terry and her sister Kate acting in The Hunchback; *Smallhythe Place.*

Lincoln green with a maroon and embroidered cape which Dame Ellen wore as Lady Macbeth in 1888.

The Lyceum Room is dedicated to her outstandingly successful twenty-four-year partnership with Sir Henry Irving at the Lyceum. There are several sketches of Irving and a remarkable set of woodcuts by her son, Gordon Craig, a showcase of Lyceum mementos and costumes worn by Dame Ellen and Sir Henry. The Bedroom remains virtually as Dame Ellen left it with portraits of her family and many intimate possessions, including a copy of the Globe Shakespeare annotated in her own hand.

Snowshill Manor Gloucestershire

The National Trust

3 miles s of Broadway

The stone Cotswold manor of Snowshill, dating mainly from c.1500 with alterations and

*Looms and spinning wheels in the Mizzen Room,
Snowshill Manor.*

additions in *c.*1660 and *c.*1720, was affec-
tionately restored in the present century by
Charles Wade (1883–1956) who then crammed
room after room, each fancifully named to
reflect something of its contents, with a
bewildering and quite fascinating variety of
objects. He was primarily concerned not so
much with the arts but with examples of
skilled craftsmanship from all parts of the
world.

In the Turquoise Hall is a collection of
Chinese bureaux and cabinets, designed as
Buddhist shrines, together with models of
Chinese junks, two Japanese clocks and early-
19th-century English musical instruments.
Between the Entrance Hall and Meridian is a
small display case containing shoes and slippers.
Zenith contains, in addition to much Oriental
export porcelain, a Friesland bracket clock, its
face embellished with angels and supported

each side by a helmet-crowned mermaid
blowing a trumpet.

A fine collection of mainly nautical interest
is in Admiral, including walking sticks made
from a narwhal tusk. Twenty-six suits of
Japanese Samurai armour stand menacingly in
the Green Room together with a fine Japanese
Buddhist domestic shrine and two Tibetan
prayerwheels.

Elsewhere are boneshaker bicycles
(1870–85); children's prams; sentimental 19th-
century coloured prints for cottage decoration;
a collection of spinning wheels; farm wagons;
tools associated with clothmaking, including
fly and hand shuttles; an oak canopied bed
with rope mattress supports and sockets in the
frame for five corpse candles, representing the
five wounds of Christ; an intriguing small
stumpwork casket, and countless other delightful and admirable objects.

Somerleyton Hall Suffolk

The Lord and Lady Somerleyton

5 miles NW of Lowestoft off B1074

'Somerleyton is a specimen of the architecture of the Elizabethan period, transformed by the purest taste into a rich and noble example of Anglo-Italian. A rich, harmonious style pervades the whole building, and a master mind can be traced in every design and in every enrichment.' These words introduced the 'Particulars of Sale', prepared in 1861 when Sir Morton Peto, a self-made railway financier who had built this spectacular Victorian house, was verging on bankruptcy. In 1863, it was bought by Sir Francis Crossley, Bt, an immensely successful carpet manufacturer and a generous benefactor to Halifax, the scene of his industry.

The panelling in the Oak Parlour is from the original Jacobean house which had first stood here, as is the wood-carving of the doorcases and round the chimneypiece. The silver gilt moulded mirror came originally from the Doge's Palace in Venice and the tapestry here is 18th-century Flemish. The Library is used as the family sitting room, an understandable choice in view of the attractive light carved oak used throughout the room and the colourful Savonnerie carpet from Paris. Each bookshelf is appropriately labelled, as for example 'Science and Mental Philosophy', and there are altogether over five thousand books.

The Dining Room contains interesting paintings, including a portrait of Admiral Sir Thomas Allin, Somerleyton's owner in the 17th century, by Kneller, two canvases of the Peninsular War by Clarkson Stanfield, one depicting the siege of San Sebastian, and a biblical study by Reni. Family portraits and works by J. F. Herring and Landseer are in the Front Hall and two huge polar bears in the dark panelled Entrance Hall; the 1st Baron shot fifty-seven in the Arctic in 1896.

The Drawing Room with its elaborate plasterwork ceiling and brilliant white paint-work enriched with gilt and its display cabinets is perhaps the most characteristically Victorian room. There is also an elaborate dolls' house.

Speke Hall Merseyside

The National Trust, administered by Merseyside County Museums

8 miles SE of Liverpool on E side of Speke airport

This splendid quadrangular Tudor black and white half-timbered manor house enclosing a courtyard was started in 1490 by Sir William Norreys and was completed about 1612, since when its exterior has been little altered. Wood was then much used for building in Cheshire and southern Lancashire because of the scarcity of stone.

The exterior makes little concession to the influence of the Renaissance then reaching these shores, but the effective use of Flemish Renaissance decorative motifs can be seen in the great wainscot panelling on the west side of the Great Hall, especially in the treatment of the classical pilasters and of the carved oak and plaster busts which may represent Roman

Detail of the genealogical overmantel, c.1560, carved in Flemish Renaissance style; Speke Hall.

emperors. Close contacts developed between England and the Low Countries in the latter part of the 16th century after the breach with Rome made direct contact with Italy impractical. The chimney breast displays various types of Gothic decoration.

Another outstanding decorative feature is the Great Parlour's plasterwork ceiling: it consists of panels of roses, pomegranates, vines and flowers, the beams decorated with hop and honeysuckle motifs; the Flemish Renaissance influence can be seen in the use of the buckler and strap motifs out of which the vines grow. Also notable is the genealogical overmantel carved in Flemish style.

In the mid-18th century, Speke fell into disrepair until it was rescued by Richard Watt, a Liverpool merchant, whose 19th-century descendants gradually restored the house, furnishing it with Victorian pieces made in 16th- and 17th-century styles and sometimes incorporating carvings from earlier periods. Some of the panelling and fireplaces are also 19th-century revivals of Elizabethan and Jacobean designs.

Springhill Co. Londonderry

The National Trust

On Moneymore–Coagh road, 1 mile from Moneymore

The martial Conyngham family from Ayrshire owned the Springhill estate of 350 acres, acquired for £200 in 1658, until the death in 1957 of Captain William Lenox-Conyngham, when the house passed to the National Trust. Built late in the 17th century, it was originally protected by a defensive barrier, which was dismantled when the house was extended in 1765.

The pleasing interior has changed little during the last 200 years except for the addition of the Dining Room c.1850. The panelled Entrance Hall and the fine oak Staircase Hall beyond are hung with family portraits by unknown artists. The Hall also contains two brass-bound Dutch East Indies export chests.

There are late-18th-century Irish ladder-back chairs in the Library, on whose shelves are fine old leather-bound books, including a rare English-Irish dictionary. The portraits of William III and Mary supposedly by Kneller, were given to Sir Albert Conyngham, who raised a regiment for the king, for services to the Protestant cause. The cabinet contains Wedgwood basalt ware.

A group of pastel family portraits by Hugh Douglas Hamilton hangs in the Drawing Room near the show-case containing a miscellany of mementos of the Lenox-Conyngham family. The Bedroom contains an intriguing medicine chest, once owned by the 3rd Viscount Molesworth, a family connection by marriage and the great Duke of Marlborough's A D C.

In the well-proportioned Dining Room, embellished with more family portraits, is a painting of a group of young men on the Grand Tour. The marquetry walnut chairs with fiddle backs are of the William and Mary period. The marble of the mantelpiece was brought from Herculaneum by the 4th Earl of Bristol, Bishop of Derry.

The firearms in the Gun Room, whose walls are hung with Chinese wallpaper of the 1720s, the oldest in Northern Ireland, include a six-feet six-inches-long muzzle-loader, used during the 1689 siege of Derry, and two late-18th-century blunderbusses.

There is an intriguing mainly 19th-century Costume Museum in a building close by.

Squerryes Court Kent

Mr J. St A. Warde

Off A25 at w end of Westerham

Standing in well-wooded grounds and facing south across its lake towards the Surrey Hills, this red-brick William and Mary manor house with its central pediment and hipped roof is today little changed from when it was first built in 1681. It was acquired in 1731 by John Warde, whose father, Sir John, and great-uncle, Sir Patience Warde, were both Lord

John Wootton The Warde Family, *c.1735; Squerryes Court.*

Mayors of London. Their descendants still live here. The paintings and furniture are of splendid quality.

The spacious Entrance Hall is dominated by Warde and Bristow family portraits by or in the manner of Riley, Dahl and Vanderbank. Here also is the royal pardon, written in Latin and signed by Charles II, which Sir Patience was granted at the Restoration after he had supported the Parliamentarians in the Civil War. The Dining Room with its elegant early-18th-century furniture, its mirrors of the same period surmounted by the Warde crest and an exotic Indo-Portuguese cabinet from Goa, *c.*1680, contains a fine collection of Dutch 17th-century paintings acquired by the second John Warde. They include a delightful family group outdoors by Van der Helst, two Ruysdaels and a Hondecoeter over the fireplace, two by Van Goyen, a fine example of Siberechts' work, and a Steenwyck, depicting Christ driving the moneylenders out of a vast Gothic church.

In the Drawing Room are more family portraits, including Wootton's Warde family group on horseback, *c.*1735, his portrait of Mrs Warde and two by Arthur Devis. There is also Barraud's 1829 portrait of John Warde, known as the father of foxhunting; on the table below is his Wedgwood punchbowl. Other family portraits are by Dandridge and Opie. Of special interest is Stubbs' canvas of a horse. Here also is more excellent early Georgian furniture and a pair of mahogany music stands in the rococo manner bearing the family arms. Three fine Soho tapestries by Joshua Morris, *c.*1730, after designs by Clermont, hang in the Tapestry Room with six embroidered late-18th-century pictures from Spain or Italy.

The paintings on the first-floor Gallery include a St Sebastian by Van Dyck, two large allegorical scenes by Giordano, a portrait of Philip II of Spain after Rubens, some fine lacquered furniture and a large early-18th-century Chinese armorial dinner service.

The Wolfe Room commemorates the great friendship between the Warde family and the young James Wolfe, victor at Quebec in 1759. Wolfe's first commission reached him while he was staying at Squerryes. Here is perhaps the only portrait for which the future General sat, painted at the age of thirteen, and other mementos.

The Museum of the Kent and County of London Yeomanry is established here.

Standen West Sussex

The National Trust

2 miles sw of East Grinstead on the Saint Hill road (B2110)

Although built in 1892–4, Standen's absence of clutter and its fresh decorative colouring gives it an anti-Victorian character. Its architect, Philip Webb (1831–1915), was a life-long friend and associate of William Morris whose influence strongly pervades the interior. The walls of the Drawing Room, Corridor and Stair Hall are hung with Morris-designed wallpapers, those of the Morning Room with his chintz, while much of the furniture and furnishing textiles were provided by the firm of Morris & Co. Webb himself designed the light fittings and some pieces of furniture recently introduced by the National Trust. There is a particularly fine carpet by Morris and Co. in the Drawing Room. In the Hall are portraits by William Nicholson of James and Margaret Beale for whom the house was built, and drawings in the Morning Room corridor by, among others, Burne-Jones, Madox Brown and Holman Hunt. Other decorative features include Japanese prints, pink lustre pottery by William de Morgan and Chinese blue and white ceramics.

Stanford Hall Leicestershire

The Lord and Lady Braye

7½ miles NE of Rugby off B5414

Sir Thomas Cave acquired Stanford Hall on the Dissolution of the Monasteries but the

Stained glass by Edward Burne-Jones at Standen.

present elegant four-square William and Mary mansion was built to designs by the Smiths of Warwick after 1690, when Sir Roger Cave, 2nd Baronet, decided to re-site the family home on the Leicestershire side of the River Avon. The house took many years to complete. The 3rd Baronet married Margaret Verney of Claydon through whom the Braye title, created by Henry VIII, came to the Cave family in 1839 after long abeyance. The rectangular stables of warm red brick, built by the 5th Baronet, stand close to the mansion which is set in mellow green parkland.

Two tall flights of steps meet outside the entrance to the *piano nobile*; its Marble Passage leads to the heart of the house and the great mahogany flying Staircase with carved balusters, the newels formed as Tuscan columns, surmounted by glass candle-holders. The walls of the Passage, the Staircase and the state rooms are hung with portraits of Elizabethan statesmen, of the royal Stuarts, and of the Cave and Verney families (whose descendants still live here), painted, among others, by Johnson, Lely, Kneller and Hudson.

The finely proportioned Ballroom has many distinguished features – its pedimented chimneypiece; its doorcases embellished with swags hanging from lions' masks and crowned with a broken pediment containing the Braye arms, supported by *putti*; the richly plastered ceiling and gilded frieze; the parquet floor and the giltwood, marble-topped 18th-century sidetables, on one of which stand Chinese export wares and fine cut-glass on the other. The portraits here are of outstanding interest, having all belonged, with one exception, to

L. Pecheux's portrait, 1770, of Prince Charles Edward, the 'Young Pretender', in middle age; Stanford Hall.

Henry Stuart, Cardinal Duke of York, younger brother of the Young Pretender, whose name is given as Henry IX on his portrait in the Marble Passage. There are also portraits of the Old Pretender, described as James III, and of the Young Pretender in middle age by Pecheux, together with a case of Stuart relics including the Cardinal's crucifix, cardcase, spectacle case and a miniature of Mary Queen of Scots which belonged to Marie de Medici, acquired after the Cardinal's death in 1807.

Fine furniture includes the pier-glass and gilt table below it in the Grey Drawing Room; the fine late-17th-century English walnut corner cupboard and the small Queen Anne writing cabinet with mirror in the Green Drawing Room; the set of six late-17th-century longback chairs with corkscrew legs and tapestry covers in the upstairs Oak Gallery; an old refectory table and a case of well-preserved 18th-century waistcoats and other garments. The oak-panelled Library contains a Gothic library table, relics of the Battle of Naseby which was fought nearby, and documents, including an eye-witness account of the trial and execution of Charles I. There is a small Roman Catholic chapel in an outhouse and an Aviation Museum named after Percy Pilcher, the first man to fly in England, who was killed here in 1899.

Stapleford Hall Leicestershire

The Lord Gretton OBE

5 miles E of Melton Mowbray, 1 mile S of B676

Three distinct building phases mark the history of Stapleford Park. The most remarkable is the earliest, namely the Tudor wing, erected about 1500 by Thomas Sherard, great-grandson of Robert Sherard to whom the estate came by marriage in 1402: it was handsomely restored in 1633. In about 1670 Bennet Sherard, 2nd Lord Harborough, added the Restoration hipped-roof mansion, parts of which were redecorated in the 1770s. The Jacobean style south wing was added after the estate had been acquired in 1894 by the present owner's grandfather. Standing in fine parkland, Stapleford (pronounced 'Stappleford') contains good paintings, furniture and decorative features.

The elegant plasterwork ceiling with its blue and ivory centrepiece and the fireplace in the 1670 Entrance Hall are late-18th century. The walls are hung with sporting pictures by John Ferneley and by J. F. and J. N. Sartorius. In the Ante-room the bold 17th-century decoration of the frieze, of the entablature over the door, of the overmantel enclosing the Victorian mirror, and on the wall panels have been attributed to Webb. This room contains an excellent Italian ebony, tortoiseshell and ivory cabinet, 1643, Louis xv commodes and good portraits by Zoffany, Reynolds and Hone. In Lady Gretton's Sitting Room is a fine William and Mary chest-of-drawers in oyster veneer walnut, a Louis xvi writing table and portraits by Lely, Cotes and Romney.

Admirable paintings in the Drawing Room include a view of the Tiber, the Castello St Angelo and the Vatican beyond by Bellotto, two fine Venetian scenes by Guardi and Dutch works by Ruysdael, Van Goyen and Van der Neer. Hone's unusual portrait of General Sherard, shown directing a battle with his ADC, hangs in the late-19th-century Saloon with likenesses by Kneller and Hudson and shipping scenes by Monamy and Berchem. More excellent Dutch works are in the Library, including portraits by Hanneman and Miereveldt. There are two very interesting full-length portraits in the vaulted Old Kitchen, by or attributed to Gheeraerts, of the 1st Lord Sherard and his wife. In the Dining Room, whose elaborately carved overmantel is by a disciple of Gibbons, are portraits by Van Dyck (*The Betrothal*), Lely and Kneller: the furniture is in the Hepplewhite manner.

The Victorian Marble Hall and Staircase contain Empire furniture, a vigorous late-17th-century Mortlake tapestry, a Church Gresley dessert service (the factory operated near Burton-upon-Trent between 1794 and 1808), a collection of seascapes, and family portraits, among others, by Birley and de Laszlo. In the Long Gallery, built in the 1890s, its walls and ceiling impressively undecorated, are two

N. Hone's painting of General Sherard with his aide-de-camp at the Battle of Bruckmuhl (1762); Stapleford Hall.

Dutch or Flemish carved-oak cabinets, a 17th-century Swedish chair covered in Spanish leather and a splendid late-18th-century French chandelier. The chimneypieces are 18th century, the further one by Rysbrack, whose impressive monument to the 1st Earl of Harborough, his wife and child is in the fascinating late-18th-century Gothic parish church in the grounds. The Balston collection of Staffordshire figures, presented to the National Trust by the late Thomas Balston, should also not be missed.

Stonor Park Oxfordshire

The Lord Camoys

On B480, 5 miles N of Henley-on-Thames

Stonor, standing on a hillside amid beechwoods, is aglow from the many shades of red brickwork with which it is faced. The oldest part of the present mansion is at least 13th century, but the Stonor family goes back still further, and has been in continual occupation of the estate for at least 800 years. In the Middle Ages the family prospered but their loyalty to Rome after the Reformation brought upon them fines, imprisonment and exclusion from public office. Undaunted, the family protected hunted priests, including Edmund Campion, and the Library contains an important recusant book collection. After the Catholic Emancipation Act, 1829, Thomas Stonor (1797–1881) entered parliament, successfully claimed the ancient Barony of Camoys, founded the Henley Royal Regatta and served Queen Victoria as Lord-in-Waiting for thirty-two years.

The extended Tudor E-shaped house, in which there are signs of much earlier building, remained little changed during the Recusancy until the mid-18th century when the Tudor forecourt, wall and lodges were swept away and the Hall was Gothicized with an ogee-shaped fire surround and a Gothic overmantel embellished with heraldry. The 14th-century Chapel of flint with stone dressings was also redecorated in Gothic style, 1796–1800. In 1790 a Staircase with a Gothic ironwork balustrade was added and in 1834 the Hall was divided into two, one half being transformed into a Drawing Room. Some of the contents were dispersed at sales in 1938 and 1975, but much of great interest remains, including the loan of furniture, portraits and tapestries by Mrs Eyre Huddleston.

The Gothic Hall contains 16th-century portraits, including members of the Huddleston and Hoby families. The stained glass includes 16th-century examples, perhaps from the Wool Hall at Ypres, as well as earlier family armorial glass. The lantern is 1757. Further family portraits in the Drawing Room, Dining Room, Library, Lady Camoys' Bedroom and the Long Gallery include works by Wissing, Kneller, Riley, Wright and Romney; Scrots, (*Queen Mary in her Youth*) and Hieronimus Custodis are also represented. There are notable Italian paintings and drawings, including works by Tintoretto, the three Carraccis and by Giambattista and Domenico Tiepolo.

The furniture is wide-ranging from the Tudor to the late Regency periods, and includes good examples from France, Holland and America, which is represented by a pair of 'New York' mahogany chairs and two sets of 18th-century wall sconces; also American are the maps of Rhode Island on the Alcove Staircase. A flamboyant element is introduced by the unusual early-19th-century shell-shaped bed, supported by mermaids and dolphins, and the set of 18th-century shell chairs in Francis Stonor's Bedroom, by the mid-18th century Baroque carved saints from South Germany, the fine pair of Venetian carved celestial and terrestrial globes by Coronelli, dated 1699, and the bronze and ormolu Louis XVI pineapple vases. The French wallpaper, 'Les Monuments de Paris', printed and coloured by Dufour in 1815, is particularly pleasing.

There is a fine collection of 15th- and 16th-century Italian bronzes, Persian rugs, an excellent Flemish depiction of Tobias and the Angel among the tapestries and some fine examples of wood carvings, especially in the Chapel and the Library.

Early-19th-century shell-shaped bed and 18th-century shell chairs; Stonor Park.

Stourhead Wiltshire

The National Trust

At Stourton, w of B3092 Frome–Mere road

Built for the Hoare family to Palladian designs by Colen Campbell in the early 1720s, this restrained classical mansion contains much splendid English 18th-century and Regency furniture, portraits, landscapes in oil and watercolour by European as well as English artists, sculpture, ceramics and objects of art. The Hoares were perceptive collectors throughout the 18th and early-19th centuries and Stourhead is one of England's great treasure houses.

The Italian landscape and classical scenes reflect the interests of Henry Hoare II and Sir Richard Colt Hoare, both of whom travelled extensively in Italy. They include oils by Nicolas and Gaspard Poussin, Vernet, Orizonte, Mengs, Zuccarelli and Rosa de Tivoli, watercolours by J. R. Cozens, 'Warwick' Smith and the Swiss Louis Ducros, much admired by Colt Hoare, and by Jacob Philipp Hackert and Carlo Labruzzi. Maratta's *Marchese Pallavicini and the Artist* was acquired in Rome. A fine triptych of the Adoration of the Magi by Jan Provost is in the Picture Gallery Ante-room; other Netherlands painters include Van Uden and the younger Teniers.

There are notable family portraits by Ramsay, Samuel Woodforde, Kauffmann, Jonathan Richardson, Leighton, William Hoare (not a blood relation), Downman, Cotes, Reynolds, Dahl and Wootton. Wootton painted the fine hunting picture with Henry and Benjamin Hoare, its frame crested with a fox's mask, hanging over the chimneypiece in the Little Dining Room, and collaborated with Dahl in the equestrian portrait of Henry Hoare II in the Entrance Hall.

Outstanding among the sculpture is Le Sueur's bronze bust of Charles I. There are also works by Rysbrack, including his busts of the old and the youthful Milton and, in the Library, statuettes and plaster busts by Cheere.

The English furniture throughout is excellent, including the pair of console tables supported by carved foxes, c.1735, and the later mahogany and satinwood oval-backed chairs in the Entrance Hall, the card table of dark San Domingo mahogany carved with a Bacchic mask and festoons of vines c. 1740 in the Music Room, and the set of dining chairs with open inverted shell-backs perhaps by Giles Grendy, 1746. Thomas Chippendale the younger was responsible for the furniture made for Colt Hoare's Library and Picture Gallery. The remarkable late-18th-century Italian cabinet in the Cabinet Room, made of ebony and faced with *pietre dure*, once belonged to Pope Sixtus V (1585–90); its stand is English, 1742.

There are interesting chimneypieces in the Library, the Music Room, the Italian Room and the Saloon, whose green and white marble structure is embellished with plaques by Flaxman. The ceramics include Chelsea, Derby, Wedgwood and Worcester pieces, some French and German examples and Chinese export wares from the K'ang Hsi period onwards.

Herbert Le Sueur's bronze bust of Charles I, c.1635; Stourhead.

Stratfield Saye Hampshire

The Trustees of the Duke of Wellington

1 mile w of A33 between Reading and Basingstoke

After Waterloo the Duke of Wellington could have acquired a finer mansion with the money voted by Parliament than Stratfield Saye, a Carolean house built *c.*1630 whose interior was much altered in the mid-18th century. Indeed the Duke at first had far more grandiose plans in mind but in spite of buying imposing Italian marble pillars for a new house in 1821, he was eventually content to retain the old Stratfield Saye and introduce water closets and central heating for the comfort of his declining years.

The Hall nevertheless has a martial air appropriate to the victor of the Peninsular War; on its walls are British and Portuguese paintings of battles and from the Gallery with its portraits of later Dukes and Duchesses hang Napoleonic tricolours, appropriately diminished by the 7th Duke's Garter banner. Much of the furniture once belonged to Cardinal Fesch, Napoleon's uncle; the green malachite *tazza* was a gift to the Iron Duke from the Emperor of Russia. Here and elsewhere thoughout the house are mementos of the Duke's campaigns and gifts from the grateful crowned heads of Europe, including porcelain from Prussia, Austria and Russia. The three Roman mosaic pavements set into the marble floor are from the nearby Roman settlement of Silchester.

The Library with its gilded frieze and ceiling in the style of Kent contains Tintoretto's *Ascension*, books from Napoleon's collection, Regency furniture, including two armchairs by or after Thomas Hope, a miniature 18th-century temple in *pietre dure* from Russia, a fine Persian carpet and many honours lavished on the Great Duke displayed in cases. The Music Room has paintings and bronzes of Wellington's renowned charger, Copenhagen, two large-scale hunting groups and Haydon's painting of the Duke showing George IV the field of Waterloo.

John Fowler restored both the Lady Charles Room, now the principal sitting room, containing companionable family portraits, and the impressive white and gold Gallery, which contains bronze busts on gold and ebony plinths, fine French furniture including Louis XVI cabinets by Levasseur and a splendid Carlin commode, brought by the Duke from Paris; its Spanish carpet is modern, woven to the 7th Duke's design. The Gallery walls are lined with prints, introduced *c.*1795, which inspired the Duke to create the adjoining Print Room that has two prints of himself, and to decorate some of the bedrooms in the same way.

Family portraits hang both in the Small Drawing Room and in the 1775 Dining Room with its bold ceiling from a design in Robert Wood's *The Ruins of Palmyra*. Hoppner's work predominates but Hogarth and Lawrence are also represented. Some of the paintings from the Spanish Royal Collection, mainly Flemish and Dutch, taken from the defeated French after Vitoria and confirmed in Wellington's possession by the Spanish monarch, are in the Drawing Room; the rest are at Apsley House, London. Busts of the 1st Duke and his contemporaries line the corridor to the Billiards Room.

The Duke's adventurous and varied life is illustrated by a fascinating exhibition in the Stables. The estate includes a country park open to the public.

Sudbury Hall Derbyshire

The National Trust

6 miles E of Uttoxeter off A50

The Vernons settled in Sudbury in the latter part of the 16th century but it was not until the return of Charles II in 1660 that a start was made on Sudbury Hall, one of the most richly decorated of all Restoration mansions. Its plan, incorporating both new fashions and such then outmoded features as the Long Gallery, indicates that George Vernon, who had inherited the estate in 1659, may himself have been the architect. The task took twenty years to complete, perhaps because he was paying for the work out of income. Once completed in

*The late-17th-century Great Staircase, Sudbury Hall, with carving
by Edward Pierce and plasterwork by James Pettifer.*

about 1680, the house remained virtually untouched except for the addition of a 19th-century east wing since converted to a Museum of Childhood. The Hall remained with George Vernon's descendants until the death of the 9th Lord Vernon in 1963 when it was transferred to the National Trust by the Treasury, which had accepted it in part payment of death duties.

The splendour of this red-brick mansion's interior decoration is outstanding. Having first used provincial craftsmen, in the mid-1670s Vernon employed from London Grinling Gibbons and Edward Pierce as carvers and Robert Bradbury and James Pettifer as plasterers. Pierce carved the magnificent pine balustrade of the Great Staircase, while the plasterwork is Pettifer's; in 1691 Louis Laguerre added the decorative paintings. The ceilings of the Saloon and the Drawing Room are by Pettifer and Bradbury; the glorious carving over the Drawing Room chimneypiece is by Gibbons but the fine ceiling painting *Psyche Received by Jupiter* is by an unknown hand. Bradbury was also responsible for the Long Gallery's stately ceiling. Here are flowers and foliage, emperors' heads, horses, shells, dragons and wild boar. The ceiling of the Queen's Room is by Samuel Mansfield, while its pink alabaster overmantel was carved by William Wilson of Leicester, *c.*1773. There are also fine doorcases, especially that at the foot of the Grand Staircase leading into the Hall, and imposing pedimented frames to the paintings in the Saloon.

Among noteworthy family portraits is that of George Vernon, Archbishop of York, by Lawrence; other portraitists represented include Kneller, Hudson, Vanderbank, Enoch Seeman, Hoppner and George Richmond, and, most important of all, a rare collection of portraits by Wright (?1617–1700) in their contemporary 'Sunderland' frames, which hang in the Long Gallery. Wright's portrait of George Vernon, the builder of Sudbury, hangs over the door in the Saloon. There is an unusual 17th-century Flemish ebony cabinet whose panels contain biblical scenes on copper by the younger Frans Francken, an excellent gilt pierglass *c.*1740 in the Queen's Room and a fine

pair of gilt eagle console tables with marble tops, *c.*1740, in the Long Gallery. John Bushman's late 17th-century long-case clock in its black japanned case stands in the Drawing Room. Greek and Etruscan vases mingle with the books in the Library and there are good examples of 18th-century Chinese ceramics.

Sudeley Castle Gloucestershire

The Dent-Brocklehurst Family Trust

At Winchcombe, 6 miles NE of Cheltenham on A46

Built from the 15th to the 17th century on a much older site, Sudeley became of historic importance when Henry VIII's only surviving wife, Catherine Parr, married the unreliable and scheming Thomas Seymour, Baron of Sudeley, who was later executed for meddling in royal politics on behalf of his niece, the much wronged Lady Jane Grey. She also stayed here and later followed him to the scaffold. Catherine's heavily restored little room, containing two cases of Roman coins found locally, looks into the Outer Courtyard. The Inner Courtyard was largely destroyed by the Parliamentarians in the Civil War – only the Dungeon Tower which is used for various purposes, including exhibitions, remains intact.

The Castle and estate were restored by the Dent family, renowned glove makers, only a small part of whose distinguished collection of paintings is on display, most of them in the North Hall. Here is Constable's *The Lock*, Turner's magical *Pope's Villa on the Thames*, Ruysdael's *Watermill*, *The Miracles of St Francis of Paola* and *The Holy Family* by or after Rubens, and the allegorical group of Henry VIII and his children, known as 'The Tudor Succession', attributed to Lucas de Heere. The Library contains Greuze's enchanting *Innocence*, Van Dyck's *The Infant Saviour embracing St John* and Claude's *Rape of Europa*.

Hogarth's *Bridge of Life* hangs at the top of the inner Staircase, while the first-floor oak-panelled Lobby contains works by the younger Teniers and by Wynants and an unusual 17th-century stumpwork dressing case. The adjoin-

ing corridor and the rooms off it are enriched with fine needlework. George Vertue's set of engravings from Holbein in the ground-floor corridor once belonged to Horace Walpole. Also of great interest is Emma Dent's collection of letters and autographs continued by the family since her death in 1900.

Sulgrave Manor
Northamptonshire

The Sulgrave Manor Board

8 miles NE of Banbury

Lawrence Washington, whose ancestors can be traced back via Lancashire to Washington Old Hall near Sunderland, had already established himself as a prosperous wool merchant when he acquired the manor of Sulgrave, originally

Portrait of George Washington by Gilbert Stuart, 1795, at Sulgrave Manor.

monastic property, for £324 14s at the Dissolution in 1539. His fine manor house, completed c.1560, was sold by the family in 1659, to be restored early in the 18th century. Three years earlier John Washington, great-great-grandson of the original builder of Sulgrave and great-grandfather of George Washington, had emigrated permanently to Virginia, his family having suffered considerably during the Protectorate for their loyalty to the Stuarts. The house was in poor condition when it was acquired to celebrate the centenary of a hundred years of peace between Britain and the USA and it was then restored, refurnished and endowed from British and American sources. At its formal opening in 1921, the Duke of Cambridge, brother of Queen Mary, announced: '... we have had one idea in mind. We want this house to be a shrine for all Americans who visit the old country and a centre from which sentiments of friendship and goodwill between the British and American peoples will forever radiate. ...'

There are portraits of the 1st President, including those by Charles Willson Peale and Archibald Robertson, but the best is by Gilbert Stuart, of which there are several versions;

there is also a good copy of Houdon's bust. In the Deed Room and Porch Room, now used as a museum, are several mementos, including autographed letters, a peace medal given by the President to friendly American Indian Chiefs and a pearwood snuff-box presented by Queen Mary. The furniture and furnishings are late-17th and early-18th-century, including a fine Queen Anne walnut settee covered with contemporary needlework and a spinet of walnut, inlaid with sycamore, c.1710, made by Thomas Hitchcock. Among other interesting pieces is George Washington's carved and painted mahogany chair in the style of Hepplewhite and the Elizabethan chest in the Great Chamber, whose Elizabethan four-poster bed has a magnificent needlework coverlet of the William and Mary period.

There is a fascinating mid-18th-century Great Kitchen, whose fittings and equipment have been brought here from a house in Weston Corbett, Hampshire.

Sutton Park North Yorkshire

Mrs Sheffield

At Sutton-on-the-Forest, 8 miles N of York on B 1363

This modest yet impressive early Georgian classical brick mansion, built on the site of an Elizabethan manor in the 1720s, to which two elegant wings were added in the mid-18th century, was designed by Thomas Atkinson. It stands in the attractive village of Sutton-on-the-Forest, with trim gardens and a well-timbered park beyond on the south side. In 1963 the present owner and her husband moved to this former property of the Sheffield family, once Earls of Mulgrave and Dukes of Normanby and Buckingham, from Normanby Hall, Humberside, nostalgically recorded in Felix Kelly's painting in the Dining Room overmantel. Much of the impeccable 18th-century contents came from Buckingham House, inherited by Sir Charles Sheffield from the last Duke of Buckingham, whose natural son he was. There is also an Ice House.

Cortese was responsible for the splendid Library ceiling and the plasterwork on the Staircase, as well as for the delicate rococo ceiling of the yellow and white Hall with its Corinthian columned screen, black and white floor, its family portraits by Kneller and Hayman and the long-case clock, the case by Chippendale. A self-portrait by the American Benjamin West hangs in the Library.

The richly carved pine panelling with fluted Ionic pilasters in the Morning Room is attributed to Flitcroft; the portrait of the Earl of Wiltshire in the overmantel is after Holbein. Excellent porcelain is everywhere, especially in the Porcelain Room, which contains glorious examples of Dr Wall Worcester, a superb Chelsea Derby chandelier after Meissen, and pieces from the Meissen, Bow and Chelsea factories. There are Lowestoft armorial pieces in the Hall passage, late-17th-century *Blanc-de-Chine* pieces and a splendid Meissen centrepiece by Kändler in the Chinese Room, with its well-preserved hand-painted Chinese wallpaper, and, on the first floor, 18th-century Dutch porcelain, *c.*1772. The furniture includes good Dutch and French as well as English 18th-century pieces, outstanding among them being the Queen Anne walnut bureau in the Chinese Room. In addition there are fine Adam-style chimneypieces and glass chandeliers.

Syon House Middlesex

The Duke of Northumberland KG

On N bank of the Thames between Brentford and Isleworth

Syon was originally a religious foundation. It was suppressed in 1539 by Henry VIII, whose rotting corpse burst out of its coffin while resting here on its last journey to Windsor and was savaged by dogs. The property was given to Henry Percy, 9th Earl of Northumberland, by the inconstant James I who later imprisoned him for fifteen years. The title went into abeyance on the death of the 11th Earl in 1670, to be revived eighty years later for Sir Hugh Smithson, the husband of his great-grand-daughter. It was he, soon afterwards created the 1st Duke, who in 1762 commissioned Robert Adam to restore Syon House, then 'ruinous and inconvenient'.

Adam scarcely touched the exterior of the rectangular castellated Jacobean mansion (surmounted by the lion of the Percy crest), which gives no indication of his remarkable neo-classical decoration within, inspired by James Stuart's Greek designs contained in *The Antiquities of Athens,* 1762, compiled in co-operation with Nicholas Revett. Adam's aim of creating a completely unified interior was more nearly attained here than at any other of his houses. The Entrance Hall, two storeys high with a black and white marble floor, creamy white walls and patterned ceiling, is coolly and majestically Roman. At one end a copy of the Apollo Belvedere stands in an apse; at the other end, steps lead past a bronze copy of the Dying Gaul and into the triumphant Ante-room, brilliant with its vividly coloured polished scagliola floor and its twelve *verdantique* columns, found in the Tiber, each crowned with an Ionic capital and a gilded sculpted figure. Two gold and blue trophy panels embellish the walls. The white and gold intricately patterned plasterwork ceiling, a circle within an octagon, is perhaps the greatest achievement of Joseph Rose Jr. The gilt marble-topped tables beneath the trophy panels and the chairs upholstered in pale blue are to Adam's design.

The apses at each end of the Dining Room are elaborately decorated above the columned screens; the pedimented overmantel, the classical figures in niches facing the windows, the giltwood seat furniture with oval backs covered in the original red (now faded pink) brocade are as fine as the splendid ceiling. The frieze panels by Casali are less successful.

The Red Drawing Room is hung with red Spitalfields silk and contains fine furniture, including a marquetry writing table with sliding lid, *c.*1750, and an exceptional carpet also designed by Adam and made by Thomas Moore of Moorfields, dated 1769. The ceiling roundels, octagon and diamond shaped, were painted by Cipriani. The portraits of the

RIGHT *The Ante-room designed by Robert Adam with plasterwork by Joseph Rose Jr; Syon House.*

Stuarts by, among others, Honthorst and Van
Dyck, include Lely's of Charles I with the Duke
of York, 1647, one of three of Charles' children
held at Syon. This may have been painted on a
visit by Charles while he was awaiting trial, on
one of the occasions when he was allowed to see
them. The Spanish mahogany doors are
enriched with ivory and ormolu; the white
marble chimneypiece is magnificently decorated by Boulton with applied ormolu.

The proportions of the celebrated Long
Gallery are harmonized by Adam's skilful use
of pilasters in groups of four and by the ceiling
patterns, again the work of Rose. The furniture
is mainly to Adam's design. There is a fine
semi-circular landscape by Zuccarelli over
both of the mirrored chimneypieces and
circular portraits under the frieze of Charlemagne and his Northumberland descendants.
In the later Print Room are portraits by Lely,
Gainsborough, Reynolds, Stuart and Phillips.
Rubens' impressive *Diana Returning from the
Hunt* hangs off the West Corridor.

ABOVE *Peter Lely* Charles I with the Duke of York,
1647; Syon House.

BELOW *Rubens* Diana Returning from the Hunt;
Syon House.

RIGHT *'Leda and the Swan', Chelsea, c.1755;
Upton House.*

Tatton Park Cheshire

The National Trust, financed and administered by the Cheshire County Council

2 miles N of Knutsford, 13 miles SW of Manchester off A537

The Tatton estate was acquired *c*.1680 by Sir Thomas Egerton, Lord Chancellor, whose descendants became Earls and Dukes of Bridgwater. A junior branch of the family settled at Tatton. The present house, with the exception of the Dining Room which was designed by Thomas Farnolls Pritchard of Shrewsbury *c*.1763, was fashioned in the neo-classical manner first by Samuel Wyatt in the 1780s, then by his nephew, Lewis Wyatt, 1808–13.

Lewis was responsible for the cool, elegant Grecian style of the Entrance Hall with its two screens of porphyry Ionic columns, one each side of the front door. It contains two superb Italian Renaissance chests inlaid with ivory and pewter, a Florentine gilt cassone and an elaborate Goan cabinet. There is a portrait of the 1st Lord Egerton by Calvert, who also depicted the Cheshire Hunt, 1839, and one of the Duke of Mantua (1569–1622) by Frans Pourbus the Younger.

The furniture of Lewis Wyatt's Music Room, hung with cherry-coloured silk, includes contemporary French pieces even though the Napoleonic Wars were then in progress, but most of it is by Gillow. The paintings include a classical landscape by Gaspard Poussin and an Italian scene by Berchem. The grandest of Lewis Wyatt's rooms is the Drawing Room, for which he designed the pier-glasses and splendid pier-tables supported by silvered swans. Gillow's gilt rococo seat furniture is carved in high relief all over, indicating that the chairs could be placed anywhere and not merely along the walls as was customary in the 18th century. There are two Venetian views by Canaletto and Bortolomeo Nazzari's impressive portrait

LEFT *The marble fireplace flanked by gilt statues in the white and gold Double Cube Room, Wilton House.*
BELOW *The late-18th-century Library, Tatton Park; the bookcases and most of the furniture are by Gillow.*

of Samuel Egerton (1711–80) who was apprenticed for a time to Joseph Smith, picture dealer and British consul in Venice, but the outstanding work here is Van Dyck's *Martyrdom of St Stephen*, c.1623.

The excellent bookcases in the handsome Library, containing one of the National Trust's most important collections of books, and most of the rest of the furniture are by Gillow. Above the bookcases is a fine collection of 17th-century Delft vases and jars.

The Dining Room is gloriously decorated in the rococo manner. The bacchic motifs of vine leaves and bunches of grapes in the frieze are repeated on the wall panels which frame family portraits by, among others, Beechey, Lawrence, Owen and Herkomer. The overmantel contains a portrait of Sir Thomas Egerton, who founded the family fortune.

A fine satinwood bookcase inlaid with ivory by Gillow is in Samuel Wyatt's Yellow Drawing Room, while the outstanding porcelain, including Chelsea 'Gold Anchor' and Worcester pieces, is in the Card Room. On the landing at the top of Wyatt's Staircase are portraits of the Gentlemen of Cheshire painted in 1720 to celebrate their decision not to support the Old Pretender in 1715. The adjoining bedrooms are furnished by Gillow.

The 4th and last Lord Egerton (1874–1958), who bequeathed Tatton Park to the National Trust, was notable as a pioneer motorist and aviator and as a traveller in eastern Asia, but he

Chippendale's neo-classical marquetry library table, 1770; Temple Newsam.

is perhaps best remembered for his game trophies from all over the world, a vast quantity of which are in the huge Tenants' Hall built to accommodate them.

Temple Newsam West Yorkshire

The Leeds Metropolitan District Council

5 miles E of Leeds; 1 mile S of A63 (near junction with A642)

This fine Tudor-Jacobean house, once the home of the Viscounts Irwin, was acquired in 1922 as a Leeds City Council Arts Museum. Its spacious rooms, some with early rococo plasterwork by Thomas Perritt and his partner, Joseph Rose Sr, are ideal for the display of its magnificent collections of paintings, furniture, silver, pottery and porcelain.

The furniture is outstanding. In the South-East Room stands Chippendale's celebrated neo-classical marquetry library table, 1770, enriched with ormolu rams' heads, originally made for Harewood House. In the North-West Room is another distinguished mahogany library table made in the Gothic taste for Lord Pomfret, 1760. Giles Grendy fashioned the scarlet and gold japanned chairs, c.1740, in the Great Hall; the mahogany commode with ormolu mounts, c.1750, is attributed to John Channon. There are also exotic Japanese lacquer wall cabinets; pieces in Sheraton and Hepplewhite styles, others by and in the manner of Kent; Chinese Chippendale chairs with the Connock crest; pieces by Vile and Cobb, including the 1761 pair of console tables and mirrors on the end wall of the Long Gallery, and by Gillow of Lancaster; examples of Spanish colonial furniture from Peru, and a Chinese rosewood chair made in Java for export. A marvellous gilt and needlework suite, 1746, is in the Long Gallery, and the Duke of Leeds' glorious day-bed and sofa in the exquisite colours of the original Genoa cut-velvet covers is in a special air-conditioned closet in the Top West Wing.

There are splendid portraits of the Irwin family and others by Knyff (a rustic 3rd Lord clock, and Chinese hand-painted wallpaper enriched with birds cut out from Audubon's famous collection of ornithological prints, *The Birds of America*.

Thurnham Hall Lancashire

Mr and Mrs S. H. Crabtree

6 miles s of Lancaster on A588

Thurnham Hall dates back to the 13th century when the original pele tower was erected; with the enlargement of the house during succeeding centuries the tower has been incorporated into the rest of the structure. Lancashire has always been a stronghold of dedicated Roman Catholic families since Henry VIII's breach with Rome, and the Dalton family which owned Thurnham from 1566 until 1973 was

The priest hole behind the Tudor fireplace in one of the bedrooms at Thurnham Hall.

Rococo candlestand with entwined dolphins, c.1760, by Thomas Johnson; Temple Newsam.

Irwin), the younger Pourbus, Mercier (the 7th Lord Irwin and his wife), Cotes, Richardson, Highmore, Reynolds (Lady Hertford) and Benjamin Wilson. Other painters represented include Pannini, Pellegrini, Ricci, Richard Wilson, Joli, Ibbetson and Henry Morland.

The porcelain includes examples of Ming, Chinese blue and white, K'ang Hsi *famille verte*, Staffordshire pottery, Leeds stoneware, the only complete Chelsea 'Gold Anchor' tea and coffee service in existence and a wide-ranging collection of creamware. Other memorable items include *cassoulets* for fresh herbs by Boulton, a pair of silver candlesticks designed by Robert Adam, a marble bust by Roubiliac of Alexander Pope, a remarkable rococo candle-stand with entwined dolphins by Thomas Johnson c.1760, silverware by Paul de Lamerie and others, an exquisite collection of gold boxes, important clocks including both Benjamin Vulliamy's temple clock, c.1791, and William Norris' late-17th-century lantern one of these. The house has a well-preserved priest hole at the back of the Tudor fireplace in one of the bedrooms and a Roman Catholic chapel which dates from 1845 and contains Victorian stained glass. John Dalton (d. 1837) was responsible for the Gothic south façade of this mainly 16th-century building, which fell into disrepair during this century and was ravaged by fire in 1959. The present owners have set about its careful restoration with the pleasing results to be seen today. The Great Hall with its handsome Tudor fireplace is now embellished with oak panelling of the same period as the original Elizabethan wainscot and the ribbed plasterwork ceiling and moulded frieze have been restored. The Jacobean staircases have also been renovated.

Tiverton Castle Devon

Mr and Mrs Ivar Campbell

On outskirts of Tiverton, next to St Peter's Church

This historic fortress dominating the River Exe was built in 1106 at the command of Henry I by Richard de Redvers, whom the King created Earl of Devon. In the 13th century, the earldom and Castle passed to the Courtenays. A key royalist stronghold in the Civil War, it fell to the Roundheads in 1645 when General Fairfax destroyed the main fortifications, so ending its military importance. Their romantic ruins now bound the garden. A new wing was added in the 17th century, but the notable medieval gatehouse is still the entrance to this family home, which has been carefully restored by the present owners, who came to the Castle in 1960.

An imposing Staircase leads up from the North Guard Room, past painted extracts from the Bayeux Tapestry, denoting the Castle's Norman origin. The Captain of the Guard's Room features military portraits, notably of Mr Campbell's ancestor, Major General Sir Neil Campbell, the British Commissioner with Napoleon at Elba. Here also is a rare contemporary broadsheet entitled 'The Taking of Tiverton Castle'.

There are interesting pieces of English and Continental furniture, carvings and hangings in many rooms, and a fascinating collection of clocks in the South-East Tower. The Chapel of St Francis, dedicated to animal welfare, is dominated by a modern dragonfly cross. However, perhaps the most intriguing room is the Joan of Arc Gallery. This features portraits and documents commemorating the other version of the Maid's life – that she was not an unknown shepherdess, but the illegitimate daughter of Queen Isabeau of France and her brother-in-law; that after her capture, she was not burned but married a nobleman of Lorraine, Sieur Robert des Armoises, and later died peacefully in her bed. There is supporting evidence from the des Armoises archives.

Towneley Hall Lancashire

The Burnley Borough Council

½ mile SE of Burnley

The Towneley family has been established in this part of Lancashire for at least 600 years. As staunch Catholics, loyal to the Stuarts, they suffered accordingly. Alice Mary, the youngest of three daughters and co-heiress of Colonel Charles Towneley, who married Lord O'Hagan, Lord Chancellor of Ireland in 1871, offered the house and parkland to the Burnley Corporation for a nominal sum in 1902; she herself lived nearby until her death in 1921. This ancient building, first started in the mid-14th century and subsequently much added to and altered, is now used as an art gallery and a museum for local crafts and industries.

Of remarkable interest is the decoration of the Great Hall. Although the struggle to bring back the Stuarts continued until the failure of the uprising in 1745 to place Prince Charles Edward on the throne, in which the Towneley family was heavily involved, Richard Towneley commissioned Vassalli in 1729 to decorate the Great Hall. The splendid Baroque plasterwork ceiling with medallions of Roman Emperors and the two figures, the 'Dancing

Charles Zoffany
Charles Towneley
among his Marbles,
1790; Towneley Hall.

Faun' and the 'Medici Venus', one standing upon each of the two elegant fireplaces at opposite sides of the terracotta Hall, are fascinating examples of Vassalli's work. Extra interest is given by busts of Roman Emperors on short green marble pillars. Here also is the eighteen-foot-long oak table with a carved frieze dated 1613. In the west wing off the Hall are two spacious Regency rooms which house temporary exhibitions.

The oak-panelled Long Gallery and adjoining bedrooms contain much good 17th-century oak seat furniture, court cupboards and chests-of-drawers, some inlaid with ebony, ivory and mother-of-pearl. Here hang paintings by de Wint, James Stark and William Shayer Sr, but the main collection is in two galleries elsewhere with oils by, among others, David Cox, Burne-Jones, Zoffany (the well known portrait of Charles Towneley in his sculpture gallery), James Webb, B. W. Leader and Vicat Cole, and watercolours by Francis Nicholson, Goodwin, de Wint, Collingwood-Smith, Ibbetson, Towne, Copley Fielding, Müller and Birket Foster.

Outstanding is the early-16th-century Towneley Altarpiece of the Antwerp School, consisting of an altar and reredos, elaborately carved in oak with scenes from the life of Christ, in the Chapel. Outside the Chapel are the Whalley Abbey vestments; dated 1390 to 1420, they form the only complete set, with one exception, of Pre-Reformation English High Mass vestments still in existence.

325

The Kitchen at Townend, with some of its original early-17th-century equipment

Townend Cumbria

The National Trust

Troutbeck village, 3 miles SE of Ambleside

A member of the Browne family is recorded to have been at Townend by 1525 and others had probably lived in Troutbeck at a still earlier date. The present farm house, however, was built in 1623 by George Browne as the condition of a marriage settlement with Susannah Rawlinson. A period of peace and prosperity followed the union of the English and Scottish crowns in 1603 which marked the end of Border strife. In Cumbria, the traditional timber-framed 'cruck' houses were being replaced by solid rough-cast stone buildings with slate roofs and today, some 350 years later, Townend is an outstanding example of early-17th-century Lakeland vernacular architecture with its structure and contents little changed.

The Brownes, firmly established among the yeomanry or lesser gentry by their vigour and independence, retained their estate until 1914, when the male line died out, and in 1947 it came to the National Trust. Today the rooms still retain much of their original character. Here in the Fire House or principal living room and in the bedrooms are fine examples of 17th- and early-18th-century carved oak vernacular furniture, including a court cupboard, armchairs and a fine cradle of 1670. In the Dower House or kitchen can be seen the fire crane, adjustable hooks, roasting spit and meat loft above what was once an open fireplace where joints were hung for curing. There are also fitted cupboards, together with clocks, collections of pottery and drinking glasses, not always easily recognizable obsolete household implements, such as candle and rushlight holders, as well as portraits by journeymen artists and fabrics woven locally in the late-18th century.

Traquair House Borders

Mr Peter Maxwell-Stuart

1 mile from Innerleithen at junction of B709 and B7062

The treasures of the House of Traquair are so intimately connected with the long history of its occupants, covering eight centuries of blood feuds, intrigues and national events as well as peaceful family life, that it is impossible to consider one without the other. For Traquair is no ordinary dwelling. Once it was a royal hunting lodge deep in the ancient Ettrick Forest, its first recorded royal visit being in 1107 when Alexander I granted a charter from Traquair Castle. During the Edwardian wars of the 13th century it was occupied by the English but reverted to the Crown with the accession of Robert the Bruce in 1306. During the next 150 years it was in the hands of a number of families and in 1478 one of James IV's favourites sold Traquair to the Earl of Buchan, the King's uncle, for just under £4 in English money. He gave it to his son Sir James Stuart, the first of

Detail of 17th-century embroidery at Traquair House.

Jacobite glasses; Traquair House.

the present line of lairds of Traquair. Close links with the monarchy by blood relationship and through service continued. The family fortunes reached their zenith in the 17th century in the time of John, 1st Earl of Traquair, who held high office under Charles I but was later fined and imprisoned under the Commonwealth and died in great poverty in 1659. His son married a lady of 'the old faith' and the family have ever since held staunchly to the Catholic traditions, sometimes suffering much in consequence.

The date of the earliest building at Traquair cannot be traced; the house mostly dates from the 16th and 17th centuries with little exterior alteration since 1698–9, when the side wings were completed and the little ogival pavilions added. The celebrated Bear Gates at the end of the long avenue were built in 1737–8. Family tradition maintains that they were closed in 1745 after the visit by Prince Charles Edward, never to be opened until a Stuart king again sits on the throne. This long association with the crown of Scotland accounts for the outstanding wealth of papers, charters, Stuart and Jacobite documents, letters and relics preserved at Traquair. There are letters from Mary Queen of Scots, who stayed at Traquair with Darnley, her second and ill-fated husband, and their baby son; letters from Charles I and Charles II as Prince of Wales and King, and a unique collection of Jacobite glasses. The 17th-century hangings at Traquair are justly celebrated, including the very fine set of embroideries done in *petit point* depicting animals and flowers.

Perhaps the most striking room is the Library, a square chamber at the top of the house created by the 4th and 5th Earls in the early-18th century. The deeply coved ceiling is decorated with a frieze painted with busts of philosophers, the books classified and beautifully bound according to a system copied from the Cotton MSS library. The Drawing Room on the first floor extends the whole depth of the building, with casement windows cut in the immensely thick walls and refined 18th-century painted panelling. About 1760 it was redecorated and painted overmantel overdoors

The restored late-17th-century carved oak doorcase in the Brown Room, Tredegar House.

added. A portrait of Dryden by John Riley, c.1685, hangs beside a group attributed to Jamesone and retouched by his 18th-century descendant, John Alexander. Two child portraits are attributed to Cornelius Johnson. More family portraits are in the Dining Room which was decorated in the 1860s. There is a portrait by Medina of the 5th Earl of Nethersdale and his wife, who rescued her husband from the Tower of London in 1716, where he had been imprisoned after the 1715 Jacobite rising.

The most distinguished piece of furniture is the state bed hung with yellow embroidered hangings brought from Terregles, another family home. There is a very fine harpsichord with its original decoration dated 1651 and made by Ruckers of Antwerp. There are some Chinese Chippendale chairs, a fine marquetry table c.1680, an ebonized Flemish cabinet decorated with biblical scenes of about 1700 and a fine set of Scottish elm chairs dating from the mid-18th century in the Stillroom which contains a good collection of English and Chinese 18th- and 19th-century porcelain.

In one of the low service wings enclosing the entrance front a Chapel was created in the 19th century. Up to this time the family worshipped in secret in the Priest's Room. Of special interest are a set of twelve 16th-century carved wood panels of the Life of Christ, Flemish in origin or possibly made by a Flemish-trained Scottish craftsman, that had been brought to a chapel at Leith used by Queen Mary of Guise Lorraine, mother of Mary Queen of Scots. During the Reformation, they were concealed and later bought by the 5th Earl, finally to be set up openly in the 19th century.

Tredegar House Gwent

The Newport Borough Council

3 miles SW of Newport near junction of M4 and A48

The Morgan family were already established at Tredegar by 1402 but the present mansion, built on a palatial scale between 1664 and 1672

Detail of the oak carving in the Brown Room, Tredegar House.

by an unknown architect, is the finest late-17th-century house in Wales. It passed through the female line in 1792 to Sir Charles Gould (1726–1806), created a Baronet in the same year, who was granted the name and arms of Morgan by royal licence on inheriting the Morgan properties. His grandson became Baron Tredegar, 1859, whose son, a generous public benefactor, became a Viscount in 1905. Tredegar House remained the family seat until 1951 when the 6th and last Baron left Wales. After serving as a school, Tredegar House was acquired by the Newport Borough Council in 1974, which is meticulously restoring and refurnishing this historic mansion.

By 1980 the State Room sequence of the Hall and the Brown Room (once the Dining Room), culminating in the Gilt Room, were largely restored as well as the Dining Room (formerly known as the New Parlour), while work was continuing on the Pink Room (above the Gilt Room) and on the bedrooms. Remodelled in the 1860s, the Side Hall with its exuberant plasterwork ceiling contains family portraits, including one of Lady Tredegar, wife of the 3rd Baron, by Augustus John. Late Stuart bolection moulded panels cover the Dining Room walls from floor to ceiling, while the broken pediments above the doors are enlivened by acanthus leaves. The more robust plaster ceiling work, consisting of a wreath of vine leaves and grapes, with flowers and fruit, is Victorian, *c.*1870. The paintings in the New Hall are mainly early-17th-century; the ceiling has yet to be restored.

The Brown Room is lavishly panelled in honey-coloured oak, each panel separated from the rest by a pilaster carved with sprawling acanthus up which *putti* are climbing. In the broken pediments above the panels are carved busts of Roman Emperors, with Augustus and Livia facing each other over the doorcases at the opposite ends of the room. The plasterwork on the ceiling was executed in the 1870s, the original having collapsed in 1848. The superbly carved shield over the chimneypiece with twenty-four quarterings is late-17th century: they represent the families with which the Morgans had intermarried, but many of them are probably mythical.

The Gilt Room is elaborately decorated. The pine panelling is grained to imitate walnut and the picture frames of allegorical figures, including Prudence, Temperance and Cybele, are heavily gilded as are the swags beneath them. The ceiling is 17th century, the only one to survive on the ground floor; within the enormous wreath of fruit and flowers is a copy from a 1647 engraving of a ceiling in the Palazzo Barberini, Rome, painted by Pietro da Cortona, which glorifies the reign of Pope Urban VIII (1633–9).

The Cedar Room, a late-17th-century closet on the first floor, panelled and fitted with shelves, is decorated with 'barley-twist' pilasters, its ceiling painting depicting cherubs at play amid floral garlands in the blue sky. Furniture and paintings of the appropriate period are gradually being collected.

Trerice Cornwall

The National Trust

3 miles S E of Newquay, via A392

Secluded in a quiet, wooded valley, the present enchanting small manor house was built of silvery grey limestone in 1572 by Sir John Arundell, since when it has remained largely unaltered. It was acquired by the National Trust in 1953. The strapwork plaster ceiling in the splendidly proportioned Hall, which rises through two storeys, is Elizabethan, as is the scrolled plaster overmantel, supported by well-moulded caryatids, and much of the glass in the great east window. Except for the Hall table, which is early-19th-century, the contents of the house are on loan or brought here from elsewhere by the Trust.

The great chest in the Hall dates from the mid-16th century and the oak furniture from the mid-17th century as does the Aubusson tapestry panel. In the adjoining Library is a fine romantic landscape by Vernet, depicting Tivoli in late afternoon. Here also are an imposing breakfront mahogany bookcase with Gothic decoration and a small satinwood Sheraton desk with cylindrical top; the dark green carpet is Donegal and the 'Chinese Lowestoft' armorial plates are Ch'ien Lung. The magnificent first-floor Solar or Drawing Room, facing south, is flooded with light, showing to advantage the splendid plastered barrel-vaulted ceiling, the great 1573 plaster armorial chimneypiece, the elegant frieze and the vast painting by Snyders of dead game. The excellent 18th-century furniture includes a Queen Anne walnut *escritoire*, Chippendale period chairs and a marquetry writing table, embellished with ormolu, together with 18th-century Chinese and English porcelain of which there is more, mainly Worcester and Caughley, in the apertured Musicians' Gallery above the Hall. The corridor Gallery contains an early-18th-century Aubusson tapestry and carpet runners from Persia.

Some excellent pieces of late-17th-century walnut furniture have recently been placed in the north wing, with clocks by Tompion and Banger and by Joseph Knibb.

Trewithen Cornwall

Mr and Mrs Michael Galsworthy

2 miles E of Probus on A390

Trewithen, a handsome manor house built of Pentewan stone, stands in Cornwall's lovely countryside surrounded by its renowned woodland garden, thickly planted with camellias, magnolias and rhododendrons. It was built in 1723 for the Hawkins family from whom the present owner has inherited through the Johnstones, and there are interesting family connections with Sir Stamford Raffles of Singapore and with the Mudges, the Plymouth clockmakers. Trewithen's exterior is both restrained and elegant. There are good portraits and examples of Hepplewhite, Chippendale and Sheraton furniture.

The Palladian-style Dining Room at Trewithen.

The Library consists of two rooms, one on each side of the narrow Entrance Hall. Here there is a wide-ranging collection of horticultural books, good examples of Chinese K'ang Hsi *famille verte*, and blue and white porcelain, mid-18th century furniture, a leather wig stand, a Jacobean coffin stool and paintings by Hondecoeter and Willement. The furniture in the Oak Room, so called from its oak panelling in Palladian style with Ionic pilasters and a broken pediment above the door, includes a satinwood *bonheur-du-jour*, the top part of which is detachable, a serpentine-fronted chest of drawers, *c*.1740, veneered with laburnum, and a writing desk of Cuban mahogany. The Drawing Room chimneypiece also shows Palladian influence in contrast with the Chinese fretwork which decorates two of its doorways. Here also are two fine mirrors in the style of William Kent, a mid-18th-century spinet by Thomas Hancock, a portrait of a market girl by Reynolds who also painted that of Kitty Mudge, and family likenesses by Northcote, Opie and in pencil and wash by Cosway. The Staircase Hall, lit by an oval skylight, contains Allan Ramsay's portraits of Sir Christopher Hawkins and other members of the Hawkins family.

The most striking room is the grey-green Dining Room, enriched with white, its length alleviated by screened arcades at each end. It has an attractive chimneypiece and above it an oval portrait of Philip Hawkins. On the walls facing the window are delicate floral swags and festoons in white stucco. The paintings here include three portraits by Allan Ramsay and two, of Dr Zachariah Mudge of Plymouth and his wife, by Reynolds.

Uppark West Sussex

The National Trust

5 miles S E of Petersfield on E side of South Harting–Emsworth road (B2146)

Uppark, a pleasing house of mellow brick and stone in the Dutch style, was built high on the South Downs, perhaps by Talman, *c*.1690, for the 1st Lord Tankerville. Matthew Fetherstonhaugh, who inherited a vast fortune on condition that he purchased a baronetcy and an estate in the south, acquired it in 1747, by which time he had also married. His son, Sir Harry, who inherited the estate in 1774, was for a time a crony of the Prince Regent, who frequently slept in the bed now in the Small Drawing Room. As an impetuous young buck, Sir Harry kept the future Lady Hamilton as his mistress for some twelve months, but settled down in his sixty-ninth year when he married his dairy maid, aged twenty. He commissioned Humphry Repton to carry out several alterations on the north side and offered Uppark after Waterloo to the Duke of Wellington, who is said to have declined with the comment, 'I have crossed the Alps once.' In the 1880s H. G. Wells, then a youth, lived here with his mother, who was housekeeper at Uppark for thirteen years.

The young Sir Matthew and his wife made extensive alterations to the house and filled it with fine paintings, furniture, carpets and porcelain. On their visit to Italy they bought sea- and landscapes by Vernet and Zuccarelli, a set of paintings illustrating the 'Parable of the Prodigal Son' by Giordano and portraits of themselves by Batoni. Eight little family portraits by Arthur Devis came to Uppark with Sarah Lethieullier, wife of Sir Matthew. They also created the enchanting white and gold double-cube Saloon, the decoration marking the transition from the Palladian to the Adam style; the festoon curtains and pelmets of ivory silk brocade are original. They chose the fine set of English giltwood chairs in the Louis x v style, but the French furniture, including the Louis x v *bureau plat* and the four Boulle pedestals by Levasseur, the large ormolu chandelier, and the bronze and marble console tables, was acquired by Sir Harry, who had a francophile taste.

The story is the same throughout the State Rooms – satisfying mahogany furniture, a good set of English commodes in the Louis x v style incorporating Oriental lacquer panels and English japanned work made in the second half of the 18th century; porcelain from the

Pagoda cabinet in the style of Chippendale, 1752–60; Uppark.

Meissen, Sèvres and Chelsea factories; and early-19th-century wallpapers now much faded by 200 years of downland sun flooding into the house.

Upper Slaughter Manor House
Gloucestershire

Mr Eric Turrell

2½ miles w of Stow-on-the-Wold

This pretty mainly Elizabethan house with its elegant 17th-century porch stands high in its Cotswold valley. The lower rooms are of an earlier period and the vaulted crypt could be 14th century. The Slaughter family for whom it was built migrated in 1738 to America and the manor was subsequently a farm house until its restoration earlier in this century. The most interesting interior features are the Elizabethan chimneypieces, showing Renaissance influence, and some of the original panelling in the Hall and Drawing Room.

Upton Cressett Hall Shropshire

Mr William Cash

4 miles w of Bridgnorth, 18 miles s e of Shrewsbury

The site of this red-brick Elizabethan manor house, with older parts dating to c.1380 and c.1480, is recorded in Domesday Book and there is a 12th-century church nearby with a beautiful chancel arch, an early Norman font and a fragment of 12th-century wall painting. Traces of a medieval village can be seen in fields close to the house.

Inside is an interesting Great Hall, c.1380, said to be one of the earliest dated aisled halls in Shropshire. Much of the work in the interior is early Tudor, but changes were made in 1580 and the Drawing Room was panelled in 1600.

Across the courtyard is a fine Elizabethan gatehouse which contains two exceptional plasterwork ceilings and an overmantel.

Upton House Warwickshire

The National Trust

7 miles n w of Banbury on A422 to Stratford-on-Avon

In the reign of James II, Sir Rushout Cullen, a rich city merchant, built Upton House close to Edgehill where the first battle of the Civil War had been fought. Subsequently this mansion of yellow Warwickshire stone passed to various families, including the Earls of Jersey, until 1927 when it was acquired by the 2nd Lord Bearsted, who reorganized its layout in order to accommodate his glorious collections of paintings and porcelain. These he most generously presented to the Trust in 1948 together with the house and grounds.

The Flemish and early Netherlands Schools are magnificently represented by such masterpieces as *The Dormition of the Virgin* by Pieter Breughel the Elder, portraits by Memlinc and by Van der Weyden, Bosch's *The Adoration of the Magi*, three paintings of saints by the Master of the St Lucy Legend (that of St Jerome is particularly fine), and works by David (*Madonna and Child*), Patenier, Provost and the younger Frans Pourbus. Dutch 17th-century paintings of distinction include Metsu's *Le Corsage Bleu*, several by Steen, among them *The Tired Traveller*, a fine church interior by Saenredam, and grey, placid scenes by van der Cappelle, Van Goyen, Ruysdael, Meurant and Wouvermans.

Fouquet's miniature gouache on vellum depicting St Michael slaying the dragon is an outstanding example of French 15th-century painting. El Greco's *El Espolio*, painted on a

Fouquet's 15th-century miniature of St Michael slaying the dragon; Upton House.

The Presentation of the Virgin *by Giovanni di Paolo, a Sienese painter active 1420–82; Upton House.*

pine panel, a small-scale version of the altarpiece in the Sacristy of Toledo Cathedral, is the most notable Spanish work. The Italian collection ranges from the 14th to the 18th century; among the earlier works is *The Last Supper* by the Florentine Master of the Fabriano Altarpiece and *The Presentation of the Virgin* by the Sienese Giovanni di Paolo. The Venetian paintings include works by Lotto, Tintoretto, Domenico Tiepolo and Canaletto, and Venetian scenes by Guardi at his best.

The British paintings illustrate the 18th-century and early-19th-century achievements in the realm of portrait painting and the pleasures of the English countryside. Portraitists include Highmore, Reynolds, Romney (*William Beckford*), Raeburn (*The Macdonald Children*), Dance (*William Weddell and William Palgrave*), Arthur Devis, Hoppner, Beechey, and Opie. There are vigorous sporting works by Marshall, J. F. Herring Sr and Francis Sartorius (especially *Peter Beckford's Hounds*). Stubbs is splendidly represented by *The Haymakers*, *The Reapers* and *The Labourers*. Here also are Hogarth's renowned *Morning* and *Night*.

The wide-ranging collection of 18th-century English and European porcelain is another of Upton's joys. The many fine examples of soft-paste wares include those of

Vincennes and Sèvres *jaune jonquille, bleu céleste, gros bleu* and *bleu-du-roi* grounds, but the English factories of Bow, Chelsea of both the 'Red Anchor' and 'Gold Anchor' periods and of Chelsea-Derby are well represented in a collection in which figure representation is prominent.

The Hall contains a set of late-16th-century Brussels tapestries representing the 'Hunts of the Emperor Maximilian' after Bernard van Orley. The 18th-century English furniture includes a fine mahogany suite of chairs and settees covered with original *gros point* and *petit point* needlework.

Vale Royal Abbey Cheshire

The Michaelmas Trust

¾ mile from Whitegate between Winsford and Northwich

Vale Royal Abbey was established in 1277 by Edward I as the largest Cistercian foundation in England. After the Dissolution of the Monasteries the property was purchased by Sir Thomas Holcroft and in 1616 by Mary, Lady Cholmondeley, widow of Sir Hugh Cholmondeley and daughter of Christopher Holford; in 1617 she entertained James I here in great state. In 1821, her direct descendant was created Baron Delamere of Vale Royal. After World War II, the property left the family and has been owned since 1977 by the Michaelmas Trust, founded in 1975 to give vocational training to the mentally handicapped. The Trust is also carefully restoring this mansion.

Sir Thomas Holcroft adapted the Abbey domestic buildings on the south and west sides of the cloister to create a house. Ransacked and one wing destroyed in the Civil War, the house was subsequently extended and altered in the late-18th century and by Edward Blore in 1833 in Jacobean style. In 1860 John Douglas received his first major commission to reface the south block, build a clock tower and re-do much of the internal plasterwork in lavish style. Later, in 1877, he remodelled the Library, incorporating fine late-medieval and 17th-

century Flemish woodwork. The Dining Room contains a good 1750s pedimented doorcase, and the Saloon a series of heraldic achievements celebrating the Cholmondeleys.

The Vyne Hampshire

The National Trust

4 miles N of Basingstoke, between Bramley and Sherborne St John

The Vyne was built of brick *c.*1500–27 by William Sandys, who served Henry VIII for over thirty years, helped organize the Field of the Cloth of Gold, was created Lord Sandys of The Vyne and subsequently became Lord Chancellor. The classical portico of the south front, the first to be added to an English country house, was designed by John Webb, Inigo Jones' son-in-law, in 1650, three years before the estate was sold by the 6th Lord Sandys to Chaloner Chute, a fearless advocate, who became Speaker of the House of Commons under Richard Cromwell. Sir John Chute, last of his line, left the estate to the National Trust in 1956.

Important changes to the house were made in the mid-18th century by John Chute, a close friend of the poet Gray and of Horace Walpole. He installed the rococo plasterwork ceilings in the Large Drawing Room, the Ante-room and the Further Drawing Room, redecorated the Ante-Chapel in Gothic style and added the Tomb Chamber, which contains Thomas Carter's impressive reclining marble effigy of Speaker Chute, to the late-Perpendicular Chapel with its magnificent 16th-century Flemish stained glass and its fine maiolica tiles, made in Antwerp by an Italian craftsman from Urbino. He converted the original stone hall and stairs in 1770 into a neo-classical staircase with fluted Corinthian columns, an achievement which Horace Walpole acknowledged by calling him 'an exquisite architect, of the purest taste, both in the Graecian and Gothic styles'.

There is excellent furniture at The Vyne, much of it acquired by John Chute, notably twelve walnut Queen Anne chairs with pierced slats, now covered with *petit point* needlework by the late Lady Chute, in the Dining Room; four single chairs by Vile and Cobb in the Chapel Parlour; an Italian *pietre dure* casket mounted with ormolu on a carved gilt stand attributed to Vile and Cobb in the Ante-room; two marquetry inlaid French-style commodes attributed to Pierre Langlois and a Louis xv writing table in the Large Drawing Room; and a Kent-style table in the Vestibule whose scagliola top bears the arms of Sir Robert Walpole.

Other outstanding contents include a fine set of painted 'Latimo' glass plates of Venetian scenes, Italian maiolica plates from Castelli, and Meissen and Oriental china in the Ante-room, the bracket clock *c.*1754 by François Simon of Paris in the Large Drawing Room and a fine Khorassan carpet in the Ante-Chapel. Noteworthy among the paintings is Rosalba Carriera's portrait of Francis Whitehead and a landscape by Andrea Locatelli. The Tapestry Room with its Soho tapestries, woven *c.*1720 by John Vanderbank, leads into the Oak Gallery with its glorious and finely carved panelling installed *c.*1526 by Lord Sandys; especially fine is the royal coat of arms over the east door and the mid-17th-century classical marble chimneypiece in the east wall.

ABOVE *Thomas Carter's marble effigy of Chaloner Chute in the mid-18th-century Gothic-style Tomb Chamber; The Vyne.*

LEFT *Early-16th-century maiolica tiles made in Antwerp by an Italian craftsman and installed in the Chapel at The Vyne.*

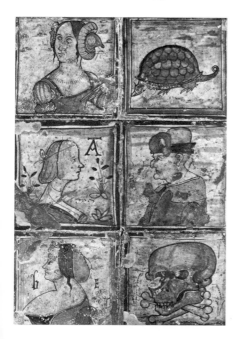

Waddesdon Manor
Buckinghamshire

The National Trust

6 miles NW of Aylesbury on A41 to Bicester

Built 1874–89 in French Renaissance style by G. H. Destailleur, a French architect, for Baron Ferdinand de Rothschild (1839–98) on a glorious site with wide views of the Chilterns, Waddesdon Manor is one of the great treasure houses of Europe. Baron Ferdinand's main interest was in rich and elaborate 18th-century art of the finest quality. This love

François Boucher Philippe Egalité as a Child, *1749; Waddesdon Manor.*

Japanese 18th-century porcelain fish, mounted as a fontaine à parfum; Waddesdon Manor.

extended to reconstructing rooms out of old materials, including panelling, and reproducing them as they had been during the reigns of the Bourbon Kings. In this way he acquired thirteen carpets from the royal Savonnerie factory, Paris, all made for French royal palaces; much of the remarkable French furniture was purchased in England. He also collected Dutch and Flemish 17th-century masters and 18th-century English portraitists.

His sister, Miss Alice, who inherited on his death, added arms and armour and much of Waddesdon's Sèvres and Meissen china. Her great-nephew, James de Rothschild, to whom she bequeathed Waddesdon, also inherited from his father resplendent collections covering much the same ground. These he amalgamated to leave them and the estate, generously endowed, to the National Trust in 1957.

Among the French painters are Watteau, Pater, Lancret, Greuze, Fragonard and Boucher. The Dutch and Flemish works by Rubens, Cuyp, van der Heyden, de Hoogh, Terborch and Van de Velde are equally impressive. There are two glorious large Venetian views and six studies of Venetian islands by Guardi. English painters include Reynolds at his best, Gainsborough, Romney and Francis Wheatley. Among the collection of gold boxes are many painted with enchanting miniature landscapes by Van Blarenberghe and leading French miniaturists of the period. The tapestries include examples from Beauvais and Gobelins. Among the sculptors are Falconet, Lemoyne and Clodion.

There are over a hundred pieces of 18th-century French furniture, many veneered with patterns in marquetry and mounted with ormolu, others lacquered or painted, many of them by such distinguished *ébénistes* as Riesener, Cressent, and the Dubois, father and son; there are several by Carlin, Lacroix and Baumhauer, mounted with Sèvres plaques. There is much fine china, including Meissen figures by Kändler, Chinese *famille rose, famille verte* and celadon wares, often mounted in ormolu; but pride of place goes to the magnificent range of Sèvres, including the dessert service in *bleu céleste* in the tented Blue Sèvres Room upstairs.

There are books remarkable for their bindings, fans, clocks, arms and armour, musical instruments, Roman, Renaissance and Baroque jewellery, German and Venetian glass, Italian maiolica, Staffordshire 17th-century slip-ware dishes, Limoges enamel plaques, miniature portraits, chandeliers and ormolu wall-lights, elaborate door-furniture, damasks and other materials many of them woven for the house, bird-cages, 18th- and 19th-century buttons of various materials, lace, and a collection of embroidered and woven textiles from Europe, Russia and the Middle East. When completed, the Waddesdon catalogue will consist of some fourteen volumes.

Wallington Northumberland

The National Trust

12 miles w of Morpeth along B6343, 1 mile s of Cambo off B6343

Wallington was acquired by Sir William Blackett, a successful Newcastle merchant, who built the present restrained quadrangular in 1688, then in a very remote area. His grandson, Sir Walter Calverley Blackett, reorganized the exterior and remodelled the interior, employing Pietro Francini of the Italian-Swiss family of stuccoists to decorate the Dining Room, Saloon and Library with enchanting rococo plasterwork. Wallington passed by marriage to the Trevelyan family of Nettlecombe, Somerset, and it was Maria Wilson, the wife of Sir John Trevelyan, 5th Baronet, who brought Wallington its great treasury of porcelain. The 6th Baronet and his wife, Pauline Jermyn, preferred Wallington to Nettlecombe and they had the courtyard converted into the enclosed Central Hall.

Friends of Ruskin, Millais and Holman Hunt, they commissioned William Bell Scott, head of the Newcastle School of Design, who was imbued with Pre-Raphaelite principles, to paint eight admirable history scene canvases which they hung on the walls of the Hall. Pauline Trevelyan and Ruskin participated in painting flowers and plants on its stone pillars.

The house passed to a cousin, Sir Charles Edward Trevelyan, whose brother-in-law, Lord Macaulay, was a frequent visitor to Wallington. Sir Charles' son, Sir George Otto Trevelyan, was also a distinguished historian, as was his own second son, G. M. Trevelyan, Master for many years of Trinity College, Cambridge. Sir Charles Trevelyan, the 3rd Baronet, who was President of the Board of Education in the two pre-war Labour governments, gave Wallington to the National Trust in 1941.

There are family portraits by Hoppner and Romney in the Hall, by Hudson and Gainsborough (that of Mrs Hudson, *née* Trevelyan, possibly altered by Reynolds) in the Dining Room and Reynolds' full-length of Sir Walter Calverley Blackett in the outstanding white and lilac Saloon. Elsewhere are works by Arthur Devis, Turner, David Cox, Ruskin, Burne-Jones and Bell Scott.

In the Hall is a remarkably fine collection of very rare Bow figures, 1752–5, two Bristol Delft bowls commemorating the 1741 parliamentary election in Newcastle which cost Sir Walter Blackett, who was returned, £6,319, and good examples of Chinese *famille verte* and powder blue porcelain. There is more fine Oriental porcelain in the Dining Room and especially in the Saloon, which contains a *famille rose* fish bowl on its mid-18th-century gilt mahogany stand with dolphin feet. The European porcelain is seen at its grandest in Lady Trevelyan's Parlour. The early Meissen includes a set of the Continents modelled *c.*1745 by J. J. Kändler and a tea-set decorated by J. G. Klinger. The small teapot (No. 44) dates from the Böttger period, made *c.*1715, some four years after the Meissen factory was founded. Other German factories and Sèvres

337

*'The Fortune Teller' by the 'Muses Modeller',
Bow, 1752; Wallington.*

and Vienna are also represented.

There are good examples of Chippendale, Sheraton and Hepplewhite furniture, a number of Dutch pieces and, in the Saloon, French commodes of the Régence period (1715–23). The desk in the Study was used by Lord Macaulay when writing his *History of England*, while Sir George Otto Trevelyan sat at the writing table to work on his *History of the American Revolution*.

Julia, Lady Calverley, stitched the ten remarkable panels of needlework in rococo frames hanging in the Needlework Room, dated 1717, and also the magnificent six-fold screen (dated 1727), the most important piece of needlework in the house. There is a fine collection of dolls' houses, mainly 19th century, in the Common Room, while upstairs is Lady Wilson's (her daughter married the 5th Baronet) Cabinet of Curiosities. This extraordinary miscellany includes stuffed birds and their eggs, fossils and bones, wax impressions, narwhal tusks and war instruments from the South Seas. Much has gone to museums; much happily remains.

Warwick Castle Warwickshire

Warwick Castle Ltd

In the town of Warwick

This dramatic stronghold, once the seat of the Earls of Warwick, was started in the 11th century but the bulk of it, including the basement or cellar area, dates from the early-14th century. The great towers and the barbican and gatehouse were all built as part of a single though protracted building programme between *c.*1375 and 1400. Additional building was done in the 17th and 18th centuries, mainly on the domestic side of the Castle, but a great fire in 1871 did considerable damage. The Great Hall was gutted and restoration work included a new high hammerbeam roof. In this Great Hall is a fine collection of weapons and armour, including armour of the Marquess of Montrose, miniature Elizabethan armour made for the young son of the Earl of Leicester and impressive equestrian armour – the rider wears Italian jousting armour and the horse German armour of the 16th century. The great Kenilworth Buffet, which was made out of one oak tree by Cookes & Sons of Warwick, was exhibited at the Great Exhibition of 1851.

LEFT *16th-century armour; Warwick Castle.*
ABOVE *The State Dining Room at Warwick Castle.*

The State Dining Room contains some fine pictures: *Two Lions* by Rubens, an impressive full-length version of King Charles I on horseback by Van Dyck and two other mid-18th-century royal portraits in extravagantly ornate frames. In the Red Drawing Room are two large Boulle type cabinets containing part of a Ch'ien Lung *famille rose* armorial dinner service, two fine Italian marriage chests, a handsome small Dutch marquetry table and some portraits by, among others, Lely and Kneller. The splendid Cedar Drawing Room, finely panelled and with an 18th-century Carrara marble chimneypiece in the manner of the Adam brothers, giltwood marble-topped tables and blue-john and ormolu candelabra by Matthew Boulton, is crowned with a late-17th-century plaster ceiling.

Notable pieces in the Green Drawing Room include a 16th-century Florentine table and four early-19th-century English giltwood tables each holding a 17th-century Japanese Imari banqueting dish. Queen Anne's Bedroom has a splendid ceiling in green and gold. The elegant marble chimneypiece is surmounted by Kneller's portrait of Queen Anne, which is flanked by gilded plasterwork panels. The walls are hung with an early-17th-century set of Brussels tapestries which depict the gardens of a medieval palace. The ceiling of the adjoining Blue Boudoir is particularly fine, as is the portrait of Henry VIII.

Washington Old Hall
Tyne and Wear

The National Trust

In Washington, 5 miles W of Sunderland

Washington Old Hall, originally built in the 12th century, is now a place of pilgrimage for all those interested in early American history

Jacobean oak-panelling and 16th-century furniture in the Panelled Room, Washington Old Hall.

and Anglo-American goodwill. It is from here that George Washington's ancestors took their name and although his particular branch of the family moved west of the Pennines in the 13th century, Washington descendants remained at the Old Hall until 1613 when it was sold, the original building partly destroyed and the present small 17th-century manor built of sandstone on the original foundations. Surrounded increasingly by industrial and mining developments, it was due for demolition when it was saved in 1936 by a local preservation committee, restored and given to the National Trust in 1957. The top floor is used by the Sunderland Metropolitan Council who are tenants of the whole property but the ground floor and a bedroom upstairs have been furnished in typical 17th- and early-18th-century fashion, helped by funds and gifts from both sides of the Atlantic.

An early-17th-century chimneypiece has been installed in the stone-flagged Great Hall which is furnished with good English and Flemish oak furniture and with paintings, mostly 17th-century Dutch, some on loan from the Bowes Museum. Its wall at the Kitchen end is medieval as are those of the Kitchen itself. An early-19th-century Staffordshire jug, bearing emblems of the United States, is in the Bedroom.

The splendid Jacobean oak panelling in the Panelled Room together with some of the furniture was given by Miss Mabel Choate in memory of her father, a distinguished American ambassador to Britain. It contains, among other objects of interest, a fine 16th-century oak buffet, a carved and marquetry fronted chest for clothes and an oak 'cricket' table, on which stand a fine stumpwork cabinet, a 17th-century Persian vase and Delft pieces.

George Washington's family tree is on the first landing. At the top of the stairs are two show-cases containing Washingtonian mementos; above them hangs the flag of the American Bicentennial of 1975. A picture of Mount Vernon, Virginia, which President Carter autographed on the back and presented to Washington Old Hall when he visited it in 1977, hangs in the Bedroom.

Detail of the Baroque ceiling painting by Giuseppe Borgnis in the Blue Drawing Room, West Wycombe Park.

West Wycombe Park
Buckinghamshire

The National Trust

2 miles w of High Wycombe off A40 to Oxford

Sir Francis Dashwood, the 2nd Baronet, who later inherited the barony of Le Despencer, began in about 1739 to alter the house he had been left in the Chilterns, a task which he continued until his death in 1781. He is perhaps best known for his association with the monks of Medmenham, otherwise the Hell Fire Club, which held its notorious meetings in a cave in West Wycombe hill. Sir Francis was, however, an arbiter of taste and a politician of some stature. In 1762–3 he served as Chancellor of the Exchequer under Bute and as early as 1745 he had suggested the reform of the House of Commons, a reform not undertaken until the 1832 Bill was passed.

The impressive interior decoration is partly Baroque, partly neo-classical, and the character of each room is evidenced by its ceiling. Giuseppe Borgnis from northern Italy painted those of the Blue Drawing Room, Saloon, Music Room and Study, the scenes based on works by Raphael, Reni and Annibale Carracci; the sumptuous biblical and allegorical figures which crowd his summer-blue skies are always lively, at times boisterous, on occasion amorous; the walls are painted in bright contrasting colours. His son, Giovanni, is more restrained, using designs from Robert Wood's *Ruins of Palmyra* on the ceiling both of the Dining Room and of the remarkable neo-classical Hall, whose stone floor was also his work, its walls and dado painted in imitation marble (as in the Dining Room) and porphyry respectively. The ceilings of the Tapestry Room and the Red Drawing Room are in classical Roman style by William Hannan, whose four topographical paintings of the house and park hang in the Red Drawing Room. The magnificent contents of the house are on loan from Sir Francis Dashwood, 11th Baronet.

The paintings, mainly Italian and Dutch, include works by Sacchi, Rosa, Orizonte and by Ruisdael, Jordaens and Wouvermans, probably collected by the 2nd Sir Francis during his European journeys. The furniture, mostly 17th- and 18th-century, is of fine quality. There are console tables in the manner of Kent, armchairs in Chippendale's 'Director' pattern and in the chinoiserie manner, two small English-made serpentine marquetry com-

One of a pair of serpentine marquetry commodes, 1760–70, by Pierre Langlois; West Wycombe Park.

modes by Langlois in the Red Drawing Room, and in the same room a glorious 17th-century Italian cabinet, described in the 1781 inventory as 'a very Curious Cabinet inlaid with Lapis Lazuli and many other Precious Stones'.

Other notable treasures include Brussels tapestries in the Tapestry Room, designed from peasant scenes by the younger Teniers, fine chimneypieces in the Saloon and in the Music Room, probably by Sir Henry Cheere; and the impressive Staircase of mahogany beautifully inlaid with ebony and satinwood and with a walnut balustrade.

Weston Park Shropshire

The Earl of Bradford

Entrance from A5 at Weston-under-Lizard, 6 miles w of Junction 12, M6 (Gailey)

Although built on a medieval site, this handsome mansion of rose-red brick with stone dressings was built in 1671 to the designs of Elizabeth Mytton, wife of Sir Thomas Wilbraham. Lely's fine portrait of her in grey and pale yellow is in the Drawing Room. This great estate passed by marriage, first to the Newports, Earls of Bradford, and then to the Bridgemans of Castle Bromwich. Sir Orlando Bridgeman was created a Baronet in 1660 and became Lord Keeper of the Great Seal to Charles II. There are two distinguished portraits of him at Weston, one by Borselaer in the Marble Hall and the other by Riley above the Library chimneypiece. In 1815, the 2nd Baron Bradford became the 1st Earl of the second creation.

The interior has undergone frequent changes, including those made with percipience by the present Countess to eradicate such Victorian anachronisms as the Billiards and Smoking Rooms, now converted into the First Salon and Second Salon respectively, and make it in keeping with the much earlier character of the house while retaining the comfortable atmosphere of a family home.

The Entrance Hall contains notable paintings including Stubbs' *Two Horses* over the fireplace and two by John Ferneley. In the Marble Hall, with its splendid white marble and black slate floor and the fine wrought-iron balustered marble staircase of 1898, are two portraits by Wright, early George II chairs with solid cartouche-shaped backs, an Italian walnut coffer and three gilt cabinets in which are displayed Chinese ceramics and Bow, Derby and Chelsea figures. The Tapestry Room contains a series of mid-18th-century Gobelins tapestries, one signed 'Boucher, 1766' and giltwood furniture covered in Aubusson tapestry. The glass cabinet contains early-18th-century Chinese porcelain.

There are three portraits by Lely in the Drawing Room in addition to that of Lady Wilbraham, and others by Kneller and Mary Beale. Here also is an excellent Louis XV desk and a small Louis XVI cabinet together with Bow china. The comfortable Library, with a Corinthian pillared screen at each end, is hung with family portraits above the bookcases by Reynolds, Romney, Hayter and Hoppner. In front of the fireplace is Sir Orlando's Purse of the Great Seal of England.

The Dining Room has been delightfully re-created by Lady Bradford and contains impressive portraits, especially those by Van Dyck and Lely, and an attractive conversation piece, *Homage to Handel*, by Pine. The West Marble Hall with its Boulle cabinet and Coalport china is dominated by Jacopo Bassano's *The Way to Golgotha*, originally presented to Charles II by the people of Holland. Here also is a selection of the 1,100 letters written by Disraeli between 1873 and his death in 1881 to Selina, wife of the 3rd Earl of Bradford; her portrait is in the Library.

The two Salons, with black and white tiled floors, are enriched with two Aubusson tapestries, fine seascapes by Storck and Vernet, paintings by Jacopo and Leandro Bassano, Brouwer, Castiglione, and, outside the Second Salon, a stuffed yellow 'cock' parrot which miraculously laid an egg on twenty-four consecutive days.

On the Landing above the Marble Staircase are portraits by Lely and Wissing and an unusual set of bird pictures on embossed *papier*

Van Dyck's portrait of Sir Thomas Hanmer, c.1638; Weston Park.

mâché by William Hayes, 1761–3. On the Stone Staircase is a Soho tapestry of Chinese design and at its foot a fine collection of Worcester porcelain. Some of the most notable portraits, mainly the smaller ones, are concentrated in the Breakfast Room. Here is Holbein's immensely distinguished *Sir George Carew*, Mor's portrait of an unknown woman and likenesses by Johnson, de Keyser, Honthorst, Riley, Kneller, Gainsborough and Hoppner and a delightful likeness, *c.*1623, by an unknown hand of Lady Diana Russell who became the wife of Francis Newport, 1st Earl of Bradford.

Wightwick Manor West Midlands

The National Trust

3 miles w of Wolverhampton up Wightwick Bank (A454)

The Wightwick manorial township is mentioned in Domesday Book and the Wightwick family, who built a Tudor manor house (now a

One of the tiles by de Morgan surrounding the Italian chimneypiece in the Drawing Room, Wightwick Manor.

windows in the Drawing Room, the Hall and the Great Parlour, and he was also responsible for the plaster frieze, the painting of the timbered ceiling and the carved stone fireplace in the last room. L. A. Shuffrey designed the plaster ceiling and frieze in the Billiard and Dining Rooms. There are tiles by de Morgan, 17th-century Flemish verdure tapestries in the Hall, and blue and white Nankin plates which were extremely popular in Victorian days. In the Oak Room is a settle designed by Bodley and decorated by Kempe, also a cupboard with panels painted by Treffry Dunn after Rossetti's pictures and with carving by T. Keynes, which once belonged to Swinburne and Watts-Dunton in Putney. There are also antique oak chests and refectory tables.

Lodge), lived here until the 19th century. The estate was acquired in the 1880s by Theodore Mander, an enlightened industrialist and keen supporter of the ideas of William Morris and the Pre-Raphaelites, and the many-gabled mansion of half-timbered construction, erected between 1887 and 1893 to designs by Edward Ould of Liverpool, constitutes an important memorial to this fascinating Victorian movement. Theodore's son, Sir Geoffrey Mander MP, and his wife Lady Mander, herself a Pre-Raphaelite authority who still lives at Wightwick, contributed paintings, furniture and other items to the original collections.

Morris's 'Dove and Rose' wall-coverings hang in the Drawing Room, his 'Diagonal Trail' in the Great Parlour, his wallpapers embellish the Morning and Billiard Rooms, the Ground Floor Passage and upstairs bedrooms, and the Billiard Room curtains and carpets in the Dining Room and Oak Room are to his design.

Wightwick's splendid collection of Pre-Raphaelite paintings includes work by Millais, D. G. Rossetti and Holman Hunt, together with that of Burne-Jones, Madox Brown, Watts, Leighton, Sandys and other Victorians. C. E. Kempe designed the painted glass

Wilton House Wiltshire

The Earl of Pembroke

In Wilton 2½ miles w of Salisbury on Exeter road (A30)

The splendours of Chatsworth and Longleat can be seen from afar but Wilton House lies hidden from the town by its wall. To enter through Chambers' Triumphal Arch, surmounted by the equestrian statue of Marcus Aurelius, raises keen expectations which are far surpassed by the actual magnificence of the house. It is built on sequestered monastic property given by Henry VIII to Sir William Herbert, later ennobled as 1st Earl of Pembroke. The outstanding qualities of the state rooms facing south arose from the ashes of a fire in 1647 or 1648, caused, according to Aubrey, 'by airing of the roomes'. The south front had probably been designed about 1636 by Isaac de Caus under Inigo Jones' supervision; its reconstruction was mainly the work of John Webb but 'with the advice' of Inigo Jones. James Wyatt altered the north and west ranges late in the 18th century and gothicized the east front Entrance Hall, which contains busts, four of them by Roubiliac. The contents of the house are superb.

In the Little Smoking Room are fine 18th-century regimental equestrian portraits by Morier, also Charles II walnut marquetry furniture. Fifty-five gouache paintings of the Spanish *'Haute Ecole'* riding school are in the Large Smoking Room as well as a glorious Chippendale cabinet bookcase.

The Staircase, hung with family portraits by Dahl, Mytens, Beechey and Lely, a splendid *Democritus* by Ribera and religious scenes by Bloemart, Cortona and Palma, leads to the State Rooms, remarkable for their painted ceilings. Sabbatini's *Birth of Venus*, surrounded by Inigo Jones' and Webb's decorations, embellishes the ceiling of the Little Ante-room. The Corner Room ceiling is the work of Giordano, its cove painted with designs by Clermont; both rooms contain distinguished 16th- and 17th-century religious and genre Dutch and Italian paintings by, among others, Claude, Rubens, Orley, Leyden, Lotto and del Sarto. The ceilings of the Colonnade Room and the Great Ante-room are both by Clermont. The former contains fine portraits by Beechey, Lawrence and especially Reynolds, while the latter possesses two portraits by Van Dyck, three seascapes by the younger Van de Velde and a portrait by Rembrandt of his mother.

The white and gold Double Cube is one of the grandest of English state rooms, its walls decorated with bold swags of fruit, flowers and classical masks, the ceiling canvases depicting the story of Perseus by Emanuel de Critz (they have also been attributed to Francis Cleyn), the cove painted by Edward Pierce, the furniture designed by Kent and Chippendale and the walls hung with Van Dyck's royal and family portraits, for which the room was designed. These masterpieces were painted in London while Charles I still reigned and were brought here during the Commonwealth. The splendid Single Cube Room also contains portraits, mainly of the family, by Van Dyck, Lely, Jonathan Richardson and Wissing. The ceiling canvas, representing Daedalus and Icarus, was painted by Giuseppe Cesari. The furniture is in the style of Kent and Chippendale. Emanuel de Critz was responsible for the dado paintings of scenes from Sir Philip

Sidney's *Arcadia* and Inigo Jones for the marble fireplace.

The Upper Cloisters that surround the interior courtyard of the house, Wyatt's early-19th-century Gothic creation, contain Richard Wilson's views of Wilton House, Samuel Scott's *Covent Garden*, a pastoral scene by Zuccarelli, ancient and 18th-century busts of Roman Emperors, mahogany chairs, lacquer cabinets and fine K'ang Hsi jars with lids.

Wimpole Hall Cambridgeshire

The National Trust

Off A603, 8 miles s w of Cambridge and 6 miles N of Royston

Wimpole Hall's mellow red-brick central block, dating from the mid-17th century, and its estate were purchased in 1710 by the Duke of Newcastle but passed almost at once to his son-in-law, Edward, Lord Harley, who succeeded as 2nd Earl of Oxford in 1724. In 1713–21, Gibbs added the two wings on either side of the original block, one containing the Chapel, and in 1730 he added the splendid Library on the north front to house the renowned Harleian collection, started by the 1st Earl and continued by his son. The plasterwork here is attributed to Isaac Mansfield and the Italian plasterer, Bagutti. When the 2nd Earl died in 1740, after his financial failure, his library consisted of 50,000 printed books, 41,000 prints and 300,000 pamphlets, all sold by his widow in 1742. His 8,000 manuscripts, bought by the nation for £10,000, formed the nucleus of the British Museum's collections.

Philip Yorke, 1st Earl of Hardwicke, Lord Chancellor 1736–56, bought Wimpole in 1740 and commissioned Flitcroft to create the noble Gallery and remodel the Saloon. He employed Artari for the plasterwork and Sefferin Alken for the wood-carving. Soane designed the T-shaped Yellow Drawing Room for the 3rd Earl in the 1790s and extended the ante-chamber to Gibbs' library to form the present Book Room. The last major additions were made in the

The Library at Wimpole Hall built by James Gibbs in 1730 to house the Harleian book collection.

1840s by H. E. Kendall for the 4th Earl.

The house was derelict and almost without contents when acquired by Captain George Bambridge in 1938. His wife Elsie, younger daughter of Rudyard Kipling, widowed in 1943, set about restoring Wimpole and collecting suitable furnishings, having demolished Kendall's additions – which still left Wimpole the largest house in Cambridgeshire. She died in 1976 leaving the nearly 3,000-acre property to the National Trust, together with the Kipling archives, now on loan to Sussex University.

The only furniture still at Wimpole when the Bambridges acquired it were some pier-glasses and tables, a series of marble-topped tables now in the Gallery, the large oak pulpit inlaid with Gothic tracery in walnut in the Library, and the set of seat furniture in the Yellow Drawing Room. The rest of the furniture was either acquired by Mrs Bambridge or is on loan. Her good taste is exemplified by the painted furniture, mostly South German, in the South Drawing Room, the furniture and the English carpet from Exeter, *c.* 1780, the largest known example of its kind, in the Library, and by the four *torchères* with rams' masks in the Yellow Drawing Room.

There are portraits by Kneller (Bishop Burnet), Reynolds (the Duchess of Manchester with her small son depicted as Cupid), Ramsay, Ben Marshall (a young girl walking her dog), Cotes and Mercier. Mrs Bambridge was greatly attracted by watercolours, by 19th-century subject pictures and small decorative paintings. George Brittain's disrespectful *Apotheosis of the Royal Family* and a group including the Prince Regent, Mrs Fitzherbert and Sheridan by the Rev. William Peters is in the South Drawing Room. Elsewhere are paintings by Bonington, David Cox, Wootton, Bogdani, Witherington and Tissot (*The Shooting Gallery*). The Lord Chancellor's Room and Dressing Room are agreeably crowded with coaching scenes, especially the latter, while Mrs Bambridge's Dressing Room has more drawings of carriages, Gillray cartoons and costume pieces.

Winslow Hall Buckinghamshire

Sir Edward and Lady Tomkins

At entrance to Winslow on A413 from Aylesbury

This imposing Baroque house at the eastern end of the quiet country town of Winslow compels immediate attention. Tall, compact, with flanking pavilions, constructed of rose-red brick with stone dressings, its hipped roof dominated by a row of majestic chimneys, there is never any doubt of its importance. William Lowndes, who had been Secretary of the Treasury, decided in 1697 to build what is in effect an urban rather than a country house on the edge of his native town. There is little doubt that the Surveyor-General, Christopher Wren, designed the building. Its detailed accounts, published by the Wren Society, show that he scrutinized the bills very closely.

The interior is comfortably furnished in a manner which is completely in harmony with the character of the house and its rooms, mostly wainscotted with oak panelling. The English furniture, mainly early-18th century, spans the period between William III and the Regency. There are also French and Italian pieces, acquired by the present owners during a distinguished diplomatic career. The paintings include works by the younger David Teniers, Van de Velde and Vernet. The main first-floor bedroom is embellished with four fantasies painted on canvas by an unknown painter, although suggestive of Daniel Marot's style; Mr E. Croft-Murray is of the opinion that they may derive from the set of tapestries of the 'Château du Roi' by Le Brun. But the chief treasure of this delightful house is undoubtedly the fine collection of early Chinese ceramics, including several T'ang camels, and jade.

Woburn Abbey Bedfordshire

The Trustees of the Bedford Estates

In Woburn, 8½ miles NW of Dunstable; M1 (exit 12)

Beyond the entrance from Repton's magnificent park to the Abbey stands Henry

Flitcroft's great grey Palladian mansion, built in the mid-18th century for the Russell family, Dukes of Bedford. It is still massive even after the 12th Duke reduced it by half in 1950 and was forced to demolish Holland's elegant riding school and tennis court because of dry rot.

Woburn Abbey came to John Russell, 1st Earl of Bedford and Lord Privy Seal, from Henry VIII in 1550. It was the 4th Duke (1710–71), one of the Whig leaders in the reign of George III and in turn British Ambassador to Paris, Lord Lieutenant of Ireland and Secretary of State, who commissioned plans for the present house from Flitcroft. He was also responsible for amassing much of the outstanding furniture, paintings and articles of virtu which fill it. Much has since been added including the fine illustrated books on natural history in the Book Room and the equestrian paintings in the Sporting Room.

The collection of 16th- and early-17th-century portraits is particularly impressive. The attributions to George Gower include the outstanding Armada portrait of Elizabeth I and portraits of Lord Russell of Thornhaugh and Anna Russell, Countess of Warwick. Gheeraerts is strongly represented with four signed works (*Sir William Russell, Lady Russell, Sir John Kennedy* and *The Duke of Schleswig-Holstein*) and three confident attributions. Further fine portraits include works by or attributed to Hieronimo Custodis, Robert Peake the Elder and John de Critz. There is a fine portrait by an unknown hand of Lord Francis Russell. Later portraitists are represented by Van Dyck, Riley, Hoppner and the outstanding collection by Reynolds in the Reynolds Room, especially his *Oliver Goldsmith*, his *Marquis of Tavistock* (1759) and his self-portrait in the white and gold pedimented overmantel.

The Library contains marvellous self-portraits by such masters as Hals, Cuyp, Tintoretto, Steen, Hogarth, Murillo and by Rembrandt, together with his portrait of an old rabbi. There are twenty-four Venetian scenes by Canaletto. Elsewhere there are notable paintings by Velazquez (*Admiral Pareja*),

Claude, Van Goyen, Teniers, Poussin, Vernet, and Bonington, fine 17th-century Mortlake tapestries, bronzes and snuff boxes.

The state rooms were decorated by Flitcroft, the fine furniture supplied by Messrs Norman and Whittle, to which have been added exquisite 17th- and 18th-century French pieces by such distinguished *ébénistes* as Montigny, Riesener and by Langlois who worked in London. The plasterwork is probably by the Rose family. The Chinese Room contains glorious hand-painted Chinese wallpaper, Chinese Chippendale furniture and Chinese 18th- and early-19th-century ceramics. A room is dedicated to the memory of the present Duke's grandmother, remarkable both for her philanthropy and for her flying achievements; she broke many flying records in the 1920s and 1930s and was killed in a flying accident in 1937.

In the Crypt are displays of Imari and Kakiemon wares from Japan, fine English 18th-century porcelain from the Chelsea, Worcester and Longton Hall factories, a superb Sèvres dinner service presented by Louis XV, and silver, silver-gilt and gold plate by distinguished craftsmen, including de Lamerie and Willaume, as well as fine collections of miniature portraits and model soldiers.

Wolfeton House Dorset

Captain N. T. L. Thimbleby

1½ miles NW of Dorchester on A37 to Yeovil

The earliest parts of this impressive grey-stone mansion, once the home of the Trenchard family, may be 14th-century but the main construction is Elizabethan. Many alterations over the centuries have involved the re-siting of much of the exuberant and enjoyable Renaissance oak carving with which Wolfeton abounds.

The tiny Chapel, now in a gatehouse turret, contains carved panels, c.1480, of the signs of the Zodiac and the corresponding occupations of the months; among its other paintings is a Greek icon of St George, c.1600. The Screens

The Armada portrait of Queen Elizabeth I, c.1588, attributed to George Gower; Woburn Abbey.

Passage, its ceiling partly embellished with 17th-century plasterwork, has both 16th- and 17th-century panelling and remarkable carved doorways into the Great Hall and the Parlour. The Parlour doorway into the Passage and the overmantel contain wooden figures flanked by large Corinthian columns. The Parlour and Dining Room also sport elaborate late-16th-century plasterwork; the latter's plaster overmantel depicts Paris awarding the apple to Venus.

Over the first-floor doorway into the Great Chamber at the top of the stone Staircase is a stone pediment supported by Corinthian side pilasters with, at its centre, a bearded head. The splendid stone chimneypiece of the Great Chamber depicts American Indians and Orientals together with Faith and Hope. Some of the furniture is 17th-century.

There are royal and family portraits in the Great Hall and on the Staircase by or attributed to Johnson, Kneller and Hudson. In the Stair Tower leading out of the Great Hall is a fascinating miscellany of views of Wolfeton, carvings from Arabia and antique pottery from Cyprus.

Glossary

ACANTHUS formalized leaves of the acanthus plant used as part of the decoration of a Corinthian capital (q.v.) and in some types of leaf carving.

AMORETTO (Italian) cupid or winged cherub.

ANTHEMION honeysuckle or palmette ornament used in Greek and Roman architecture, usually in cornices and neckings of Ionic capitals (*see* Order).

ARABESQUE mural or surface decoration in colour or low relief, composed in flowing lines of branches, leaves and scrollwork fancifully entwined.

ARCADE a range of arches supported on columns or piers, attached to or detached from the wall.

ARCHITRAVE the lowest of the three main parts of the entablature (q.v.). Also the moulded frame surrounding a door or window.

BALUSTER a small pillar or column, often of fanciful outline.

BALUSTRADE a series of balusters supporting a handrail on staircase or balcony.

BAROQUE florid and exuberant artistic style intended to impress, originating in Italy in the 16th century and flourishing in the 17th and early-18th centuries; the hallmark of the Papacy, the courts of royalty and the nobility.

BARREL VAULT a continuous plain arch, semi-circular or pointed; the simplest form of vault, also called tunnel or wagon vault. Barrel vaulting may also be divided into bays by transverse arches.

BLANC-DE-CHINE white porcelain made at the Tê-hua kilns of Fukien province, China, perhaps the most beautiful ever made. Probably first fashioned towards end of Ming Dynasty (1368–1643); much was exported to Europe in late-17th and early-18th centuries.

BLUE-JOHN a decorative fluorspar, marked with blue, purple and brown, mined in Derbyshire. Used extensively in mid and latter part of 18th century.

BOLECTION a raised moulding round a panel.

BOMBÉ (French) an exaggerated swelling shape often given to the fronts of rococo chests of drawers.

BONHEUR-DU-JOUR (French) a small writing table with drawers or pigeon-holes.

BOULLE fine inlay work used in cabinet-making with complicated designs of brass, gold or bronze combined with ivory, ebony or tortoiseshell. The Parisian *ébéniste* André Charles Boulle (1642–1732) first developed this style during the reign of Louis XIV; it was widely imitated and revived in the 19th century.

BREAKFRONT term used especially to describe a bookcase where the side sections are in line but the central portion protrudes.

BUFFET an open, doorless, three-tiered sideboard, often elaborately carved, on which food, cups, etc., were placed. Developed in the 16th century.

BUREAU-PLAT (French) a flat-topped writing desk with drawers.

CABOCHON an oval gem polished but uncut.

CABRIOLE a curved leg bending outwards at the knee and tapering inwards towards the foot, which may be club, scroll, claw-and-ball, etc.

CANTILEVER a beam, girder or projection supported at one end only. A cantilever bridge has a central portion suspended between two cantilever arms.

CAPITAL head or top part of a column (*see* Order).

CAPRICCIO a fanciful or whimsical composition on canvas, board, ceiling or wall.

CARTOUCHE a decorative tablet, often used to carry an escutcheon (q.v.) of arms.

CARYATID a bust, demi-figure, three-quarter or full-length female figure supporting an entablature (q.v.).

CASSONE Italian Renaissance 15th- and 16th-century chest, very heavily carved or decorated with views, scenes, etc.

CHIAROSCURO (Italian) a pictorial art in which only the light and shade are represented, i.e. black or sepia and white.

CHIMNEYPIECE frame surrounding a fireplace; often includes an overmantel of ornamental woodwork or marble, sometimes enclosing a painting or mirror.

CHINOISERIE European imitations or evocations of Chinese art in buildings, follies, interior decoration, furniture, etc. First appeared in the late-17th century and was very popular in the 18th.

CLASSICAL architecture or decoration, based on the forms developed in ancient Greece and Rome (*see* Palladian and neo-classical).

CLERESTORY upper part of the walls of a church nave with windows above the roofs of the aisles.

CLOISONNÉ enamel in which colours of pattern are kept apart by their outline plates.

COASTER usually a low round stand used to circulate food or a decanter round a table.

COFFEUSE French term for a dressing table.

COMMODE (French) a piece of furniture with drawers and shelves.

CONFIDENT French term for a sofa curving forward to enable two people to half-face each other.

CONSOLE used to describe a table standing against a wall supported on brackets or by an eagle, etc. Also a scroll-shaped bracket.

CORBEL a bracket, projecting horizontally to support a beam or another feature.

CORNICE the top projecting part of an entablature (q.v.) in classical architecture. Also any projecting ornamental moulding.

COROMANDEL heavy, hard and jet-black wood, sometimes with brown or yellow streaks.

COVING convex curving space between the wall and ceiling.

CUIRASSE a piece of armour to protect the body down to the waist.

CUPOLA a small dome, crowning a roof or turret.

DOMESDAY BOOK The census of England completed in 1086 on the instructions of William the Conqueror.

DOORCASE the case lining a doorway on which the door is hung.

DRESSINGS stones worked to a smooth or moulded edge and set round an angle, window or any feature of a building.

ÉBÉNISTE a cabinet-maker in France.

ENTABLATURE in classical architecture, the horizontal top part of an order (q.v.). An entablature consists of an architrave (q.v.), frieze (q.v.) and cornice (q.v.) and is sometimes supported by columns.

ESCRITOIRE a cabinet fitted with drawers enclosed by an upright flap used for writing.

ESCUTCHEON an armorial shield.

ÉTAGÈRE (French) a set of shelves.

FAN VAULT vaulting where solid concave-sided semi-cones meet or almost meet at the apex of the vault. The cones and centres are decorated with panelling and ribs.

FAUTEUIL (French) armchair.

FOIL a lobe or leaf-shaped curve formed by the cusping of a circle or an arch. A prefix indicates the number of foils, e.g. trefoil, quatrefoil, etc. Used in Gothic tracery.

FRIEZE the middle division of an entablature (q.v.) in classical architecture. The decorated band along the upper part of an internal wall below the ceiling or cornice.

GAMELAN Javanese musical instrument.

GATEHOUSE the main entrance to the courtyard of a house. When leading to an inner court, it will have a tower and contain fine rooms.

GESSO a white mixture of glue and chalk. It was used in the early-18th century on furniture, then carved and gilded or silvered.

GIRANDOLE a branched support for candles or lights, fixed to a wall or to a mirror.

GOTHIC medieval architectural style, mainly 13th to 16th centuries, chiefly dependent upon the use of the pointed arch.

GOTHIC REVIVAL the style based on the growth of knowledge of medieval architecture which followed the neo-Gothic (q.v.) of the 18th century.

GOUACHE painting executed with opaque colours ground in water and mixed with gum and honey.

GRISAILLE monochrome painting in shades of grey.

GROS POINT canvas embroidered in cross stitch, formed by two threads crossing at right angles.

GROTESQUE a stylized form of decoration with human figures or heads and animal forms surrounded by flowers and architectural fancies; derived from Roman wall paintings.

HAMMERBEAM a horizontal roof bracket, which usually projects at the level of the base of the rafters to carry arched bases and struts and is itself supported by braces.

HIPPED ROOF a roof with sloped instead of gabled ends.

INTAGLIO a stone or gem with incised carving.

IONIC *see* Order.

JACOBEAN pertaining to the reign or times of James I (1603–25).

JAPANNED varnished or lacquered.

JARDINIÈRE an ornamental stand or receptacle for plants.

KAKIEMON a type of pottery made in Arita, Japan, whose characteristic asymmetrical designs became popular in 18th-century Europe, where they were copied.

LACQUER an oriental varnish, perfected in China in the 4th century BC, applied to wood, leather and other materials.

LINENFOLD panelling of early to late 16th century decorated with conventional representation of linen in vertical folds. One piece of 'cloth' fills each panel.

LUNETTE a semi-circular opening; possibly filled with a painting or a sculpture.

MACHICOLATION a projecting gallery or parapet of a castle wall with holes in the floor to enable the defenders to drop missiles or boiling lead on attackers.

MAIOLICA Italian pottery coated with an opaque white enamel ornamented with metallic colours: glazed wares, mainly Italian.

351

Glossary

MANTELPIECE the ornamental structure of wood, marble, etc., above and around a fireplace.

MARQUETRY designs cut from veneers of various woods and fitted together, sometimes with such other materials as ivory, pewter, mother-of-pearl, to form a figurative or floral pattern.

METOPE the space in the classical frieze between the tryglyphs (blocks with vertical grooves).

MULLION uprights of wood or stone which divide a window.

NEO-CLASSICAL a style which developed after 1750, based upon the direct study of Greek and Roman buildings, as opposed to Palladianism (q.v.). The Greek revival at the end of the 18th century was a late development of neo-classicism.

NEO-GOTHIC the conscious choice of what was thought to be medieval Gothic style, which became fashionable after 1750, when Strawberry Hill, Twickenham, was built for Horace Walpole, and continued into the first quarter of the 19th century in England.

NETSUKE a small piece of ivory, wood, etc., carved or decorated, worn as a bob or button on the cord by which articles are suspended from the girdle of Japanese national dress.

NEWEL-POST the principal post at the end of a flight of stairs or on a landing.

NIELLO a black composition, consisting of metallic alloys, for filling in engraved designs on silver or other metals.

ORDER in classical architecture an order comprises a column, with or without a base, a shaft, capital and entablature (q.v.), decorated and proportioned in one of the accepted modes: Doric, whose frieze is punctuated by tryglyphs (q.v.); Tuscan, simple; Ionic, with a scrolled capital; Corinthian, with a capital of acanthus leaves; and Composite, with both leaves and scrolls.

ORIEL a bay window on an upper storey or storeys.

ORMOLU bright gold-coloured alloy of copper, tin and zinc, gilded bronze or lacquered brass. Furniture ornaments made or applied with ormolu were widely used in French cabinet-making in the 17th and 18th centuries.

PADOUK a kind of rosewood from Burma; a marked red wood.

PALLADIAN architectural style derived from publications and buildings of Andrea Palladio, the 16th-century Italian architect, and introduced into England by Inigo Jones. Revived in early 18th century.

PARCEL-GILT silver-gilded only in parts, popular in late 17th and 18th centuries.

PARQUETRY a form of veneer laid in a geometrical pattern that sometimes achieves a three-dimensional effect.

PEDIMENT in classical architecture usually a low pitched triangular gable above a portico (q.v.), formed by running the top of an entablature along the sides of the gable. Also a similar feature above doors or windows. A broken pediment has a gap in the upper mouldings.

PETIT POINT canvas embroidered with tent stitch (q.v.).

PIANO NOBILE principal floor of a house containing the state or reception rooms, placed above the basement or ground floor. The ceilings are usually higher than those on other floors.

PIER solid masonry support, usually rectangular, as distinct from a circular column.

PIER-GLASS looking glass hanging on a pier between windows.

PIETRE DURE Italian term for semi-precious stones such as agate, amethyst, cornelian, jasper, lapis, etc. Of Roman origin but revived in Italy in the 16th century, especially in Florence, where they were worked into slabs of mosaic and used as table tops and for the decoration of cabinets.

PILASTER shallow pier or engaged column projecting from a wall.

PORPHYRY a hard red volcanic rock quarried anciently in Egypt, capable of taking a high and beautiful polish; associated with the Roman emperors. Black and green porphyries also exist.

PORTICO a roofed space, open or partly enclosed, often forming the entrance and centre piece of the façade of a temple, church or house.

PRESS a cupboard in which clothes were stored.

PUTTO (Italian) a plump, naked infant which, unlike a cherub or cupid, is without wings. Used in Baroque ornament.

QUAICH a shallow drinking-cup formerly common in Scotland.

QUATREFOIL see foil.

QUOINS dressed stones at the angle of a building, usually laid so that the exposed faces are alternatively large and small.

RÉGENCE the first phase of the French rococo or Louis XV style c.1710–30.

REGENCY the English late neo-classical style, predominant from the 1790s to the 1840s, though strictly it applies to the regency of George Prince of Wales, 1811–20.

RENAISSANCE the revival of classicism which came about in Italy, particularly in Florence, in the early-15th century, later spreading in turn to France and England.

REREDOS structure behind and above an altar.

ROCOCO a form of decoration developed in the 18th century from the late Baroque, but more light-hearted, fanciful and elegant.

ROMANTICISM the movement, first developed in the 18th century, characterized by the subordination of form to theme and by imagination and passion. In architecture it encouraged revivals of every known style.

RONDEL or ROUNDEL a round moulding or aperture, usually in a wall surface.

RUSTICATION masonry (usually dressed) cut in large blocks, with recessed joints, normally used on the lower part of a wall. Also applied to columns.

SABRE-LEG curved to resemble the blade of a cavalry sabre.

SCAGLIOLA (Italian) imitation marble, composed of cement or plaster and marble chips or colouring matter, often used for columns and in interior decoration in 18th-century classical architecture.

SCONCE candle holder, often attached to wall, with polished back plate to reflect light.

SCREENS PASSAGE the space or corridor at the service end of a medieval hall, dividing it from the buttery, pantry and kitchen.

SEAWEED MARQUETRY an intricate and even design of marquetry generally used on small panels; it was fashionable in England and Holland during the 1690s and the early years of the 18th century.

SECRÉTAIRE À ABATTANT (French) drop-front writing desk with drawers and pigeon-holes.

SERPENTINE fronts of furniture with an outward curve in the centre flanked by concave curves.

SOLAR living room in an upper storey of a medieval castle or house.

SPANDREL the space between the side of an arch and the vertical of its springing. Also applied to the surface between two arches in an arcade.

STRAPWORK a decoration of interlaced, scrolling or curling bands, similar to leather or iron straps; originating in the Netherlands about 1540, it became popular in Elizabethan and Jacobean England.

STRAWBERRY HILL GOTHIC *see* neo-Gothic.

STUMPWORK modern name for relief embroidery in which human figures and other subjects are worked over shaped blocks of wood or padding; a favourite technique of the Stuart embroiderers for such articles as needlework pictures, miniature cabinets and mirror frames.

STYLE GALANT romantic 18th-century style.

TALLBOY a tall chest of drawers, often raised on legs.

TENT STITCH needlework consisting of groups of parallel stitches arranged diagonally across the intersections of the threads.

TESTER a flat canopy, usually over a bed.

TORCHÈRE (French) torch holder, tall candelabrum, hall-lamp.

TREEN made of 'tree'; wooden household objects such as bowls, spoons, etc.

TROMPE L'OEIL (French) painted deception, giving three-dimensional impression.

TRYGLYPH *see* metope.

TURKEY WORK English knotted-pile fabrics made between the 16th and 18th centuries with the same technique as Turkish rugs and used principally for table carpets, cushions and upholstery.

TYMPANUM semi-circular space between the lintel (stone bridging an opening) of a doorway and the arch above it.

VENETIAN WINDOW a triple window whose central section is heightened and arched.

VERRE ÉGLOMISÉ (French) glass decorated with a layer of engraved gold.

VERNACULAR native to a particular country or locality with no pretensions to imitating cosmopolitan fashions.

WAINSCOT timber suitable for lining or panelling walls; hence panelling.

Index

Index